INTEG
INFRASTRUC ENT

Two week

Editors

Kulwant Singh
HSMI Human Settlement Management Institute, New Delhi

Florian Steinberg
IHSP Indian Human Settlements Programme, New Delhi

Nathaniel von Einsiedel
UMP Urban Management Programme for Asia and the Pacific,
Kuala Lumpur

INTERMEDIATE TECHNOLOGY PUBLICATIONS 1996

Intermediate Technology Publications Ltd., 103–105 Southampton Row, London WCIB 4HH, UK

© Copyright Reserved

A CIP catalogue record for this book is available from the British Library

ISBN 1 85339 354 1

Originally published in India by Oxford & IBH Publishing Co. Pvt. Ltd., 66 Janpath, New Delhi 110001. Typeset at Radiant Printers, New Delhi. Printed in India at Baba Barkha Nath Printers, New Delhi.

FOREWORD

It is a privilege for me to provide a foreword to a publication that stands out as an example of collaborative efforts betweeen urban management support groups and networks. The partnership between Indian Human Settlements Management Institute, the Netherlands Government supported Indian Human Settlements Programme and the UNCHS/IBRD/UNDP Urban Management Programme in the conceptualization and production of this book is a good example of productivity utilizing complementarities in urban management related international technical cooperation efforts.

The idea for this book originated when the editors and myself in late 1994 reviewed the contributions to the International Seminar on "Integrated Urban Infrastructure Development" held in Delhi in February 1995. It struck us at the time that the seminar contributions comprised a significant number of cases of good practice in integrated urban infrastructure development in Asia, which would be worth disseminating to a wider audience than just the seminar participants. The present shape of the book vindicates this, as it not only contains updated country case studies, but also thematic papers and overview papers which endeavour to generalize common lessons of experience.

The publication of this book is timely, as we are currently less than a year away from the Second United Nations Conference on Human Settlements (Habitat II), which will be held in Istanbul, Turkey in June, 1996. One of the two conference themes is: sustainable human settlements development in an urbanizing world.

The models and practices of integrated urban infrastructure development as they have emerged in the countries reviewed in this book clearly make a major contribution to advancing the cause of sustainable urban development. In that sense the planning and programming for integrated urban infrastructure development has proven to be a very powerful entry point for addressing a whole range of conditions for sustainability.

Embarking on such an integrated investment programming approach, for instance, stimulates policy makers to develop sustainable municipal financing patterns, to develop conducive institutional structures, and to seriously strengthen local capacities to conduct investment programming and monitor the implementation of ensuing investment plans. In some cases all these issues have led to even much broader issues being addressed, such as issues of terms and conditions for civil service employment.

Such linkages are highlighted in the country contributions and amplified particularly in the thematic and overview contributions in this book. Therefore, it is my conviction that this book will make for stimulating reading for urban managers and scholars of urban development alike. I also feel that it comprises an important Asian contribution to the global Habitat II effort to document and disseminate experiences of good urban management practice.

Emiel A. Wegelin,
Coordinator, Urban Management Programme,
UNCHS (Habitat), Nairobi, 2 October 1995

PREFACE

Between 1 and 4 February 1995 the Human Settlement Management Institute (HSMI) and the Indian Human Settlements Programme (IHSP), with support by the Ministry of Urban Development[1], Government of India, the United States Agency for International Development (USAID) and the Economic and Social Commission of Asia and the Pacific (ESCAP) organized an international seminar on "Integrated Urban Infrastructure Development" in New Delhi. This seminar brought together a wide range of experiences from various Asian countries, viz., Bangladesh, India, Indonesia, Laos, Myanmar, Nepal, the Philippines, Sri Lanka, Thailand, Turkey and Vietnam.

The seminar was a unique gathering of about 120 professionals and functionaries from these countries, representatives of international agencies and organizations like ESCAP of the United Nations, the Urban Management Programme (UMP) in Nairobi, the Urban Management Programme for Asia and the Pacific (UMPAP), United Nations Children's Fund (UNICEF) in Delhi, Regional Housing and Urban Development Office (RHUDO) in Delhi, USAID and the Institute for Housing and Urban Development Studies (IHS), Rotterdam, the Netherlands. Such wide participation reflected the keen interest of policy makers, professionals and planners towards innovative approaches for integrated provision of urban infrastructure.

Encouraged by the success of the seminar, and the particular interest of Dr. Emiel A. Wegelin, Coordinator, UMP, Nairobi, it was decided to publish revised versions of some of the seminar papers and of the seminar recommendations to make these accessible to a wider professional audience not only in Asia but- the world over.

This volume tries to be as representative as possible in the selection of country experiences of integrated urban infrastructure provision. In addition to the papers available at the time of the seminar, the editors

---

[1] Since April 1995 the Ministry of Urban Development has been renamed as Ministry of Urban Affairs and Employment.

have also been able to obtain some new theme papers which had not been available at the time of the seminar.

Most of the initiatives taken by different countries in the Asian region have some commonalities and address similar types of issues. For example, the Integrated Development of Small and Medium Towns (IDSMT) of India, Integrated Urban Infrastructure Development Programme (IUIDP) of Indonesia, Urban Development through Local Efforts (UDLE) of Nepal, Regional Cities Development Programme (RCDP) in Thailand, the Programme for Essential Municipal Infrastructure, the Local Government Investment Fund (LGIF) in the Philippines, and the convergence approaches of the Indian Urban Basic Services for the Poor (UBSP) in conjunction with the *Nehru Rozgar Yojana* (NRY) poverty alleviation scheme and the Environmental Improvement of Urban Slums (EIUS), all try to improve availability of urban infrastructure. Similarly, the Metro Manila Capital Investment Folio (CIF) of Philippines and Cukorova Metropolitan Region Urban Development Project of Turkey focus on upgradation of infrastructure in a wider context of metropolitan regions. Considerable work has been done at local, regional and national levels to conceptualize, design, implement and evaluate these programmes and schemes. These experiences deserve to be discussed in a multi-country context to expedite the process of experience sharing and transfer of knowledge.

During the seminar it was recognized that an international exchange on the present experiences and practices of integrated urban infrastructure planning has started, and this in itself is a very positive development. Therefore, it is recommended that the various experiences be seen as mutually reinforcing, and different countries may review the cases presented in this volume for their relevance in their own context. It is hoped that this volume is able to encourage more institutions in various countries to promote a convergence and reinforcement of the elements applicable for their own integrated urban infrastructure projects and programmes.

The editors would like to thank for contributions from the Ministry of Urban Development (MoUD), Housing and Urban Development Corporation (HUDCO) of India, the Urban Management Programme (UMP), and the Dutch government-sponsored Indian Human Settlements Programme (IHSP) which have made it possible to publish this volume.

The editors would also like to acknowledge the valuable support of the following seminar rapporteurs and colleagues in the compilation of the proceedings and recommendations of the Seminar: Gita Dewan Verma (HSMI), Karin Borgman (IHS), Sudipto Mukherjee, Forbes

Davidson (IHS), Harry Mengers (IHSP), Sanjib Sarma (HSMI), S.K. Gupta (HSMI), J.S. Marwaha (HSMI) and P.P. Singh (IHSP).

March 1996

Dr. Kulwant Singh,
Executive Director, Human Settlement
Management Institute (HSMI), New Delhi

Dr. Florian Steinberg,
Project Leader, Indian Human Settlements
Programme (IHSP), New Delhi

Nathaniel von Einsiedel,
Regional Coordinator, Urban Management
Programme for Asia and the Pacific
(UMPAP), Kuala Lumpur

CONTENTS

Foreword   iii

Preface   v

List of Tables, Figures and Boxes   xiii

Acronyms and Terms   xix

Notes on Authors   xxv

1. Introduction   1
   Kulwant Singh, Florian Steinberg,
   and Nathaniel von Einsiedel

PART I: OVERVIEW ARTICLES

2. The Multi-sectoral Investment Planning Approach   17
   for Integrated Development of Urban Services
   Kulwant Singh and Florian Steinberg

3. To Integrate or Not to Integrate: Developing a   33
   Model for Effective Integration
   Forbes Davidson and Michael Lindfield

4. The Urban Management Programme and   47
   Integrated Urban Infrastructure Development
   Emiel A. Wegelin

PART II: COUNTRY PAPERS

Indonesia

5. The Integrated Urban Infrastructure Development   75
   Programme in Indonesia
   Achmad Lanti and Robert van der Hoff

Philippines

6. The Local Government Infrastructure Fund in   103
   the Philippines
   Apolo C. Jucaban

7. The Capital Investments Folio: An Innovative   119
   Approach to Metropolitan Management in the Philippines
   Nathaniel von Einsiedel and Victoria de Villa

8. The Programme for Essential Municipal Infrastructure   143
   Utilities, Maintenance and Engineering Development
   Apolo C. Jucaban and Bituin B. Torte

Thailand

9. The Regional Cities Development Programme in   159
   Thailand: Developing Urban Infrastructure
   Banasopit Mekvichai and C. Ridhiprasart

10. Songkhla Fishport: Structuring and Implementing a   177
    Public-Private Partnership Project
    Michael Lindfield

Nepal

11. Integrated Action Planning Experience: The Experience 193
    in Nepal
    David M. Irwin and Jibgar Joshi

India

12. The Integrated Development of Small and Medium   213
    Towns Programme in India
    K. Dharmarajan

13. The Integrated Development of Small and Medium   233
    Towns in the Punjab
    Gopal Krishan

14. The Municipal Urban Development Fund of   243
    Tamil Nadu: Operations and Experiences
    R. Sundararajan and K. Mukundan

15. Integrated Infrastructure Planning and Programming: 259
    A Five-Year Capital Investment Model for Small and
    Medium Towns
    B. Bhaskara Rao and N. Nageshwara Rao

16. Integrated Provision of Basic Services in Urban India 279
    Harjit S. Anand

Turkey

17. The Cukurova Metropolitan Region Urban Development   299
    Project
    Nihat Sayinalp

PART III: GENERAL THEMATIC PAPERS

18. Municipal Finance and Integrated Urban Infrastructure   315
    Development
    Kyung-Hwan Kim

19. Institutional Issues of Urban Infrastructure Financing   329
    Michael Lindfield

20. Training for Integrated Urban Infrastructure Development   349
    Forbes Davidson, Harry Mengers and Hans Teerlink

21. Environment Mapping for Integrated Development   373
    Dinesh Mehta, Usha P. Raghupathi and Rajesh Sharma

22. Land Management for Integrated Urban   395
    Development in Asian Cities: Implementing the
    Formula L + P + F + Ni = SUD
    Ray W. Archer

PART IV: LOOKING AHEAD

23. Integrated Urban Infrastructure Development: 420
    Whither Now ?
    Kulwant Singh, Florian Steinberg and
    Nathaniel von Einsiedel

ANNEXURE

Recommendations of the International Seminar   427
on "Integrated Urban Infrastructure Development"

LIST OF FIGURES, TABLES AND BOXES

2. The Multi-sectoral Investment Planning Approach for Integrated Development of Urban Services: *Kulwant Singh and Florian Steinberg*

FIGURE
— 2.1 : Multi-sectoral Investment Planning

3. To Integrate or Not to Integrate: Developing a Model for Effective Integration: *Forbes Davidson and Michael Lindfield*

FIGURES
— 3.1 : Dynamics of Integration
— 3.2 : Integration Generates Resistance
— 3.3 : Success Needed to Maintain Integration
— 3.4 : Levels of Integration of Requirements
— 3.5 : Elements of Integration
— 3.6 : Dimensions of Integration

BOXES
— 3.1 : Environmental Improvement of Urban Slums: A Case from India

4. The Urban Management Programme and Integrated Urban Infrastructure Development: *Emiel A. Wegelin*

BOXES
— 4.1 : Integrated Public Investment System, State of Baja California, Mexico
— 4.2 : Decentralization and Inter-sectoral Planning in the State of Karnataka, India
— 4.3 : The Municipal Management Improvement Programme in Sri Lanka
— 4.4 : IUIDP in Indonesia
— 4.5 : Planning Manual for Local Authorities in Sri Lanka
— 4.6 : Integrated Action Planning (IAP) in Nepal
— 4.7 : Calcutta Metropolitan Development Authority
— 4.8 : The Community Construction Contract System in Sri Lanka
— 4.9 : Action Plan Seminar on Partnerships, New Delhi, 1994

5. The Integrated Urban Infrastructure Development Programme in Indonesia: *Achmad Lanti and Robert van der Hoff*

TABLES
- 5.1 : List of "Urban Projects" (*Repelita II - III*)
- 5.2 : Total Investments for the IUIDP
- 5.3 : Sources of Funds for Government Spending in the Regions (*Tk.I and Tk.II*)

6. The Local Government Infrastructure Fund in the Philippines: *Apolo C. Jucaban*

FIGURES
- 6.1 : The Philippine Islands and Administrative Regions
- 6.2 : Geographical Distribution of LGIF Projects
- 6.3 : Percentage Sharing of Project Funds
- 6.4 : Percentage Sharing of Funds Per LGU
- 6.5 : Map Showing Integration of Various Urban Infrastructure Projects Funded by Various Sources
- 6.6 : Map Showing Integration of Various Urban Infrastructure Projects Funded by Different Sources
- 6.7 : Map Showing LGIF Integrated Projects with Private Sector, LGU, World Bank and USAID Funding

TABLES
- 6.1 : Grant Fund Allocation
- 6.2 : Proposed Fund Matching Scheme
- 6.3 : Funding Contribution from Various Sources for the LGIF Projects in Pangasinana, Philippines
- 6.4 : Funding Contribution from Various Sources for LGIF Projects and Other Foreign Funded Projects, Province of Guimaras, Philippines

7. The Capital Investments Folio: An Innovative Approach to Metropolitan Management in the Philippines: *Nathaniel von Einsiedel and Victoria de Villa*

FIGURES
- 7.1 : The CIF Planning Process
- 7.2 : The Project Evaluation Process
- 7.3 : The CIF Process

TABLE
- 7.1 : Possible Path of Development

8. The Programme for Essential Municipal Infrastructure Utilities, Maintenance and Engineering Development: *Apolo C. Jucaban and Bituin B. Torte*

FIGURES
- 8.1 : PREMIUMED Institutional Set-up

— 8.2 : Traditional Institutional Set-up for a Typical Loan
     Programme
— 8.3 : MDF-PREMIUMED Fund Flow Concept

TABLE

— 8.1 : World Bank-assisted Urban Development Programme (in
     the Philippines)

9. **The Regional Cities Development Programme in Thailand:
   Developing Urban Infrastructure**
   Banasopit Mekvichai and C. Ridhiprasart

FIGURES

— 9.1 : Location of Regional Urban Growth Centres, by Rank
— 9.2 : Administrative Organization of the Regional Cities
     Development Programme Project

TABLES

— 9.1 : Types of Urban Development Projects by Regional Growth
     City
— 9.2 : Project Investment Funds, RCDP Phase I

10. **Songkhla Fishport: Structuring and Implementing a Public–Private
    Partnership Project**: *Michael Lindfield*

FIGURE

— 10.1: The Project Process of the Songkhla Fishport Development

11. **Integrated Action Planning: The Experience in Nepal:**
    David M. Irwin and Jibgar Joshi

FIGURES

— 11.1: Integrated Action Planning Approach
— 11.2: Location of Muncipalities That Have Received IAP in Nepal

TABLE

— 11.1: Multi-sectoral Investment Programme for Dhullkhel

12. **The Integrated Development of Small and Medium Towns
    Programme in India**: *K. Dharmarajan*

TABLES

— 12.1: Project Costs
— 12.2: Organizational Set-up of IDSMT
— 12.3: Release of Central Assistance to IDSMT
— 12.4: IDSMT Components
— 12.5: Categories of IDSMT Towns
— 12.6: IDSMT Financing Patterns

13. The Integrated Development of Small and Medium Towns in Punjab: *Gopal Krishan*

TABLES
— 13.1 : Towns Covered under the IDSMT Programme
up to September 1994 in the Punjab
— 13.2 : Profile of the Towns Covered under the IDSMT Programme
in the Punjab

14. The Municipal Urban Development Fund of Tamil Nadu: Operations and Experiences: *R. Sundararajan and K. Mukundan*

FIGURES
— 14.1 : MUDF—Flow Chart Showing Fund Flow
— 14.2 : Implementation of MUDF

TABLES
— 14.1 : TNUDP Cost Estimates
— 14.2 : Disbursements From the Fund
— 14.3 : Disbursements by Sector
— 14.4 : Recovery of Debts
— 14.5 : Madras Corporation Forecasts versus Actuals
— 14.6 : Forecast versus Actual—Smaller Municipalities
— 14.7 : Performance of Selected Remunerative Schemes

15. Integrated Infrastructure Planning and Programming: A Five-Year Capital Investment Model for Small and Medium Towns in India: *B. Bhaskara Rao and M. Nageshwar Rao*

FIGURES
— 15.1 : Analytical Process of IIPP
— 15.2 : Flow Process of IIPP
— 15.3 : Water Supply Service Development
— 15.4 : Financial Appraisal Process for a Project

TABLES
— 15.1 : Capital Costs of Service and Remunerative Projects
— 15.2 : Summary of Iterations of the FOP for Hassan

16. Integrated Provision of Basic Services in Urban India: *Harjit S. Anand*

FIGURE
— 16.1 : Community-led Integrated Development Model

20. Training for Integrated Urban Infrastructure Development: *Forbes Davidson, Harry Mengers and Hans Teerlink*

FIGURES
— 20.1 : Relationship between Capacity Building for Urban
Development Operations
— 20.2 : Relationship between Physical Development and
Institutional Development

— 20.3 : Relationship between Training and Other Forms of Capacity Building

— 20.4 : Relationship between Training and Technical Assistance

— 20.5 : Organization of Training

— 20.6 : Training Approach in Karnataka

TABLE

— 20.1 : Target Groups and Training Programmes During the First Years

21. **Environment Mapping for Integrated Urban Infrastructure Development**: *Dinesh B. Mehta, Usha P. Raghupathi and Rajesh Sharma*

FIGURES

— 21.1 : Delhi: Landfill Sites

— 21.2 : Delhi: Sewage Treatment Plants

— 21.3 : Delhi: Traffic Problem Areas

— 21.4 : Bombay: Sewage of Water Supply

— 21.5 : Bombay: Sewage Outfalls

— 21.6 : Bombay: Landfill Site

— 21.7 : Ahmedabad: Ground Water Level

— 21.8 : Ahmedabad: Sources of Water Supply and Distribution Network

— 21.9 : Ahmedabad: Ward Wise Distribution of Dilapidated Housing—1990

— 21.10 : Vadodara: Per Capita Availability of Water

TABLE

— 21.1 : Analytical Framework for Urban Environmental Mapping

22. **Land Management for Integrated Urban Development in Asian Cities: Implementing the Formula L + P + F + Ni = SUD**: *Ray W. Archer*

BOXES

— 22.1 : Meaning of the Formula : L + P + F + NI = SUD

— 22.2 : Justification of the Formula : L + P + F + NI = SUD

FIGURES

— 22.1 : The Suburban Road Pattern in the Ladprao/Ramintra "Superblock", A Chaotic Maze of Subdivision Project Roads

— 22.2 : The Stages of Urban Land Development as a City Expands

— 22.3 : Layout of Nava Nakorn New Town

— 22.4 : Minburi Land Pooling/Readjustment Project

— 22.5 : The Bang Kapi Special Assessment Project

ACRONYMS AND TERMS

ADB	:	Asian Development Bank
AIDAB	:	Australian International Development Assistance Bureau
AIT	:	Asian Institute of Technology
APO	:	Area Project Officer
ARVs	:	Annual Rateable Values
ATI	:	Administrative Training Institute
BOLT	:	Build, Operate, Lease and Transfer
BOO	:	Build, Operate and Own
BOT	:	Build Own Transfer
BOT	:	Build Operate and Transfer
CBOs	:	Community Based Organizations
CDC	:	Community Development Council
CDP	:	Comprehensive Development Plan
CDS	:	Community Development Society
CIDM	:	Community-led Integrated Development Model
CIF	:	Capital Investment Folio
CMC	:	City Management Committee
COs	:	Community Organizers
CPO	:	City Project Officer
CS	:	Chief Secretary
CUDP	:	Calcutta Urban Development Project
DCB	:	Demand Collection Balance
DUDA	:	District Urban Development Agency
EBO	:	Elected Bureaucratic Organization
EDI	:	Economic Development Institute
EIUS	:	Environmental Improvement of Urban Slums
EJBUDP	:	East Java and Bali Urban Development Project
EPM	:	Environmental Planning and Management

ESCAP	:	Economic and Social Commission of Asia and the Pacific
EWS	:	Economically Weaker Sections
FIRE	:	Financial Institutions Reform and Expansion
FOP	:	Financial and Operation Plan
GLD	:	Guided Land Development
GNP	:	Gross National Product
GOI	:	Government of Indonesia
GTZ	:	Gesellschaft für Technische Zusammenarbeit
GUD	:	Guided Urban Development
HMS	:	Humanitarian Municipal Services
HRD	:	Human Resource Development
HSMI	:	Human Settlement Management Institute
HUDCO	:	Housing and Urban Development Corporation
IAP	:	Integrated Action Planning
IATWG	:	Inter-Agency Technical Working Group
IBRD	:	International Bank for Reconstruction and Development
ICB	:	International Competitive Bidding
ICDS	:	Integrated Child Development Services
IDAP	:	IUIDP Development Assessment Plan
IDP	:	Institutional Development Plan
IDSMT	:	Integrated Development of Small and Medium Towns
IHS	:	Institute for Housing and Urban Development Studies
IHSP	:	Indian Human Settlement Programme
IIPP	:	Integrated Infrastructure Planning and Programming
IMR	:	Infant Mortality Rate
IRR	:	Internal Rate of Return
ITA	:	International Technical Assistance
IUIDP	:	Integrated Urban Infrastructure Development Programme
IUPA	:	Institute for Urban Policy Analysis
KIP	:	*Kampung* Improvement Programme
LGAD	:	Local Government Affairs Division
LGIF	:	Local Government Investment Fund
LIDAPs	:	Local Institutional Development Action Plans
LIDP	:	Local Institutional Development Plan
LP/R	:	Land Pooling/Readjustment

LRCs	:	Learning Resource Centres
LSG	:	Local Self-Government
MDAs	:	Metropolitan Development Authorities
MDF	:	Municipal Development Fund
MIP	:	Multi-Year Investment Planning
MIS	:	Management Information System
MMC	:	Metro Manila Commission
MMIP	:	Municipal Management Improvement Programme
MOF	:	Ministry of Finance
MOHA	:	Ministry of Home Affairs
MOI	:	Ministry of the Interior
MOPW	:	Ministry of Public Works
MOUA&E	:	Ministry of Urban Affairs & Employment
MoUD	:	Ministry of Urban Development
MSIP	:	Multi-sectoral Investment Planning
MUDF	:	Municipal Urban Development Fund
NCC	:	National Cadet Corps
NCU	:	National Commission on Urbanization
NDC	:	Neighbourhood Development Committee
NEDA	:	National Economic and Development Authority
NFE	:	Non-formal Education
NGOs	:	Non-Governmental Organizations
NIC	:	Neighbourhood Infrastructure Committee
NILG	:	National Institute of Local Government
NIMBY	:	Not-In-My-Backyard
NPA	:	National Programme of Action
NPV	:	Net Present Value
NSS	:	National Sample Survey
NUDS	:	National Urban Development Strategy
O&M	:	Operation and Maintenance
OBM	:	Office of Budget and Management
OCF	:	Commissioner for Finance
OCP	:	Commissioner for Planning
ODP	:	Outline Development Plan
OSR	:	Own-Source Revenue
OUD	:	Office of Urban Development
OVG	:	Offices of the Vice-Government

PAFPAK	:	Programming and Financial Planning, Analysis, Control and Coordination
PAP	:	Policy Action Plan
PEDP	:	Physical and Environmental Development Plan
PERT	:	Programme Evaluation and Review Technique
PHC	:	Public Health Care
PIUs	:	Project Implementation Units
PJM	:	*Program Jangka Menengah*
PMG	:	Project Management Group
PMO	:	Project Management Office
PMUs	:	Project Management Units
PO	:	Project Officer
PPO	:	Professional Project Organization
PPPs	:	Public-Private Partnerships
PRIMU	:	Project Review Implementation and Management Unit
PTC	:	Bus - Pallavan Transport Corporation
PWD	:	Public Works Department
RCDP	:	Regional Cities Development Programme
RCDP	:	Regional Cities Development Projects
RCVs	:	Resident Community Volunteers
RDA	:	Regional Development Account
RHUDO	:	Regional Housing and Urban Development Office
RIAP	:	Revenue Improvement Action Plan
RIAPs	:	Revenue Improvement Action Plans
RIC	:	Resident Infrastructure Volunteer
RIP	:	Revenue Improvement Plan
RIVs	:	Resident Infrastructure Volunteers
RMDP	:	Regional Municipal Development Projects
SCP	:	Sustainable Cities Programme
SHASU	:	Scheme of Housing and Shelter Upgradation
SIP	:	Slum Improvement Programme
SPAs	:	Special Provincial Administrations
SUDA	:	State Urban Development Agency
SUDAP	:	Strategic Urban Development Action Plan
SUME	:	Scheme of Urban Micro-enterprises
SUWE	:	Scheme of Urban Wage Employment
TA	:	Technical Assistance

TEK	:	Turkish Electricity Authority
TNUDP	:	Tamil Nadu Urban Development Project
TOCs	:	Trainers-on-Calls
TOT	:	Training-of-Trainers
TRAMP	:	Traffic Management and Transport
UBS	:	Urban Basic Services
UBSP	:	Urban Basic Services for the Poor
UD	:	Urban Development
UDLE	:	Urban Development through Local Efforts
UIP	:	Universal Immunization Programme
ULGs	:	Urban Local Governments
UMP	:	Urban Management Programme
UMPAP	:	Urban Management Programme for Asia and the Pacific
UNCHS	:	United Nations Centre for Human Settlements
UNDP	:	United Nations Development Programme
UNICEF	:	United Nations International Children's Emergency Fund
UPACAR	:	Urban Poverty Alleviation through Community Action Resources
URDI	:	Urban and Regional Development Institute
USAID	:	United States Agency for International Development
USL	:	Urban Sector Loan
WJSSCUDP	:	West Java and Sumatra Secondary Cities Urban Development Project

NOTES ON AUTHORS

Dr. HARJIT S. ANAND is Managing Director, Haryana State Small Industries and Export Corporation, Chandigarh, India. Earlier he was Director (Urban Development), Ministry of Urban Development, New Delhi, India.

RAY W. ARCHER is Professor of Urban Land Economics and Management, Asian Institute of Technology, Bangkok, Thailand.

FORBES DAVIDSON is Senior Staff, of the Institute for Housing and Urban Development Studies (IHS), Rotterdam, The Netherlands.

K. DHARMARAJAN is presently with the World Bank, India Office, as Co-ordinator, Urban Management Reforms. He was formerly Joint Secretary (Urban Development), Ministry of Urban Development, Government of India, New Delhi.

NATHANIEL VON EINSIEDEL is Regional Coordinator, Urban Management Programme for Asia and the Pacific (UMPAP), Kuala Lumpur, Malaysia.

ROBERT VAN DER HOFF is Senior Staff and Regional Representative of the Institute for Housing and Urban Development Studies (IHS), Rotterdam, The Netherlands, based in Jakarta, Indonesia.

DAVID M. IRWIN is Advisor of the Urban Development through Local Efforts (UDLE) Project, Kathmandu, Nepal.

Dr. JIBGAR JOSHI is Director General, Department of Housing & Urban Development, HMG, Kathmandu, Nepal.

APOLO C. JUCABAN is Executive Director, Local Government Investment Fund (LGIF), Manila, The Philippines.

Dr. KYUNG-HWAN KIM is Urban Finance Advisor, Urban Management Programme (UMP), United Nations Centre for Human Settlements (UNCHS), Nairobi, Kenya.

GOPAL KRISHAN is Professor of Geography, Panjab University, Chandigarh, India.

ACHMAD LANTI is Acting Director for Programme Development, Directorate General of Human Settlements, Ministry of Public Works, Jakarta, Indonesia.

MICHAEL LINDFIELD is Senior Research Fellow of the Australian Housing and Urban Research Institute, Brisbane, Australia. He was formerly Senior Staff of the Institute for Housing and Urban Development Studies (IHS), Rotterdam, The Netherlands.

Dr. DINESH B. MEHTA is Director, National Institute of Urban Affairs (NIUA), New Delhi, India.

Dr. BANASOPIT MEKVICHAI is Assistant Professor, Department of Urban and Regional Planning, Chulalong Korn University, Bangkok, Thailand.

HARRY MENGERS is Project Leader (Karnataka) of the Indian Human Settlements Programme (IHSP), Bangalore/Mysore, India and a Senior Staff of the Institute for Housing and Urban Development Studies (IHS), Rotterdam, The Netherlands.

K. MUKUNDAN is Director, Kirloskar Consultants, Madras, India.

USHA P. RAGHUPATHI is staff, National Institute of Urban Affairs (NIUA), New Delhi, India.

B. BASKARA RAO is Professor of Urban Planning, and Chief Executive of Symbiosis of Technology Environment and Management (STEM) Consultants, Bangalore, India.

N. NAGESHWARA RAO is with Symbiosis of Technology Environment and Management (STEM) Consultants, Bangalore, India.

C. RIDHIPRASART is the Director, Local Government Development Affairs Division, Department of Local Administration, Ministry of Interior, Bangkok, Thailand.

NIHAT SAYINALP is Director of PRIMU, Bank Iller, Ankara, Turkey.

RAJESH SHARMA is staff of the National Institute of Urban Affairs (NIUA), New Delhi, India.

Dr. KULWANT SINGH is Executive Director, Human Settlement Management Institute (HSMI), New Delhi, India.

Dr. FLORIAN STEINBERG is Project Leader, Indian Human Settlements Programme (IHSP), New Delhi, India and a Senior Staff of the Institute for Housing and Urban Development Studies (IHS), Rotterdam, The Netherlands.

R. SUNDARARAJAN is Senior Economist, Project Management Group (PMG), Madras, India.

HANS TEERLINK is Senior Staff of the Institute for Housing and Urban Development Studies (IHS), Rotterdam, The Netherlands.

BITUIN B. TORTE is consultant to the PREMIUMED Programme, Manila, The Philippines.

VICTORIA De VILLA is staff of the Local Government Investment Fund (LGIF), Manila, The Philippines.

Dr. EMIEL WEGELIN is Coordinator, Urban Management Programme (UMP), based at the United Nations Centre for Human Settlements (UNCHS), Nairobi, Kenya.

INTRODUCTION

Kulwant Singh, Florian Steinberg and Nathaniel von Einsiedel

Integrated urban infrastructure development is an approach which is being tried out in a wide range of Asian countries since more than a decade (Wegelin, 1990; Peterson, Kingsley and Telgarsky, 1994).[1] An international seminar was conducted in February 1995 in New Delhi, India, with the intention to: (i) compare and discuss the methodologies for planning, programming, implementation, operation and maintenance of integrated infrastructure programmes; (ii) identify unmet challenges, shortcomings as well as the impact of integrated infrastructure programmes; and (iii) define possible avenues for improvement of the existing infrastructure programmes by learning through a regular exchange of programme experiences. The countries represented in this seminar included Bangladesh, India, Indonesia, Myanmar, Nepal, the Philippines, Sri Lanka, Thailand, and Turkey. The issues of particular interest in the seminar were: acceleration and higher efficiency of service provision; improvement of local revenues; improvement of local institutional capabilities; reduction of negative environmental impact; and access of the urban poor to urban services.

Pursuant to wide-ranging discussions it is increasingly being realized that "integrated urban development" is a necessary strategy to govern our cities better and create a better foundation for economic development and extended basic amenities to the urban poor. Integrated urban development is also a very complex issue and will not only take a long time to materialize but also take many avenues in which it will emerge.

During the last few years urban managers and policy makers have become increasingly concerned with the adequacy of infrastructure.

---

[1] The approach or elements of it are also being implemented in a number of Latin-American and African countries such as Argentina, Brazil, Colombia, Gambia, Mexico, Nigeria, Venezuela (see Wegelin, 1995).

In the context of economic liberalization and macro-economic development, infrastructure plays a crucial role and provides an enabling environment for the productivity of households and firms. The role of social infrastructure is equally important in a wider context of equity and affordability.

In the current phase of economic development the urban sector has to play a major role. In most countries the contribution of the urban sector in the national income is significantly higher than the size of their urban population. About 60 per cent of the gross national product (GNP) of developing countries is generated from urban areas. This is particularly important in the context of developing countries which are undergoing rapid urbanization. It is estimated that by the year 2000, 50 per cent of the world's population will live and work in urban areas; and Asia is also rapidly advancing toward these levels of urbanization. In fact, more than 60 per cent of the world's expected urban growth is occurring in Asia. Many cities and towns in Asia are seriously affected by overcrowding, environmental degradation, social disruption, underemployment and poor housing, infrastructure and services. The magnitude of urbanization is accompanied by a host of inadequacies related to the delivery of land, shelter, infrastructure and environmental management. Environmental problems originating from production and consumption, in particular the manifold impact of water, air and soil pollution, as well as the growing threat from solid, liquid and radiating wastes endanger the sustainability of urban life and prosperity (World Bank, 1994).

However, the normative base of urban infrastructure among developing countries is low. Nearly 30 to 40 per cent of the urban population of Asia resides in sub-standard housing—including slums and squatter settlements—with 34 per cent of the urban population living below the absolute poverty line. Sizeable chunks of urban population in Asian countries do not have access to basic infrastructure facilities such as safe water, sanitation and garbage disposal. Between 20 and 60 per cent of urban population residing in Nepal, Bangladesh, Myanmar, Indonesia and Thailand do not have access to safe water. The situation with respect to sanitation is no better—at least 50 per cent of urban population belonging to Nepal, Bangladesh, India and Myanmar do not have access to safe sanitation. Countries like Turkey, Indonesia and the Philippines still have to provide sanitation facilities to 5 to 20 per cent of their urban population. Almost 30 to 50 per cent of garbage in most countries remains uncollected. Urban infrastructure development of this magnitude and initiation of appropriate schemes and programmes aiming at upgradation of the urban infrastructure, pose a serious challenge to national governments of such countries.

There is an increasing awareness that the potential role of the urban sector in the macro-economic development can be made more effective through appropriate investments in urban infrastructure. The investment requirements to meet the backlog of urban infrastructure across Asia are so high that normal budgetary allocations are woefully inadequate. Meeting such a backlog will require stimulation of local revenues to finance a cost-effective development of urban infrastructure. At the same time the flow of loan finance has to be increased many times over to meet the demands of the urban infrastructure sector. Urban infrastructure is invariably linked with productivity of urban economies and macro-economic development. This is why upgradation of urban infrastructure has received increasing attention over the past few years. The focus on urban infrastructure is particularly visible among developing countries which are making serious efforts to enhance the productivity of their economies through better provision of infrastructure (World Bank, 1991 and 1993).

Internationally, the urban policy agenda has been orientated towards five priority areas: (i) alleviation of urban poverty; (ii) strengthening of municipal administration; (iii) provision of shelter, urban infrastructure and services; (iv) improvement of the urban environment; and (v) promotion of the involvement of non-governmental organizations (NGOs), community-based organizations (CBOs) and the private sector (United Nations Development Programme, 1991).

Thus the management of urban growth should aim at achieving social justice, ecological sustainability, political participation, increased economic productivity and a culturally vibrant urban life. Promotion of new policies and strategies for managing urbanization and integrated infrastructural development to improve the living environment and the quality of life is of crucial importance.

This change in the policy perception has forced the national governments in the Asian region to pay more attention to the adequacy of urban infrastructure in terms of the efficiency in the delivery of municipal services, which have been left "orphaned" for a long time. However, since a few years, urban management by local governments is being viewed as one of the most important leverages for the provision of (basic) services. Also, the need to abandon the "project approach" to urban development has been understood, and this brings forward the notion of accountability and transparency as part of urban services delivery. In this context it is extremely important to strengthen local governments, the municipal finance situation and resource base of municipalities. At present, too many cities of Asia are not at all equipped to handle the impact of the expanding neo-liberal market economies, and to meet the challenges of providing land, housing and infrastructure which are needed to cope with the urban future, and to avert the suffering of the urban poor (Dillinger, 1994).

It is in this context that many national, state or provincial governments and municipal bodies have been pondering over how they can better integrate the supply of environmental infrastructure and services, and to reach higher levels of efficiency and assured sustainability.

The experiences of integrated urban infrastructure development in Asia presented in this book illustrate a good degree of variation, outreach and impact. We now provide an overview of the characteristics of some of these. The most important of these which we can choose from India, Indonesia, Nepal, the Philippines, Thailand and Turkey.

A few principles for "integrated urban infrastructure development" should be highlighted as they emerge from the examples of the Integrated Development of Small and Medium Towns (IDSMT) of India; the Integrated Urban Infrastructure Development Programme (IUIDP) of Indonesia; the Urban Development through Local Efforts (UDLE) of Nepal; the Regional Cities Development Programme (RCDP) in Thailand and the Programme for Essential Municipal Infrastructure, the Local Government Infrastructure Fund (LGIF); the Metro Manila Capital Investment Folio (CIF) in the Philippines; the Cukorova Metropolitan Region Urban Development Project of Turkey; and the convergence of approaches of the Urban Basic Services for the Poor (UBSP), *the Nehru Rozgar Yojana* (NRY) and the Environmental Improvement of Urban Slums (EIUS) in India.[2]

General Principles of Integrated Urban Infrastructure Development

Integrated infrastructure planning and programming implies integration of technical, spatio-environmental, financial and institutional issues. Integration should be aimed only to the extent necessary for clear benefits and not for its own sake, and should proceed incrementally so as to be pragmatic and to allow for building upon existing capabilities. Following the orientation towards municipal development, integrated infrastructure development not only needs to be fully based on the local context, but also be located in a broader, planned framework. The linking of policy levels, however, should be attempted in a flexible way.

---

[2]   Unfortunately, it was not possible to get any contribution of the Sri Lankan Municipal Management Improvement Programme (MMIP) which recently seems to be facing serious implementation problems.

Integration and coordination require a spirit of cooperation in order to succeed, and integrated infrastructure provision requires a reorientation of existing approaches so as to be more participatory and evolutionary to allow for a convergence of efforts by various actors. Hence, it is necessary that local governments become the key actors in integrated infrastructure development. For this, decentralization needs genuine commitment from higher levels and there needs to be consensus regarding the discretion that local governments have in bringing about integration in programmes. For local governments to effectively emerge as lead actors, there is a need for appropriate and adequate capacity building through carefully designed, phased and promoted training as well as technical consultancy in initial stages of the adoption of integrated approaches.

Further, political support is necessary for ensuring allocation of resources and commitment to implementation, operation and maintenance. External assistance should be designed to avoid sustainability problems and various donor agencies should coordinate their efforts to promote integration. Financing agencies need to explore ways of using infrastructure finance to reinforce integrated infrastructure planning, and education and training curricula should respond to the need for reorientation.

Multi-sectoral Investment Planning

Financial integration merits maximum attention and therefore Multi-sectoral Investment Planning (MSIP) should be used as a tool for prioritization and decision-making on investment programmes. The well-structured integration of information on committed and planned expenditures is a vital step towards gradual and comprehensive integration. MSIP should link local needs and effective demand and existing commitments with potential resources. MSIP needs to be as broad-based as possible and a variety of partnerships should be explored to allow for sufficient and articulate involvement of key stakeholders. An incremental approach is needed as there are several possible levels of complexity and sophistication. Linkages with wider urban regional development policies can be forged only over a period of time. There should also be an increased emphasis on rapid approaches to planning and information collection, and demand-driven action planning needs to become an accepted mainstream planning process rather than a peripheral approach.

Services for the Poor

Integrated infrastructure planning should pay special attention to the provision of basic services to the poor and marginalized groups and bring this concern into the mainstream of urban development by focussing on integrated projects rather than conventional "low-income" projects.

Instruments like an Urban Poverty Fund can help in bringing together funds for coordinated service delivery for the poor. Creative financial management can ensure that remunerative uses subsidize non-remunerative ones. Innovative cost-efficient technologies can make for greater access to the poor and, by facilitating improved cost recovery, can make service delivery for the poor sustainable.

All programmes should strive for effective community involvement at all stages and articulate community development interventions aimed at community empowerment. The right kind of NGOs need to be promoted to provide specialized services in a manageable number of settlements and their functioning integrated through settlement-level networking.

Advocacy and training for orienting government agencies and officials towards creating a participatory environment and to more responsive interventions is crucial. Structural changes, such as the creation of an Urban Poverty Alleviation cadre and measures to secure coordination between funding agencies so that projects of different donor agencies are convergent rather than competitive also merit attention.

An adequate and user-friendly Management Information System (MIS) on urban poverty that is owned by all concerned needs to be developed and regularly updated, preferably by an independent research institution.

Municipal Finance

Municipal finance issues merit urgent attention through a range of interventions aimed at improving financial performance and setting up municipal finance programmes and instruments. Innovative municipal finance windows need to be set up and can be located within any sort of urban (infrastructure) finance institution. Instruments like municipal development funds can potentially converge public and private resources available for urban infrastructure.

The basic expertise for preparing budgets can be built upon so that budgets become developmental tools. Creative financial management can result in a viable mix of remunerative and non-remunerative projects. In this context, rationalization of tariffs and service charges is essential.

Capacity building in municipal bodies is needed both in support of resource augmentation and for the optimum use of resources. This can be achieved through training as well as by locating incentives like committed funds and performance-related eligibility criteria for lending in municipal finance programmes. Municipal financial performance improvements can be constrained if all windows do not reflect a unity of purpose in laying down minimum performance efficiency criteria for eligibility. Likewise, lack of political will can constrain necessary rationalization of tariff structures. Advocacy for addressing such external constraints is needed.

Capital Markets

Emerging possibilities of capital market financing of infrastructure investments call for special attention. Project bonds would be viable but can also generate a bias in favour of components for which beneficiaries are identifiable and where fees can be charged. General bonds would answer the requirements of those components of infrastructure which do not have a steady or sufficient rate of return. However, these should be introduced only after a local agency has demonstrated its capability in improving efficiency in infrastructure provision and established its credibility as an economically viable entity. Given the complex nature of urban infrastructure, it may be more useful to combine project viability and general municipal affordability in various degrees in alternative packages.

In the short run, an intermediary is needed to provide credibility, do institutional packaging and use a mix of funds. In the long term, however, local agencies should tap the capital market directly if they choose using directed credit or budget allocations for resource mobilization through the capital market.

Environment and Land

Current planning practices have created a situation where the poor are paying more for less services, and the environment in urban areas is steadily degenerating. Reorienting existing planning, development and regulatory practices assumes significance in this context.

Development controls in general need to be more responsive; regulations resulting in constraints to land supply in particular need to be scrapped or at least significantly modified; planning procedures—especially those relating to land transactions—need to be simplified and made more transparent; and planners need to move away from guiding to managing development, and this needs to reflect in academic and training curricula.

Demand-driven action-planning needs to become a mainstream planning process rather than a peripheral approach. Even if not applicable in totality to a different context, experiences with, for instance, land pooling, do serve as lessons that can be of use in formulating worthwhile intermediate techniques pending necessary long-term institutional changes.

Environmental mapping can be very useful for making a quick overall assessment which would help local governments in making more rational investment prioritization, assessing risks and working out routes for service networks.

Many traditional practices merit attention as a complementing, if not substituting, system of infrastructure provision at the local level. Opportunity costs of land utilization need to be viewed against the benefits, i.e., not only the physical services but also economic opportunities.

Public and Private Partnerships

Integrated infrastructure provision requires the convergence of efforts of all actors through organized partnerships. Local governments need to take the initiative in this regard. Well designed regulatory mechanisms and contracting procedures are pre-requisites for the success of partnerships. A level playing field, transparency and accountability are equally essential. Special care is needed in designing regulatory mechanisms and contracting procedures which secure access for the poor through infrastructure provision partnerships.

The Contributions and Structure of This Book

This book is divided into four parts: First, there are a few conceptual overview articles. The second part presents country experiences and detailed case studies. The third part comprises a number of thematic papers on issues of integration. The fourth part takes a brief look at the future of the concept and approach of integrated urban infrastructure development. The recommendations of the International Seminar on Integrated Urban Infrastructure Development are presented in the Annex of the book.

K. Singh and F. Steinberg set out explaining the basic model of integrated infrastructure planning, describe goals and expected benefits of multi-sectoral investment planning (MSIP), and stress the need for revenue improvement planning and institutional development. The establishment and widespread adoption of MSIP is considered a long process, with the actual yields of decentralization and participation of the private sector and the community becoming visible only in the longer run. **F. Davidson and M. Lindfield** argue that integration should not be aimed at like an end in itself, but as a means to achieve additional benefits from investments. They support this argument with several cases. "In short, for integration to work it is necessary to ensure that: 2+2 = (at least) 5." **E.A. Wegelin** gives an overview of the Urban Management Programme (UMP) and its support for urban infrastructure management. Integration and the application of MSIP figures prominently in these promotional efforts of UMP. It is argued that cities can start the MSIP process initially with a few investment activities, and then gradually expand the scope of integration as the system gains maturity and is institutionalized.

A. Lanti and R. van der Hoff provide a review of the evolution of the Integrated Urban Infrastructure Development Programme (IUIDP) in Indonesia over 10 years. The IUIDP may represent one of the most refined approaches to MSIP, with many well-developed instruments. However IUIDP implementation in Indonesia has faced serious challenges from high inflation and very rapid increase in the urban population. This has brought down the actual per capita investments in the early 1990s. There are considerations that the sectoral scope should be extended. But as long as the full institutionalization of the MSIP is not achieved, it appears more appropriate to wait and to root the IUIDP "culture" more firmly. **A.C. Jucaban** details the Local Government Infrastructure Fund (LGIF) in the Philippines which is aimed at inducing local and private initiatives in planned infrastructure development through provision of seed capital. The LGIF approach has shown the merit of converging available resources, and stimulating private investments in remunerative components. It is, however, being realized that for more capital-intensive investments (which are often the more critical ones) the model may have to be adjusted. **N. von Einsiedel and V. A. de Villa** present the Metro Manila Capital Investment Folio (CIF) as an interesting approach to synchronization of planning, programming, budgeting and resource mobilization. CIF has succeeded in taking care of both big (Ministries of Transport, Public Works, Housing, etc.) and small spenders (Ministries of Health, Education, etc.). However, equity and affordability concerns are not the explicit objectives of the CIF. In the case of the Programme for Essential Municipal Infrastructure Utilities, Maintenance and Engineering Development (PREMIUMED) in the Philippines, **A.C.Jucaban and B.B. Torte** explain that municipal finance issues are the most crucial ones. Through its Municipal Development Fund (MDF) PREMIUMED is able to raise and combine funds from a mix of sources, and make these available to municipalities. In this context it is necessary to explore other forms of resource mobilization through tax collection, user charges, and land-based charges. In order to achieve these goals it is necessary to create the necessary management capacities at municipal levels. **Banasopit Mekvichai and C. Ridhiprasart** elaborate on the Regional Cities Development Programme (RCDP) in Thailand, which follows the policy of developing medium-size cities into industrial growth centres. In terms of integration the RCDP illustrates that different organizational and political levels require different degrees of integration. Technical and spatial integration proved to be a realistic short-term target, but financial integration ran against vested financial and political interests. **M. Lindfield** further illustrates the RCDP by citing the case of the development of a "fishport". This explains on the basis of a concrete case the approach of integration of physical, financial and institutional aspects of project formulation and implementation for shifting of port activities and using the area rendered surplus for commercial and residential development through the private sector. **D.M. Irwin and J. Joshi** present the approach and tools for Nepal's Integrated Action Planning (IAP) which has provided technical and financial support for a number of small and medium size towns. IAP has the potential to be effective, decentralized, demand-driven and fairly rapid in planning. Municipalities do have sufficient capacities to participate in the planning exercise and are supported by technical assistance teams. **K. Dharmarajan** provides a critical assessment of the 15 years of experiences with the Integrated Development of Small and Medium Towns (IDSMT) scheme which until March 1995 has reached out to some 750 Indian towns. This programme is not considered to be a very big success as it falls short in achieving a sufficiently broad degree of integration, and its impact remains limited. Nevertheless, it is remarkable that this programme, which is regularly reviewed and improved, represents a challenging vision and many local governments depend on the programme's existence. In the context of decentralization and devolution of powers the IDSMT will assume an even more important role for municipal services development. These points are also underlined by **G. Krishan's** review of the IDSMT scheme in the Indian state of Punjab. In terms of the turnover of funds, Punjab seems to have utilized well the available funding of the IDSMT. But on the ground level the impact of the resulting investment is not too apparent. This has, however, not discouraged planners from attempting to improve the IDSMT scheme, and thus the programme has become an exercise of sustained "learning-by-doing". **R. Sundararajan and K. Mukundan** present yet another Indian scheme of integrated investment packages stipulated by the Municipal Urban Development Fund (MUDF). This fund invites municipal bodies to prepare MSIPs consisting of remunerative and non-remunerative projects, and to present these schemes with a proper assessment of feasibility, cost recovery and implementation capability. It is expected that the MUDF financing window will shift from a government sponsored body to a private financial institution and thus open new avenues of public-private partnerships. **B. B. Rao and M. N. Rao's** model for Integrated Infrastructure Planning and Programming (IIPP) is applied to five-year capital improvement for small and medium towns in Karnataka state, India. The IIPP experience shows that capital improvement plans can bridge the gap between "no action planning" at the local level and "non-resource based long-term master planning" at the state level. IIPP produces feasible investment packages for municipal development. **H.S. Anand** reviews India's urban poverty alleviation programmes and illustrates how an initiative for "convergence" and integration in the Urban Basic Services for the Poor (UBSP) provides physical and social infrastructure for the poor. The backbone of this experience is community and women's participation, and the experience has prompted many states to work on the establishment of Urban Poverty Funds which would resemble an even higher level of institutionalization of integration. For the case of Turkey, **N. Sayinalp** elaborates on the experience of the multi-city scheme of the Cukurova metropolitan region. The Cukurova project is, despite good intentions and a fair amount of technical support, a scheme which illustrates well the constraints of replicability when there is insufficient political support. The lesson of the Turkish experience is that local capacity building in terms of technical, administrative and financial management skills is a pre-requisite for the success of decentralized initiatives. Where this is not (yet) available, extended consultant support is required.

In the section of "General Thematic Papers" **K.-H. Kim** states that integrated urban infrastructure development provides an excellent context for raising cost awareness, reducing costs as well as mobilization of more revenue. According to him maximization of impacts can only be achieved through decentralization with accountability and private sector participation. In this context it is essential to develop an incentive system for municipal efforts, and that municipalities obtain greater autonomy over their finances so that they effectively can plan for integration. **M. Lindfield** explores the linkages between institutional development and successful financing of urban infrastructure projects. He claims that adequate institutional strengthening needs to go hand in hand with the development of integrated urban infrastructure, and this combines with the need for technical support to (local and other) agencies to formulate their programmes. He proposes to link institutional development efforts with financing streams to gain maximum credibility and legitimacy. **F. Davidson, H. Mengers and H. Teerlink** point out that for the purpose of integration there is also a need for new attitudes and skills of interdisciplinary working. Training support needs to address the changing needs of local (and higher level) agencies, and should be orientated towards support of decentralized decision-making and inter-agency cooperation. Performance improvement of interdisciplinary teams being the ultimate goal, there is a good chance to optimize the impacts of technical assistance programmes if these are combined with training support. **D. Mehta, U.P. Raghupathi and R. Sharma** explain how environmental mapping can be very useful for quick assessments which help municipalities to prioritize their investment decisions more rationally keeping environmental concerns in mind. The requirement is, however, a timely collection and availability of geo-referenced data on environmental risks. In the case of small and medium towns this goal may not be easily attained due to lack of human and managerial resources. On the issue of land for integrated urban development, **R. W. Archer** presents the "land + plans + finance + network infrastructure" formula for sustainable urban development. He highlights the need for forward looking land development techniques which utilize land pooling and other instruments to structure and guide urban expansion and growth. This implies that development planning requires more flexible, simplified and transparent land development procedures.

In the final section **K. Singh, F. Steinberg and N. von Einsiedel** attempt to look ahead to the future of integrated urban infrastructure development. It is highlighted that short-term planning cannot stand alone anymore. The complexities and long-range needs of our cities today require more medium-term planning tools for technical, social and economic development. In doing so, multi-sectoral investment programmes shall be built on consensus and participation at decentralized levels. Although the various schemes discussed in this book have their own objectives, targets, financial modalities, components, procedures and schedules, we need to aim at the integration of these at local levels so that cross benefits can be obtained. Comprehensive investment packages, however, cannot remain an end in themselves, but need to be backed by a strengthening of municipal bodies.

BIBLIOGRAPHY

Dillinger, W. (1994), *Decentralization and its Implications for Urban Services Delivery*, Urban Management Programme, Publication #16, The World Bank, Washington, D.C.

Peterson, G.E., Kingsley, G.T. and Telgarsky, J.P. (1994), *Multi-sectoral Investment Planning*, Urban Management Programme (UMP) Working Paper Series No. 3, UNCHS, Nairobi.

United Nations Development Programme (1991), *Cities, People and Poverty: Urban Development Cooperation for the 1990sA UNDP Strategy Paper*, UNDP, New York.

Wegelin, E. A. (1990), 'New Approaches in Urban Services Delivery: A Comparison of Emerging Experience in Selected Asian Countries', *Cities*, 7 (3): 244-258.

Wegelin, E. A. (1995), 'IUIDP in a Comparative International Context', in Suselo, H., Taylor, J.L. and Wegelin, E.A. (eds.), *Indonesia's Urban Infrastructure Development Experience: Critical Lessons of Good Practice*, UNCHS, Nairobi.

World Bank (1991), *Urban Policy and Economic Development: An Agenda for the 1990s—A World Bank Policy Paper*, World Bank, Washington, D.C.

World Bank (1993), *Municipal Development Sector Review: Political Decentralization and its implications for Urban Service Delivery* (a draft report), World Bank, Washington, D.C.

World Bank (1994), *World Development Report 1994: Infrastructure for Development*, World Bank, Washington, D.C.

PART I

OVERVIEW ARTICLES

THE MULTI-SECTORAL INVESTMENT PLANNING APPROACH FOR INTEGRATED DEVELOPMENT OF URBAN SERVICES[1]

Kulwant Singh and Florian Steinberg

Introduction

Many urban practitioners have come to the conclusion that unless an integrated and holistic approach to urban development and infrastructure development planning is applied, the current sectoral and segmented planning and urban management practices will continue to result in haphazard and unplanned development.

Of course integration of investments is already an approach recommended by many (Wegelin, 1990; Dimitriou, 1991; Peterson, Kingsley and Telgarsky, 1994) but there are only a few instances of its implementation. Certain experiences with integrated projects and programmes also indicate that the difficulties in implementing integrated programmes may not be justified by the results achieved. This suggests that integration should only be aimed at when the expected additional gains through the "integrated" manner of programme planning and implementation outweigh opposing forces.

This paper proposes an approach of integrated, i.e., "Multi-sectoral Investment Planning" (MSIP)—as in the common terminology of the UNCHS/UNDP/World Bank-sponsored Urban Management Programme (UMP)—which is particularly based on experiences in the context of Indonesia's Integrated Urban Infrastructure Development Programme (IUIDP), the Integrated Action Planning (IAP) approach of Nepal and the Integrated Infrastructure Planning and Programming (IIPP) in

---

[1] Much of this paper draws from Institute for Housing and Urban Development Studies (IHS)/Steinberg (1993).

Karnataka state, India. Such an approach entails infrastructure provision which is not sector-specific but integrative, and attempts to support urban managers with a planning process for coping with the growing demands for infrastructure and services in the cities of the developing world.

The MSIP approach departs from the conventional spatial planning bias of master planning which seldom provided financially viable investment packages, and also the compartmentalized practice of the "project-by-project" approach. The MSIP approach is orientated towards strategic performance in local government and defines different but complementary roles of the existing government levels (local, provincial/regional, central) in the process of MSIP, and stresses the need for the strengthening of local management capabilities.

Understanding of Integrated Infrastructure Planning

The approach of integrated infrastructure provision aims at the planning, programming, implementation, and operation and maintenance of urban infrastructure through integrated means. In particular this "integration" is intended in technical or physical matters of projects as well as in the financial and institutional sense.

The concept of MSIP is related to the existing forms of urban master planning. However, MSIP as an action-orientated infrastructure planning tool requires a quick appraisal and confirmation of the main directives of the urban development strategy. Further, the principles of pooled or integrated financing of multi-sectoral investment plans, and the policy objective of increased local revenue creation and cost recovery for infrastructure services are highlighted. The approach of integrated urban infrastructure provision also aims to provide improved institutional capabilities and encourages local governments to apply this strategic planning approach (Zaris, Carter and Green, 1988: Baross, 1991).

MSIP is a methodology for the formulation of a multi-year and multi-sectoral investment programme which aims at the integration of urban infrastructure programmes and projects. These programmes and projects are to be executed under the responsibility of local governments with the possible additional help of higher government levels at provincial (or state) levels and at the national level. The main goals of the MSIP methodology are to:

1. Increase efficiency in the utilization of resources available for infrastructure development, avoiding duplication of similar

activities by various urban sector agencies, and undertaking activities with maximum stimulation and additional benefits for urban development.

2. Increase effectiveness in generating local resources for the financing and management of local infrastructure development. The provision of urban services is to be driven by more performance orientation and business-like attitudes (World Bank, 1991 and 1994).

The expected benefits of MSIP are:

1. Urban infrastructure investments can be better oriented and match better the local requirements for improvements in urban infrastructure and the urban settlements field, and be better in accordance with the development priorities that are defined by the local governments, by community consultations and real demand studies.

2. Participation of the local governments, private sector and the community takes place during the planning, formulation and execution of the multi-year programme.

3. Integration of planning and programming of sectoral projects (for instance water supply, sewerage, drainage, solid waste management) can be realized.

In other words, MSIP is a development programme specially formulated for urban infrastructure. It has the elements of planned and integrated provision of services, the setting of relevant priorities, the planning of management responsibilities for implementation, and the integration of financial resources. The integration further refers to "bankable project packages", to geographical location, and to the implementation period. Further, the aspect of integration takes into account the wider framework of regional development priorities and the development priorities set out in provincial (state) medium- or long-term development plans.

Among the **direct benefits** there are services which can be "sold" to the urban community which will benefit from the services and infrastructure provided. Financial contributions of the community (for instance in the form of taxes and fees) will increase with the betterment of physical results (as expressed in the quality of land, roads, buildings, etc.) or non-physical components (for instance trade activities, commerce and services, industries and communication). It is this accumulation of public resources and income which will express progress of physical and welfare aspects of the quality of urban life. Among the **indirect benefits** of improved services is the increased productivity of people due to better services, as also the better functioning of the urban living environment.

As a local government programme, MSIP can be complementary to other national/regional/ provincial scale programmes (such as national roads or transport schemes).

Typical MSIP sectors can comprise the following:

- Drinking water supply.
- Sewerage, human waste and sanitation.
- Drainage and flood control.
- Solid waste management.
- Urban roads.
- Neighbourhood improvement programmes.
- Core housing, sites-and-services programmes.
- Urban renewal, resettlement.
- New settlements and satellite settlements.
- Urban land provision and guided land development (GLD).
- Public housing.
- Market infrastructure improvement.
- Public transport terminals.
- Electricity provision.
- Telephones and telecommunication.
- Social infrastructure (education, sport and health facilities, etc.).
- Cemeteries.

However, not all major urban infrastructure development sectors can be covered by a MSIP (as the small list of Indonesian IUIDP components shows[2]). In general, such a list of sectors for the MSIP will combine responsibilities of a variety of agencies for the implementation of the MSIP which entails improvement of the local revenue situation and the local institutional capabilities.

Physical and Environmental Development Planning: The preparation of a MSIP is preceded by a physical and environmental analysis which focuses on urban development trends and urban environmental profile. The findings may be laid down in base maps and environmental profile maps. Initial findings of the physical and environmental review are seen against existing plans in order to identify shortcomings (Heinrichs, 1993;

---

[2]   The Indonesian IUIDP covered water supply, sewerage and human waste, solid waste, drainage and flood control, urban roads, neighbourhood improvement (KIP) and market infrastructure improvement. For a review of the IUIDP, see Dimitriou, 1991; Hoff and Steinberg, 1992 and 1993; Suselo, Taylor and Wegelin, 1995.

Joshi and Lojewski, 1993). The physical and environmental analysis defines the urban development scenario and strategy, provides maps of the physical and environmental characteristics and problems, and outlines the required regulatory provisions and bye-laws. The urban development scenario and strategy is intended as a quick exercise in structure planning which provides the gross framework for urban development, but excludes detailed land-use and zoning plans. The maps of the physical and environmental characteristics and problems are based on rapid urban surveys. The required regulatory provisions and bye-laws are formulated with implementation and operation and maintenance in view, and are based on the provisions of the Institutional Development Plan (IDP) which aims at the strengthening the management capacity at city level and improved operational mechanisms for urban services delivery, and operation and maintenance.

The conclusions of any earlier analysis of physical and environmental problems are considered in conjunction with the projects prioritized to form a plan of guidance for future urban development while protecting the environment.

An important element of any Physical and Environmental Development Plan (PEDP) is a phased programme for the urban expansion of the city. Where appropriate, PEDP presents recommendations for land development schemes such as guided land development, sites and services, and land pooling.

Revenue Improvement Planning: The formulation of a strategy to increase local revenues is one of the objectives of the MSIP approach and is accomplished through a Revenue Improvement Plan (RIP). The financial development strategy helps in sustaining the provision of services, providing new, additional infrastructure facilities, and building up capital reserves. Local resources shall increasingly be mobilized locally to pay for local urban infrastructure development, and operation and maintenance. This increases local autonomy and reduces expenditure burdens on central government budgets. For this reason the process of programme formulation is also combined with relevant choices and priorities of programme/project packages which are cost-efficient and can contribute to the mobilization of (a certain degree of) cost-recovery.

MSIP clarifies for each sector project its priority and location as well as the available or possible financial resource allocation. Each organization involved in the financing of urban infrastructure knows from the draft MSIP the volume of its own expected contribution and the contribution of other organizations in the realization of the total infrastructure development programme. As a multi-year planning approach the MSIP also anticipates and defines the annual contributions for all urban stakeholders (public sector, private sector, community) during the given planning period. Urban infrastructure development which is systematically and carefully planned provides several direct and indirect benefits for urban development and the quality of urban life.

Institutional Development Planning

The process of preparation and implementation of integrated urban infrastructure programmes in the form of multi-sectoral investment plans involves a number of organizations and institutions which operate and manage their affairs at their specific levels. Thus, the formulation of an institutional development plan (IDP) to ensure the implementation and management capabilities is required. IDPs address deficiencies in manpower, institutional resources, and operational rules and bye-laws which restrain the provision of infrastructure and urban management.

Institutional development planning includes the following levels of government:

The local government (or municipal) level: This usually possesses several service departments (for instance, public works offices) and service agencies (for instance, post and telecommunications agencies) which are responsible to build, manage, operate and maintain their respective infrastructure components in accordance with local requirements and available financial resources. In the implementation of their tasks local government agencies will be supported by provincial (or state) and central government level agencies.

The provincial-regional (or state) government level: This becomes responsible to assist local governments in the execution of those projects which are beyond the handling and financial capacities of local governments. The role of the provincial-regional- (or state-) level agencies is to: (i) appraise local MSIP proposals and combine these in a provincial (or state) programme package for annual and multi-year investments; (ii) assist local governments (or municipalities) in the preparation and implementation of MSIPs; and (iii) appraise and monitor the implementation of MSIPs with respect to their relationships to provincial (state) plans and programmes for urban development. Apart from the technical assistance by provincial (or state) government agencies, there may also exist the possibility of financial assistance for integrated programme packages.

National government level: At the national government level there are ministries (such as the ministry of planning, of urban development, ministry of public works), and other national agencies (national electricity board, etc.) which set the standards for the urban infrastructure development, and define the development budget requirements.

The role of the central government agencies is to: (i) appraise and monitor the implementation of MSIPs with respect to their relationship with national plans and programmes for urban development; (ii) appraise provincial MSIP packages and agree on central government budget contributions; (iii) coordinate central government agencies which play a role in the implementation of the MSIPs; (iv) publish MSIP guidelines explaining the mechanisms, procedures and components of the programme, as well as the appraisal criteria; (v) arrange for technical assistance as far as this is financed through bilateral or multilateral external aid agencies; and (vi) to formulate and implement supportive programmes such as training, research, and information and communication support. Additionally, some of these national institutions are (usually) also directly involved in some type of programme/project execution through the collaboration with provincial (or state) level agencies. Such involvement of national or central government agencies is particular for certain demonstration or pilot project schemes which need to be tested before they are delegated to lower government levels for routine implementation.

By now it is evident that there are many organizations which contribute to the planning, programming, construction, management, operation and maintenance of urban services, which provide technical and financial assistance. This coordination and integration of all their efforts is needed in order to maximize efficiency and effectiveness (McGill, 1994).

The Process of Integrated Infrastructure Planning

The process of planning and implementing a multi-sectoral and multi-year investment programme entails a number of steps which are determined by the existing institutional set-up and guiding laws. However, the following steps provide a generally applicable sequence (also see Figure 2.1):

1. Define a local government lead agency for the planning exercise and assign authorities of inter-agency coordination with this lead agency. In addition, define which higher level agencies the planning process needs to refer for appraisal or approval.
2. Take existing national and regional development plans into account and review existing urban master plans (if available) in order to define through a rapid urban appraisal the expected urban development scenario.
3. Identify infrastructure needs on the basis of this urban development scenario, and already known and forecasted future deficiencies.

Figure 2.1. Multi-sectoral Investment Planning

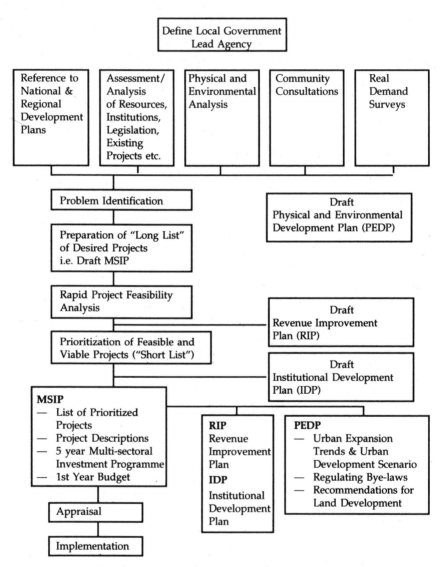

Conduct community surveys ("real demand surveys") and hold community consultations.

4. Compile information about ongoing and already committed projects and investments. Assess and analyse the existing resources, institutions and relevant legislation.

5. Develop a Physical and Environmental Development Plan (PEDP) on the basis of the physical and environmental analysis.

6. Prepare a "long list" of the desired multi-sectoral investment programme (i.e., the draft MSIP). Prioritize projects for each sector and take community benefits and cross-sectoral project priorities into account while prioritizing.
7. Undertake rapid project feasibility analysis of the proposed projects.
8. Develop a Revenue Improvement Plan (RIP) which will help to raise local income within the planning period.
9. Tally draft MSIP ("long list") with projected revenue and subsidy position of the local government. Take into account the expected results of the Revenue Improvement Plan (RIP), and prepare a realistic "short list" of prioritized projects for the final version of the MSIP.
10. Prepare an Institutional Development Plan (IDP) which takes into account the coordination and integration of various local agencies for the implementation of the investment programme and for the RIP. The IDP outlines measures for the strengthening of local institutions.
11. Compile the final Multi-sectoral Investment Plan which incorporates the PEDP, the RIP, and the IDP for approval at the city level.
12. Conduct with the assistance and supervision of higher levels of government(s) and/or financial institutions an appraisal of the multi-sectoral investment programme.
13. Make necessary, additional institutional and legal arrangements for the implementation of the programme by establishing (temporary) project management and monitoring units.

Confirmation of Major Urban Development Policy Components

The initiation of the integrated MSIP approach needs full endorsement of central or national agencies as part of a national policy towards development, management, operation and maintenance of urban infrastructure. Such a policy decision implies that local governments (or municipalities) receive an increased degree of responsibility for the planning, programming, provision, management, operation, management and financing of their own infrastructure programmes and projects within the area of their respective jurisdiction. In order to respond effectively to this task, local governments need to deal with all phases of the infrastructure development cycle in an integrated manner. This requires:

— Building and maintaining urban infrastructure facilities at such a level as considered necessary within the context of a specifically defined and endorsed urban development scenario, with sufficient attention towards the relationship and inter-linkages of different infrastructure sectors.

— Mobilizing and managing the financial resources and the managerial capabilities of the local agencies, and involving the community and the private (commercial) sector.

The urban development policy needs to reinforce the MSIP approach and focus on the following principles:

1. Urban infrastructure development and maintenance is a responsibility of the local governments, assisted and guided by provincial and central government agencies.

2. Planning, programme formulation and the decisions on investment priorities are based upon a participatory planning approach, involving local governments and, where possible, the urban community, including non-governmental organizations (NGOs) and community-based organizations (CBOs) and the private sector.

3. Mobilization of financial resources and optimization of their utilization for infrastructure investments under the MSIP approach is better than under conventional approaches.

4. The system of local (municipal) finance for infrastructure development is improved, and new possibilities of loan financing (through local or foreign sources) are made available.

5. The local institutional management capabilities are improved, fulfilling the objectives of more autonomy and local responsibilities.

6. Coordination and consultation between relevant and related agencies, the commercial and non-commercial private sector organizations, and the community is facilitated.

7. A functioning management information system is built up which helps to monitor and assess the performance of institutions, urban process and urban products, i.e., urban infrastructure and services delivery.

Financing Patterns of Integrated Multi-sectoral Investment Plans

The implementation of integrated multi-sectoral investment plans will rely to a large extent on the existence of a favourable financial and taxation policy. With the evolution of the paradigm that provision of urban services should increasingly be self-financing and be covered by fees and taxes of the beneficiaries, a new policy and public understanding of the relationship between adequate services provision and user charges as well as (a certain degree of) cost recovery for these services need to be established.

Cost recovery for multi-sectoral investment plans can be achieved through several ways including:

— **Direct means** such as direct payments for tariffs, for instance for water or for the usage of public community sanitation facilities. Such tariffs can include the costs for operation and maintenance (O&M). Differentiated water tariffs can help to cross-subsidize water consumption of poorer parts of the urban community.

— **Semi-direct means**, such as garbage fees, without making a difference of quantities of garbage accounted for, but differentiating between household and commercial/industrial solid waste. Differentiated garbage tariffs can help to cross-subsidize fees of poorer parts of the urban community.

— **Indirect means** such as taxes for land and property or for vehicle ownership. Such taxes have also a high potential to allow for cross-subsidies. Water consumption fees can also provide cross-subsidies for sectors that are difficult to charge for (for instance sewerage, drainage, etc.) as these services are not directly felt as "consumerables".

Thus, local governments will need to clarify within the context of the multi-sectoral investment plan which sources of finance are accessible to cover non-recoverable costs (direct subsidies from central or provincial government levels) and which service sectors have the potential to be (partly) self-financing. The integration of resources requires a pooling of:

- Expected user fees and services charges.
- Other local revenues which can be fed into urban infrastructure development.
- Community self-help contributions to building or operation and maintenance of certain infrastructure components.
- Private sector financing of certain profitable infrastructure components.
- Provincial- or state-level subsidies.
- Central government subsidies.
- Local/national loan finance.
- International (bilateral/multilateral) loan finance.

The different components of finance for different service sectors have to be identified according to the following criteria in order to establish financing plans and budgets for the integrated multi-year investment plans: (i) who finances what ?; (ii) what percentage of estimated project costs is covered ?; and (iii) whether financing is done through loans, subsidies or direct income ? In principle, multi-sectoral investment plans are formulated as five-year programmes, but these multi-year programmes need to be broken down in annual MSIP budgets for the respective local government budgeting process.

Multi-sectoral Investment Planning: What Future ?

With respect to integrated urban infrastructure development as an innovative approach, planners and politicians have to assess critically what are the possible achievements, shortcomings and backlogs in terms of: acceleration of provision of services; improvement of local revenues; improvement of local institutional capabilities; reduction of environmental impact of major infrastructure investments; and access of the poor to urban services.

Integrated urban infrastructure programmes will also have to deal with a plethora of issues which can only be partly resolved by the approach of integrated planning. However, the success of integrated urban development will depend on a more positive development of aspects such as urban management and training, environmental sustainable urban development, management of land, local resource mobilization, community participation and decentralization.

Urban Management and Training

Within the framework of the integrated urban development process a new perception and practice of urban management needs to be evolved. This is a concern for management as a process of interventions involving negotiations and consensus-finding between institutions and representatives of different urban actors (private and public, in general), between the local, provincial and central government levels and the affected and participating public.

Training must be considered as one of the most important long-term leverages for the strengthening of urban management capacities, as it is always "people" and professionals who will determine the course and speed of developments. Without appropriate human resource development, innovative projects and (urban) development policies as well as institutional changes will remain meaningless and without the necessary human resource basis to transform innovations into sustainable, regular activities (Sidabutar, et al, 1991).

Environmental Sustainable Urban Development

During the last few years the notion of "sustainable development" has been widely discussed. From the early "limits to growth" perspective the discussion on environmental development has now broadened with the understanding that development has to ensure the basic needs of all, especially the poor. This implies that infrastructure delivery is seen as one of the most important aspects in ensuring sustainable development. Additional paradigms for the understanding of "sustainable development" have stressed "affordability, cost recovery and replicability" and the improvement of urban productivity and poverty alleviation as a precondition for the protection of urban environment. This has led to a more systematic inclusion of environmental issues into urban programmes and projects.

The Management of Land

Land as an essential resource for the development of human settlements and for the generation of infrastructure services is a major problem in many cities. Land is not only required for the development of services such as water supply, human waste, drainage/flood control, solid waste management, slum upgrading and urban roads, but land management issues have an influence on housing schemes, urban renewal or resettlement programmes, land consolidation and guided land development (GLD). Additionally, where urban projects have an impact on land outside of certain governmental boundaries there is often a need for cooperative arrangements between local governments.

Local Resource Mobilization

Local resource mobilization is predominantly an issue of municipal financial management. Potential resources exist, but they must be tapped more adequately. This also relates to issues of municipal management in revenue administration, tariff setting, tax mapping and tax collection. Capacities of local governments in the mobilization of resources need upgrading through a series of operational measures including implementation of the property tax, improvement of local government revenue administration, improvement of local water enterprises' management, revenue performance, and reforms of the local taxes and charges. Additional initiatives need to be orientated towards the introduction of more user charges for urban services (as also tried in the health, education and transport sectors). But so far, cost recovery ("remunerative") schemes have been limited to water services and markets and shopping complexes.

Public Private Partnerships

The private sector can invest much more in urban services than it has done so far. It could play a role in low-income housing, urban public transportation, water supply, urban sanitation, solid waste management and guided land development. To make the Public-Private Partnerships (PPPs) successful, the actors involved will have to consider a number of important requirements such as mutual trust and good relations, convergence of interests, capital and profit-sharing; risks of projects borne by all partners involved, commitment and decision-making according to clear procedures; a business-like market-oriented approach of local governments; coordination of policy actions of different government institutions and levels of government; and, last but not least, continuity.

Community Participation

The non-commercial private sector communities—NGOs as well as CBOs—can participate more effectively than they have done so far. Although communities cannot contribute much cash, they can nevertheless help governments to save large amounts of money. Equally, NGOs/CBOs also do not contribute cash, but they can assist local governments in managing urban development as intermediaries between the communities and local governments.

Decentralization

In the coming years, integrated development of municipal infrastructure in central government technical assistance for local governments will require to build firmly on decentralization as its cornerstone. This would involve transferring basic responsibilities for project planning, programming, implementation and supervision to local governments. The role of central governments will gradually shift to one of giving general guidance and support and to acting as a catalyst for development finance, and to coordinating inter-agency cooperation (Mabogunje, 1993; World Bank, 1993).

The present experiences with integrated programmes indicate that it is not easy to quickly institutionalize these and make them part of routine operations. Implementation experience of MSIPs has, in fact, shown that there is often a time lag of many years between new ideas and their incorporation into public policy and, after that, into routine practice of local governments. It is known that conventional solutions and approaches will neither help to make up the deficits in physical and social infrastructure, nor provide for the stimulation needed for accelerated urban economies. Increased pressure from local governments may be a good indicator that technocratic and managerial skills are being developed at local levels and that the time is appropriate for more decentralization. It should also be stressed that decentralization may in the beginning be rather costly and not yet cost-effective. The actual yields of decentralization may only become visible in the medium- or long-term. However, as is well known, decentralization is not a "quick fix" (Rondinelli, Nellis and Shabbir Cheema, 1983).

A critical issue that will remain so, is the involvement of the private sector, non-governmental organizations and communities in urban development through public-private partnership projects or through people's direct participation. The nature of the integrated urban development approach provides an excellent opportunity for increased public-private partnership and community participation, but these will require right and sensible stimulation. The multi-year planning process of "bottom-up" planning, with its many complicated steps, needs to be opened up for more participation of formal and non-formal private sector groups. Such groups need strong encouragement and guidance in order not to become disorientated in the working of the planning machinery. On the other hand, it appears that the ambitious development goals of any integrated urban development strategy and of special infrastructure programmes can only achieve their intended strength and impact if an effective partnership between public, private and community sectors is built up.

BIBLIOGRAPHY

Baross, P. (1991), *Action Planning*, IHS Working Paper No. 2, Rotterdam.

Dimitriou, H.T.(1991), 'An Integrated Approach to Urban Infrastructure Development: A Review of the Indonesian Experience', *Cities*, 8 (3): 193–208.

Institute for Housing and Urban Development Studies (IHS)/Steinberg, F. (1993), *Training Manual for Integrated Infrastructure Planning*, Unpublished draft, IHS, Rotterdam.

Joshi, J. and Lojewski, H.V. (1993), 'Urban Planning Methods in Nepal II—Further Experiences with the Integrated Action Planning Approach (IAP) in Nepal', *TRIALOG*, 39: 20–25.

Heinrichs, B. (1993), 'Urban Planning Methods in Nepal I—The First Application of the Integrated Action Planning Approach (IAP) in Nepal', *TRIALOG*, 39, 18–19.

Hoff, R. van der and Steinberg, F. (eds.) (1992), *Innovative Approaches to Urban Development: The Integrated Urban Infrastructure Development Programme in Indonesia*, Aldershot, Avebury.

Hoff, R. van der and Steinberg, F. (1993), *The Integrated Urban Infrastructure Development Programme and Urban Management Innovations in Indonesia*, IHS Working Paper No. 7, Rotterdam.

Mabogunje, A. (1993), 'Infrastructure: The Crux of Modern Urban Development', *Urban Age*, 1 (3): 3–6.

McGill, R. (1994), 'Integrated Urban Management: An Operational Model for Third World City Managers', *Cities*, 11 (1): 35–47.

Peterson, G.E., Kingsley, G.T. and Telgarsky, J.P. (1994), *Multi-sectoral Investment Planning*, Urban Management Programme (UMP) Working Paper Series No. 3, UNCHS Nairobi.

Rondinelli, D.A., Nellis, J.R. and Shabbir Cheema, G. (1983), *Decentralization in Developing Countries: A Review of Experience*, World Bank Staff Working Paper No. 581, Washington, D.C.

Sidabutar, P., Rukmana, N., Hoff, R. van der and Steinberg, F. (1991), 'Development of Urban Management Capabilities: Training for Integrated Urban Infrastructure Development in Indonesia', *Cities*, (Oxford), 8(2), 142–150.

Suselo, H., Taylor, J.L. and Wegelin, E.A. (1995), *Indonesia's Urban Infrastructure Development Experience: Critical Lessons of Good Practice*, UNCHS, Nairobi/Jakarta.

Wegelin, E. (1990), 'New Approaches in Urban Services Delivery: A Comparison of Emerging Experience in Selected Asian Countries', *Cities*, 7 (3): 244–258.

World Bank (1991), *Urban Policy and Economic Development: An Agenda for the 1990s*, World Bank Policy Paper, Washington D.C.

World Bank (1993), *Municipal Development Sector Review: Political Decentralization and Its Implications for Urban Service Delivery*, A draft report, World Bank, Washington D.C.

World Bank (1994), *World Development Report 1994: Infrastructure for Development*, World Bank, Washington D.C.

Zaris, R., Carter, I. and Green, I. (1988), 'An Action Planning Approach to Strategic Urban Development', *Habitat International*, 1 (4): 13–19.

3

TO INTEGRATE OR NOT TO INTEGRATE: DEVELOPING A MODEL FOR EFFECTIVE INTEGRATION

Forbes Davidson and Michael Lindfield

Overview

Integration is a much proposed, but little implemented concept (Wegelin, 1990). There are strong reasons for integration—the most important being that it can make better use of scarce resources; put another way, programmes can be more effective in reaching their objectives. This is very important if it means that more families get access to basic services, or that a town's economy can function better.

However the performance of integrated programmes is often considerably less than optimal in terms of: (i) the sustainability of their organizational structure; (ii) the effectiveness of relationships between professionals; and (iii) the efficiency in the use of resources. This leads to the question of why are integrated programmes all that effective. In many cases the integration process is not sufficiently thought through. The tensions arising from the attempts to integrate are often counter-productive. Integration should only be attempted when the benefits are so clear that they outweigh the pressures that tend to oppose integration. These pressures include opposition from officials who perceive that they lose power in the process of integration.

This article attempts to review some of the major international experiences in integration. It assesses their effectiveness and derives what lessons can be learnt. On the basis of the international experiences assessed, a model is proposed. This model sees integration as a means towards an objective rather than an objective in itself. The various dimensions of integration are then described and used as a basis for improvement of practise.

The Reasons for Integration

Why Integrate?

Integration allows for more effective and efficient use of scarce resources. And although "effectiveness" is now a fashionable word, but the concept in itself is very important. By effectiveness is meant whether a programme is actually succeeding in meeting its objectives. By "efficiency" is meant whether a programme is using resources well in order to achieve its objectives. Integration is essentially aimed at promoting efficiency in order to make the programmes more effective. This is achieved through:

— Allowing for effective planning and implementation through the possibility of trade-offs and acquiring potentially higher overall benefits from a given amount of resources spent on a programme;
— Enabling implementing organizations to perform more effectively; and
— Helping to identify and mobilize additional financial and human resources.

What Happens If We Don't Do it Well ?

Inappropriate attempts to integrate can waste time and resources. This happens when one:

— Tries to achieve uniform or coordinated technical inputs for no significant net gain in output and to achieve uniform or coordinated outputs which contribute little or nothing to programme impact;
— Creates the need to establish or restructure organizations with no significant net gain in efficiency or effectiveness of outputs; and
— Establishes or restructures funding systems with no net gains.

In effect, inappropriate integration does not result in lower cost and more accessible products and services being delivered in a more timely manner. In fact, it can even result in more expensive products delivered at a later point in time.

Lessons from International Experience

The Regional Cities Development Programme, Thailand

The objectives of the Regional Cities Development Programme (RCDP) were essentially to divert development from Bangkok and improve the standard of living in the regional cities (Sinclair, et al., 1983, 1986). In order to achieve these objectives there was a perceived need to integrate the organizations involved in the RCDP—specifically the municipalities and the public works department (PWD). To achieve this the Office of Urban Development (OUD) was created within the Local Government Affairs Division (LGAD) of the Ministry of the Interior (MOI). Both OUD and PWD were under the same ministry, MOI. However the PWD had been established much earlier, was much larger, both in staff and resources, and had much greater institutional hierarchy than the LGAD. The municipalities however, were clearly under the control of the LGAD.

In these circumstances, OUD could "cooperate" with PWD but could relatively effectively "coordinate" the activities of the municipalities. The external "glue" applied to this structure was the World Bank/Australian International Development Assistance Bureau (AIDAB) funding for RCDP, which "required" OUD for implementation of the project.

When the second RCDP failed to materialize, OUD reverted to the LGAD, losing its status as an independent bureau. Financial monitoring systems, both at the municipal level and at OUD, were much improved as a result of the RCDP. However, an attempt to integrate the municipality-controlled Municipal Development Fund into the funding structure of the RCDP—a good idea from a technical point of view—was resisted by the mayors of the municipalities and ultimately rejected (Lindfield, 1987).

Effectiveness: In terms of its first objective of diverting development from Bangkok, the programme achieved very little because the cities chosen were too far from the capital and only the infrastructure in the cities, not their links to the primate and to their hinterland, were considered. It terms of its other objective of improving the quality of life in the regional cities, however, significant improvements were made.

Key lessons: One can derive the following lessons from this programme:
1. Different levels of "integration" are appropriate in different organizational and political contexts.
2. Integration persists only as long as the organizations involved see tangible benefits accruing from it.
3. Technical and spatial integration—achieved in the RCDP by AIDAB-funded consultants and continued by OUD—is perhaps easier to achieve in the short term.
4. Financial integration in the face of vested interests, except in respect to financial systems, is difficult unless substantial effort, backed by

political will, is mobilized and maintained. It is also important that integration does not work against objectives involving decentraliza-tion of financial decision-making powers.

The Integrated Urban Infrastructure Development Programme, Indonesia

The Programme: The Integrated Urban Infrastructure Development Programme (IUIDP) has many objectives. But they may be characterized primarily as: (i) upgrading the standard of living in urban areas in an efficient manner by undertaking comprehensive upgrading of infrastructure; and (ii) strengthening the urban management institutions in order to sustain this improvement process.

In order to achieve these objectives there was a perceived need to integrate the technical sections of the central Ministry of Public Works (MOPW) and the local governments. To achieve this, the Human Settlements Department of MOPW was strengthened. The Ministry of Home Affairs (MOHA) which is nominally in control of local govern-ment was initially excluded from this process as fund flow was through the Human Settlement Department. Because of its control over resources, and backed with the ability to obtain legislative changes which bound MOHA, the Human Settlement Department was able to implement substantial changes in the organization and funding systems of local governments.

In these circumstances, the Human Settlement Department could effectively "integrate" certain parts of local government into its opera-tions. Again, the external "glue" applied to this structure was the assistance of the World Bank, Asian Development Bank and other agencies which "required" integration for implementation of the project (Hoff and Steinberg, 1992; Davidson and Watson, 1995).

As decentralization has become more of an objective in Indonesia, MOHA has been brought more into the IUIDP process—in particular—in the process of strengthening local governments. Financial monitoring systems, at the municipal level and at both the Human Settlement Department and MOHA were improved as a result of the IUIDP. However, an attempt to create a Regional Development Fund to finance infrastructure for cities—again a good idea from a technical point of view—was resisted by many parties within the Indonesian government and is a "lame duck" (Suselo, Taylor and Wegelin, 1995).

Effectiveness: Substantial improvements have been made in the infra-structure of the cities in Indonesia as a result of the programme. These improvements have focussed on bulk infrastructure as well as slum upgrading—areas which are under the control of the Human Settlement Department and were considered too narrow a focus to enable comprehensive integrated development of urban areas. However, less impact has been achieved in making organizations responsible for providing and maintaining this infrastructure at the local level. Some progress has however, indeed been made in upgrading the standard of local consultants to the point where they can support the local governments in implementing infrastructure investments.

Key lessons: The difficulty of getting different departments to integrate was recognized. In response to this a major long-term programme of training and communication support was started. Problems were more in the central government than in the local government, where integration is more natural as programmes come together in a limited area. Further, the elements of integration—technical, financial and organizational were recognized after some years and formalized in requirements for plans which comprise three main components: the integrated infrastructure plan; the Revenue Improvement Action Plan (RIAP) and the Local Institutional Development Plan (LIDAP).

A shortcoming of the programme was that the benefits of integration, and who would benefit, were not sufficiently emphasized. This made the "sale" of the programme to local government even more difficult.

The Integrated Development of Small and Medium Towns, India

The programme: The Integrated Development for Small and Medium Towns (IDSMT) is a programme aimed at promoting the development of smaller towns through funding strategic projects. The development of these towns was hoped to help stem the tide of migration to the big cities. The programme has been running for some 15 years, and by 1992 some 515 towns had been involved in the programme through three plan periods (Ribeiro, 1987; Edelman and Banerjee, 1994). Funds are provided by the central government as concessionary loans on a matching basis with state or local government. Typically the programmes include land development for shelter (e.g. sites and services), road and traffic improvement and commercial or industrial development (e.g. a market building which provides stimuli to the town and a source of revenue for the municipality). Complementary stimuli to this was state and local funding of other programmes such as slum improvement, which should be planned in an integrated manner. Plans have most often been developed by state governments, though in theory, local government should play a strong role. The most recent phase of the programme has included part of the funding from "official finance organizations", such as the Housing and Urban Development Corporation (HUDCO). With these loans, much higher interest rates are paid and there are no grace periods.

Effectiveness: A considerable amount of infrastructure has been built, and market buildings developed, which provide some revenue to the local government. However, the results of the programme have been disappointing from the viewpoint of good performance arising from the use of an integrated approach. Land programmes were often held up by litigation. Commercial development programmes were often ill-advised. The role of local government was often too weak to make for good, strategic decision-making, and local government itself was weak as a manager. Often, local government would be bypassed in decision-making and sometimes even not informed (Edelman and Banerjee, 1994).

Key lessons—India: Among the lessons learnt from the experiences of IDSMT are:

1. Decision-making has been too centralized—normally at the level of state government. Integration of programme elements at that level was very difficult (Prasad et al., 1988). It also meant that it was not possible for local government to make good decisions on the dimensions of integration.
2. Local government in many states is very weak, with only limited capacity to plan and manage.
3. The level of investment has often been too low to make a major impact.
4. The investment has not been well focussed locally to promote economic development (Development Administration Group, 1989);
5. Support and training programmes for local government and state government were recognized in the original planning, but were only weakly implemented. The benefits from integration were not stressed, were seldom planned, and were not appraised.
6. The original objectives for the national strategy were probably unrealistic.

Analysis of International Lessons

The key lessons to emerge from this brief review of three experiences in integrated programmes are:

1. Integration is often seen as an end in itself, rather than a means towards producing better services.
2. There is an underestimation of the tensions and resistance arising from integration efforts which require strong management if they are not to undermine programmes.
3. The questions of the desirability of different degrees of integration and the elements of integration such as finance, organization, technical and spatial elements, have not been well considered.
4. The benefits from integration need to be clear and should be clearly communicated to those concerned (Figures 3.1 and 3.2).

Figure 3.1. Dynamics of Integration

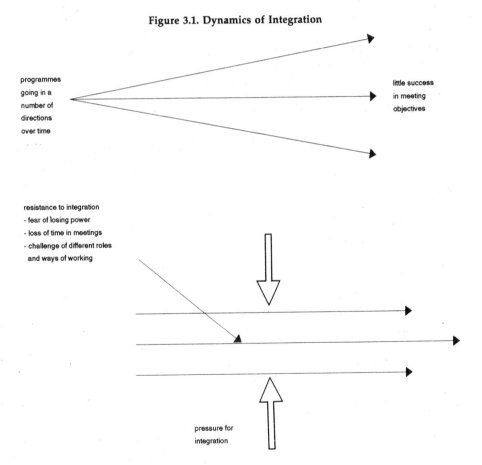

A Model of Integration

In order to improve the performance of integration, it is useful to understand the dynamics and dimensions involved. Dynamics relates to what forces are operating when we try to integrate. Dimensions refers to the nature of integration itself. First we will look at the dynamics.

Dynamics of Integration

Integration is *relatively* simple when one body holds all the money and covers all the technical sectors concerned. However, this is seldom the case. When integration entails that organizations or departments have to give up control over programmes or projects, then resistance can be expected. This is illustrated in Figure 3.1, where programmes are diverging in their aims. Figure 3.2 indicates pressures for integration being resisted by fear of loss of power, loss of time and the unknown factors involved in different ways of working. Figure 3.3 indicates the need for success to provide the motivation to maintain pressure for integration.

Figure 3.3. Success Needed to Maintain Integration

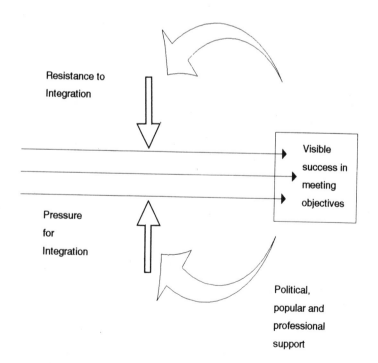

Resistance to
Integration

Visible
success in
meeting
objectives

Pressure
for
Integration

Political,
popular and
professional
support

Dimensions of Integration

Dimensions of integration refer to ways that we can look more closely at what integration actually means. Professionals often use the word "integration" very loosely. However, it is useful to look more closely at the concept of integration, and subdivide it to achieve a more meaningful understanding of the term. This can be done in two ways: the first, which we call "levels" describes how integrated a project programme is, and how integrated it needs to be. The second dimension, which we call "element" describes what is integrated spatial and technical aspects, financial aspects and organizational aspects.

Levels

It is useful to look at the three main levels of working together. These are cooperation, coordination and integration. They represent an increasing intensity of working together, an increasing potential of greater efficiency and also an increasing chance of conflict. All levels share the need for the motivation that comes from sharing common objectives. These levels and their requirements are illustrated in Figure 3.4.

Cooperation: This requires a willingness to work together and modify plans in order to meet a common objective. It depends on good motivation, itself founded often on understanding based on good information. It is very much contingent on personal relations and trust rather than rules and regulations. A lot of effort is needed to establish this, and needs continuity of goodwill in order to sustain. On its own it is often sufficient. It is also the foundation for coordination and integration. Without it, they will not work.

Figure 3.4. Levels of Integration and Requirements

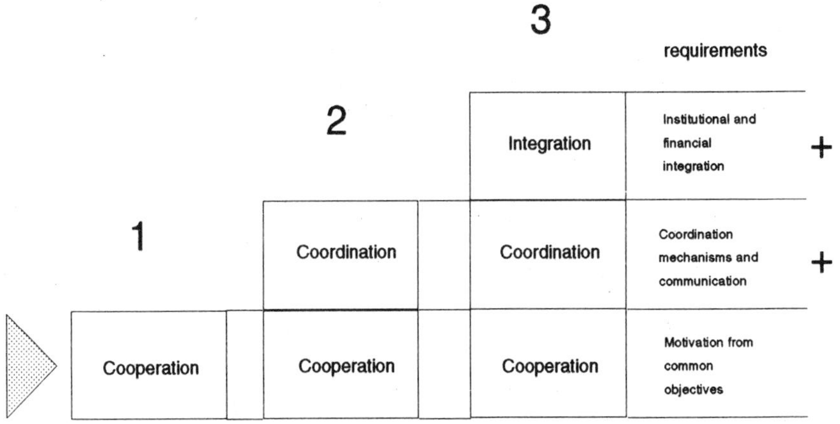

Coordination: This requires that certain procedures are established to regularly consult and discuss issues. It is more formal and takes more time, but may be necessary, especially where issues are complicated and where bureaucratic organizations are involved.

Integration: Integration means "bringing together into one". An example is a project that deals with a number of different sectors by planning, financing and managing their implementation together. To work, not only does it require cooperation and coordination but also needs a formalized decision-making system and procedures to enable this system to work efficiently and effectively.

Elements

The second way of looking at integration in a detailed is to examine the forms that it takes. Four main elements can be identified: institutional, technical, spatial and financial. Figure 3.5 represents these four elements.

Figure 3.5. Elements of Integration

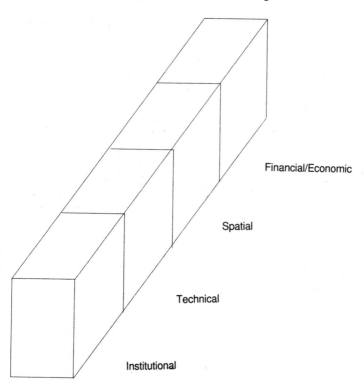

Financial/Economic

Spatial

Technical

Institutional

Institutional integration: This refers to the relationships between the institutions concerned and their motivation and ability to work together. "Institution" refers to governmental, non-governmental, private and community-based organizations. Within organizations it can include working together between disciplines. Forms of institutional integration can include partnerships. This area is one which is very often overlooked and which needs particular attention here. If there is no clear idea of why to work together and no clear perceived benefit, then any level of integration is likely to be undertaken reluctantly. Under these circumstances the results are likely to be ineffective.

Technical integration: This involve links between different sectors, for example, linkages between water supply and drainage. This is a very important area, giving the possibilities of efficient and effective working. From this it is possible to create positive links, for instance, between drainage and solid waste collection, so that increased benefits can be obtained.

Spatial integration: Related to technical integration but deserving of separate consideration is geographic or area-based integration. Creative links between different programmes are possible when they are carried out in the same location. Demands for spatial integration include spatial planning, design and understanding of land and property markets. The case of Mehboobnagar, Andhra Pradesh, in India illustrates a case where lack of integration resulted in less effective development (Box 3.1).

Box 3.1. Environmental Improvement of Urban Slums: A Case from India

In Mehboobnagar, in Andhra Pradesh a slum was being improved under the Environmental Improvement of Urban Slums (EIUS) programme. There was not enough money to complete more than half of the access improvement. The programme was implemented by contractors. At the same time the community had been organized under another programme—the Urban Basic Services for the Poor (UBSP). However, no link was made between the programmes. This was a lost opportunity. If the community had provided labour, the access paths could have been completed.

Financial integration: Integration of different elements is always difficult if there is no financial integration. Conversely, it is often the integration of budgets which creates the major opposition to integration. For example, different departments such as roads and water may normally have their own budgets and the advantages of power and perks that go with them. They also have their own systems for tendering and managing contracts. To have this pooled in the budget of an integrated programme creates a situation where these departments stand to lose power. Without financial integration, however, it is difficult to achieve the trade-offs and efficiencies that allow major savings.

Summary of the Model

Integration is important as it has the potential to increase the efficiency of projects and programmes, and through this, to increase their effectiveness. However, the higher the level of integration, the more is the pressure which is likely to be against it. For this reason, the benefits to be gained must be very clear to all concerned. The best level of integration is likely to be the lowest but which still gives clear benefits. All levels, however, require a foundation of common objectives which integration can help achieve.

The four main elements of integration—organizational, technical, spatial and financial/economic—must all be taken into account if integration is to be successful. This is illustrated in Figure 3.6.

Figure 3.6. Dimensions of Integration

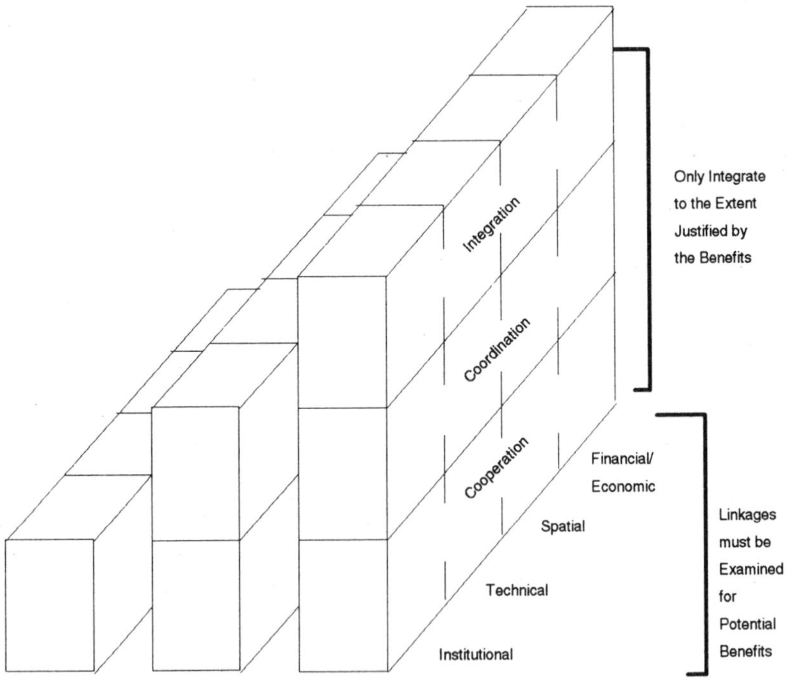

Practical Implications of the Model

Requirements for Integration

For good use of resources, some level of integration is desirable. It is essential that all parties involved have clear common objectives. This suggests that they should all be involved in the planning process from as early a stage as possible. The higher the level of integration, the more difficult the process is likely to be. For this reason particular attention should be directed to ensure that the level of integration is commensurate with the benefits likely. Further, integration should link together the institutional, technical, spatial and financial elements. Procedures should be built into programme planning and appraisal to ensure that the dimensions of integration are properly considered. It needs to be ensured that an appropriate institutional setting is created in order to implement the solution and operate any resulting investment, systems, etc., (institutional integration). Appropriate technical inputs are brought to bear in order to achieve the optimal physical/social solution (technical integration). Elements are considered spatially so as to derive the maximum possible advantage of their relationships, or to avoid negative relationships (spatial integration). There are appropriate financial inputs to fund this solution in the long term (financial integration).

Implications for Programme Design

This model has two major implications for modifying current programme design practice:

— Preparatory projects should only be formulated so as to involve broad-based participatory processes such as working groups or fora which structure a wide range of stakeholder inputs to identify, prioritize and find solutions to problems and issues. Required levels of integration should be decided by working groups.

— The preparatory process should be resourced and monitored by an independent parallel group which: (a) acts to raise issues to introduce new concepts and different forms of organizational structure and additional financing sources; and (b) acts as a "ginger group", and (c) monitors the preparatory process. This group would basically raise the potentials for integration (in the interests of the more effective execution of the project).

Conclusion

Integration has the potential to mobilize scarce resources more efficiently, and for this reason it is a very important approach. However, in project formulation and appraisal there is a need to specifically test the degree of integration proposed to ensure that it is necessary. This means assessing the potential stress and relating this to the potential gains. The gains must be significant and clear to all parties involved to make it worth the effort of going for full integration.

In short, for integration to work it is necessary to ensure that:

2+2 = (at least) 5

BIBLIOGRAPHY

Davidson. F. and Watson, D. (1995), 'Training for IUIDP: Ideas, Integration and Implementation', in Suselo, H., Taylor, J.L. and Wegelin, E.A. (eds.), *Indonesia's Urban Infrastructure Development Experience: Critical Lessons of Good Practice*, UNCHS, Nairobi.

Development Administration Group (ed.), (1989), *Generating Economic Development in Smaller Towns of Gujarat, India*, Series on Indian Urban Management No. 38, University of Birmingham.

Edelman, D. and Banerjee, R. (1994), 'Case Study of India's Integrated Development of Small and Medium Towns Programme in Karnataka State', Paper present at the ISOCARP Conference, Prague.

Hoff, R. van der and Steinberg, F. (1992), *Innovative Approach to Urban Development: The Integrated Urban Infrastructure Development Programme in Indonesia*, Aldershot, Avebury.

Lindfield M. (1987), 'Integrated Urban Projects', Paper presented at the 7th International NHA-IHS-ATI 'Seminar on Integrated Development Programme: A Support Strategy for Housing Development', Asian Institute of Technology (AIT), Bangkok.

Prasad, D.R. *et al.* (1988), *Integrated Development of Small and Medium Towns in Karnataka and Tamil Nadu—An Evaluation*, Regional Centre for Urban and Environmental Studies (RCUES), Osmania University, Hyderabad.

Ribeiro, E.F.N. (1987), 'Role of Medium and Small Towns in the Human Settlements System of India', Paper presented at the 7th International NHA-IHS-ATI 'Seminar on Integrated Development Programme: A Support Strategy for Housing Development', Asian Institute of Technology (ATI), Bangkok.

Sinclair Knight and Partners Pvt. Ltd. (1983), *Feasibility Studies for the Regional Cities Development Project*, Songkhla, Vol. 6, Ministry of Interior, Bangkok.

Sinclair Knight and Partners Pvt. Ltd. (1986), *Songkhla Fishport and Industrial Estate Development: Management and Marketing Plan*, Ministry of the Interior, Bangkok.

Suselo H., Taylor, J.L. and Wegelin, E.A. (1995), *Indonesia's Urban Infrastructure Development Experience: Critical Lessons of Good Practice*, UNCHS.

Wegelin, E.A. (1990), 'New Approaches in Urban Services Delivery: A Comparison of Emerging Experiences in Selected Asian Countries', *Cities*, 7 (3): 244–258.

4

THE URBAN MANAGEMENT PROGRAMME AND INTEGRATED URBAN INFRASTRUCTURE DEVELOPMENT

Emiel A. Wegelin

Overall Programme Scope and Operation

The Urban Management Programme (UMP) is a long-term global technical cooperation programme (initially funded for the ten-year period 1986-1996) designed to strengthen the contribution that cities and towns in developing countries make toward human development, including economic growth, social development and reduction of poverty. The UMP is a partnership between the United Nations Development Programme (UNDP), the United Nations Centre for Human Settlements (UNCHS-Habitat) and the World Bank. It is presently also supported by 12 bilateral external support agencies, and as such it is the largest global multi-agency technical assistance programme in urban development in the world. It involves a partnership of many actors in developing countries at the regional, national, municipal, non-governmental and community levels.

The UMP Phase 1 (1986–1992) — for which the World Bank was the executing agency and UNCHS-Habitat the associated agency — focussed mainly on the development of "generic" policy framework papers, discussion papers and tools with global validity and applicability in the areas of municipal finance and administration, urban land management and urban infrastructure management. From 1991 onwards it also focussed on urban environmental management.

The UMP Phase 2 (1992–1996) — which started in mid-1992 and which is executed by UNCHS-Habitat, with the World Bank as the associated agency—is translating the results of the Phase 1 into operational support for policy action planning and programming at the national, provincial and city levels. This phase of the programme is characterized by three key operational principles:

— It is **demand driven.**
— It is **operationally decentralized through regional offices and networks of expertise.**
— It **brings together the creative efforts and experience of the international support community in urban management.**

The key actors are those at the regional, national, municipal and community levels in the developing countries themselves. The ultimate beneficiaries of the programme are the citizens who live in and use cities and towns, particularly the urban poor, who will receive better-managed services and more accountable, participatory and transparent urban management. To achieve this, local, national and regional expertise will be strengthened.

UMP Phase 2 thematically covers the five substantive areas:

— municipal finance and administration;
— urban infrastructure management;
— urban land management;
— urban environmental management; and
— urban poverty alleviation.

The programme relies on two mutually supportive processes to facilitate capacity building in these theme areas:

a) **City and country consultations**: These bring together national and local authorities, the private sector, community representatives and other stakeholders within a country to discuss specific problems within the UMP theme areas enumerated above and to propose reasoned solutions. In doing so, UMP thematic policy framework papers, discussion papers and technical tools, as applicable, are used as starting points for the discussion. Consultations are held at the request of a country or city and are intended to provide a forum for discussion of a cross-section of issues, generally resulting in a concrete action plan for policy programme change. As noted above, the UMP in Phase 2, as a matter of principle, responds to **articulated demand** for support, rather than proffering its potential for assistance.

b) **Regional networks of experts**: The second process is the development of regional networks of experts in each of the five UMP theme areas for the purpose of providing technical advice and cooperation to ensure sustained capability to support consultations and follow-up thereafter. This follow up includes facilitating the implementation of action plans and the mobilization of resources required for it. Typically, these regional experts become the foundation of the human resource base in the programme after having participated in several country or city consultations in their specific area of competence.

These processes are spearheaded by the UMP regional offices in Africa, the Arab states, Asia and the Pacific, and Latin America and the Caribbean, through which the UMP seeks to strengthen urban management by harnessing the skills and strategies of regional networks of experts, communities and organizations in the public and private sectors.

Through its core teams in Nairobi (UNCHS) and Washington (World Bank) the UMP supports the regional programmes and networks by synthesizing lessons learned; identifying best practices; conducting ongoing state-of-the-art research; and disseminating programme-related materials. In principle, this covers all the five UMP themes noted earlier.

UMPs Policy Focus in Urban Infrastructure Management

The inability of cities to provide and maintain adequate infrastructure severely affects the productivity, and the living and working environments of their populations, especially of the urban poor. The traditional supply orientation to infrastructure policy has tended to produce an overemphasis on facilities rather than a focus on services, emphasis on public sector provision (which often requires the coordination of many institutional actors) and politicized decision-making regarding types of investments and pricing of services. These developments, in turn, have resulted in haphazard investments in new assets (often based on inappropriate standards of provision), inadequate operation and maintenance, non-sustainability and unreliability of services, constraints to economic productivity and environmental degradation. Infrastructure investments also have too often been made without adequate attention to cross-sectoral linkages. As a result, many cities are burdened with capital projects that no longer can function at their designed capacity, are located in the wrong places for today's economic activity, or require so much funding that they displace other, more useful projects. Investments need to be coordinated across sectors, fit within a multi-year development plan and be consistent with the financing constraints that a locality faces.

Therefore, the UMP promotes an urban infrastructure service delivery approach that provides and maintains adequate infrastructure services which respond to effective demand and emphasize affordability, inter-sectoral linkages, appropriate standards and partnerships between the public, private and community sectors in demand identification and service delivery. It is noted that service demands differ widely across cities, countries and industries along the dimensions of accessibility, capacity, diversity, quality, time, condition and price. The traditional focus has been on capacity, but demands are increasingly shifting to other service dimensions. Delivery plans must be in place to meet demands that differ along each of these dimensions both within and across cities.

Urban Management Programme Information

The UMP produces a number of publications which present the findings of case studies, research, and the insights and broad recommendations developed under the work of the UMP to date, and illustrate instruments, techniques or examples of good practice and procedures that the UMP has found useful in addressing the issues surrounding the five components. The UMP issues a formal publications series that consists of discussion papers, policy framework papers, and management tools. With respect to infrastructure the UMP has published a policy framework entitled "Strategic Options for Urban Infrastructure Management" (Fox, 1994) and a tool paper entitled "Utility Mapping and Record Keeping for Infrastructure" (Pickering, Park and Bannister, 1993). In addition the UMP publishes working papers, which have a more operational focus. The working paper series seeks to highlight examples of good practice in urban management. This ranges from case studies of one or more aspects of urban management in a particular city to regional and even global syntheses of experiences. Complementary to the policy framework on infrastructure management the UMP therefore published a working paper on MSIP (Peterson, Kingsley and Telgarsky, 1994). This paper is now discussed in brief as it highlights some vital issues.

Multi-sectoral Investment Planning[1]

General Considerations

Investment priority setting lies at the heart of a community's planning for its future. Infrastructure systems, like roads or water networks, and public facilities, like school buildings or health clinics, have useful lives of 25 years to as long as a century or more. Investments in these facilities

---

[1]   This section draws heavily on Peterson, Kingsley and Telgarsky (1994). This paper is meant as reference for officials charged with decision-making on capital planning and selection of priorities for investment at the local level. The paper provides an overview of existing practice and possible options, which then can be built into operational policy and daily management. The paper is primarily based on experiences in the cities of developing countries as is expected to be used by the concerned individual there.

shape the development of a community or an entire urban region. They help determine the directions in which population growth will occur, the cost competitiveness of business operations in the community, and the satisfaction of citizens with the public services they receive.

MSIP is a process for setting investment priorities. It has roots both in the physical planning traditions of master plans and in the budgeting tradition of the annual operating and capital budgets. Its product is a multi-year capital plan, showing what investments will take place across sectors, how this investment will be financed, and the repercussions of investments on the operating and maintenance budgets of local public agencies. When the MSIP process is taken seriously, and the resource constraint is acknowledged realistically, the resulting plan provides a framework both for public sector decisions and for private sector investment.

Traditional urban planning has often produced plans that are too ambitious or too prescriptive, or that fail to take into account users' willingness to pay for public facilities. As a result, there is a history of unrealized plans—not just project designs that are never built, but basic frameworks that are never taken seriously by real-life investors, whether in the public or private sectors. However, MSIP is not the magic solution within urban management. It should be seen as just one of the tools to improve the management of local capital investment decision-making.

Multi-sectoral investment planning begins with four injunctions:

1. Investment planning should be demand-driven. Users' interests are paramount. The role of planners and other public agencies when setting investment priorities is to accurately detect demand, steer development toward areas where it can be accommodated most efficiently, and take into account the financial and social costs of proposed capital improvements.

2. All public agencies with a significant role in investment decisions should be part of the local multi-sectoral investment planning process. Success of the process depends upon effective interaction between planners and budgeting officials, on the one hand, and line agencies that are responsible for supplying services, on the other. In the end, household and business demand is for the *services* that infrastructure facilities provide, but as the durable skeleton of the urban area, the facilities have impacts beyond the sector-specific satisfaction of today's service demands.

3. When an MSIP process is inaugurated, every step should be simplified as much as possible. It is far more important to put in place a broad priority-setting approach that gathers and analyses information

across sectors, and uses both "demand" and "cost" factors, than to try to perfect any single step of the process. *Few MSIP processes have ever failed because they took practical shortcuts. Most have failed because they never got off the ground. The preparatory work has been so detailed and time-consuming that participants lose interest, especially if they observe that the elements in place are not influencing actual investments.*

4. Comprehensiveness is critical to a well-functioning MSIP process. There should be a strategy for allocating scarce investment resources across all sectors and all projects. This does *not* imply, however, that a central planning group needs to assess and prioritize all potential projects. Some investment decisions are best entrusted to markets; others can be decentralized to line agencies; still others can be decentralized to community or neighbourhood associations. In fact, the MSIP process cannot function effectively unless decentralization is used to relieve the burden on the central planning and budgeting group.

Implementing a Multi-sectoral Investment Planning Process

The exact design of the MSIP process must be adjusted to the institutions and planning practices of each country, as well as to the size and complexity of municipal authorities. However, similar steps typically are involved in establishing a workable approach. These steps can serve as a guide to establishing MSIP systems.

1. **Establish an inter-agency steering group and lead agency that will have responsibility for investment prioritizing.** All of the principal agencies involved in planning, building, paying for, and operating major public facilities should be represented on the inter-agency steering group. The role of the steering group, relative to political authorities, in making final investment choices should be clearly established.

2. **Decide on the mechanisms that will be employed for measuring user demand and incorporating this information within the priority setting process.** User demand can be measured in many ways. For some kinds of facilities, markets provide the best vehicle for transmitting demand signals. For other kinds of facilities, household and business surveys or other techniques can be used to capture demand. In the past, however, user demand has been underrepresented in government priority setting. More attention has been given to supplier preferences or the jurisdiction's physical plans. A systematic strategy is needed for incorporating "demand" into capital planning and budgeting.

3. **Identify the capital improvements priorities of the community through surveys and other techniques.** Informed priority setting requires as much information as possible on the critical needs of the community, both objectively expressed as infrastructure service inadequacies and subjectively expressed as citizen perceptions of priorities and willingness to pay for capital improvements. Measurement of service coverage, capital stock condition and household willingness to pay provide the background picture from which informed investment choices can be made.

4. **Obtain information on investment activities already underway or about to be started.** One advantage of a coordinated MSIP process is that it provides monitoring investment activity. In the absence of such a system, the potential arises for vast duplication between local government investment and state or central government investment in the same region, or for incompatibilities between city-wide infrastructure systems and the local improvement efforts undertaken by neighbourhood associations and community groups.

5. **Prepare lists of prioritized projects by agency or individual sector.** The priority setting process begins with the instructions given to line agencies and other institutions responsible for preparing investment proposals and delivering services. These instructions should clarify the criteria that are to be used in ranking capital projects in order to reinforce common development goals.

6. **Decide on cross-sectoral project priorities.** A core group of agencies' prioritized projects will then be referred to the steering group for cross-sectoral comparison. A number of evaluation systems have been used by different communities to rank capital projects. These range from common sense methods, intended to insure that systematic consideration is given to all projects, to elaborate scoring systems, designed to leave less room for political judgments in priority setting. None of these ranking systems should be allowed to operate on automatic pilot. However, as modified to fit local conditions, they can be of great value in clarifying local objectives for the capital programme and ensuring that individual projects serve these objectives.

7. **Plan for the revenue side of the MSIP budget.** Investment planning traditionally has given more attention to priority setting on the expenditure side of the capital budget than to revenue analysis. However, revenue constraints provide a reality check for all

investment plans. The multi-year capital plan should be elaborated on both the expenditure and revenue side, so that financing requirements are clear. Potential sources of financing then can be systematically examined, together with indications of citizen-taxpayer willingness to pay for any increase in local capital spending.

Local Investment Planning in an Inter-governmental Setting

This section focuses on MSIP at the local level. However, local authorities do not exist in a vacuum—they are part of an inter-governmental system. Investment priorities for urban development may be set by national or provincial levels of government. A large part of local investment funding will continue to come, either directly or indirectly, from these higher levels of government.

Sharing Information on Capital Projects between Levels of Government

In many countries, central government provincial ministries still bear the principal responsibility for local-level investment. At a minimum, local authorities need to be informed accurately and in time about these projects. They then can plan the local capital budget around the major investments being put in place by others. In any kind of integrated planning process, decisions about land development or water and drainage systems need to be coordinated with new road construction (see Box 4.1).

Box 4.1. Integrated Public Investment System, State of Baja California, Mexico

The problem of inter-governmental information regarding public works projects is being addressed by the State of Baja California in its Integrated Public Investment System. The system generates monthly reports on the status of all public works underway or planned for construction in the state. It is used as a diagnostic tool for the timely delivery of public works. The data generated by the system is used to prepare executive reports for the Governor and state authorities, and poster-sized information sheets displayed in public buildings throughout the state. The system is now being modified so that, following each monthly update, information on individual urban areas in the state will be automatically downloaded to the city planning authorities in larger cities.

Priority setting for local projects will be greatly influenced by the kinds of complementarities that are possible with the large-scale infrastructure systems being installed by a national government. Perhaps of even greater importance is the fact that, if local authorities know that a major local investment is planned by higher authorities, they can monitor its progress and help shape the project to fit locally defined needs. A routine system of inter-governmental notification should be established. Without it, experience shows that central ministries will, from time to time, neglect to inform local authorities in time about their plans.

Support for Cross-sectoral Local Planning

Practical urban problems do not fall into mutually exclusive sectoral categories. Nor do they respect the administrative divisions built into central government ministry structure. They logically require a cross-sectoral planning and action response. Local authorities often are able to see these connections, but their ability to respond through public action is hampered by the fact that they must obtain funds or authority to act from central government agencies which are focussed exclusively on their individual sectors (see Box 4.2).

Box 4.2. Decentralization and Inter-sectoral Planning in the State of Karnataka, India

> In 1985, the Karnataka state government transferred development responsibilities to district-level administration. The state government also appointed a number of senior civil service officers to staff each council to build up their capacity. Most importantly, the representatives of central line ministries in each district were made directly responsible to the district council.
>
> District councils then were given responsibility for formulation and implementation of the district development plan, formerly a state responsibility. Under this arrangement, district councils can identify cross-sectoral needs, draw up plans to respond to them, and enlist the support of the different line ministries through their representatives who report to the council. The system has produced a good deal more flexibility for cross-sectoral planning. However, local investment planning is still subject to national- and state-level sectoral norms.

Even in routine investments, the functional separation of central ministries may impede common-sense coordination and prioritization at the local level. In Ghana, roadside drains are installed by the Transport Ministry at the time it builds roads. Other types of drains are the responsibility of another ministry. The Transport Ministry has received more capital funding than other agencies. As a result, in most of Ghana's cities, the only drains to be found are alongside roadways, even though this has produced a drainage system that leaves most of the cities' needs unattended. In most countries in the Asian region, basic responsibility for investment in most urban services is devolved to the local government, which is responsible for establishing the cross-sectoral linkages it believes are critical. However, full decentralization of this responsibility is unlikely to occur. Even so, other kinds of inter-governmental arrangements can support local inter-sectoral planning. The basic requirement is that local authorities be encouraged to tackle problems across sectoral lines, and then be free to recommend solutions that involve coordination among different central-level ministries.

Supporting Local Budgetary Flexibility

A well-functioning MSIP system requires that local authorities have discretion over the size of the capital budget, as long as they are willing to finance project expansion from their own resources. Some additional revenues almost always can be raised from better tax administration. Integrated programmes of urban management improvement typically assist cities in improving tax collections and expanding the tax base simultaneously with the introduction of new capital planning methods. However, cities also need the flexibility to raise tax rates, should this be appropriate, and to employ market-based financing mechanisms such as user fees or betterment taxes. Often central governments still restrict local control over this part of the local budget. A case in point is the property tax—the authority to locally set local property tax rates is not given to local governments in most countries in the region, where such tax is legally still a national (e.g., in Indonesia) or provincial (e.g., in Pakistan) tax.

Governments have followed different strategies in enhancing local authorities' ability to generate revenues. Often, decentralization has involved increasing the national revenue-sharing amounts to which local governments are entitled. Such steps have strengthened local government finances, and increased their ability to perform capital planning and investment. However, these measures do not address local governments' right to choose the size of their budget to be financed from their own sources. In some countries, devolution of service responsibilities to the local level has also been accompanied by granting local authorities new discretion to set tax and fee rates or to tap additional tax bases. In some instances, central governments have gone so far as to provide significant incentives for greater local revenue-generation. In Pakistan, for instance, the 1991 National Finance Commission award adopted a one-for-one matching grant system. Every additional rupee that a local authority generates through restructuring of its local tax system, central government matches with an additional rupee of transfer payments (see Box 4.3).[2]

Inter-governmental Cooperation in Establishing New Investment Planning Approaches

Actions of the kind described in the preceding paragraphs help set the framework for local multi-sectoral investment planning and project selection. Except for the seconding of central ministry staff, they do not

---

[2] For a comprehensive discussion of financial issues related to decentralization, see Dillinger (1994). This report identifies inter-governmental transfer reform as one of the most important areas for action on the decentralization agenda.

Box 4.3. The Municipal Management Improvement Programme in Sri Lanka

In 1985 the Government of Sri Lanka embarked on an ambitious programme to improve municipal management in its 51 Urban Local Authorities (ULAs) within a broader policy of decentralization and strengthening of local government. Support inputs in the programme are largely technical assistance and training, managed and coordinated through an Urban Programme Unit (UPU) specially established for this purpose in the Ministry of Local Government, Housing and Construction.

One of the key features of the programme is that it seeks municipal management and finance performance improvement before significant new capital investments are made. For each ULA participating in the programme performance improvement plans are drawn up: a multi-year plan and a short four-month plan. The plans contain a base line review identifying problems and potential solutions. Based on this an action plan is designed for improvements in areas like local revenue-generation, financial reporting, management procedures, staffing, operation and maintenance, as well as for preparation of investment plans, if required. For each such action area targets as well as dates for completion are set. The plans are formulated in a process of discussion and negotiations between the ULA and a technical assistance team from the UPU.

In implementing the programme the government relies on an incentive strategy, in which it allocates an increasing portion of central government grants for local government development to municipalities which have demonstrated increased performance in the above areas. At the same time substantial technical assistance and training (advocacy/dissemination as well as technical training) is provided to support the initiation and continuing implementation of the programme. Both these features underscore the strong government commitment to the programme which is assisted by United Nations Development Programme (UNDP) and International Bank for Reconstruction and Development (IBRD).

by themselves address the problem of inadequate capacity at the local level, or local authorities' lack of familiarity with the kinds of planning methods suitable for an environment where they have greater control. To change actual practice a more direct collaboration between central and local authorities is needed.

A good example of this comprehensive approach to planning change is the Integrated Urban Infrastructure Development Programme (IUIDP) in Indonesia. Until the mid-1980s, virtually all urban infrastructure in Indonesia was planned by central government agencies in Jakarta (primarily by the Ministry of Public Works) and implemented by their field offices in the provinces. The programmes of one central office (e.g., water supply) were seldom coordinated with those of another (e.g., drainage), either spatially or temporally, and local officials had little chance to influence them.

As cities and towns began to grow much more rapidly, there was recognition that this approach could not be sustained logistically, let alone respond sensitively to the varying needs of different urban areas. Increasingly central government officials came to believe that the only satisfactory long-term solution would be for local governments to assume full responsibility for providing (and largely financing) their own urban services. This approach was endorsed in the National Urban Development Strategy (NUDS). However, it was also clear that few of Indonesia's local governments then had the capacity to assume this role effectively. The IUIDP was a response to this dilemma (see Box 4.4).

Box 4.4. IUIDP in Indonesia

The IUIDP is a phased approach to integrated investment programming and decentralization in which the central government supports local capacity building at the same time that it works with existing local staff in planning and implementing investment programmes. In its idealized form, the process entails the following steps:

1. Meetings are held with provincial governments to review NUDS analyses and prioritize cities for attention.
2. Project teams in the selected cities (local staff with technical assistance provided from the centre) review and update local master plans or develop a new "structure plan" where none is available.
3. Teams then use those plans as a guide in developing a proposed local multi-year investment programme PJM integrated across several sectors and constrained by likely resource availability during the PJM period.
4. The teams are also required to prepare a complete financing plan based on projected resource availability during the PJM period (including a plan that covers the possible enhancement of local revenues) and on responsible local government borrowing as well as on probable support from the central budget and/or external donors.
5. Plans are also prepared for building a commensurate capacity of local government to assume increasing responsibility for infrastructure development, operation and maintenance.
6. On the basis of the multi-year PJMs, individual cities prepare annual budget requests.
7. The programmes and budget requests so defined are reviewed at the provincial and central levels and decisions are made about the allocation of central loan and grant funds.

To date, IUIDP has been limited to functions that traditionally had been the responsibility of the Ministry of Public Works, Directorates General for Human Settlements— department of *Cipta Karya* (water supply, sanitation, drainage, *kampung* improvement, etc.) and roads and highways—department of *Bina Marga* (urban roads). It was reasoned that trying to cover more functions at the start would add more complexity and threaten programme viability. Other functions could be added later, after the validity of the IUIDP approach had been proved.

IUIDP has been implemented nation-wide under guidelines initially issued in 1985 and periodically updated since then. PJMs have been prepared for urban areas in all 27 provinces, covering 56 per cent of the urban population by the end of 1993.

Efforts have been made on a continuing basis to improve the process. For example, the initial guidelines and manuals have been regularly revised based on operating experience. A new emphasis on operations and maintenance was introduced through the Performance Oriented Operations and Maintenance Management System (POMMS), which was designed and tested in eight cities. Also notable was the effort by Directorate General Bina Marga (not initially included in the original programming) to shift virtually all urban road planning into the IUIDP framework.

Partly because initial targets were so ambitious, there have been a number of problems in IUIDP implementation. Particularly in the early years, central-government-sponsored consultants often dominated MSIP preparation, in a number of cases without providing adequate opportunity for meaningful involvement of local officials. To date, many local governments have not internalized the process or developed the capacity to operate it effectively. It also became clear that the initial guidelines were too cumbersome and did not permit enough flexibility to adapt to varying local needs and priorities.

Nonetheless, IUIDP has generally been regarded as a major accomplishment. Its basic characteristics (integrated planning across sectors based on city-specific conditions, the linkage to financial discipline through the revenue improvement action plans (RIAPs) and capacity building through the local institutional development action plans (LIDAPs) in and of themselves have been a dramatic improvement over the approach of the past. Also, efforts continue to be made to rectify problems as they are identified by revising IUIDP guidelines (see Box 4.4).

A number of steps have been taken at the national level to reinforce and institutionalize the process. The Ministry of Home Affairs presently requires that local governments that have them, use their MSIPs and RIAPs, developed through IUIDP, as the basis for their submissions in the traditional annual budget negotiations with the central government. Similarly it now prescribes the development of LIDAPs as a routine requirement for all local governments. Ministry of Public Works instructions now require that all agencies within the Ministry conform their own investment plans to local MSIPs where they exist. Perhaps more important than instructions on paper is the political power which the existence of a locally developed MSIP creates. In the early 1980s, when local governments had no coherent capital improvement programmes of their own, they had little rationale for complaining about a central agency's implementing a project in their territories without sufficient prior negotiation. Now, when a MSIP exists, there is a sound basis for appealing to any central agency initiative that does not conform to it. Interviews indicate that such appeals generally are upheld and that, accordingly, central agencies are progressively less likely to try to initiate projects inconsistent with MSIPs.

Although Indonesia's planning reforms are specific to its institutional setting, the approach to inter-governmental collaboration can be applied in other settings. It is not sufficient for central government to merely hand over responsibilities and funding to local authorities. They also need to support a programme of capacity building which equips local authorities to perform their new functions (for example see Boxes 4.5 and 4.6). Indeed, a number of similar initiatives have been embarked on,

Box 4.5: Planning Manual for Local Authorities in Sri Lanka

The Urban Development Authority of the Ministry of Policy Planning and implementation in 1990 issued a planning manual under the theme "Planning for Action" (based on UMP material) to: (i) *provide guidelines to improve the level of planning* in local authorities. Rather than set a formula for local planning, options at different levels of detail that could be implemented incrementally were proposed. Thus, each council could tailor its planning activities to its own resources and increase the complexity of planning activities as capacity increases, and (ii) *provide guidelines for better coordination of physical and economic planning* since at that time, development plans were often made without an understanding of the cost implications of proposed activities. If physical and economic planning and budgeting were coordinated, officials would need to evaluate projects and set priorities to accomplish the most vital activities. Also, a more rigorous planning process could provide local authorities with a strong base for working with other agencies and levels of government to achieve their plan objectives.

Some of the advantages of the new planning structure were:

- **Timely collection of relevant data.** Traditionally, data that was collected and analysed did not have a strong correlation to the final conclusions and recommendations of the development plan. Often data was not current, thus drawing into question conclusions based on the data. The procedures suggested types of data most relevant to the process and methodologies of obtaining current data.

- **More efficient planning process.** With streamlined procedures at various levels of planning activity, more efficient planning would result in less time to carry out the process and a greater number of completed plans. The emphasis would be on establishing a document to guide actions that could be accomplished realistically by the local authority in the near future.

- **Greater flexibility.** The new procedures would give greater flexibility to professionals and officials in responding to constantly changing conditions in urban areas. Since plans would not specify one solution—but options—for development, councils would not be locked into uncompromising positions and would still have guidelines for making planning decisions.

- **Regular updating of plans.** Once planning capacity had been established in a local authority, it would be possible to update the plans to reflect urban growth as well as changing needs and priorities.

The manual's objectives of coordination of physical planning with economic planning included:

- **A clear understanding of the financial implications of development options.** Cost estimates must be made for desirable capital investments. This would establish the general magnitude of funding required to accomplish planning objectives.

- **Identification of potential funding sources.** This should include not only funds directly under the control of the local authority but also funds available from other agencies and ministries. The local authority should also increase revenue sources over time, thus making funding available for increased capital expenditures.

- **Prioritization of projects.** Since in most cases the cost of desired projects would be greater than available resources, it was necessary to establish project selection criteria. Procedures to identify projects providing benefits to the majority of residents and/or revenue to the local authority were set out.

Box 4.6: Integrated Action Planning (IAP) in Nepal

The framework for developing a very comprehensive package of Operational Guidelines for Integrated Action Planning was prepared by the Department of Housing and Urban Development (DHUD) supported by the Urban Development through Local Efforts (UDLE) Project (with German Technical Cooperation/GTZ support) (UDLE) specifically for use during the third cycle of the programme of planning support to municipalities. The guidelines are continuously subject to corrections, additions and changes as per the requirements of the integrated Action Planning cycles and the growing experience of the Planning Teams. The IAP Guidelines were originally developed on the basis of UMP material on IAP. The first draft of the comprehensive IAP operational guidelines was produced by the participants in the preparatory workshop for the second cycle of the planning support programme for municipalities. . In this workshop, the guideline framework made available through UDLE was used to identify those priority components which the participants considered in need of special attention prior to commencing the fieldwork in Dharan and Tulsipur. Selected sets of activities (sub-components) were thoroughly examined in the context of the experience in applying IAP operationally during the life cycle.

both in the Asian region and elsewhere, having similar features of multi-sectoral investment programming, inter-governmental collaboration decentralization of responsibilities and local capacity building.[3]

Inter-governmental Coordination at the Local Level

Vertical integration between different levels of government is not the only challenge to inter-governmental planning. Coordination is equally important between the different independent jurisdictions that comprise an urban area.

No fully satisfactory solution to the problem of horizontal integration has been found. The Metropolitan Development Authorities (MDAs) created in several of the large urban regions of South Asia have been an attempt to force coordination by combining in a single master agency the responsibility for planning, financing and actually building all of an urban region's major infrastructure works, as well as owning and developing the region's open land. Some of the Metropolitan Development Authorities have grown to be large and powerful organizations. The Karachi Development Authority, for example, in 1991 had 8,996 employees and, over its lifetime, has had ownership and development responsibility for some 800,000 building plots. However, the experience with MDAs demonstrates that consolidating capital-related functions under a single roof does not guarantee effective coordination. Moreover, the MDAs have come to be viewed as monopolistic bureaucracies, disdainful of elected local government. Even their financial survival

---

[3] For a range of examples, see IUIDP in a comparative international context, in Suselo, Taylor and Wegelin (1995).

now is in question. The MDAs have relied to a great degree on profits from land sales to sustain operations. As the explosion in land prices has cooled in some metropolitan areas, as a result of financial liberalization in competing markets, some of the seemingly guaranteed income of the MDAs has disappeared.

It now appears that the answer to horizontal coordination lies not in the creation of massive institutions responsible for all development-related activities throughout the metropolitan region, but rather in simplification of duties. There is need for some institution at the metropolitan level to take responsibility at least for compiling a single capital investment programme from the project lists of individual jurisdictions, wrapping these in an explanatory text with accompanying maps, and enunciating the basic policies that are shaping investment selection. This body should simultaneously have strong links with the local government and with the national/state government. It need not necessarily have infrastructure construction and financing responsibilities, or be charged with metropolitan-wide land development.

Once the entire set of planned capital projects affecting an urban region has been laid out in a single document, conspicuous incompatibilities among projects can be pinpointed and attacked. Appropriate strategies for tying together sectoral investments can be debated. The appropriate institutional framework for doing this will vary by urban region. At the start, an *ad hoc* structure to support voluntary cooperation is preferable to the creation of yet another formal institution. Under India's current decentralization efforts, the Calcutta MDA has itself evolved in this direction, shedding many of its direct construction responsibilities and becoming a metropolitan planning agency, responsible for area-wide coordination (Box 4.7).

Simplifying the Design and Implementation of MSIP

Coordination and integration of sectoral planning always has held appeal in principle, but attempts to implement the vision often have led to a maze of bureaucracy. Like attempts at multi-year, inter-sectoral national economic planning, some of the more complex physical planning coordination structures have collapsed of their own weight.

Local MSIP design needs to learn from this experience. A simple MSIP structure stands a much better chance of being sustained and put to use than a complex one. Every opportunity should be seized to disaggregate the global project list of a city into smaller, more manageable parts, as long as it is possible to do so without violating the objective of making better informed trade-offs between investment possibilities. Fortunately, there are a number of simplifying principles that can be

Box 4.7: Calcutta Metropolitan Development Authority

The Calcutta Metropolitan Development Authority (CMDA) is one of the largest capital development agencies in the world. Among its 5,000 employees, it has 100 qualified planners, 500 graduate engineers, 3,000 junior engineers, and many economists, financial experts and social scientists. The CMDA has had the statutory obligation of coordinating and integrating urban development activities for the metropolitan region. It has controlled virtually all financial flows for public investment, acting to channel national and state grants and loan programmes to municipalities in the region, and issuing its own development bonds. It has overseen the preparation and coordination of the capital budgets of local governments, the metropolitan sewer and water authority, the land development agency, and others.

Even in this arrangement, however, there have been complaints about coordination. The planning sector (of CMDA) is ignored by the operation sectors; its programme development more often than not is side-stepped by project implementing departments. The appraisal, monitoring and evaluation unit (which performs economic appraisals of projects) ... is an anathema that the CMDA had to accept at the insistence of the World Bank, but never took seriously ... (It) cannot play the critical role of linking planning with implementation. Faced with the technocratic and financial power of CMDA, local government lost control over priortization of development projects. Community as well as municipal participation in planning has been meagre.

applied to the priority setting process which will actually enhance the efficiency of capital allocation. These are now described.

Many community improvement projects can be integrated and prioritized at the community level. They do not have to go through the municipal MSIP. Small-scale community improvement or squatter upgrading projects account, in the aggregate, for a substantial share of local public investment. In Mexico in 1992, the PRONASOL programme of community investment financed more than $2.5 billion worth neighbourhood projects. As in a number of other countries, these works were co-financed by central government and the communities, the latter making their contributions in the form of labour, supervision and modest financing.

In Mexico's case, municipal governments operate at the margin of PRONASOL. They need to be aware of the community works that are programmed and plan for their integration into city-wide infrastructure networks. Some cities choose to use city funds to accelerate the community investment process. When they do so, they typically follow the model of community partnership established by the federal programme, but apply it to additional neighbourhoods.

However important the role of municipal government, it is the essence of such community programmes that investment priorities are set by the community itself, acting through its own organizations. External advice on the technical complementarity between different types of infrastructure facilities may be provided, but in the end coordination is a community responsibility (see Box 4.8). The "empowerment" created by having the community go through its own process of project prioritization to allocate investment resources cannot be achieved if a central steering group makes final investment choices. The steering group's only involvement in this kind of investment should be to ensure that the connection between community networks and city-wide networks is properly planned and that different neighbourhoods of the same income level are treated equitably.

Box 4.8: The Community Construction Contract System in Sri Lanka

Parallel to the increasing involvement of the formal private sector in the delivery of urban services, which is a major trend in many countries, the residents of informal settlements will have to rely increasingly on their own initiative and improve their situation on a self-help basis and, where necessary and possible, with the participation of the informal private sector.

Under the Million Houses Programme in Sri Lanka the populations of slums and shanty settlements work together with a public-sector agency, the National Housing Development Authority (or NHDA), to plan, construct, operate and maintain basic urban infrastructure. The three core principles of the community construction contract system are:

- The delegation of the responsibility for the provision of infrastructure in low-income settlements from the government to the end-users of the infrastructure.
- The development of a sense of responsibility among the end-users for the maintenance and management of that intrastructure as a result of their involvement in its provision.
- The commitment of the government to providing all technical support, training and information required by the end-users to carry out these responsibilities.

The approach developed was called the community action planning and management approach or CAP. The approach sees people as the main resource for development rather than as purely an object of the development efforts or as mere recipients of benefits. The objective of the approach is to motivate and mobilize the population of an urban low-income settlement. The role of the NHDA and the urban local authorities is to support this process where necessary, but the community is expected, through this process, to develop its ability for self-management and eventually to take its development in its own hands.

The first step in the process of CAP for an urban low-income settlement is the two-day community action planning workshop. This workshop is the core activity of the CAP approach. Participants include community leaders and representatives of the various interest groups in the settlement, NHDA staff, the urban local authority and other organizations concerned. The key to the workshop is the options-and-trade-off technique, because a problem may be solved in several ways and each solution may call for different trade-offs. The planners have an important role to play in the workshop because they have to clarify the trade-offs for the community. However, the selection of the option is left entirely to the community and the individual families. Issues-specific workshops are subsequently organized to help the community deal with various specific problems and issues in the implementation of the action plan decided upon.

Delegation of priority-setting for community-scale projects does not violate any of the principles of MSIP. In fact, the community processes used to select projects tend to closely resemble the procedures recommended for municipality-wide MSIP in smaller towns.

Self-financing activities funded through user fees, betterment taxes or benefit charges may also be removed from centralized project ranking. Investment levels for self-financing services provided on a market-like basis should be determined by consumers' willingness to pay. Decentralized market principles should take precedence over centralized planning. As long as customers want and are willing to pay for better water service, better trash removal or local road paving, the public suppliers of these services should respond to their customers' demands.

The MSIP process needs to take into account only the "spillover" effects these activities have on other domains. Part of this spillover may be financial. If the water authority or solid waste authority is seeking capital funds from the city general budget, these requests should be subjected to the same MSIP ranking process as other capital project proposals. There may also be cross-sectoral spillovers. Satisfying the full demand of consumers for water consumption may trigger liquid waste disposal problems that the city is not equipped to handle. These particular spillovers are so common that many jurisdictions have combined sewer and water responsibilities within a single agency, and required that the agency levy a single water consumption fee that covers both the costs of water provision and the costs of water removal in accord with sanitation standards. Still, large water and sewer projects should be examined for the implications they have for other sectors, and for this reason should be examined, if not ranked, within the MSIP process.

It may appear that by excluding self-financing projects from MSIP prioritization, the process itself is diminished. On the contrary, as long as a system is truly self-financing and fee levels are set to cover the system's incremental costs, no planning group should spend its time attempting to second-guess the demand-driven allocation of capital financed by the system's users. In practice, the great majority of urban water and waste-water systems in the developing world do not come close to covering incremental costs. Therefore, they will fall under city-wide MSIP procedures through their requests for general-purpose capital assistance.

Often, project rankings can be performed most meaningfully across sub-sectors within a common sectoral framework, or across sectors in the context of a single programme having clear objectives. Project priority setting within a sector, or within a single multi-sectoral programme, often can have a much clearer focus than priority setting across the entire universe of potential projects. For example, within the transportation sector projects can be ranked by the impact they have on average journey-to-work times, or according to other criteria that have been identified in sectoral studies as having critical importance. Within a multi-sectoral environmental programme designed to improve human health, potential sub-projects can be ranked quite precisely according to the human health improvements they produce per dollar spent.

When projects are disaggregated sectorally or by programme in this manner, MSIP becomes a two-step process. In the first step, the steering group and budgetary authorities must decide how much capital funding will be allocated to a sector or programme as a whole. Then sub-projects proposed in a programmatic framework can be ranked by how effectively they accomplish programmatic goals. At both stages, the most difficult task is to reach clear consensus as to what the priority sectoral or programmatic goals are, so that criteria for project selection can be formulated.

Indonesia's IUIDP is a case in point, with programme components confined to a typical public works sectoral scope, including water and sanitation (comprising solid waste management as well as drainage), urban roads flood protection and *kampung* improvement; while this limitation has often been criticized, it has meant that it has been possible to focus on the technical complementarities between programme components and ensure that these are fully exploited in investment priority-setting.

Once the MSIP process has been established, the steering group can promulgate criteria for project ranking, allocate sectoral or agency capital budgets in conjunction with the budget office, and allow agencies to rank their own project proposals according to the criteria established. All projects do not have to go through the central review group.

A concentrated effort, involving large amounts of staff time, will be needed to change a city's capital planning and budgeting procedures to install a workable MSIP. A one-time effort can command this scale of resources because rationalization of local investment programming is seen as having high and immediate pay-off in terms of results.

It is unreasonable, however, to expect to be able to sustain a similarly high level of commitment over time from a mayor, chief city planner or central government ministers. The steering group responsible for continuing operations typically will involve officials one level down from this chief executive level. The steering group's membership can be expanded and replenished over time by reaching outward beyond municipal government, as is described in the next section. Still, in view of the additional demands likely to be placed on the inter-sectoral planning process, as it expands into activities other than direct municipal investment, it is advisable to look for ways to simplify routines for municipal project ranking.

One approach to simplification is to have the MSIP process, once it has been well established, function in a more decentralized manner. The steering group can establish project ranking criteria, as it normally does, and assign weights to the criteria if it chooses to use a formalized rating system. However, instead of ranking all projects itself, it can delegate to line agencies the responsibility for rating their own projects according to the inter-sectorally established criteria. Large projects, involving capital expenditures above some threshold level, can automatically be forwarded to the steering group for its consideration. Agencies can be instructed to review all project proposals for spillovers, whether financial or sectoral, beyond the sponsoring agency, and also require that all projects of this kind be submitted for central review.

Cities can start the MSIP process with certain core activities, then gradually expand as the system gains capacity. Because local government staff capacity in developing countries is weak, designers of new systems need to start from a simple core and plan to expand functions over time.

The Integrated Urban Infrastructure Development Programme of Indonesia illustrates such an incremental approach. IUIDP's first stage is much simpler than a full-fledged MSIP. It started with only a few infrastructure elements (i.e., water, sanitation, solid waste disposal) with the notion that others would be added in later years after the process had proved itself and developed political momentum. Also, project identification and prioritization are done in a quite simple manner the first time a city goes through the exercise, with the expectation that more sophisticated techniques can be applied once staff capacity has been strengthened. In the beginning integrated planning involved only those functions managed by one Directorate General of the Public Works Ministry, greatly simplifying inter-governmental relations. This avoided additional inter-departmental coordination issues which would have arisen immediately if the programme scope, for instance, had covered all infrastructure and municipal services which are notionally a local responsibility, including communications, primary health care and primary education.

Incremental development of this kind is advisable throughout the lifetime of MSIP. If the MSIP process proves successful, it can gradually be broadened, for example, to include organizations not included in the original, core steering group. There are at least three candidate groups for inclusion in such an expanded process:

1. Other public agencies that make capital investments but for a number of possible reasons (e.g., reliance on different funding sources) are not included in the initial local capital budgeting process. Examples of this are public housing and land development agencies or parastatals that may be developing facilities in the locality.

2. Private institutions whose investments are encouraged by (often subsidized by) the public sector, e.g., private firms that develop land or construct facilities on a turn-key basis for government or under some other kind of public-private partnership.

3. Other major private investors and developers active in the locality. These could include public interest-oriented NGOs and CBOs as well as private firms.

At first, such participation might only entail listening to and commenting on presentations regarding the strategy and analytical foundations underlying the multi-year capital plan and current-year capital budget. The chances for conflicting actions by the private and other public sector investors should be reduced if this strategy is discussed. Open discussion would in fact address what is often an important problem. Private developers in a number of countries complain that uncertainty about the location and timing of government infrastructure investments is one of the major risks they face.

In the next stage, the MSIP staff might collect data on the tentative investment plans of other such institutions before final reconciliations begin. Also, these other institutions might be allowed to participate in sessions that set the capital budget strategy and criteria to be used in project selection (being able to make comments and discuss alternatives even if they have no role in final decision making). Where this occurs, the regular capital budget planners would have a better basis for decision making. Even though the process would not legally bind the outside institutions it seems likely that their own plans would be influenced. The adjusted plans of the other public agencies and public-private partnerships might be published as an informational addendum to the final public capital programme. Private sector participation in a broad MSIP process also would pave the way for direct involvement of the private sector in meeting local infrastructure needs, through concessions from the municipal government or other kinds of authorization for private investment.

UMP Regional Support Activities

For reasons mentioned in earlier paragraphs the UMP tries to include an integrated approach in almost all of its infrastructure-related activities. However, the UMP supports several activities which specifically relate to Integrated Urban Infrastructure Development. Examples of activities related to this field include:

— **An UMP regional seminar on partnerships in municipal infrastructure services** as held at the National Institute of Urban Affairs in New Delhi between 7 and 11 February 1994, with some 75 participants from nine countries and several external support agencies. The seminar concluded that the Urban Management Programme in the region could facilitate the country-level action agenda by initiating certain specific actions. These are summarized in Box 4.9. Similar regional seminars are planned in Latin America/Caribbean region and Africa in 1995.

— **Environmental Planning and Management (EPM) demonstration in Madras:** This activity is designed to provide local authorities and their partners in the public, private and popular sectors with an improved environmental and management capacity. The overall development objective of the project is to promote environmentally sustainable socio-economic development and growth in Madras by: (i) enhancing availability and efficiency of use of natural resources and reducing exposure to environmental hazards in and around the city; and (ii) strengthening local capacities to plan, coordinate and manage sustainable urban development.

More specifically, the project will:

— Identify and develop key environmental planning and management strategies and action plans, within the framework of and incorporated into the overall strategic development plans for Madras, including systems to operationalize these strategies such as spatial planning, economic planning, sectoral and agency financial planning, sector investment programmes, and legal and administrative adaptations.

— Strengthen the capacity of local institutions to plan, coordinate and manage sustainable urban development and growth, with emphasis on environmental considerations, multi-sectoral coordination, and effective participation of public, private and popular sectors.

— Develop the key environmental planning and management strategies and action plans into well prepared ("bankable") capital investment and technical cooperation projects and "packages"

Box 4.9: Action Plan Seminar on Partnerships, New Delhi, 1994

1. *Research Dissemination*: It was felt that the country-specific partnership experiences presented at the seminar provided adequate descriptions of the current status but did not give sufficient details of the processes that the national and local governments had to go through to put the partnership in practice. The impacts of such partnerships were also not discussed in sufficient details. The following cross-country comparative studies were proposed:

- Cost analysis of municipal services under partnership arrangements.
- Review of legislations for facilitating partnerships.
- Pricing mechanisms and their impacts on the poor.
- Compendium on norms of urban infrastructural services and costs of urban services in the region.
- Performance indicators on cost, maintenance quality, coverage, revenues, manpower and environmental parameters.
- Compendium of contract documents used by various countries.

2. *Information-sharing*: It was felt that the rich experience of some of the countries in the region needed to be disseminated widely among the countries in the region on a long-term basis. The following specific information needs were identified:

- National action plans/policies/legislations on partnerships in municipal infrastructure.
- Contract management documents, procedures and codes.
- Process related description of partnerships.
- Performance monitoring of partners and institutional arrangements.

3. *Capacity Building*: The action agenda also identified facilitation of the local capacity building for initiating partnerships within the Asia-Pacific Region for municipal information. From the country presentations, the following emerged as the specific needs:

- Advocacy and awareness workshops at national level to initiate partnerships.
- Enhancing managerial capacities for:
  — Financial management (debt servicing).
  — Institutional development.
  — Demand assessment.
  — Contract arrangement skills.

suitable for direct financial support from a variety of local, central, and external agencies, thereby attracting extra funds from additional sources to supplement investment programmes already underway.

— These objectives of the "Sustainable Madras" Project must be understood as being basically parallel and interactive—not compartmentalized and sequential. The fundamental approach of "Sustainable Madras" is concerned with the *process* of environmental management viewed as an iterative and cumulative activity.

— **Metropolitan Management in Manila—Delineation of Tasks and Organizational Arrangements:** The Urban Management Programme and the World Bank have been assisting the Government of the Philippines to address the problems of Metro Manila. A Metropolitan Management Workshop was held in February 1993. During the course of consultation and discussions following the workshop, the government leaders sought further assistance from the UMP and the World Bank in detailing the necessary work to aid the legislative process to provide for an effective metropolitan institution. Because of the multi-sectoral nature of metropolitan management some sectors will be considered for an integrated approach, including solid waste management, traffic and transportation, flood control and drainage, environmental management and strategic land use planning.

It was found that there was a lack of consensus on these functions to be performed by a metropolitan government. Delineation of the various tasks, scope and responsibilities of the subjects are essential to establish more clearly the consensus and the government's willingness to proceed further with the legislative and administrative actions necessary to create appropriate financial and institutional arrangements.

Conclusion

Better systems of capital investment planning and capital budgeting are an important part of improving urban management capacity to meet such demands. Recent experience from different parts of the world brought together by the UMP illustrate the principal design choices that officials face in building a capital Multi-sectoral Investment Planning (MSIP) system, and offers step-by-step suggestions on how a multi-sectoral investment planning process can be constructed. Emphasis is given to simplicity, for experience demonstrates that a straightforward system of capital project selection, easily understood by professionals and the public alike, stands the best chance of being sustained and of actually changing the way investment decisions are made.

BIBLIOGRAPHY

Dillinger, W. (1994), *Decentralisation and its Implications for Urban Services Delivery*, Urban Management Programme (UMP), Publication # 16, Washington D.C.
Fox, W.F. (1994), *Strategic Options for Urban Infrastructure Management*, Urban Management Programme Policy Paper #17, The World Bank, Washington D.C.

Peterson, G., Kingsley, G.T. and Telgarsky, J.P. (1994), *Multi-Sectoral Investment Planning*, Urban Management Programme (UMP) Working Paper No. 3, UNCHS, Nairobi.

Pickering, D., Park, J.M. and Bannister, D.H. (1993), *Utility Mapping and Record Keeping for Infrastructure*, Urban Management Programme Discussion Paper #10, The World Bank, Washington, D.C.

Suselo, H., Taylor, J.L. and Wegelin, E.A. (1995), *Indonesia's Urban Infrastructure Development Experience: Critical Lessons by Good Practice*, UNCHS, Nairobi.

PART II

COUNTRY PAPERS

Indonesia
Philippines
Thailand
Nepal
India
Turkey

5

THE INTEGRATED URBAN INFRASTRUCTURE DEVELOPMENT PROGRAMME IN INDONESIA

Achmad Lanti and Robert van der Hoff

Introduction

A large number of cities in the world have suffered from rapid and sometimes uncontrolled growth since World War II. In the 1950s and 1960s, for the first time in human history, megacities emerged, each having more than 10 million inhabitants. Some cities started doubling in size every 10 years. Predictably, this urban sprawl was not matched with provision of adequate infrastructure and social services because only the richest and best-governed cities could mobilize the resources to respond to what seemed an insatiable need for land and amenities. In the 1970s, baffled by urban pollution, skyrocketing land prices, crime and poverty, many people started to worry that large cities would not be sustainable in the long run. Many advocated the abandon of urban life in favour of a simpler and healthier form of village life. As cities were also centres of employment very few families ventured into rural areas to find a future.

People came to understand that despite all their perceived evils and disadvantages, cities were here to stay, and that they were an essential part of societal and economic development. Cities were for people, the reasoning went, and thus people had to manage to make good cities somehow. The same people had to admit, however, that in the absence of unlimited resources, they did not quite know how to turn cities into clean, pleasant, safe and profitable places to live. One thing was certain: the old way of managing cities did not yield the desired results, and change in one form or another was definitely needed. In many developing countries, governments and international aid agencies were disappointed with the results of their efforts to improve cities. For many years, enormous amounts of money had been spent on water supply, electricity and housing schemes, but the results were meagre. Not enough people benefited, especially not the urban poor, whereas a few benefited too much. Many projects appeared to be out of touch with actual needs; others appeared to be randomly and poorly implemented. Citizens wondered, for instance, why so often roads were paved only to be broken up again to dig ditches for ducts and cables? And why did services always have to break down for the lack of proper maintenance? There was also disillusionment with most city master plans that looked wonderful on paper but were never implemented.

This paper deals with one of the recent attempts to create better cities. It reflects beliefs cherished by a large number of people who over the past decade have contributed a lot of creative energy to invent and test new ways for developing and managing our cities. It also reflects a lot of painstaking effort to make it happen. The job certainly isn't finished yet. As the story will show, there is still a long way to go in creating cities that our children will like to grow up in and have kids of their own.

Not surprisingly, Indonesia is one of the countries that faces rapid urbanization. Each year, more than three million people are added to the urban population of Indonesia. In other words, each year another city the size of Surabaya is put on the map. By the end of this century, urban dwellers may constitute one-third of the total Indonesian population of about 200 million people. With the precipitous drop in world oil prices in the 1970s and 1980s and the resulting decline in central government revenues, there was an urgent need to dramatically increase local government revenues for meeting ever-expanding urban infrastructure demands. Although official estimates vary, it is generally assumed that the order of magnitude of Indonesia's total infrastructure investment need is around US$ 1 billion annually. In comparison, during the period 1990-1991, the Directorate General of Human Settlements of the Ministry of Public Works planned for approximately US$ 500 million worth of investment, of which it could realize about 70 per cent.

This paper deals mostly with the role of the government in city development because the subject of this paper—the Integrated Urban Infrastructure Development Programme (IUIDP)—started as a government initiative. Part of this initiative, however, was to incorporate the contributions of the commercial and non-commercial private sector into urban development planning because they finance a large part of urban development—if not the largest part.

The original idea underlying the IUIDP was developed by officials in the Directorate General of Human Settlements in the Ministry of Public Works in Jakarta, and was quite simple. If long-term city master plans have to be implemented step by step and year by year, these people asked themselves, how come there is no link between the city master plans and local governments' annual development budgets? Would it not be possible to make an intermediary programme that translates the master plans into infrastructure projects and financial projections for several years, from which then annual budgets for infrastructure construction, operation and maintenance can be derived? Wouldn't such a programme be more sensitive to local needs, and thus create a more solid basis for medium-term infrastructure development and more local "sense of ownership"? Most of all, would it not result in more strategic investment planning, more synergy and spin-offs, and be attractive to private investors as well?

Most people thought it would, and the idea caught on. Quite soon, however, the initiators realized that it was easier said than done. For one, it would require a neat meshing of sectoral plans, otherwise it would not be possible to put together a comprehensive medium-term programme. It would also require coordination of various sources of funding. Local governments could hardly be expected to make financial projections if they could not project their own revenue for the next couple of years, or if they could not estimate how much the private sector and communities would invest, and if they did not know how much money they were going to receive from central government next year. It would also require local governments to formulate the most likely development scenario for their cities, but it was feared that very few people in local government would be capable of doing so. Furthermore, it would require local governments to assess the current state of their infrastructure and to make realistic projections of medium-term needs. In fact, it was doubtful that most city governments would be capable of putting such a medium-term programme together without a lot of expert assistance. And since the implementation of such a medium-term programme would result in loans and contracts, what would its legal status be? And how much freedom would local governments have in taking initiatives in the temporary absence of detailed guidelines and instructions for this programme? Apparently, there were a lot of "ifs and buts" in the approach.

In fact, there is more to the IUIDP than can be covered in this paper. Since its inception over 10 years ago, hundreds of reports, dozens of papers and several books have been published on the topic; this paper refers to a few selected publications only. It briefly discusses the history of urban development projects leading to the IUIDP approach, the policy context of IUIDP, its main components, and its preparation and implementation experience. This includes a discussion of coordination arrangements and the framework for financing urban infrastructure, focussing on methods for improving local revenues. Finally, the paper concludes by looking at the future of the IUIDP, outlining the probable further institutionalization of the IUIDP within the context of decentralization. It also outlines the possible broadening of the IUIDP's scope to encompass additional sectors and private sector participation.

Urban Infrastructure Development

Prior to *Repelita I* (1969-1974)[1] the Government of Indonesia (GOI) provided basic urban services as rapidly as possible to needy communities through central government sectoral project financing. The Directorate General of Human Settlements in the Ministry of Public Works took care of sub-sectors such as water supply, drainage, sanitation, garbage collection and public housing. Given the limited pool of financial and human resources—which moreover was largely concentrated in Jakarta—it was understandable that there was a serious backlog in the development of infrastructure. As yet, very little thought was given to decentralization and devolution of responsibilities and authority for infrastructure development to Indonesia's 27 provincial (first level or *Tk.I*) governments and some 300 local (second level or *Tk.II*) governments.[2]

The sectoral approach to infrastructure provision implied that each sector was planned and implemented largely on its own, with relatively little coordination or integration between sectors. For example, there was no coordination between the construction of urban roads and the construction of drainage systems because they belonged to different sectoral departments. The shortcomings of this fragmented approach were recognized, and a more integrated approach was tried out by the Directorate General of Human Settlements when it launched the *Kampung* Improvement Programme (KIP) in Jakarta during *Repelita I*. The KIP provided basic urban services to low-income urban neighbourhoods (*kampung*) as an integrated package. The programme concentrated on upgrading and/or providing walkways and access roads, drainage, public water taps, communal latrines, washing facilities and other amenities while retaining most of the existing housing stock. The KIP was later expanded into a national programme, but it remained operational at the neighbourhood level. The integration of basic services did not extend beyond the *kampungs*.

---

[1]   *Repelita* : National Five-Year Development Plan.
[2]   *Tk.I* or Level I refers to provincial government administration; *Tk.II* or Level II refers to government administration at local level, either regency or municipality. Regional government comprises both provincial and local government.

Later, during *Repelita II* (1974-1979) and *Repelita III* (1979-1984), the GOI started broadening its approaches to urban infrastructure development. Realizing that the KIP's neighbourhood-level amenities needed somehow to be connected to city-wide infrastructure, a series of pilot projects were started to extend the integrated approach to the entire urban area. This emerged as the next phase in Indonesia's efforts to plan and implement infrastructure and came to be referred to as the "Urban Project" approach. The GOI obtained financial support from the International Bank for Reconstruction and Development (IBRD) and Asian Development Bank (ADB) to implement it. The major projects undertaken in the "Urban Projects" programme are listed in Table 5.1.

Table 5.1: List of "Urban Projects" (*Repelita II - III*)

Project Name / Location	Donor
Urban Project 1 - Jakarta	IBRD
Urban Project 2 - Jakarta, Surabaya	IBRD
Urban Project 3 - Semarang, Solo, Surabaya, Ujung Pandang	IBRD
Urban Project 4 - Padang, Palembang, Pontianak, Banjarmasin, Samarinda, Yogyakarta, Denpasar	IBRD
Urban Project 5 - (same as Urban Project 3)	IBRD
Bandung Urban Development Project (BUDP)	ADB
Medan Urban Development Project (MUDP)	ADB
Central Java Small Town Urban Development Project (STUDP)	ADB

Source: Suselo, Taylor and Wegelin, 1995, p. 14.

These "Urban Projects" had some interesting features in common. First, an urban infrastructure was planned on a more integrated basis through coordination between physical sectors and financial resources. Moreover, the GOI required that local governments assume an increasing share of financing, both from their own sources and by borrowing from foreign donors through central government (on-lending). In addition, the central government provided assistance in carrying out planning and feasibility studies conducted largely by centrally recruited and supervised consultants. Also, the GOI began to focus more on the institutional aspects associated with the project components. All projects included a KIP component. Thus, many of the basic elements of what later became known as the IUIDP—including more integrated physical and financial planning and implementation, and shared responsibility between local and central levels of government—were beginning to take shape.

The Beginnings of a Breakthrough

The "Urban Project" approach was limited to the cities listed in Table 5.1. Thus, it could not really be considered a national programme. As the approach was based on centrally set physical development targets along sectoral lines (KIP, urban roads, etc.), it was not quite suitable for the GOI's next objective, which was to expand the approach into a national and more decentralized programme.

> "National urban policy makers came to realize that setting sectoral targets was not sufficient: there was a necessity to formulate infrastructure investment programmes which met the unique needs of each city. This required a major conceptual change in urban development policy from the project approach to a programme approach. The crucial question was how to balance sectoral and national targets with location-specific area needs in which all sectors could be planned in an integrated way" (Suselo, Taylor and Wegelin 1995, p.15).

The GOI started preparing a National Urban Development Strategy (NUDS) which provided clear guidance to national urban development issues, established a large urban database, and identified hundreds of strategic urban development centres for which in principle priority allocation of limited national resources for infrastructure provision could be considered. Then, by the mid-1980s (end of *Repelita III*), the IUIDP came into being, in which the GOI proposed to shift planning and programming of urban infrastructure from a sectoral, largely "top-down" and centralized approach towards a more integrated, "bottom-up" and decentralized approach. This required the GOI to assume a different role:

"In this context the government's new role is perceived as an 'enabler' rather than as a provider of all resources and services. With limited resources or capacities the following strategic approaches to urban intervention are suggested:

- To concentrate on those services which can have the greatest strategic impact, and those which cannot be organized efficiently by the private sector, community organizations or individuals;
- To give the private sector and community organizations the appropriate 'enabling' framework and structures to contribute on their own to services provision;
- To encourage the private sector—through deregulation, appropriate pricing and fiscal policies, through land management and guided land developments, or through contracting of tasks such as

construction, waste collection and disposal etc.—to contribute to the strengthening of services provision" (Hoff and Steinberg, 1992, p. 7).

As the rather weighty words "decentralized" and "integrated" have already been used several times in this paper, it might be useful to describe their meaning in the Indonesian context before further discussing the IUIDP.

The GOI adheres to three main principles of devolution of responsibility for government affairs: de-concentration, co-administration and decentralization. "De-concentration" means central government functions and responsibilities distributed in the region through regional offices; "co-administration" basically means functions and responsibilities implemented jointly by the central and regional governments; and "decentralization" in general means regional discretion in implementing government functions and responsibilities. The GOI itself uses the term "regional autonomy". The extent to which any of Indonesia's regencies and municipalities is decentralized, de-concentrated or co-administered, as well as the "mix" between the three, can vary widely depending on size, population, economic function and other factors. Although the principles of decentralization were already laid down by law in 1974, they have—after 20 years—been only partly implemented, amongst others because of practical complications in dealing with the country's enormous geographic spread and diversity. Starting in 1995, "regional autonomy" is being tried out in 26 selected regencies, one in each province except for the Capital Region of Jakarta, covering about 20 million people.[3]

A classification system is applied by which regencies and municipalities are graded on the basis of population and economic performance. They can be classified as "beginner", "medium" or "advanced", which in turn will determine the extent to which they can become decentralized. Whatever model the GOI applies, it can be argued that decentralization is largely demand-driven. As a general rule of thumb, regional governments seeing a potential advantage will push for "regional autonomy", while poorer and isolated regencies and municipalities will prefer to remain dependent on central government grants and subsidies, and will tend to be unresponsive to the decentralization process. It will also be clear that "medium" and "advanced" municipalities are often NUDS strategic development centres, and will have the best chances of obtaining finance for urban development, including for the IUIDP.

The word "integrated" has been used so often for everything ranging from health care to home decoration that its meaning has largely

---

[3] For comparison, the Netherlands (total population 16 million) gave its own decentralization process in all 12 provinces a 20-year trial run (1972-1992).

been lost. In the context of the IUIDP, however, it is understood to have the following connotations:

- Logical operational linkages between long-term (20–25 years), medium-term (5 years) and short-term (annual) infrastructure investment planning.
- Matching of the spatial, technical, financial and institutional aspects of city infrastructure investment.
- Effective planning coordination between the public and private sector actors involved in all stages of the infrastructure development process.
- City-wide consistency between infrastructure investment initiatives by local, provincial and central government agencies, as well as proposals forwarded by local communities and private developers.
- Efficient assessment, mobilization and application of the various public and private sources of infrastructure investment funding.
- City-wide coordination and compatibility between infrastructure sub-sectors such as water supply, drainage, roads, and garbage collection, with the understanding that other sub-sectors and sectors can be included, and that an integrated plan can include any desired number of sectors and sub-sectors that together constitute a logical whole.
- Effective management of the entire investment cycle including planning, programming, financing, construction, operation and maintenance.

From the start, it was accepted that total "integration" in the sense that everything is linked to everything else was neither feasible nor desirable, as the approach would be bogged down in endless consultations and decision-making loops. The IUIDP approach was meant to accelerate the provision of urban services, not to slow it down. In the end, sectoral agencies will each have to build, operate and maintain their infrastructure components more or less independently from each other. The basic idea was, however, that infrastructure investment would become more systematic, transparent, and effective in meeting a city's needs:

"The programme has been greeted with most enthusiasm by the municipalities. Local officials have longed for control over their own affairs. They know their cities' problems. They want to solve them. They have yearned for more town planning, training, and experience. For years, they have been frustrated by the implementation of programmes from Jakarta with little relevance to their people's needs.

They have been embarrassed and annoyed by the waste of central government resources. They have felt, given half a chance, they could plan and implement better programmes themselves" (Jellinek, 1988, p. 26).

The Medium-term Investment Plan

The newly created Medium-term Infrastructure Investment Plan[4] became the principal tool for linking long-term master plans with annual investment budgets. It follows a number of required steps to arrive at a bankable package of infrastructure projects. The main steps include:

- First, an IUIDP Development Assessment Plan (IDAP) is prepared. This plan makes a rapid assessment of the current master plan or, in the absence of such a plan, provides an urban development scenario on a 20-year horizon, assesses current levels of infrastructure, and projects future infrastructure needs.

- On the basis of the IDAP, a rough medium-term infrastructure plan is prepared that lists the sub-sectors to be included, as well as approximate volume and location of projects for the next five years.[5] Different sub-sectors can have different time frames for implementation. Great importance is attached not only to appropriate new projects, but also to rehabilitation, operation and maintenance of existing infrastructure. Apart from physical projects, the list can also contain non-physical projects such as mapping, surveying, feasibility studies, land acquisition and other activities that are closely related to infrastructure provision.

- On the basis of this rough projection, a quick assessment is made of the city's financial resources and institutional capabilities required to implement the infrastructure investment plan, and actions plans are prepared for improving resource availability up to the required level. The Local Institutional Development Action Plan (LIDAP) and the Revenue Improvement Action Plan (RIAP) spell out what needs to be done to build the capacity and acquire the resources needed to implement the PJM. For smaller towns, it is possible that

---

[4]   In Indonesian: *Program Jangka Menengah* (PJM)

[5]   For the time being, the scope of the IUIDP is limited to eight sub-sectors under the responsibility of the Directorate of Human Settlements, Ministry of Public Works: water supply, sanitation, roads, drainage, flood control, garbage collection, market improvement and *kampung* improvement. The period of five years is indicative, as a PJM can span a period of anywhere between three and seven years, depending on need.

available resources are so limited that the PJM consists mainly of a RIAP and LIDAP.

- The draft PJM, RIAP and LIDAP are made consistent with each other through an iterative consultation process which mostly takes place at the local government level. When this process is completed, the programme for the first one or two years is worked out in more detail, including feasibility studies and environmental impact assessments, if required.

- Then the PJM is ready for appraisal by technical agencies such as provincial planning and public works agencies, central government ministries, and international financing agencies. In principle, no external appraisal is required if a city self-finances its infrastructure development, but this is seldom the case. The programme is appraised as a whole, but individual projects and project components are also appraised individually where necessary.

- Once funding for a PJM has been approved—wholly or partially— by the appropriate technical agencies, a loan is prepared that enables the city not only to implement the PJM, but also to operate and maintain the infrastructure it has built. For economy of size, the donor agency usually prefers to put together a number of cities and towns located in the same province into a single loan package.

The PJM is meant to be a rolling plan, meaning that annual reviews, updates and adjustments are made, and that development budgets can be adjusted forward and backward in time. This overcomes the limitations of the traditional annual "frozen" development budgets. In principle, it is even possible to add new projects halfway. By becoming a rolling plan, the PJM avoids the inherent rigidity of packaged and fixed multi-year plans and becomes an annual review exercise that is part and parcel of a city's regular planning and budgeting activities. On the other hand, a rolling plan's inherent flexibility and lack of specificity beyond year three or four makes it much harder to appraise and package for loan funding than a fixed plan. Apart from being an investment planning tool, the PJM is also meant to be an enabling tool by giving local governments the means to empower themselves:

"The power of enabling lies in its capacity to anticipate, to be dynamic, to steer away from undesirable development and to steer towards desirable development. In this respect, the PJM is an enabling instrument because it is (or should be) one of the main instruments for decentralized planning at local level. It is a document that commits local governments to a common course of action for a number of years, and its RIAP and LIDAP are the main instruments to give it the desired punch. The infrastructure it proposes to build, operate and maintain is supposed to anticipate and facilitate development, not just to run after facts and catch up with the backlog. From the perspective of the IUIDP, the PJM will become an important tool when it is specifically designed to enable, and when local governments and communities can, to some extent, empower themselves through their PJM" (Hoff and Steinberg, 1993, p.33).

Driving Forces

Some important factors conducive to the development and acceptance of the IUIDP were:

- The dramatic decline in the world prices of oil meant that the GOI's financial resources were shrinking steadily over the years. This meant that the size of sectoral grants to local governments had to be drastically reduced as well. As a result, local governments were forced to start mobilizing a greater local share of resources required to finance their own infrastructure.

- Decentralization, though not fully implemented under the 1974 law, has been official GOI policy for about 20 years, and is becoming increasingly operational with the passage of further regulations and instructions. At the outset of the IUIDP, it was already almost certain that with or without the IUIDP, fully "autonomous" local governments were going to emerge before the end of the century.

- The IUIDP approach builds on Indonesia's Constitution and subsequent legislation for decentralization, justly underlining that it is inherently proper for local governments to be responsible for basic urban infrastructure provision and management even if they need financial and technical support by higher levels of government.

- As the country became more industrialized and increasingly complicated to manage, decentralization emerged as an absolute necessity, even though some viewed it merely as a necessary evil.

As can be deducted from the above, the forces working in favour of the IUIDP approach were quite strong, and the emergence of the IUIDP not only triggered off renewed interest in fiscal and administrative decentralization, but also accelerated its implementation.

Constraints

From the start, the GOI faced several institutional constraints that hampered application of the IUIDP approach. As new approaches require new knowledge, skills and attitudes, they had to be introduced nation-wide and "sold" to all the parties concerned. As very few people were available to do this, lack of qualified human resources became the first and foremost constraint. Another big constraint — exacerbating the first one—was the country's enormous geographic spread. It is much cheaper, quicker and easier to train a local government official in Jakarta than a couple of thousand kilometres away in the province of Irian Jaya. Although it would have been nice to try out the IUIDP in a few select locations near Jakarta, and gradually expand it from there, it was decided from the start that the IUIDP was to become a national programme, in line with national development policy and the National Urban Development Strategy. Anything less than a national programme even when it was only "national" on paper might create resentment among local governments who would consider themselves neglected or even excluded from submitting a PJM. Other constraints demonstrated mainly that "old ways die hard". These included the following:

- The National Development Planning Agency continued to have a relatively conservative "set-target" approach to infrastructure planning tied to the annual and five-year development budget cycle.

- Many engineers in the Ministry of Public Works opposed the approach largely because the required changes would lead to a significant loss of power and control on the part of the central government bureaucracy.

- The Ministry of Home Affairs, ostensibly the chief proponent of decentralization, gave mixed signals as to its commitment to bring it into full force and effect.

- The Ministry of Home Affairs also felt unhappy about the fact that the donor agencies viewed the IUIDP mainly as a technical programme and gave practically all funding to the Ministry of Public Works. According to the Ministry of Home Affairs, the IUIDP was a local government programme, and therefore Home Affairs was its natural counterpart.

- The Ministry of Home Affairs also argued right from the beginning that the IUIDP was too limited in scope, and that all 18 development sectors applied by the GOI should be included in strategic urban development planning. Therefore, it was argued, the IUIDP should not be limited to only Ministry of Public Works infrastructure, and the programme should be reorganized and renamed the Integrated Urban Development Programme or IUDP. It was also argued that the PJM—invented by the Ministry of Public Works—had no legal status as a planning document in regional government, with the result that local governments would be very reluctant to invest time in preparing them.

- Perhaps the primary institutional constraint was at local government level itself. Most regencies and municipalities had in the past become highly dependent on the centralized system of planning, financing and managing urban infrastructure. As a result, and in spite of their apparent desire to have more control over their own destinies, they were quite reluctant to assume the burden of these additional responsibilities. For instance, they did not like the idea of having to use own revenue to finance the rehabilitation, operation and maintenance of infrastructure. They also preferred the familiar project approach because their modus operandi was often driven by the overheads and commissions derived from projects. Thus, instead of viewing the PJM as a means to self-empowerment, they often treated it more like a shopping list for central government funding.

- Even if local governments were sufficiently motivated, bottlenecks occurred. Quite a few local governments became disappointed with the IUIDP approach, not because they did not recognize its merits, but because they did not appreciate the way it was done. Some local governments resented the fact that central government, citing lack of competence at local level, did all the negotiations with the donors and hired all the consultants. Some others, having enthusiastically prepared PJMs without help of consultants, became disenchanted when told that their programmes were too poorly done to qualify for donor-funding. Others became disappointed when they found out that the centrally hired consultants hardly bothered to consult with them, and produced English reports and PJMs that few local government officials fully understood.

As is evident from the foregoing, most of the constraints were not really technical in nature, but related to appropriate institutional arrangements, training, information and communication. Looking at the constraints, the GOI became aware that several preconditions would have to be met for successful IUIDP implementation, the most important being:

- As opposition to the integrated and decentralized approach was inevitable from some quarters, there was a need to achieve consensus among central and local government agencies; therefore, considerable patience, political will and long-term commitment would have to be generated from all sectors and levels of government.

- Given the lack of management capacity at the local level, top priority had to be accorded to a broad-based and extensive capacity-building effort.

- The decentralization effort had to be given renewed impetus if it was to stay ahead of the IUIDP and truly support accelerated infrastructure provision. Local governments had to be weaned away from overdependency on centrally provided projects to sustain themselves.

It should be noted that meeting these requirements was probably the hardest task facing the IUIDP. The technical side of infrastructure investment planning was not all that difficult. It did not involve any new technology or know-how that was not already available in the country or could not be provided by qualified advisors. The main problem was that too few people had a good grasp of the financial and institutional implications of the new approach. This resulted in unnecessary guessing about its real meaning and importance, a distinct "wait-and-see" attitude, hence considerable loss of momentum.

The First Steps

Between 1985 and 1990, the GOI undertook a number of steps to prepare for IUIDP implementation. These included:

- As it was believed that the overall programme could not be established without substantial external financial resources, the GOI sought international donor assistance in preparing the IUIDP in several provinces. International technical assistance (TA) became an essential vehicle for programme implementation.[6] Perhaps ironically, the GOI became highly dependent on this support.
- The GOI strove to develop institutional capacity, especially in local (*Tk.II*) government so it could assume more responsibility for the preparation of PJMs. The UNDP and the UNCHS provided technical assistance for capacity building in six provinces[7] prior to combining PJMs into "bankable packages" for implementation.
- In view of the lack of qualified staff in *Tk.II*, as well as the need to introduce the new approach to provincial and local cadres, the Ministry of Public Works launched the IUIDP Training Project, supported by the Government of the Netherlands.
- Technical assistance was also provided for IUIDP preparation support and IUIDP implementation support. This assistance focussed on building up provincial and local capacity for project

---

[6]   The packages financed in the beginning were the ADB-supported West Java and Sumatra Secondary Cities Urban Development Project (WJSSCUDP) and the IBRD-supported East Java and Bali Urban Development Project (EJBUDP).

[7]   Central Java, Yogyakarta, Bali, North Sumatra, West Sumatra and South Sumatra.

management and monitoring of the implementation of the PJMs. Several donors participated in this effort.

The GOI soon discovered that against all intents and purposes, the IUIDP was quickly becoming a much more cumbersome process than intended. It took several years to prepare local PJMs and "bankable" project packages, whereas it was initially thought to take only a year at most. This lack of expediency can be explained by several factors:

- Capacity-building for the local government required more time and effort than anticipated and required substantial assistance by consultants and donors for whom the IUIDP approach was also new; everybody was learning by doing.
- Some donors were not willing to approve loans for PJMs without complete and sophisticated feasibility studies, special institutional arrangements (PMUs, PIUs)[8] and other additional technical work completed beforehand. The IBRD in particular wanted everything tied up in the beginning, making the preparation process difficult and lengthy. This led some to conclude that the donor agencies were too sectorally oriented to undertake the IUIDP, and some advocated a return to the familiar sectoral approach to urban development.
- The GOI continued to act as a "provider" and was apparently not yet comfortable with its new role as "enabler" of development at local level. Although central government staff had to re-focus increasingly on providing overall supervision and guidelines, the entire IUIDP process was still managed at the central level with consultants hired by central government; local government had little say in the preparation of *PJMs* and did not fully understand them as they were produced in English.
- Consultants and local government staff were also slow in developing mutually supportive roles. The consultants rarely displayed an understanding attitude to help build local capacity, whilst local officials had yet to learn how to use consultants in a process that they were supposed to guide and control.
- The Ministry of Public Work's initiative in training, information and communication was not only insufficient, but even created resentments in other central government departments because there was no natural institutional "home" for the IUIDP training (Sidabutar, et al, 1991). As the training cut across agencies, the big question became where to vest the institutional responsibility for IUIDP training.

---

[8] PMUs are Project Management Units at provincial government level; PIUs are Project Implementation Units at local government level.

Related to this was another question: Who would accredit IUIDP training, as only accredited training programmes were attractive to local government staff, as opposed to project-based *ad hoc* courses that leave no traces, no credit points and no career prospects once the project is over?

- Despite the legitimate need for an improved institutional apparatus for project execution, the creation of non-structural project management and implementation units (PMUs and PIUs) solely for the purpose of IUIDP project implementation created problems. These project-based units were meant to be temporary and later to be absorbed by routine functions of provincial and local government as soon as sufficient experience with the IUIDP was acquired. Regional governments, however, often found it easier to depend on central government for project management and monitoring. In addition, some regional governments viewed these units as an unnecessary imposition into the provincial and local government structure.

The first experiences were thus quite mixed, and the period can best be described as one of trial and error. In addition, the size of the country, the number of international and national consultants involved, and the infant stage of official government guidelines caused the IUIDP approach to diversify as different donors, consultants and government officials each developed their own style of PJM.

The Urban Sector Loan

The advent of the IUIDP allowed the GOI to apply for "urban sector" lending. In return, the GOI committed itself to implement a Policy Action Plan (PAP) for the urban sector which essentially represented a continuation of ongoing GOI policies, and not a new set of measures imposed by the donor. The PAP reinforced the position of the IUIDP as the basic approach for programming and managing urban infrastructure. The PAP acted as a hook for bilateral assistance as well. The Urban Sector Loan (USL) and other donor assistance thus gave much more credibility to the IUIDP as it brought finance at a time when it was urgently needed. The Urban Sector Loan of approximately US$ 250 million provided by the IBRD from 1987 to 1989 had some distinct advantages:

- It was not tied to traditional sub-sectors such as water supply and drainage but provided support to the entire urban sector, covering all projects and activities associated with urban development.

- It was not tied to specific projects and could be expended in *Rupiah*, which could be used as part of the normal government budget for a range of activities in the urban field.

- It was "fast-disbursing" on the basis of progress in implementation of the PAP rather than against proof of project-by-project expenditures, as had been normal practice.

Looking back, the USL did not completely meet expectations, because it failed by and large to take into account the need for capacity building, and could therefore not accelerate the construction of infrastructure as was hoped it would do. In other words, it could pump more money into the preparation of PJMs, but it could not improve management capability quickly enough to significantly accelerate or increase the volume of infrastructure construction.

From Preparation to Implementation

During 1989 and 1990, the first generation of PJMs was "packaged" and made ready for implementation. The new packages were "programmatic" in the sense that the donor did not appraise all individual cities and all project components or sectors, but only a sample of five or six selected urban areas, and came to an agreement on criteria for selection of appropriate components and sectors to be included in the package.[9]

The implementation of PJMs really did not get underway until the early 1990s (*Repelita V*), based mostly on "programmatic" packages put together with foreign donor support. Starting with the WJSSCUDP and the EJBUDP, they later included the Sulawesi and Irian Jaya IUIDP, the Kalimantan IUIDP and an IUIDP for selected metropolitan and large cities. Table 5.2 shows the projects undertaken under the IUIDP umbrella.

An expanded set of IUIDP preparation activities was introduced for each *Tk.II*. These included not only the PJM, but also a revenue improvement action plan (RIAP) and a local institutional development action plan (LIDAP). The LIDAP and RIAP were coming into their own as full-fledged studies on institution-building and financial development at local level. These studies could now be undertaken independently, whereas before they had not been more than rapid assessments attached to a PJM. Already, a trend was developing towards more

---

[9]   These packages began with the IBRD-funded East Java and Bali Urban Development Project (EJBUDP) and the ADB-funded West Java and Sumatra Secondary Cities Urban Development Project (WJSSCUDP).

Table 5.2: Total Investments for the IUIDP

(in million US$)

Name of Project	Local currency	Foreign exchange	Total investment
Sulawesi and Irian Jaya Urban Development Project	87.5	100.7	188.2
Eastern Islands Urban Development Project	57.0	85.0	142.0
Bandar Lampung Urban Development Project	14.1	33.0	47.1
Second Jabotabek Urban Development Project	110.5	238.1	348.6
Third Jabotabek Urban Development Project	30.0	67.0	97.0
East Java and Bali Urban Development Project	188.9	184.5	373.4
Semarang and Surakarta Urban Development Project	123.0	173.7	296.7
West Java and Sumatra Secondary Cities Dev. Project	50.5	120.0	170.5
Bogor and Palembang Urban Development Project	79.9	154.8	234.7
Botabek Urban Development Project	126.5	80.0	206.5
Second Medan Urban Development Project	175.0	33.4	208.4
Second Bandung Urban Development Project	50.0	132.4	182.4
Central Java and DI Yogyakarta Urban Dev. Project	100.0	150.0	250.0
Total	1192.9	1552.6	2745.5

Source: Ministry of Public Works, 1995, pp. 75–104.

strategic and comprehensive studies on local economic development that could provide a solid basis for PJM preparation.

IUIDP Implementation guidelines were drafted for the first time for the EJBUDP. Maybe not surprisingly, the institutional and financial aspects of the IUIDP were coming to the fore as the issues that required most attention, rather than the identification and design of infrastructure projects which had received the most attention till then. It was a period marked by a large number of consultative meetings at central government level to work out the details of the implementation guidelines for PJMs. The result was a set of bulky documents that were comprehensive, but hard to digest for local governments without extensive briefing seminars.

A Framework for Coordination

Since the inception of the IUIDP in the mid-1980s, several institutional arrangements have been made for the purpose of coordinating urban development at the central government level. During the period 1984-1987, the Ministry of Finance took the lead in establishing the Institute for Urban Policy Analysis (IUPA). The IUPA was an effective consultative body due to good informal relations between key officials in the major ministries, but lacked executive powers to implement its policy recommendations.

In 1987, the GOI established the inter-ministerial Coordination Team for Urban Development (TKPP)[10] to replace the IUPA. The TKPP was set up concurrently with the GOI's Policy Action Plan (PAP), which in turn was largely driven by the USL. With the TKPP, the central government's coordination role shifted from the Ministry of Finance to the National Development Planning Agency. The TKPP was split into several working groups to implement the PAP. Working groups were established on the subjects of Urban Programmes, Urban Policy, Municipal Finance and Urban Institutional Development. In practice, however, only the Urban Programmes working group could be considered active because it coordinated a number of Urban Development Projects under the IUIDP.

At some stage the National Development Planning Agency considered that the TKPP was becoming unwieldy, was dominated too much by the Ministry of Public Works, and was increasingly encroaching on its role as the agency responsible for urban policy formulation. In 1990, it took the decision to streamline the TKPP. The working groups were replaced by a new body, the IUIDP Management Group (IMG). This did not prevent the IMG from becoming as preoccupied with programme and project coordination matters as its predecessor, while the steering committee of TKPP rarely convened to implement the urban PAP.

It is not easy to devise appropriate institutional arrangements for something as inter-sectoral as the IUIDP. Although the IUIDP has benefited from both TKPP and IMG for programme and project coordination and implementation purposes, it still lacks essential support regarding urban policy and such aspects as financial and institutional development that are required to support further development of the IUIDP. This lack of support can be attributed mainly to the persistent sectoral differences in inter-ministerial coordination procedures.

---

[10]   In Indonesian: *Tim Koordinasi Pembangunan Perkotaan.*

A Framework for Financing

Any discussion of Indonesia's IUIDP experience would be inadequate without at least some treatment of activities for improving the financing of urban development. This section provides a brief overview of local government finance in Indonesia, touching on some of the specific activities being undertaken within the framework of the IUIDP to improve urban development finance.

Table 5.3 shows the relative importance of funding sources during 1990-1991 of total routine and development expenditures at provincial (*Tk.I*) and regency and municipal (*Tk.II*) levels of government. This includes expenditures by regional governments (both provinces, and regencies and municipalities), as well as sectoral project expenditures of the central government agencies in the regions. The most notable features of regional government finance in Indonesia, as shown by this data, are twofold. First, is the high level of dependence on grants and subsidies from the central government. The table shows that 69 per cent of regional government revenues come from central government grants

Table 5.3: Sources of Funds for Government Spending in the Regions (*Tk.I* and *Tk.II*)

Source of funds	1990-1991 Total (billions of Rupiah)	Share of local Govt. revenue (%)	Share of total spending in regions (%)
Local Government Revenues (*Tk.I* and *Tk.II*)			
Own-source revenue (OSR)	3,135	27.4	14.0
(Local taxes, user charges, property tax)			
Other local revenue	400	3.5	1.8
Central government subsidies and grants to local governments			
Local discretionary funds	1,633	14.3	7.3
(Untied subsidies, block grants)			
Central discretionary funds	6,265	54.8	28.0
(Tied subsidies, earmarked grants)			
SUBTOTAL	**11,433**	**100.0**	**51.1**
Central government projects in the region (*Tk.I* and *Tk.II*)			
Public works and communications	4,477		22.0
Education and health	1,567		7.0
Other sectors	4,906		19.9
SUBTOTAL	**10,950**		**48.9**
TOTAL	**22,383**		**100.0**

Source: Ministry of Finance, 1994, p. 3.

to regional governments, and 49 per cent of total expenditure in the regions was for projects budgeted and executed by central government agencies. Second, is the very low proportion of total expenditures under the discretionary control of regional governments to decide to which priority sectors the funds should be allocated. Regional governments only have freedom of sectoral allocations for expenditures financed by own-source revenue (OSR) and other local revenue (14 per cent of total expenditure) and the relatively flexible block grants to provinces, municipalities and villages (7 per cent of total expenditure).

In line with the GOI's policy of decentralization combined with the IUIDP, there are three obvious priorities for increasing local government responsibility and discretion within the general area of regional finance. The first one is to channel a larger proportion of development funds through the local government-administered system of earmarked and block grants, rather than through sectoral project budgets. The second one is to modify the grant system to allow broader local government discretion for allocating grants to sectors based on local priorities. The third one is to increase local government own-source revenue through a variety of measures.

In the framework of the IUIDP, several activities have been undertaken to improve the financing of urban development in Indonesia. These activities can be divided into: (i) planning and programming tools, (ii) local government debt financing, and (iii) increasing OSR from specific sources. The following undertakings are worth mentioning:

- The local RIAP, a planning and programming tool which grew directly out of the IUIDP and the PJM, explores and details specific actions that local governments should take to strengthen their financial base and to increase the utilization of local revenues for urban infrastructure and related development. Local governments are required to prepare RIAPs (together with PJMs) in order to be eligible for donor support under the IUIDP.

- Another planning and programming tool for local governments is Programming and Financial Planning, Analysis, Control and Coordination (PAFPAK), a comprehensive capital programming and budgeting system that has been tried on a pilot basis in several municipalities.

- The Strategic Urban Development Action Plan (SUDAP) is an attempt by the Ministry of Home Affairs to provide a comprehensive local economic development action plan based on all development sectors rather than on the limited set of IUIDP infrastructure sectors. The SUDAP is now being tried on a pilot basis, and is expected to provide a more solid basis for PJM preparation than the current RIAP.

- The Regional Development Account (RDA) is a lending window in the Ministry of Finance from which local governments can borrow for projects which are (at least partially) cost recoverable. Other activities being considered for future use in the area of debt financing include the issuance of municipal bonds for infrastructure and development of a secondary mortgage market for housing.

- Finally, pending legislation would limit local government taxes and user charges to the more lucrative ones, doing away with others that cost more to levy than they earn. A special financial package, Mannual for Regional/Local Revenues (MAPATDA), provides a concrete set of guidelines for increasing yields from selected taxes and fees. Another major ongoing activity calls for improved revenue performance of the property tax through better valuation and tax administration systems.

As is apparent by now, the current menu of efforts is somewhat fragmented, as several government agencies and donors are testing out various approaches. A more comprehensive approach to the improvement of central-local financial relations is urgently needed and is likely to receive priority attention in the coming years.

Taking Stock

Experience with the introduction of fundamental changes through national programmes has shown that there is often a 10 to 20 years time lag between new ideas and their incorporation into public policy, and after that, into routine practice of local governments. So far, there are widely varying views as to how successful the IUIDP has been. Some believe it is doomed because its planning and packaging system has become too complex, and because decentralization is not keeping pace with developments in the IUIDP. Some have been calling for a "back-to-basics" movement that will focus on the original objectives of the IUIDP, doing away with all the ballast that made it so cumbersome over the years. Others believe that it has already contributed significantly to more integrated planning and implementation of urban infrastructure provision, and played an important role in helping to give local municipalities the needed urban management tools.

So far, about 170 out of the planned 400 cities scattered over the 27 provinces of Indonesia have an appraised PJM in hand, while the others are still working on it. Dozens of PJMs have been implemented, although the pace of implementation has been very uneven. In some local governments, output actually exceeded what was specified in the PJMs, whereas in other local governments there were substantial delays in implementation. A case study of implementation experience in two local governments in the WJSSCUDP, for example, showed that PJM implementation cost overruns reached as much as 63 per cent (current *Rupiah* values), largely due to increases in unit costs. Volume and specifications of completed projects, however, were still quite close to those proposed in the PJMs. Hence, despite several problems (some of which will be briefly mentioned later), the experiences of these towns were quite positive. On the other hand, available data on the overall level of actual spending on urban infrastructure within the past few years throughout Indonesia shows that:

> "In the environment of both rapid inflation and rapid growth of urban population, it is relevant to also track the trends in real per capita annual investment in urban infrastructure and services. Apparently, this peaked at *Rupiah* 11,700 [US$ 6] per capita in 1988/89, coinciding with major USL expenditures, and has deteriorated substantially since then, given the bottlenecks in IUIDP project implementation and disbursement. The 13% nominal growth in total urban infrastructure investments from *Rupiah* 790 billion in 1991/92 to *Rupiah* 892 billion in 1992/93 was totally offset by the 7% inflation and an urban population growth rate of almost 6%. Thus, the real per capita investment remained essentially flat at about *Rupiah* 8,000 per capita in 1984/84 constant *Rupiah*. This was equivalent to *Rupiah* 14,200 per capita in current 1992/93 prices" (Ministry of Finance, 1994, p.16).

Apart from inflation and population growth, the main implementation problems that surfaced during the early 1990s and which in part account for this decline in overall per capita investment include:

- Policy differences and technical problems between foreign donors, central government and provincial governments have led to substantial delays in finalizing package loan agreements. For example, certain IBRD requirements delayed signing of the EJBUDP for at least two years; delays in finalizing the WJSSCUDP loan agreement between the ADB, the central government and the government of the province of West Java postponed that province's implementation start-up by one year. A major drawback of the up-front workload was that local governments sometimes were not allowed to invest their own resources until the package was assembled and the loan had become effective, which meant a serious loss of productivity and delays in infrastructure investment.

- There were numerous technical delays in implementing specific sectors: For example, the ADB required international competitive bidding (ICB) procedures for procurement of solid waste trucks and other equipment, and central government insisted on centralized detailed engineering design for many water supply projects.

- One of the most severe implementation bottlenecks has been the shortage of qualified project managers and, to a lesser extent, technical personnel at the local government level. This has negatively affected the speed, quality and volume of urban infrastructure construction. Despite the establishment of a special IUIDP Training Unit, the training, information and communication activities could not keep up with demand and suffered from underfunding and understaffing.

- Institutional arrangements have still not been completely sorted out, including the elimination of inconsistencies and contradictions between existing and new guidelines and regulations.

- *PJMs* are still not prepared routinely by all local governments, and its legal and executive status as a plan is still not formally recognized by all government departments. The *PJMs* are also still not "rolling" because local governments are not able to review them annually without assistance by outside experts, but do not have the resources to hire such people.

It will be evident that the IUIDP is still having teething problems, as complications not only emerged in the IUIDP preparation stage, but surfaced again in the implementation stage. Despite inevitable confusion and delays, however, it also has become clear to most people that the IUIDP has somehow changed the environment and that there is little desire to revert to the status quo and increasingly untenable old ways of doing things.

The IUIDP appears to be evolving or transforming itself from something desirable but not very realistic into something desirable and reasonably practical, without straying too much from the original concept. It seems that this evolutionary process is indicative of the programme's relative success in achieving its initial objectives.

To be honest, the IUIDP still has not managed to accelerate the provision of urban infrastructure or to reduce the existing backlog. As pointed out, annual investment per capita is still more or less at the same level as it was at the outset of the IUIDP. However, other gains have been made that in the end may prove to be more valuable than the direct physical improvements achieved in the construction, operation and maintenance of urban infrastructure. Such gains could best be described in terms of changed perspectives, increased awareness about decentralization, improved motivation to put it into full force and effect, maybe even more empowerment and democracy. The IUIDP has unchained a process of rethinking the future.

The Future of the IUIDP

It may be fair to state that the IUIDP's days of experimentation should be over and that the programme is in dire need of consolidation and institutionalization. The future of the IUIDP clearly converges in five main themes—decentralization, capacity building, private sector and community involvement, sectoral expansion and institutionalization of the PJM—and each one has tangible indicators for success:

Decentralization

There is as yet no clearly defined "model" for decentralization in Indonesia. For example, there is little consensus on the pace at which it should take place, or to what extent local governments should be allowed to control a programme like the PJM. Should local governments be allowed to borrow directly from national and international financing agencies? Some advocate more rapid decentralization, while other prefer a "go-slow" approach. Both sides have valid arguments. On the one hand, decentralization is long overdue, but on the other hand, not everybody is ready for it. The very concept is still quite alien to a large number of local government staff who have been spoon-fed with instructions, grants and subsidies since Independence and who almost automatically refer all problems to a higher authority. If devolution of responsibility to local government is to become a reality as stipulated by present public policy the resulting decentralization should be manifest by certain critical indicators. The prime indicator is without doubt financial: a "critical mass" of revenues for investment in urban infrastructure and services should be earned and controlled by local governments.

Capacity Building

Despite all efforts to increase capabilities at all levels of government, capacity building is still suffering from a piecemeal approach and severe under-funding. Although the cost of training is estimated to equal at least 1 per cent of investment in infrastructure, investment in training has not reached even 0.5 per cent over the last decade. There has been reluctance on the part of certain donors to invest heavily in IUIDP training in the absence of clear government policies with regard to such crucial aspects as local government career development, job descriptions, staff transfers, institutional responsibility for regular training programmes, and accreditation. Thus, a clear indicator for the future of the IUIDP will be whether a regular manpower development programme targeted for local government staff is available, including an accelerated and accredited training programme and provision of upgraded career echelons, salary scales and other personnel incentives. As a result, one would expect to see an adequate proportion of project managers for IUIDP implementation originate from and operate at local government rather than be provided from higher levels of government.

Private Sector and Community Involvement

At present, there is still an absence of a genuine dialogue between government, private investors and communities in search of a decent place to stay. Although there are formally established "bottom-up" planning consultation procedures from the neighbourhood level up to the municipal and provincial level, these procedures do not yet function the way they should in order to make the IUIDP effective. One reason is the lack of time available for consultations. A system for channeling information between the public and private stakeholders through other means than face-to-face consultations has not yet been developed.

The participation of commercial private investors in urban infrastructure provision would provide the double advantage of reducing the government's management burden while at the same time increasing supply without burdening public resources. Still, the GOI wants to safeguard access of low-income households to basic amenities. Since private firms are inevitably driven by the profit motive, they are more interested in providing infrastructure for those who can afford it, and less interested in servicing the poor. It is important that somehow private investors become involved in PJM formulation, but the mechanisms still have to be worked out.

Not only private investors, but also non-commercial community-based organizations (CBOs) should be able to mobilize resources to provide certain services for themselves. This is already occurring to some extent in sub-sectors such as garbage collection and disposal—where community institutions frequently provide collection services—and in the field of neighbourhood pathways and drainage construction and maintenance. Hence, some of the technically simpler and smaller scale infrastructure can be provided by local community organizations, with direct cost recovery managed at the local level. This is also an area in which the IUIDP has not made significant gains yet, despite a well-established tradition of community participation (*gotong royong*). Here also, the GOI is examining how communities, whether or not assisted by non-governmental organizations (NGOs) can most effectively participate in PJM formulation. If viable partnerships between local government agencies and communities fail to materialize, the PJM will remain a weak document as it fails to take realities into account. After all, approximately 80 per cent of all housing in Indonesia is built by individual households without any government assistance. The clearest indicator for the IUIDP's future is therefore the emergence of PJMs that are planned by, for and with the people and are based on appropriate public-private partnerships.

Sectoral Expansion

If IUIDP planning and implementation procedures could be applied efficiently to more sectors than those of the Ministry of Public Works, the programme would probably become more attractive to local governments. Some of the sectors which might be added include public parks, cemeteries, slaughterhouses, transport terminals, electricity and telecommunications facilities. The scope could eventually be expanded to include virtually all public capital facilities, turning the IUIDP into the IUDP (Integrated Urban Development Programme) and bringing it in line with the development scope of the Ministry of Home Affairs. Tempting as expansion may be, limiting the programme to the present Human Settlements sub-sectors has helped to keep the IUIDP manageable in size. As the Directorate General of Human Settlements has been the IUIDP's chief sponsor, it is logical that the programme's scope has been limited to the sub-sectors under that agency's authority. In fact, there is little point in expanding the scope of the IUIDP as long as its "culture" has not yet been firmly established. A good indicator for the future is therefore that this "culture" evolves into a regular programmatic activity, after which one expects to see other sectors attached to it one by one as local capacity to manage expanded programmes increases.

Institutionalization of the PJM

Recent PJMs have institutionalized an expanded set of documents to be formulated by each participating local government. These have included not only the PJM itself, but also the Revenue Improvement Action Plan (RIAP) and Local Institutional Development Action Plan (LIDAP). Supervision of RIAP and LIDAP preparation is being transferred to the Ministry of Home Affairs as a routine, ongoing activity whose scope can be readily enlarged to encompass sectors wider than public works infrastructure. The RIAP might eventually be expanded into a SUDAP (Strategic Urban Development Action Plan). The logical explanation for this development is that the Ministry of Home Affairs bases its planning on all 18 development sectors identified by the GOI. Thus, an important indicator for the future of the IUIDP will be the emergence of these documents as a solid basis and main reference for commitment and action by all agencies involved. Another good indicator would be that PJMs become really "rolling".

Finally, it should not be forgotten that the IUIDP is not an isolated activity, and is bound to evolve under the pressure of outside forces. Emerging global concerns help shape and influence urban development and management policies. As a result, the GOI is gradually incorporating concerns of enabling strategies for shelter development, urban environmental management, urban land management, urban poverty alleviation, local economic development, and eventually, sustainable urban development into the orbit of the IUIDP. At this stage it is not clear what the end result will be, but if the IUIDP is properly managed, the future might look rewarding indeed.

BIBLIOGRAPHY

Hoff, R. van der and Steinberg, F. (eds.) (1992), *Innovative Approaches to Urban Management -The Integrated Urban Infrastructure Development Programme in Indonesia*, Aldershot, Avebury.

Hoff, R. van der and Steinberg F. (1993), *The Integrated Urban Infrastructure Development Programme and Urban Management Innovations in Indonesia*, IHS Working Paper No. 7, Rotterdam.

Jellinek, L. (1988), The Urban Challenge in Indonesia, *Indonesia Magazine*, July.

Ministry of Public Works, Directorate General of Human Settlements, Directorate of Programme Development, IUIDP Training Development Unit (1995), *Glossary of Terms and Abbreviations Used in Human Settlements Program and List of Urban Development Projects (UDP)*, Jakarta.

Ministry of Finance, Bureau for Regional Financial Analysis, Agency for Financial and Monetary Analysis (1994), *Monitoring Indicators of Repelita V Urban Policy Action Plan Implementation Results*, Jakarta.

Sidabutar, P., Rukmana, N., Hoff, R. van der and Steinberg, F. (1991), 'Development of Urban Management Capabilities: Training for Integrated Urban Infrastructure Development in Indonesia', *Cities*, 8 (2): 142-150.

Suselo, H., Taylor, J.L. and Wegelin, E.A. (1995), *Indonesia's Urban Infrastructure Development Experience: Critical Lessons of Good Practice*, UNCHS, Nairobi.

6

THE LOCAL GOVERNMENT INFRASTRUCTURE FUND IN THE PHILIPPINES

Apolo C. Jucaban

Introduction

In the last two decades urbanization has substantially out-paced the delivery of urban infrastructure and services in the Philippines. By the end of the century, the urban population is expected to be about 50 per cent of the total population. The Philippines comprises three major island groups. Luzon in the North, Visayas in the Centre and Mindanao in the South. For effective planning and administration, the country has been divided into 12 administrative regions, exclusive of Metro Manila which is the National Capital Region (see Figure 6.1). More recently, two autonomous regions have been reclassified out of the existing ones.

During the same period, planning, implementation and management of urban projects underwent significant changes, particularly, in foreign-assisted projects. In the 1970s the projects implemented were aimed at expanding physical assets and increasing the capacities of the infrastructures. Building up the capacities of local institutions was not a central objective among these projects as national agencies were principally responsible in the implementation of projects. Also, projects were basically sectoral.

In the early 1980s, inter-agency coordination began to evolve with the advent of the series of World Bank-funded urban development projects. Interrelated urban infrastructure projects were integrated into a single programme with a lead agency overseeing the various sectoral projects. This was the first attempt for an integrated urban infrastructure approach. The focus though was on housing and land titling in a poor sector of the Metro area. The principal actors were still the national agencies. Local government participation was very minimal. Private sector participation was nil.

Figure 6.1: The Philippine Islands and Administrative Regions

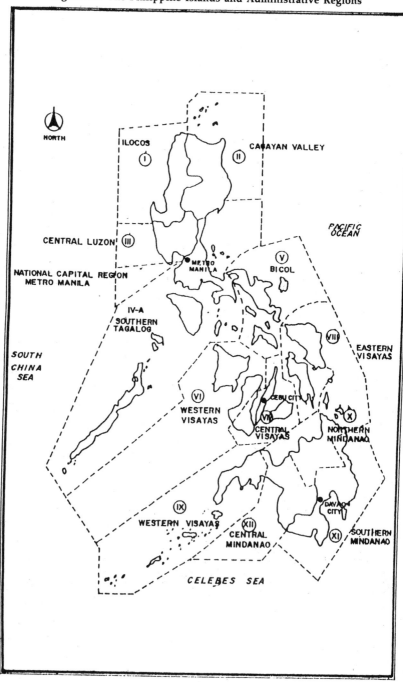

Picking up from past experiences during the last two decades, the United States Agency for International Development (USAID) initiated the Local Government Infrastructure Fund (LGIF) programme which incorporates innovative approaches to urban infrastructure planning, implementation and management (Department of Public Works and Highways, 1994; United States Agency for International Development, 1994).

Project Objectives and Scope

The LGIF is a USAID grant given to selected Local Government Units (LGUs) as "seed money" for implementation of basic municipal infrastructures. The project was conceptualized amidst efforts of the national government to devolve greater powers to the local governments. In this project the new role of local governments as key actors of development in their localities is being highlighted. Also, the exercise of its proprietary function is being tested. With funds sourced from the USAID the local governments identified critically needed municipal infrastructures, and together with the private sector, whenever possible, raised matching funds for the construction of the basic infrastructures. Where other similar foreign-assisted infrastructures were directly administered through a national agency, the LGIF projects are directly supervised by the LGUs. The LGIF-Project Management Office (PMO) though has been established under the Department of Public Works and Highways to oversee and coordinate the LGUs in carrying out the projects.

Mobilization of private sector participation is a primary aim of the LGIF programme. Of major concern is the integration of resources (particularly, financial, technical and physical) among agencies/ institutions, both government and private.

To avoid sophisticated environmental impact assessment and economic feasibility studies, projects eligible for LGIF assistance are limited to one-storey public markets, bus/jeepney terminals, municipal roads and bridges. An education component is added to the programme, which is designed to provide 12 science high schools called Learning Resource Centres (LRCs), with dedicated classrooms for general science, biology, chemistry, physics and computer science which are fully equipped with modern laboratory equipments, computers and experiment materials.

Project Financing

Under the Project Assistance Agreement between the USAID and the Philippine Government, a total grant of US $100 million is to be disbursed within a five-year period, starting 1991. However, due to the global reduction in USAID funding, it was scaled down to $27.2 million. Tables 6.1 and 6.2 show the allocation of USAID grant and financing plans respectively. The original programme could have financed 180 projects, including 12 science high schools, located in about 80 LGUs. Due to substantial cutdown, only 30 projects could be funded in about 15 LGUs. However with the "seed money" cum LGU-private sector matching fund concept, the number of projects were more than doubled

Table 6.1: Grant Fund Allocation

Category	Allocation ($ Millions)
1. Sub-projects (civil works)	
• Markets, bus/jeepney terminals, roads/bridges	16.129
• LRCs	1.560
	17.938
2. Feasibility studies	.800
3. Commodities/equipment (LRCs)	1.802
4. Technical assistance	5.975
5. Training (for LGU officials/staff)	0.534
6. Monitoring, evaluation and audit	0.150
TOTAL	27.199

Table 6.2: Proposed Fund Matching Scheme

Categories	USAID Grant	LGU/Private Matching Fund
I Projects		
(a) Public market	100%–NIL	0–100%
(b) Bus/jeepney terminal	100%–NIL	0–100%
(c) School		
i buildings	75%–25%	25%–75%
ii equipment/materials	100%	NIL
II Feasibility studies		
III Technical assistance	100%	NIL
IV Trainings	100%	NIL
V Monitoring, evaluation, audit	100%	NIL

and the number of LGUs increased to 21. The Geographical distribution of projects is shown in Figure 6.2.

The science schools were deleted since the primary objective of the programme is to initiate a private-sector led economic growth. However, due to strong representations made by the LGUs and the Education Department, three schools were put back into the programme, but the USAID grant for the building construction and site works was reduced from 100 to 75 per cent; the remaining 25 per cent had to be shouldered by the LGU. The clamour for the additional LRCs was still strong that some LGUs offered to finance 75 per cent of the civil works. Three more LRC's were accommodated.

To complement the LGIF grant the LGIF-PMO exhorted the LGUs to explore other funding schemes such as bank loans, municipal bonds and private investments. In fact, private sector involvement served as one of the primary criteria for the LGUs to be recipients of the grant. Funding counterparts from the LGUs and private sector ranged from 35 per cent to 75 per cent of the total project cost. As shown in Figure 6.3, the LGIF is financing 51.3 per cent of the total project cost while the matching fund raised by the LGUs from their own budgets and the private sector are 30.4 per cent and 18.3 per cent, respectively. It is heartening to note that in four instances, the private sector share exceeds the LGU investment as shown in Figure 6.4. Most of the LGUs were amazed to find out that the local private entrepreneurs are willing to directly participate as stakeholders and risk their capital in partnership with the LGUs. Just three years ago this was taboo to private investors.

Private sector participation could range from total (i.e. 100 per cent) financing to cost sharing or equity participation, and could be in kind such as land or in cash. Direct private sector cooperation constituted approximately $5.729 million, directed mostly to the construction of public markets, and bus/jeepney terminals whose return on investment is better than in roads or schools. The LGUs were urged to consider other modes of private participation like build-operate-transfer, credit financing and bond flotation. On one occasion, a private business conglomerate proposed to fully finance LGIF projects in San Jose City, a secondary urban centre in Central Luzon, in exchange for the lease of 7,000 sq. metres of adjacent land to put up a shopping mall. In this instance, the LGIF grant can be re-aligned by the city for other municipal infrastructures.

Coordination with banks and lending institutions was pursued by the LGIF-PMO to assist the LGUs access credit financing. In appreciation of the efforts of the LGIF-PMO, these institutions agreed to waive

Figure 6.2: Geographical Distribution of LGIF Projects

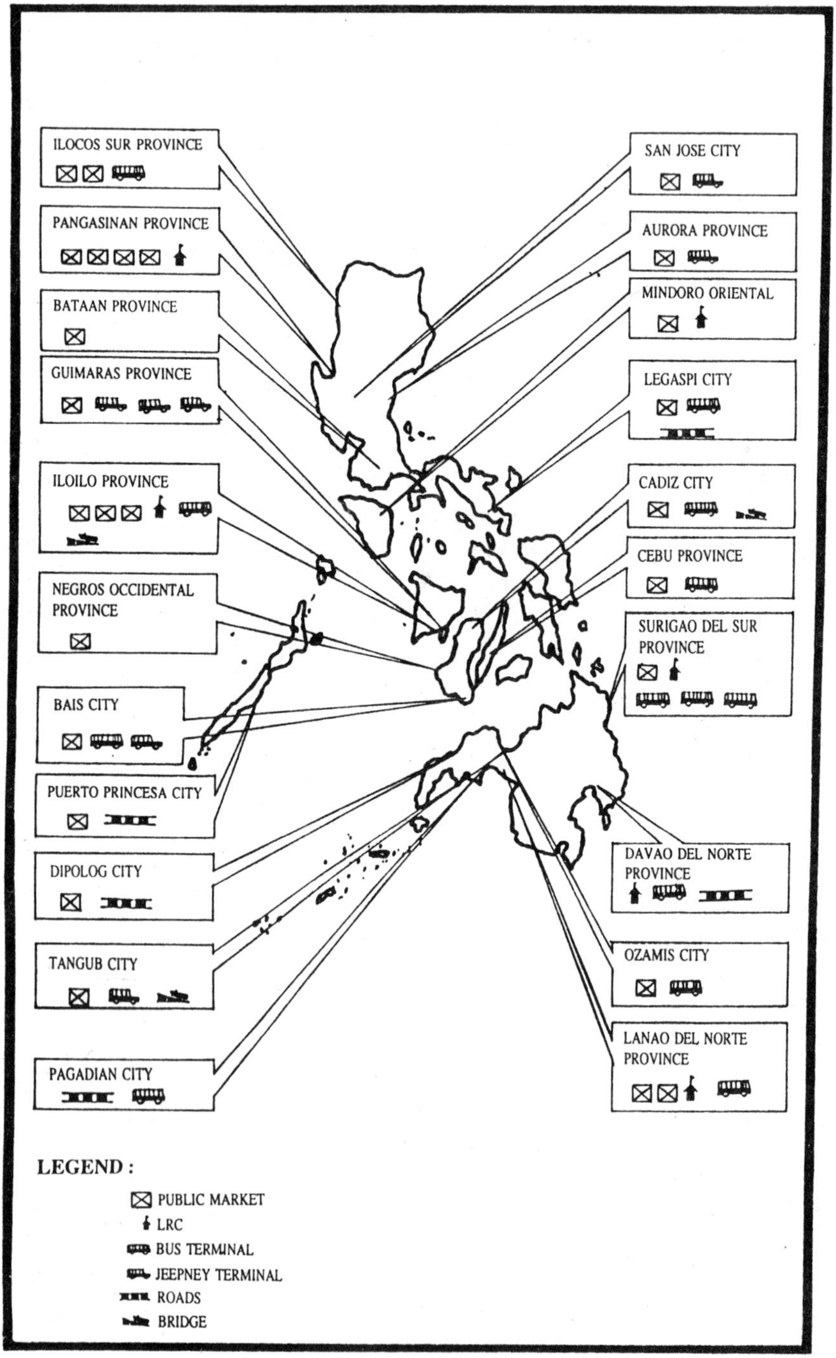

ILOCOS SUR PROVINCE

SAN JOSE CITY

PANGASINAN PROVINCE

AURORA PROVINCE

BATAAN PROVINCE

MINDORO ORIENTAL

GUIMARAS PROVINCE

LEGASPI CITY

ILOILO PROVINCE

CADIZ CITY

CEBU PROVINCE

NEGROS OCCIDENTAL PROVINCE

SURIGAO DEL SUR PROVINCE

BAIS CITY

PUERTO PRINCESA CITY

DAVAO DEL NORTE PROVINCE

DIPOLOG CITY

TANGUB CITY

OZAMIS CITY

LANAO DEL NORTE PROVINCE

PAGADIAN CITY

LEGEND :

⊠ PUBLIC MARKET
⚓ LRC
🚌 BUS TERMINAL
🚐 JEEPNEY TERMINAL
▮▮▮ ROADS
🌉 BRIDGE

Figure 6.3 Percentage Sharing of Project funds

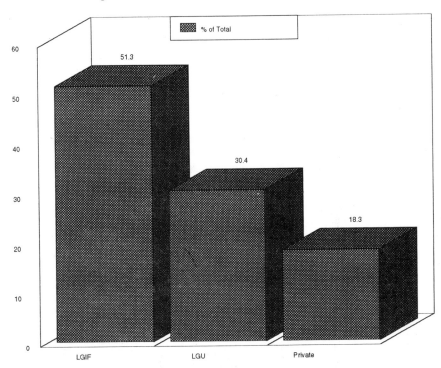

the feasibility study requirements as long as the LGIF-PMO favourably endorsed the application of the LGUs.

Arrangements have also been made by the LGUs and the private sector to operate and maintain the facilities upon completion. This is a development from the traditional set up where the LGUs were tasked to maintain completed projects. Experience shows that with very limited budget, inadequate skills, bureaucratic rigmaroles and lack of authority to make decisions, the infrastructure maintenance could better be left to the private sector. This has the added benefit of more money being recycled into active and productive circulation.

Integrative Aspects of the LGIF

The LGIF programme bears all the trademarks of an integrated urban infrastructure development in as far as financial, institutional, physical and even political aspects are concerned. Intra-project and inter-project integration is also a siginificant feature of the programme.

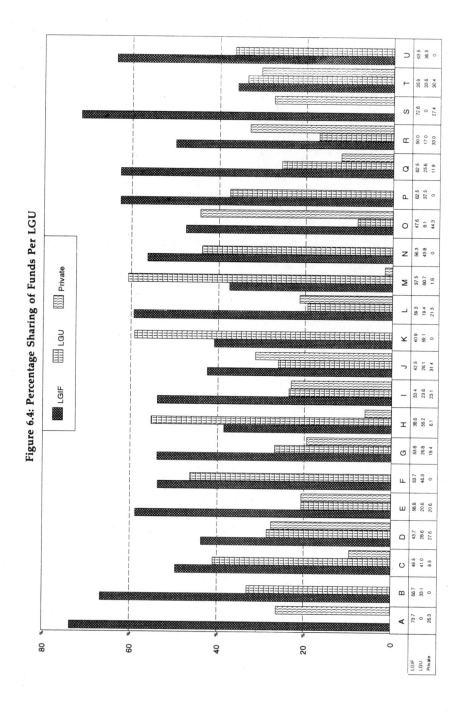

Figure 6.4: Percentage Sharing of Funds Per LGU

In terms of financial integration, the "seed money" became the integrative force in the pooling of funds including non-traditional sources such as private capital, banks and municipal bonds. It will be observed that in three LGUs, various governmental organizations, i.e., the province, congress and national agency, pooled their funds as shown in Tables 6.3 and 6.4. The latter also shows the other projects of the province funded from other foreign sources, namely the two port projects which are interlinked to the LGIF jeepney terminals, market and road projects. The economic impact and efficiency of these interrelated infrastructures are optimized by being integrated into interacting components of urban development. Table 6.3 has more than financial integration to crow about. More significantly, it marks a major milestone in integrated approach, that is, in terms of political and institutional aspects. Traditionally, a politician would not share her/his resources with other politicians, especially if they belong to different parties. It is pleasing to note that in this case the Governor of the province, the Mayor, a congressman, and a senator involved in the project, although not belonging to the same political party, agreed to pool their resources. And surprisingly, the three agreed to let the Governor be the lead actor and the "purser".

In another LGU, in the Visayas region, a lady senator contributed a substantial portion of her Countryside Development Fund to finance the construction of the bridge connecting the new LGIF public market and bus terminal site to the main town centre although she was a bitter critic of the administration and a leading oppositionist. Yet, knowing the importance of her contribution to the project, she cast off political differences and supported the administration's LGIF project. Without the bridge the public market cum bus terminal project would have been a white elephant.

The physical aspect of integration in the LGIF project can be amply exemplified by two LGUs. Figure 6.5 shows the inter-project integration between USAID bus and jeepney terminal and World Bank public market projects in the municipality of Tagum, Davao province. Both projects are highly complementary with each other. Their effectiveness is enhanced by the development of the roads leading to the provincial capital, business district and main transport routes. The support of other private organizations is vital such as the electric cooperative and local water district which readily agreed to extend their utility lines into the area. This is an example of technical-cum-institutional (or techno-institutional) integration. On the other hand, Figure 6.6 shows integration of LGIF projects with the other development projects in another LGU, the City of Legaspi, province of Albay. This is the first, under the LGIF programme that successfully floated municipal bonds to finance a

Table 6.3: Funding Contribution from Various Sources for the LGIF Projects in Pangasinana, Philippines

PROJECT	Undaneta Learning Resource Center (Science School)	Asingan Public Market	Rosales Public Market	Malasiqui Public Market	Lingayen Public Market	Construction Supervision	Total
Municipal	$ 38,462	$ 88,462	$ 150,000	$ 150,000	$ 146,154		$ 573,078
Provincial	$ 65,385					$ 57,692	$ 123,077
National (Dept. of Education Culture and Sports)	$ 19,231						$ 19,231
Congressional	$ 38,462	$ 38,462					
LGIF	$ 315,385	$ 61,538	$ 250,000	$ 288,462	$ 250,000	$ 92,308	$ 1,257,693
Total	$ 476,925	$ 150,000	$ 400,000	$ 438,462	$ 396,154	$ 150,000	$ 2,011,541

Table 6.4: Funding Contribution from Various Sources for LGIF Projects and Other Foreign Funded Projects, Province of Guimaras, Philippines

PROJECT / FUNDING	LGIF-PMO Projects							Other Foreign Assisted Projects		Total
	Buenavista Public Market	Hoskyn Jeepney Terminal	San Miguel Jeepney Terminal	Nueva Valencia Terminal	Pina-Suclaran Road Phase i	Pina-Suclaran Road Phase ii	Construction Supervision	Hoskyn Port	Suclaran Port	
Provincial	$ 34,615				$ 311,538		$ 34,615			$ 380,768
National (Dept. of Public Works and Highways)						$ 207,692				$ 207,692
Private (Bank Loan)		$ 61,538								$ 61,538
LGIF	$ 153,846		$ 115,385	$ 115,385			$ 46,153			$ 430,769
Others/German Grant (KfW)								$ 584,615	$ 384,615	$ 969,230
Total	$ 188,461	$ 61,538	$ 115,385	$ 115,385	$ 311,538	$ 207,692	$ 80,769	$ 584,615	$ 384,615	$ 2,049,997

Figure 6.5: Map Showing Integration of Various Urban Infrastructure Projects Funded by Various Sources

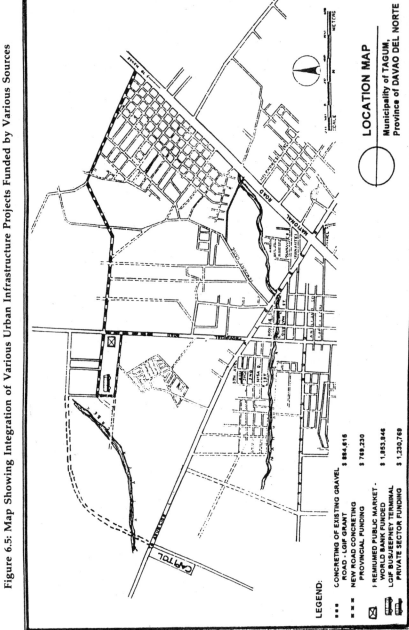

Figure 6.6: Map Showing Integration of Various Urban Infrastructure Projects Funded by Different Sources

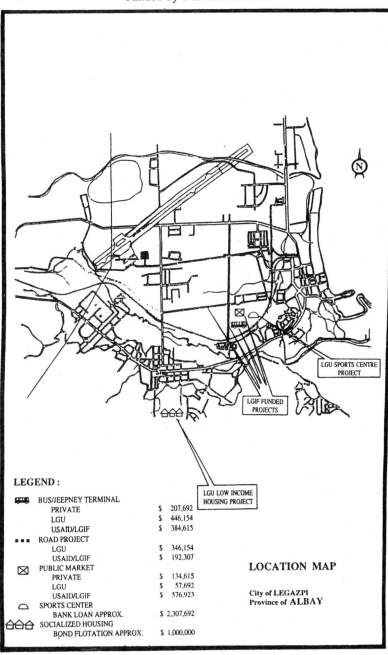

LGU SPORTS CENTRE PROJECT

LGIF FUNDED PROJECTS

LGU LOW INCOME HOUSING PROJECT

LEGEND :

BUS/JEEPNEY TERMINAL		
PRIVATE	$	207,692
LGU	$	446,154
USAID/LGIF	$	384,615
ROAD PROJECT		
LGU	$	346,154
USAID/LGIF	$	192,307
PUBLIC MARKET		
PRIVATE	$	134,615
LGU	$	57,692
USAID/LGIF	$	576,923
SPORTS CENTER		
BANK LOAN APPROX.	$	2,307,692
SOCIALIZED HOUSING		
BOND FLOTATION APPROX.	$	1,000,000

LOCATION MAP

City of **LEGAZPI**
Province of **ALBAY**

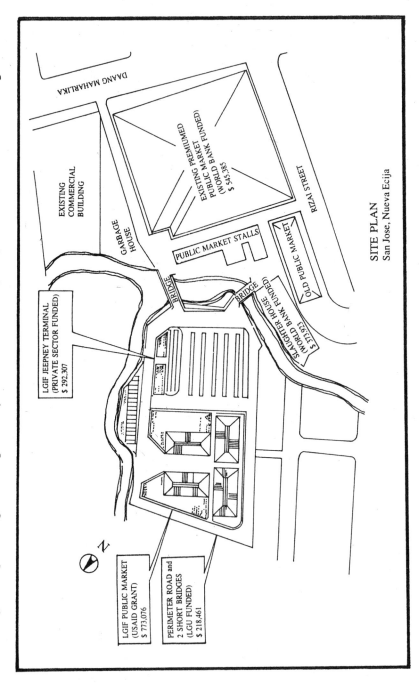

Fig 6.7: Map Showing LGIF Integrated Projects with Private Sector, LGU, World Bank and USAID Funding

DAANG MAHARLIKA

EXISTING COMMERCIAL BUILDING

GARBAGE HOUSE

EXISTING PREMIUMED PUBLIC MARKET (WORLD BANK FUNDED) $ 545,385

PUBLIC MARKET STALLS

RIZAI STREET

OLD PUBLIC MARKET

SLAUGHTER HOUSE (WORLD BANK FUNDED) $ 373,923

BRIDGE

BRIDGE

LGIF JEEPNEY TERMINAL (PRIVATE SECTOR FUNDED) $ 292,307

LGIF PUBLIC MARKET (USAID GRANT) $ 773,076

PERIMETER ROAD and 2 SHORT BRIDGES (LGU FUNDED) $ 218,461

N

SITE PLAN
San Jose, Nueva Ecija

low-cost housing project and secure a bank loan for the multi-purpose sports centre. This is also a case where the LGU is opening up new land for development which generated an upsurge of interests from the local investors especially that a new road has been constructed under the LGIF programme. Again, the electric co-op and water district readily confirmed the extension of their services to the area. It should be stated that prior to the LGIF-PMO approving the application of the city for LGIF grant, integration of other vital services and utilities was a prerequisite.

Multi-institutional integration, aside from physical, is shown by the LGIF project in San Jose City (see Figure 6.7). Here, the LGU provides the site, the private sector, the capital and the user (cooperatives) managing the facility.

Concluding Observations

There is no doubt that integration is the key to an effective urban infrastructure development. The effectiveness and beneficial impacts of integrated urban infrastructure development have been clearly demonstrated by the LGIF programme.

It appears also that integration of resources for urban development is better managed at the local level where the LGUs are the lead actor and the overall coordinator of resources and inter-agency efforts.

The success of project implementation also depends substantially on the integration of all elements (institutional, physical, technical, financial) and commitments of key actors as early as the preliminary planning and feasibility stages. This has been amplified in several instances where assurance of support services, such as power and water, is a pre-condition for the eligibility of LGU to receive LGIF grants.

Equally important is the fact that after project implementation, efficient operations and maintenance of the completed structures is assured. Needless to say, here too integration of inputs and resources of principal actors is most desirable.

By and large, it can be concluded that the LGIF project is a good example of integrated urban infrastructure development.

BIBLIOGRAPHY

Department of Public Works and Highways (ed.) (1994), *LGIF Annual Report 1994*, LGIF—Project Management Office (PMO), Manila.
United States Agency for International Development (1994), Project Assistance Agreement, LGIF-PMO, Manila (unpublished).

7

THE CAPITAL INVESTMENTS FOLIO: AN INNOVATIVE APPROACH TO METROPOLITAN MANAGEMENT IN THE PHILIPPINES

Nathaniel von Einsiedel and Victoria de Villa

Introduction

In the mid-1980s the Philippines experienced a negative growth rate which required in-depth re-examination of government priorities against a very uncertain future. It was during this time that the need for a new approach to resource management was strongly felt in a very real sense to develop a realizable public investment strategy capable of meeting a very different and difficult future.

To meet this challenge, an innovative approach to urban management was pioneered in Metro Manila, known as the Capital Investment Folio (CIF). This was designed to produce a broad consensus on government's investment priorities across all sectors over a period of five years, based on a realistic assessment of public investment resources and clearly reflecting government's stated objectives. This has shown to be a formidable approach to more efficient resource allocation in the particular circumstances of Metro Manila.

Since its inception in 1982, the implementation of the CIF was affected by several political changes like the overthrow of President Ferdinand Marcos and, in recent years, the revision of the Local Government Code which grants greater powers to the local government units. The changes in the political leadership put the CIF on hold from 1986 to 1990. And with the devolution of wider responsibilities and resources to the local government units with the enactment of the new Local Government Code in 1992 (Republic of the Philippines, 1992), a number of approaches and systems in the planning and financing of development projects have been explored.

Changes in the national economic climate also occurred recently. From a negative growth rate in the 1980s the economic momentum started in 1993 and accelerated in 1994. Real Gross National Product, adjusted for inflation, grew by 5.1 per cent in 1994, significantly exceeding the 2.6 per cent growth in the previous year (Republic of the Philippines, 1995a). Despite these developments, the need for innovative approaches to metropolitan planning and management relevant to developing city environments remains strong.

As the economy improves and power shifts from central government agencies to the local governments, the Capital Investments Folio exercise is perceived to remain relevant. For one, the scenarios and illustrations in the 1980s referred to in this paper offer prospects for progress on changing the existing rigid planning systems by which projects are developed and implemented. Much can be learnt from this experiment and it is in this spirit that this paper is written.

Metro Manila: Evidence of a Problem

Classified by the World Bank as a "lower middle-income" country, the Philippines had consistently been one of the poorer-performing economies of Asia.

Metro Manila is the capital and by far the largest urban area of the Philippines with a population of about 9 million, 13 per cent of the national population, and growing by around 230,000 each year. It produces one-third of the national GNP and close to half by value of all manufacturing and services sectors output in the economy. Situated on low-lying flood-prone land, it is a massive metropolis with formidable and complex problems, not atypical of many large cities in the developing world.

Since the mid-1970s the economy of the Philippines has proved less and less able to generate growth. In the 1980s, serious problems arose— in large part from high overseas borrowings for infrastructure projects which apparently did not increase productivity in the economy.

Metro Manila did not escape the implications of these changes; indeed, the priority in capital investments given to the provinces to stimulate agro-industrial development and the increasing problem of urban poverty surfaced most acutely in Metro Manila.

These prospects had profound implications for the government's investment activities and changed the whole environment in which projects were planned and implemented. Investment funds were clearly very limited. At the same time, the expected future demands for public services changed dramatically. Demands on sectors such as water, power and transport have reduced while those on other sectors—such as shelter and social services—increased. The structure of public sector investment therefore, had to change in order to reflect the changing demands.

What has happened is no less than a complete reappraisal of the government's objectives and ways of achieving them. The annually updated National Plan sets the necessary context for this; and the CIF process has been the mechanism for effecting change within the country's National Capital Region.

Public Administration in Metro Manila (1970-85)

Until 1970, public services were delivered by the national government together with the four cities and 13 municipalities which comprised Metro Manila. Increasing dissatisfaction and the awareness that many problems and their solutions had a metropolitan dimension, resulted in the mayors of the 17 jurisdictions forming a Metropolitan Mayors Coordinating Council (1972). But with limited technical resources and strong political conflicts this never became an effective forum for change. Finally, in 1975 the Metro Manila Commission (MMC) was promulgated by Presidential Decree and vested with the powers to act as the "central government" for Metro Manila.

There is now general agreement that the hopes vested in this change have not been realized in practice. The powers of the national government were unaffected by the change and it was the local governments whose powers were reduced—notably their taxing powers—causing continuing conflicts with their often powerful Mayors. After several years during which interim arrangements were made, it was only in 1979 that the MMC Offices of the Vice-Government (OVG), the Commissioner for Finance (OCF) and the Commissioner for Planning (OCP) were formally created. In the absence of a Commissioner for Operations, these activities—institutionalized in a number of Action Centres—were assumed by the Vice-Governor. The Finance Office was responsible for supervising local government assessment and treasury operations and for the review and approval of local budgets; and the Planning Office was responsible for preparing the Metropolitan Development Plan, enforcing the land-use plan and zoning regulations, and supervising the preparation of local city and municipal plans through the local Development Planning Offices.

The revenues of the MMC were derived from three major sources: allotments from the national government; taxes, fees and charges; and a 20 per cent contribution from the general fund of the cities and municipalities comprising Metro Manila.

Typically half of total revenues were derived from the 20 per cent allocation by local governments; and half of the MMC's expenditure was allocated to one Action Centre, for the collection and disposal of garbage throughout the metropolis.

The MMC was mainly involved in environmental sanitation; enforcement of building, land-use and zoning regulations; real property assessment; assistance to national agencies in traffic management; health service delivery; and minor infrastructure development. The national agencies and their very powerful corporations continued to provide all major sectoral services like water and sewerage, drainage and flood control, highways and transportation, power, shelter, education and health, and most other social services.

By 1981 there was widespread dissatisfaction with the existing arrangement, not least because the MMC structure had not adapted to provide for political inputs to its activities during a time of progressive national democratization; and there was much discussion on restructuring the Commission.

The Capital Investment Folio process thus evolved at a difficult time of substantial institutional fluidity when: (a) the powerful national government agencies continued to have a major influence in Metro Manila, (b) there were continuing difficulties in bringing local governments into the planning process, and (c) the Commission had no formal political mandate and was under severe public scrutiny.

Investment Planning in Metro Manila

At the national level public sector investment planning was the responsibility of the National Economic and Development Authority (NEDA), advising an inter-agency Investment Coordinating Committee which, in turn, reports to the Cabinet. Funds for the government budget were raised by the Ministry of Finance (now Department of Finance); while the release of funds to line agencies was the responsibility of the Ministry of the Budget (now called Department of Budget and Management) who pay heed to the deliberations of the Investment Coordinating Committee but are not controlled by it. The timing of releases for individual projects in particular, was heavily circumscribed by a wide range of political and other factors. As the economic crisis deepened and budget cutbacks became pervasive, the influence of this Ministry increased.

Public corporations tended to undertake their own financial management and planning largely independent of one another and of the central government machinery, and in Metro Manila they had a dominant influence on public investment. Eight large corporations, dominated by the Metropolitan Water Works and Sewerage System and the National Housing Authority, accounted for an estimated 80 per cent of public capital investment in 1984 and for two-thirds of all investment proposals for the next five years. Local government expenditures, similarly, were largely independent of central controls, although accounting for only a tiny proportion of capital expenditure.

Hitherto the funding requests of individual implementing agencies had been subjected to technical evaluation by the NEDA based on the project's economic rate of return, its overall capital requirement, the foreign exchange implications and a group of criteria collectively described as "sociopolitical sensitivity" (this is a measure jointly of the political importance of the project, its regional impact and other benefits which were not readily quantifiable). Few guidelines were issued to agencies to ensure the consistent evaluation of projects. Systematic attention had not been given to assessing the inter-relationships between projects in separate economic sectors. Nor had there been much formal recognition of regional—as distinct from national—resource limitations. In particular, there had been no mechanism for establishing investment priorities across sectors and only rudimentary coordination of investment programmes in individual regions.

In Metro Manila, as in other regions, a Development Plan—a form of outline structure plan—was intended to provide the framework for project identification and evaluation for all government agencies; but in practice the Metro Manila Plan had not been specific enough to perform this function effectively.

Evidence of a Problem

Five major problems resulted from the then existing system of planning and administration. These provided the context for the evolution of the CIF process.

Sectoral isolation of planning: The first, and probably the most crucial, problem was the narrow sectoral basis of planning which resulted both from the way resources were allocated nationally to the main government ministries, and from the role of the largely autonomous government corporations. Many problems in large urban areas are complex and necessarily demand inter-sectoral solutions (the improvement of health requires potable water, which requires a waste water disposal system, which may require drainage/flood control measures, which will require garbage collection measures, etc.). Without close inter-sectoral coordination over the location and time of investments it is extraordinarily difficult to formulate any area-based strategy. In the absence of this, planning reverts to *ad hoc* sectoral initiatives—which are often ineffective in their impact—causing much frustration in the implementing agencies and elicits a feeling of general cynicism with the planning system.

Inadequate involvement of local governments: The creation of the Metro Manila Commission had apparently subjugated the ability and/or enthusiasm of the 17 local government bodies positively to initiate high-impact projects in their areas and plan ahead, without replacing it with new initiatives. In particular there had been no successful attempt to introduce innovative funding schemes, including cross-subsidies between the richer and poorer authorities. Meanwhile, the main national agencies had been implementing major infrastructure projects or more localized slum or services upgrading projects, sometimes with little consultation with the local governments, resulting in problems of implementation, handover and beneficiary acceptance. The absence of active local government participation in investment planning was reflected in an emphasis on annual budgeting but little medium-term capital programming.

At a time when many of the major infrastructure projects in the main urban area were nearing completion (water supply, sewage system, rehabilitation, flood control) the opportunity for high-impact local projects (markets, health centres, area upgrading, local services improvement, etc.) was probably greater than ever before. Changes were clearly needed to allow the local governments to play a major role in developing, implementing and operating these projects and programmes.

Inadequacies in methods of planning: The system of planning produces certain types of projects at certain times in certain places, and if "appropriate" projects are to be initiated and implemented in a coordinated way this requires some common elements to the planning of different sectors and a relevant approach to project development. In practice, the planning system was found to be seriously deficient in both respects.

The main deficiency was the universal view of planning as a deterministic process based on reliable forecasts of key parameters—what we termed "planning under certainty". The GNP, the key parameter which drives most demand models, was assumed to increase by 6 to 7 per cent per annum for the foreseeable future, while only 3 to 4 per cent per annum turned out to be realistic. The result of producing a GNP which would treble or quadruple, rather than double, over a 20-year period was that very high fixed-demand levels were forecast and high supply options evaluated with little or no analysis of flexibility or robustness of projects under alternative futures. Some "white elephant" projects which resulted have left a difficult legacy. The corollary to devoting planning resources to inappropriate projects was that projects relevant to the changed perceptions of the future were often not identified. The need for a change in direction posed a major challenge to many agencies.

More generally there had been little attempt to develop and enforce common assumption and procedures in the identification and evaluation of projects, so that even for projects where ranking should have been relatively straightforward—for example those subject to cost-benefit analysis it was rarely the case in practice, even for projects within a single agency.

Weaknesses in the system of resource management: Disbursement decisions were crucial to which projects proceeded, and how quickly. The inability to forecast disbursement decisions made forward planning extremely difficult and inter-sectoral coordination very problematic. The problem arose partly because of difficulties by the spending agencies in forecasting resource requirements while they were facing high inflation, successive devaluations and contractors who were often unable to complete projects profitably. This was partly because of the inability of government to provide counterpart funds for internationally contracted loans; partly because of a weak linkage between the planning function as exercised by the NEDA and disbursement function as exercised by the Ministry of the budget; and partly because of the many political influences which in practice impinge on disbursement.

Thus it was common for agencies to be given the authority to proceed with projects only to find the actual disbursements to be only a fraction of those committed, with a resultant over-run of years in many cases.

Institutional fragmentation: In the Philippines, as elsewhere in the developing world, a project approach to development had led to the establishment, within individual sectors, of a number of individual projects and programmes mostly implemented by central government agencies and their corporations. In practice, many of the agencies tended to pursue totally independent paths, each developing fresh projects and taking different policy initiatives as needs were newly perceived and new agencies were commonly formed. Since the mandates of each of these agencies tended to be rather loosely defined, their roles became increasingly diffuse. As a result, programmes within a single sector could in part duplicate each other and yet, taken together, failed to meet stated objectives. In course of time, with new projects being added to the panoply of existing ones, the principles required to sustain a coherent programme tended to become increasingly indistinct, and no overall strategy for the sector existed or could be shown to relate to government objectives. This problem was more acute in some sectors, such as shelter, than in others.

The results of this formidable array of problems varied from sector to sector. For one such sector—transport—substantial resources had been invested in 16 major transport studies between 1971 and 1984, yet very little had actually been implemented. Furthermore, those projects which had been implemented had sometimes not resulted from these studies, or had been implemented in such a way as to bring into question their original justification. This picture was not a reflection of inactivity by government in the transport planning field—on the contrary, government efforts had been strenuous—but was the result of the ineffective nature of the planning process itself.

The CIF process evolved alongside this complex and formidable array of problems.

The Capital Investment Folio Approach

Evolution of the Capital Investment Folio Process

The consequences of this disjointed approach to investment planning were beginning to be recognized by the late 1970s. Then the Philippine government, with the assistance of the World Bank, took a number of initiatives to improve the situation. One of these developed into the Capital Investment Folio (CIF) process.

The CIF process was designed from the outset to be acceptable to the key agencies involved in resource allocation, and to be an overlay on the existing resource allocation activities of the NEDA, Office of Budget and Management (OBM), Ministry of Finance (MOF) and the existing sectoral planning activities of the implementing agencies. The process was therefore essentially an evolutionary development of existing systems.

Initiated in 1978 as the Metro Manila Financing and Delivery of Services (METROFINDS) project within the powerful Ministry of Public Works, Transportation and Communications, the first stage of development was the assembly of investment programmes of all government agencies to provide the first metropolitan overview of investment plans for the metropolis, the first CIF being produced for 1979. In 1980 this function was transferred to the Metro Manila Commission where it became, and still is, the responsibility of the office of the Commissioner for Planning. The first technical assistance study was undertaken in 1982 with the aim of developing the CIF into a system which could positively assist government in improving decisions on the nature, timing and location of public sector capital investment in Metro Manila.

Significant advances were made in establishing the physical and financial characteristics of all projects proposed by government units in Metro Manila, in improving inter-agency dialogue, in establishing a more formal institutional framework for carrying the work forward and in formulating and introducing a project evaluation system as an integral part of the folio preparation.

In 1984 a "window of opportunity" opened for the CIF process to exert considerably more influence than earlier. This situation arose for two main reasons. First was the impact of the rapidly deepening economic crisis on the perceptions of virtually all involved in the government. Large and repeated cuts in investment programmes, together with the realization that long-cherished projects may not now be relevant or were unlikely to be funded for many years, and a real questioning of how government should respond, provided a unique opportunity to influence decision-makers (Metropolitan Manila Commission, 1984).

Second, the World Bank had programmed a mission to Manila to finalize three major loans—in the shelter, urban transport and drainage, and environmental improvement sectors. The importance of government influencing the size and project composition of these loans, which would in practice be the major influence in Manila for the remainder of the decade, demanded that a major step forward be attempted—namely that a five-year investment strategy be formulated for the metropolis with the objective of achieving broad consensus both within government and with the Bank.

The CIF Process

The CIF process is designed to remedy many of the identified problems associated with "conventional" planning. It is a planning system involving an annual cycle of activities linked to the national budgeting system and its major output is a five-year rolling investment programme of projects and programmes which are consistent with expected available investment funds and are a clear reflection of government's goals and objectives. The process focusses on three major components of the planning process and on their interlinkages (see Figure 7.1).

The main features of the approach are:

Figure 7.1: The CIF Planning Process

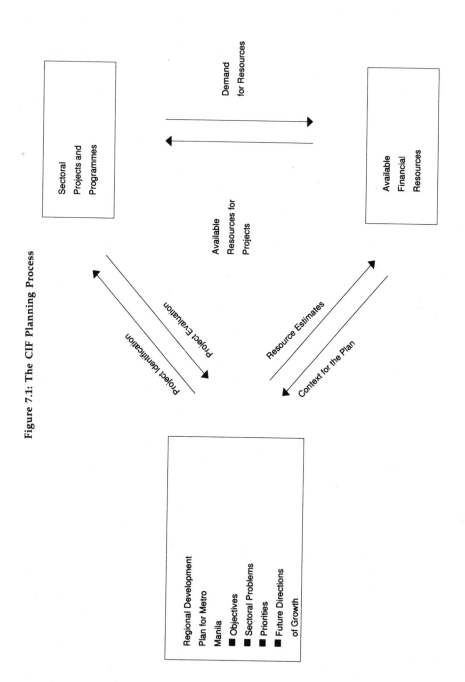

1. The formulation of a Development Plan for Metro Manila recognized by major agencies, which provides the basis for relevant policies and projects to be identified and evaluated.
2. The identification of proposed expenditure on all public sector projects and programmes in Metro Manila; and separately the estimation of likely available funding for such projects.
3. The development of an evaluation procedure to establish priorities between projects such that the demand for funds (as represented by projects)—which had always considerably exceeded available funds—could be cut back until demand and availability were in balance.

The CIF is the financial representation of the Development Plan, being the group of high-priority public sector projects most likely to contribute to government's objectives.

Institutional Framework

The cornerstone of such a new planning process is the development of appropriate institutions, and the CIF process posed particular institutional problems. Because resources were allocated nationally by sector, resource allocation to an area, such as a city, was problematic. Without changing fundamentally the national system of resource allocation this could apparently only be achieved either by giving the city government the *power* (over government ministers) to dictate what should happen within its area; or by devising some form of inter-agency body comprising the city government and the major national resource allocation and spending agencies, reliant for its effectiveness on *persuasion*.

In Metro Manila's case there was no prospect of the first of these options being effective, or desirable, but there was a promising background of inter-agency contact at senior officer level which suggested that the persuasive approach offered potential. Accordingly a senior-level Inter-Agency Technical Working Group (IATWG) was formed comprising senior representatives of all key resource allocation and spending agencies and chaired by the Commissioner for Planning, MMC. This Committee was, and is, the centre of influence of the CIF process.

The system of government in the Philippines concentrates power in the hands of a relatively few individuals, and experience has demonstrated that the achievement of influence requires access to these individuals and a good technical case to put forward. In practice the former requirement for access has demanded the presence at IATWG meetings of these key individuals from government's resource allocation and spending agencies; and the latter requirement had demanded strong technical support to the Group which had been provided in the main by the Office of the Commission for Planning, MMC.

Applying the CIF Process

Identifying Projects and Programmes

All those projects and programmes which require public funding and would benefit the people of the city should first be identified. All investing agencies should be included (government-line ministries, public coporations and local government); and all public capital investments are included, whatever their source of funding. As much information as possible should be established about each project as a preliminary to evaluation—from available feasible studies, discussions and line agencies and site visits.

The coherent assembly of financial descriptions of the projects is not likely to be an easy matter. Certain agencies probably have no medium-term investment plans. Many use different time horizons, will have expenditure projections based on varying rates of domestic inflation, or use different assumptions on anticipated changes in the rate of foreign exchange. Some agencies will go out of their way to work with an inter-agency team in developing the base information, especially those who can use this information to advance their own work; others—particularly some of those which are traditionally out of government's financial control—will initially view the process as a potential threat to their independence.

Projects should be categorized as either *on-going* (under construction, with funds committed); or *new*. Financial requirement for each project and totals for each category should be indicated.

Evaluating Available Resources

Funds for public sector projects normally come from the revenues of central and local governments and government corporations, and from borrowing. Available funds depend on the expected future state of the economy and on government policies for allocating available resources. In many developing countries, the government does not usually prepare area-based investment statistics on which estimates of available resources can be directly based. However, the sum of official pronouncements as reported by the media could be seen to amount to a declaration of specific expenditure objectives for specific areas such as the capital city.

In situations of severe economic crisis there may be GNP forecasts anticipating a sharp fall of economic growth, in which case there may be prescriptions for a cut in government budgetary expenditure as a proportion to GNP. This may be accompanied by a requirement for public corporations to increase their internally generated resources. All these imply a substantial cut in national investment expenditure. There may also be statements of government's intent to reduce inequalities in regional balance and at the same time to give priority to upgrading agricultural production and to the processing of agricultural produce both requiring a shift in expenditure priorities away from the main urban areas. All these indicate that there is considerable uncertainty about the future performance of the economy in many developing countries.

Using the full range of GNP forecasts, public resources available for capital investments for a future period will result in a corresponding range in absolute amounts, that is, a low figure for the low GNP forecast and a high figure for the high GNP forecast.

It will not be surprising to discover that in all probability, the majority of the proposed investment summed up in the activity mentioned in the preceding section will not be funded. Moreover, there will be a need to closely examine *on-going* projects which threaten to crowd out any investment in new projects. These are the main issues addressed in the evaluation.

Developing Sectoral Strategies

The necessary preliminary to project evaluation is the development of outline sectoral strategies—combinations of policy measures, investments and institutional measures which together are considered likely to provide appropriate governmental response in any situation. Given a clear understanding of the rationale underlying these strategies, the evaluation of projects becomes relatively straightforward; conversely, evaluation in the absence of this framework cannot be particularly meaningful.

This stage in the CIF process is particularly positive and may be contrasted to the more reactive evaluation stage. It allows *existing* policy options to be reviewed and *new* options—*policies which are often alternatives to capital investments*—to be discussed with the agencies before attempting to evaluate investment projects. It enables areas for possible release of public sector funds through private sector intervention to be identified. And it allows gaps in sectoral programmes to be identified—for example, there may be an existing serious garbage disposal problem with dump sites close to or already exceeding capacity, yet the only project to expand capacity may be unaffordable to the local government. A new low-cost project may then be identified, producing a coherent strategy in this sector.

This stage in the process is also crucial in that it involves the *formulation of sectoral strategies in consultation with the agencies*, thereby ensuring that the evaluation did not produce untenable results. It is not difficult to conceive of situations where the evaluation rejected all projects in one sector (perhaps because they are all high cost), leaving a vacuum and no tenable strategy to "sell" to the agencies and public. Clearly, the evaluations will achieve little respect (and will deserve little) unless it can be shown to result in acceptable strategies.

Evaluation Leading to Recommended Core Investment Programmes: Figure 7.2 outlines the nature of the project evaluation process. "Government Goals and Objectives", as defined in the national and city development plans, are to be pursued through "Projects and Programmes" subject to the constraints of "Available Resources" and "Institutional Considerations" and within the context of "Sectoral Strategies".

The primary output of this evaluation is the Core Investment Programme of high-priority projects and programmes which are compatible with the realistic estimate of available resources. The procedure to be formulated to prioritize projects should ideally be a development of similar systems already in use by national government usually applied to large infrastructure projects. The Planning under Uncertainty process has a four-step evaluation procedure.

Step 1 : Screening Evaluation: Because some projects are not likely to be well developed (being more of project "ideas") or have no possible funding source, an initial screening is carried out. This results in some projects possibly being deferred for further examination while the remaining projects could probably be realistically implemented and potentially beneficial.

Step 2 : Evaluation of On-going Projects and Programmes: No project should be considered to be so firmly committed that its implementation is inevitable. Political commitments of goverment can in practice be reinterpreted, and agreements with donor agencies can always be realigned.

Some on-going projects may be substantially or nearly complete and small additional investments could produce large benefits—it is important that these are completed as programmed. Others may have

Figure 7.2: The Project Evaluation Process

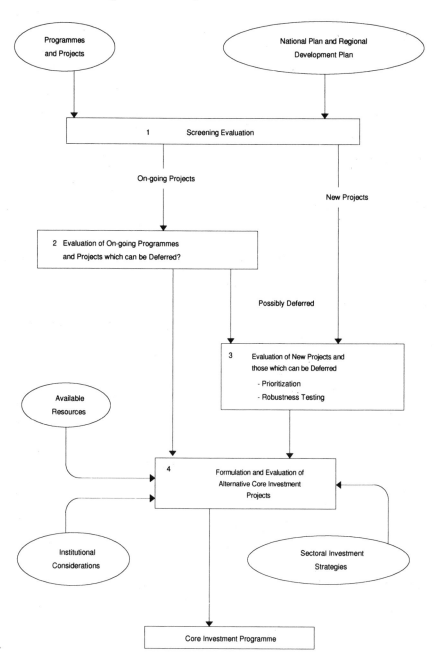

only commenced and some may require very large investments over many years before any benefits are realized—these should be examined in detail to establish whether these investments should be deferred, thereby releasing funds for higher-priority new projects.

All on-going projects should be evaluated against an agreed upon criteria (this is discussed in the next step) to categorize them as to whether they should be implemented or deferred for further examination. Projects under this latter category should be evaluated on a common basis with the "new projects to establish priorities within and between each group of projects."

Step 3 : Prioritization of New Projects and On-going Projects Which Could be Deferred: As mentioned earlier, this should be a development of similar systems in use already by the national government in order to facilitate acceptance. It should be based on a point-scoring system usually applied to major national infrastructure projects. Under this system, projects are scored on a scale of 0 to 10 against a number of evaluation criteria and the criteria weighted to give a project score. Substantial differences between scores could be taken to separate "first priority" projects from "second" and "third", and to concentrate attention on marginal projects. The weights between criteria should be representative of future "scenarios", and by changing these weights, the performance of a project under a number of different scenarios could be established—hence a view could be formed of whether government investment in a given project was likely to be risky or could be undertaken with confidence.

This latter aspect of the evaluation can be very powerful. In view of the profound uncertainty facing many developing countries, it is the most critical element of the CIF process. It will indicate that new types of projects are needed, those which are robust under a wide range of future scenarios, and projects which are flexible and could match incremental expenditures with the realization of benefits and/or revenues. This is probably something new to many developing countries but the evaluation can provide the vehicle to demonstrate their relevance in a practical setting. It can be quickly appreciated especially in countries where the usual problem of defining what government's objectives actually are in terms of weighted criteria is a pervasive one; and where the formulation of alternative future scenarios can defuse the issue.

A certain number of scenarios (say, five) can be defined, each representative of an identifiable future path of development. Similarly, a certain number of distinct criteria can be defined, each reflective of government's objectives (Table 7.1). These criteria can range from the compatibility of the project to the city's development plan, to the

Table 7.1: Possible Path of Development

(in per cent)

Criterion	High Growth	Moderate Growth		Low Growth	
		1	2	1	2
Socio-political acceptability	20.0	25.0	45.0	55.0	70.0
Government budgetary requirement	10.0	25.0	17.5	17.5	10.0
Debt service requirement	15.0	25.0	17.5	17.5	10.0
Economic profitability	55.0	25.0	20.0	10.0	10.0
Total	100.0	100.0	100.0	100.0	100.0

Note: Evaluation projects under the different scenarios will show that certain projects will score well under virtually all criteria and thus are "good" projects whatever set of weights are applied: these are the "first priority" group of projects. Equally, there will be a "third priority" group of projects which will perform consistently badly and are clearly not suited to the city need's over the coming years.

impact of robustness and flexibility characteristics of the project on its estimated economic return or cost-effectiveness. Because there is such uncertainty about the future, a wide range of scenarios may be defined — for example, the social and political acceptability criterion may be seen to account for 20 per cent of total weights under the high-growth scenarios but 70 per cent under the low-growth scenario.

Step 4: Formulation of Core Investment Programme: Additional considerations may be required for the analysis so as to formulate realistic alternative Core Investment Programmes (CIFs) for evaluation. These may include an appraisal of the institutional impact of each project, an aspect which is not susceptible to quantification. This considers, among other things, whether a project is designed to enhance the implementation capability of the organization; whether the agency is in fact capable of undertaking the project without significant further strengthening; or whether totally foregoing the project would undermine the strength of the organization to the extent that it could be revived in the event of an economic recovery.

Another consideration may involve an examination of the affordability of certain components intended for implementation by several local authorities. In a number of developing countries, local authorities are required to meet the development costs, including loan servicing of a group of projects formulated by themselves, by government line ministries and by the national housing authority. These projects normally include settlement upgrading, local roads and basic urban infrastructure, among others. Experience has shown that many of these local authorities are unable to afford repayment of the project costs under existing systems of local government financing, being constrained by the usual inflexibility of revenue resources which is exacerbated in conditions of accelerating inflation. Assuming that the financing system will not be altered, the scope of the relevant projects and hence the capital costs may have to be reduced to a level that can be afforded from traditional local revenues.

A wide range of alternative CIFs may be formulated, depending on judgments about the feasibility of cutting expenditure on projects already under construction, and on the likelihood of new funding mechanisms being introduced for local government projects. At one extreme, there may be no cutbacks and no changes in funding. However, given the feasibility of major cutbacks to on-going projects this picture can change dramatically. If these cuts are not made, it may be difficult to justify any major investment on "new" projects and programmes.

Ensuring the Acceptance of the Approach

Many aspects of the CIF approach will be valid in any large developing city, although the mechanism for effecting change will naturally need to reflect the particular circumstances of each. The changes that will be made will not be cost-free and would involve substantial investment of time. A central question facing developing cities is how the returns from this type of investment compare with those from conventional project planning. In many developing cities, the achievements of "conventional" project planning are so bad that investing in the CIF approach appears in many ways as a pre-requisite to better project planning.

Each step towards rationality in resource allocation is of course at the expense of personal patronage and influence. It is therefore crucial that requirements for a cooperative approach to urban planning exist. There must be a strong and genuine desire in government to invest wisely to improve the conditions of its people, and simultaneously there should be the natural desire within each agency to see that its projects are implemented and are effective. Demonstrably, inappropriate projects satisfy few people, and the CIF process can be effective in pursuing both sets of objectives. In countries where these views strike a cultural response, opportunities for major progress are likely to be substantial. In other countries they may be more limited.

The power balance in a developing country will dictate how, how far and how fast the CIF process should proceed. Given that it cannot directly control any major investment, it has to be devised to exert influence without attempting to take away each agency's room to manoeuvre. The main "pressure points" in a developing country are usually the major spending agencies, together with the national agencies responsible for economic planning and the disbursement of resources. The active involvement of major donor agencies can allow this influence to become more effective.

It is of course crucially important that such "influence" is (and is perceived to be) positive. If its sole objective is, for example, to evaluate prepared projects, giving the go-ahead to some and rejecting others, it is unlikely to be supported or deserves to be supported. The CIF process should seek to provide the implementing agencies and the local governments with the necessary information for them to identify and develop relevant types of projects and programmes; and to provide the necessary inter-sectoral context for sectoral programming. Thus, the logic of the process is to encourage progressive alignment of their projects and programmes towards a nearly optimum allocation of resources. Those aspects of the CIF process which are likely to be widely acceptable are:

1. Relating the demand for resources (i.e., government's projects and programmes) to likely available resources and to government's objectives—in other words providing the tight analytical framework which demands a new perspective on investment and project justification.
2. The formulation of sector strategies as a preliminary to evaluation. These can bridge institutional weaknesses and identify programme inconsistencies, duplications and missing elements.
3. The system of evaluation and the mechanism for incorporating uncertainty in the planning process.

Of particular importance in applying the process are:

1. Establishing in very substantial detail the physical and financial characteristics of projects. Only by becoming fully conversant with projects can they be sensitively evaluated.
2. Establishing the realistic level of available resourcemost governments tend to plan on the basis of sheer optimism; this has been shown to lead to inappropriate projects. In developing cities in particular, governments need to develop projects and programmes which at least provide basic services in the event of low resource availability.

3. Establishing the institutional strengths and weaknesses in government and using projects to build on the former and avoid the danger of the latter.

While the importance of developing a process which becomes institutionalized into the material resource allocation process should be stressed, it is of crucial importance to retain the dynamism of the system and to be ready to respond quickly to events. Only in this way will the relevance of the process be maintained.

In many developing cities potential projects and programmes far outstrip available resources (i.e., that much planning is inevitably wasted), but there is often no shortage of "good" projects in which government can invest in confidently. This is undoubtedly important in generating consensus in government—indeed it is very difficult on rational grounds to question an evaluation which produces a high ranking for a project, virtually whatever weights of criteria are identified. If this is not so, there would be much more focus on which scenarios should be used for evaluation - for example, may be a subset of the five shown in Table 7.1.

It is clear that the ideas of this approach to urban management are often very new and are difficult for sectoral agencies to grasp. Experience in applying the approach in a number of developing cities has demonstrated the importance of training seminars and workshops in addition to day-to-day contact to contribute to this broader understanding—which is at the root of ensuring that the approach becomes effective in practice (see Figure 7.3).

Conclusion: Opportunities for Future Progress

The main achievement of the CIF is the establishment of a practical and rational system of urban planning and administration in Metropolitan Manila (Republic of the Philippines, 1995b). The system is practical in that it can be made to work progressively and be accepted. It is rational in that it addresses the key issues in the city—for example, the likely available resources of central and local governments, how to interpret government objectives in a very uncertain future how to build up institutions. It is a system in that a team of professionals can be trained to operate an annual cycle.

In essence the CIF approach provides a new perspective on forward planning in a developing country environment. The two key issues it throws a new light on are "affordability" and "uncertainty". A new understanding of affordability leads to a more general appreciation of opportunity costs. The tight analytical framework of the approach

Figure 7.3: The CIF Process

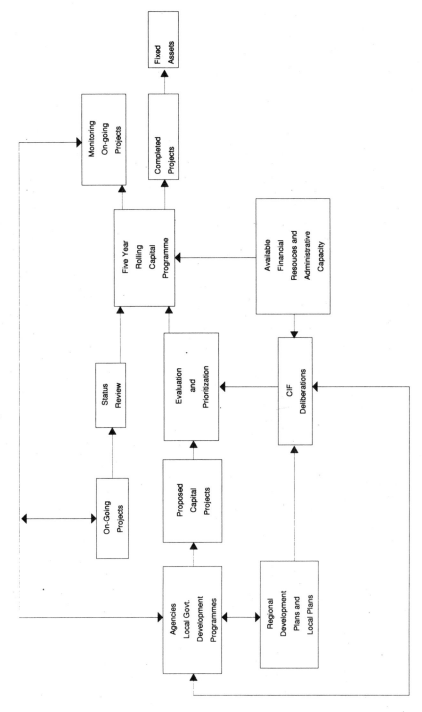

demands that proponents of projects justify them in the context of competing projects for scarce resources.

A new understanding of the need to relate changes in expectations of the future to the very deterministic system of project planning developed in earlier decades and are still widely applied, is a major step forward in project planning. The challenge of how to plan under conditions of considerable uncertainty is facing developing countries even more directly than the developed world. The formulation through the CIF approach of an evaluation process which formally incorporates "robustness" and "flexibility" in project selection marks a considerable advance.

In addition to what has been achieved, the CIF also recognizes that the view on infrastructure building is changing. Equal attention should be given to the quality of services derived from the facilities as to the quantity of infrastructures delivered. Implementors have realized that infrastructure development is not merely adding a new physical asset but also ensuring and maximizing service delivery. Maintenance and upkeep should be integrated in the infrastructure development of the national agencies and the local governments.

In terms of resource availability the CIF should also consider the additional funds that are being leveraged from private sector resources. Both the national agencies and the local governments could engage the private sector to build and operate facilities. Instruments like Build-Own-Transfer (BOT) scheme are being applied by the local authorities which could lead to inter-local arrangements among cities and municipalities that will develop metropolitan-wide infrastructure services as a form of coordinating development efforts.

The CIF process was evolved at a time when the capabilities of Metro Manila's 17 local governments to implement projects were limited. With the enactment of the Local Government Code the responsibilities of the local governments were increased along with their power to raise revenues. The local governments empowered with proprietary and corporate functions could, through their local chief executives, negotiate and contract loans and create forms of indebtedness, sign bonds, contracts and other obligations to carry on their mandated tasks. The enlarged powers of the local governments have therefore afforded them to plan and manage larger and varied expenditures.

The 1984 CIF exercise exerted "pressure points" on large investments being implemented by the national agencies and government corporations. The considered view was that development in Metro Manila is largely shaped by major infrastructures and private sector-led development. Now that the governments could mobilize bigger resources it is important to introduce some form of rationality into the planning and programme formulation of their investments. Most influence can be exerted over new projects, however.

With the recent approval of a law creating the Metropolitan Manila Development Authority (MMDA), a stronger metropolitan governing body will be installed. Its effectiveness however lies in the quality of decisions it makes. A number of these decisions requires that an objective basis exists and that an acceptable approach at arriving at them is installed. Such basis and the opportunity for integration and joint discussions among the various stakeholders in Metro Manila exist through the CIF.

To achieve greater influence it is necessary to consolidate new practices, concepts and ideas into the CIF process and allow them to be fully assimilated by the participants of the CIF process. The agencies should be regularly involved not only in the work of the process itself but in the seminars and workshops being organized by the CIF team to gain an understanding of and commitment to the process.

The CIF offers an alternative tool for investment decisions in a metropolitan set up when the tradiitional approaches to planning seem to have been found inflexible. Other cities with similar problems may find CIF's integrated approach useful. The CIF process could be developed further, and support to it should be sustained to maintain its effectiveness as a tool for urban planning and administration.

BIBLIOGRAPHY

Metropolitan Manila Commission (1984), *Towards an Investment Strategy for Metro Manila*, Manila.

Republic of the Philippines (1992), *Local Government Code of 1991 (Republic Act No.7160)*, February 6, Manila.

Republic of the Philippines (1995a), *The President's 1994 Socio-Economic Report*, National Economic and Development Authority, Manila.

Republic of the Philippines (1995b), *CY 1995 Infrastructure Program*, National Economic and Development Authority, Manila.

8

THE PROGRAMME FOR ESSENTIAL MUNICIPAL INFRASTRUCTURE UTILITIES, MAINTENANCE AND ENGINEERING DEVELOPMENT

Apolo C. Jucaban and Bituin B. Torte

Introduction

The Philippines has one of the highest urbanization rates in Asia with a high average growth rate of 5.14 per cent per annum. Rapid urban growth brings about problems of traffic, insufficient water supply, sanitation and deterioration of other basic infrastructure services. Lack of regular maintenance works has compounded the problem of insufficient basic services.

The national government is pursuing a decentralization programme to provide local autonomy and increased responsibilities to the local governments.

The decentralization programme of the government is embodied in the 1991 Local Government Code and under this programme the national government agencies would continue to be responsible for executing larger infrastructure projects while the local governments would be responsible for the construction and maintenance of minor, local roads and drains, operating municipal enterprises like, market, slaughterhouse and bus terminal, providing garbage collection and disposal and other municipal services.

Prior to the enactment of the Local Government Code of 1991, the Government, with the assistance from the World Bank, initiated the First Municipal Development Project (MDP I) also known as Programme for Essential Municipal Infrastructure Utilities, Maintenance and Engineering Development (PREMIUMED I) in 1984 and approved the Second Municipal Project (MDP II) or MMINUTE II-FRINGE in 1990.

The success demonstrated by the first and second Municipal Development Projects (MDP I&II) brought about the preparation of the Third Municipal Development Project (MDP III) or PREMIUMED II.

Brief Urban Development Profile in the Philippines

In early 1975, Urban Development Projects were initiated in the Philippines with assistance from the World Bank. The First Urban Development Project became effective in 1976 and was soon followed by other World Bank-assisted Development Programmes, i.e., Urban II in 1979, Urban III in 1980 and Urban IV in 1983.

The first four Urban Development Projects concentrated their investments in Metro Manila and substantial investments were made in housing, land development and distribution, sites and services. Basic urban infrastructure was given attention under Urban III and IV.

These Urban Projects have multi-project components and are implemented separately by different agencies. There is no single lead agency for overall programme supervision. There are as many implementing and lead agencies with corresponding project offices as there are project components or categories, i.e., housing authority for shelter, land development for slum upgradation and on-site infrastructure, public works agency for off-site infrastructure, human settlements for sites and services, and metro and local governments for municipal services.

The project areas are fixed and project components are specifically defined, described and pinpointed by agencies and by cities (Figure 8.1).

Management is highly centralized at the national level except in Urban IV wherein the cities are allowed to prepare plans and designs of market, slaughterhouse and bus terminal. The Local Government Units (LGUs) were also included in construction supervision. LGUs have not been involved in planning, project selection and design, although community and citizen participation have been maximized in Urban I.

The four Urban Projects encountered various problems such as delays in implementation, slow disbursement, very low performance in cost recovery, high loan repayment defaults and sometimes withdrawal of LGUs from the programme (Ramos and Jucaban, 1987).

Because of separate and independent project offices implementing the various components, problems of synchronization of activities and implementation schedules cannot be avoided, although there is an inter-agency steering committee for each of the Urban Development Projects.

Figure 8.1: PREMIUMED Institutional Set-up

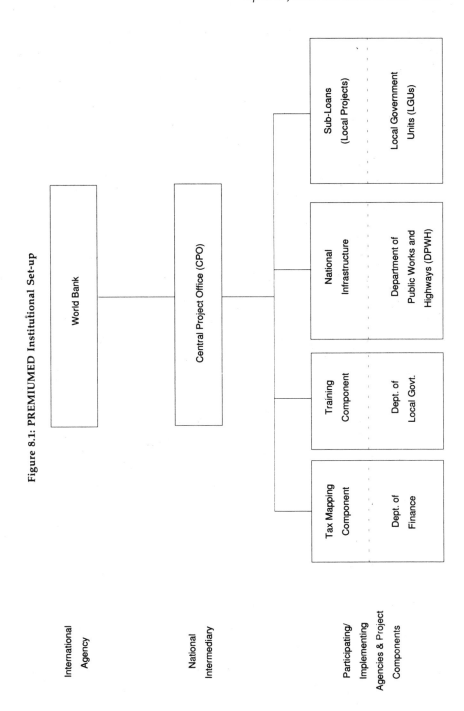

Cognizant of the problems experienced in the first four Urban Projects the government and the World Bank embarked on a project to assist LGUs finance and deliver basic municipal infrastructure and services which is: "(i) flexible in methodology and management, (ii) directed toward complete devolution of responsibilities to LGUs, (iii) responsive to the dynamic political and economic structure of LGUs, (iv) supportive of the strategy of strengthening technical and financial capabilities of LGUs leading to self-reliance, and (v) targeted to reach and cover greater number of urban centers as much as possible whenever feasible" (Jucaban, 1987a, 1987b). By 1983, a World Bank loan package was completed and in 1984 the loan agreement for PREMIUMED I or Municipal Development Project (MDP I), as officially known in the World Bank, was signed. MDP I was implemented between 1983 and 1993 and after its completion, MDP 3 or PREMIUMED II was approved in 1992 and will be implemented between 1993 and 1999 (Table 8.1).

Table 8.1: World Bank-assisted Urban Development Programme (in the Philippines)

Project	Estimated Project Cost				Project coverage
	Total	Government counterpart	World Bank Loan	Effectivity	
Urban I	$ 67.8 M	$ 35.8 M	$ 32.0 M	1976	Metro Manila: housing, slum upgrading, sites and services land acquisition, off-site and on-site infrastructure, community facilities (schools, health centres, etc.) and technical assistance.
Urban II	69.9	37.9 M	32.0 M	1979	Housing sites and services in Metro Manila and 3 regional cities; off-site and on-site infrastructure, community facilities (schools, health centers, etc.) and technical assistance.
Urban III	120.8 M	48.8 M	72.0 M	1980	Housing and land titling, basic services and house improvement loans to low-income unserviced settlements, upgrading of basic sanitation-oriented infrastructure to low income areas, sites and services, livelihood, solid waste management and technical assistance.

(Table 8.1 contd.)

(*Table 8.1 contd.*)

Project	Estimated Project Cost				Project coverage
	Total	Government counter-part	World Bank Loan	Effectivity	
Urban IV	111.2 M	44.7	67.0 M	1983	Shelter and land titling; basic infrastructure municipal enterprise (markets, slaughter-houses, etc.) projects in four regional cities outside Metro Manila.
MDP I/ED PREMIUM ED I	I78.8 M	38.8M	40.0 M	1985	Basic infrastructure and utilities, essential municipal-urban services and facilities, maintenance and equipment depot upgrading (including procurement and repair of equipment), tax mapping, training and technical assistance covering 15 to 20 cities and municipalities outside Metro area.
CVURP	—	—	—	1987 (?) Subject to further government decision	Similar to Urban I, II, III, IV but on a regional basis and integrated with the regional-rural development programme in Reg. VII (Central Visayas) with Metro-Cebu as the main focus and other cities within the region.
MDP II/ MMINUTE FRINGE	68.0 M	28.0 M	40.0 M	1992	Basic infrastructure and municipal urban services and facilities, maintenance and equipment depot upgrading, tax mapping for 40 cities and municipalities in Metro Manila and fringe areas.
MDP III/ PREMIUM ED II	113.7 M	45.7 M	68.0 M	1992	Basic infrastructure and utilities, essential municipal-urban services and facilities, maintenance and equipment depot upgrading (including procurement and repair of equipment), tax mapping, training and technical assistance to about 60 cities and municipalities outside Metro Manila.

Elements of PREMIUMED

PREMIUMED I and PREMIUMED II have basically the same objective, to assist the local government to provide infrastructure and improved municipal services.

For PREMIUMED I this objective was achieved by:

— Establishing a mechanism to provide local governments with direct access to long-term development finance on reasonable terms under the MDF.
— Establishing a permanent national-level technical intermediary (CPO) to:
  1. Assist local governments in identifying infrastructure management facilities;
  2. Evaluate project proposals for financing;
  3. Monitor and control the programme;
  4. Act as a principal liaison with the Bank and other external funding agencies in promoting urban service improvements throughout the urban hierarchy.
— Strengthening local technical and financial capacity for project implementation and service management through implementation of a broad-based Municipal Training Programme (MTP) and through organizational and fiscal reforms (RPTA).

PREMIUMED I has a total project cost of US$ 68.8 million with a loan allocation of US$ 40.0 million of which US$ 28.2 million was passed on as sub-loan to pre-qualified cities and municipalities to finance local projects. The amount of US$ 11.8 million was distributed to the various central agencies to finance the mapping, training, technical assistance and capitalize front-end fee. Counterpart funds was provided:

— By the national government through the Department of Public Works and Highways (DPWH) for the national project component, the Finance Department for mapping, and the local governments for training and technical assistance; and
— By the LGUs.

By 1993 when PREMIUMED I was completed, it had achieved the objective of assisting 42 local government units to expand and upgrade their urban infrastructure.

For PREMIUMED II, its aim of assisting cities and municipalities to expand and upgrade their infrastructure services and facilities is made by :

— Strengthening the national governments institutional framework for assisting local governments;
— Strengthening the local government's investment planning, financing and implementation capacity;
— Strengthening the local government's maintenance capacity; and
— Improving local fiscal performance.

PREMIUMED II also supports further evolution of the system established under PREMIUMED I to promote local government development and improve local government access to credit financing.

Urban and municipal infrastructure projects (national and local) included in both PREMIUMED I and II are :

— Municipal Enterprises—markets, slaughterhouse, bus terminals;
— Sanitation—provision or improvement of flood control and drainage system, community water facilities, shore protection and solid and liquid waste collection and disposal facilities;
— Transport—improvement or provision of roads, streets, and traffic system;
— Area Improvement—provision/improvement of community services and facilities in depressed, low-income neighbourhoods *(barangays)* such as footpaths, micro-drainage, public toilets, with baths and laundry areas;
— Maintenance—rehabilitation and maintenance of infrastructure, utilities, repair or upkeep of equipment and improvement or construction of equipment depots and provision of maintenance equipment and repair shop tools; and
— Other facilities—health centres and school buildings.

Other non-infrastructure but major components are:

— Tax Mapping—updating cadasters, appraising properties, improvising records management and increasing annual revenue collection to strengthen municipal finance; and
— Training—to strengthen and equip local officials and technical staff with skills and techniques in their respective jobs related to the planning, implementation and management of PREMIUMED and other World Bank-assisted urban projects.

Under PREMIUMED II, technical assistance is also provided for the conduct of the following studies:

— Municipal Lending Institutional Review; and
— Urban Environmental and Solid Waste Management Study.

The PREMIUMED II is estimated to have a total project cost of about US$ 113.7 million. The World Bank loan is US$ 68.0 M of which US$ 34.4 M would be lent on through the Municipal Development Fund (MDF). Counterpart funding would be provided as follows:

— LGUs for the local projects, maintenance programme and RPTA;
— DPWH for the national projects; and
— The MDF for the 30 per cent of the sub-loan which will be taken from accumulated payment of interest and principal.

About 60 cities and municipalities all over the Philippines are expected to benefit from PREMIUMED II.

Based on the financing plan and project coverage for both PREMIUMED projects, it can be seen that substantial assistance is directed toward the LGUs, with the national agencies providing direct support—the Department of Public Works and Highways (DPWH) for national infrastructure components, Department of Finance for tax mapping, and Department of Local Government for training.

Project Organization and Implementation Arrangement

The two central elements of the PREMIUMED are the Central Project Office (CPO) and the Municipal Development Fund (MDF)

The CPO has been established primarily to serve as the national technical intermediary between the Bank (the lender), and the LGUs (as borrowers) as compared to the set-up of the first urban projects (Figure 8.2). Aside from day to office operations and management (administrative, financial, accounting, planning, etc.) the CPO has to:

1. Pre-qualify and evaluate financial and borrowing capabilities of the cities and municipalities;
2. Evaluate and appraise their project proposals;
3. Assist LGUs in planning, project identification and packaging, project implementation and supervision and managing urban and municipal finances;
4. Oversee and monitor the entire programme and evaluate performance of LGUs and other participating agencies; and
5. Act as the principal liaison with the World Bank and possibly other external funding institutions engaged in urban development project.

The CPO is under the administrative supervision of the Department of Public Works and Highways, but takes policy guidance and direction from an inter-agency Project Steering Committee (PSC) composed of

Figure 8.2: Traditional Institutional Set-up for a Typical Loan Programme

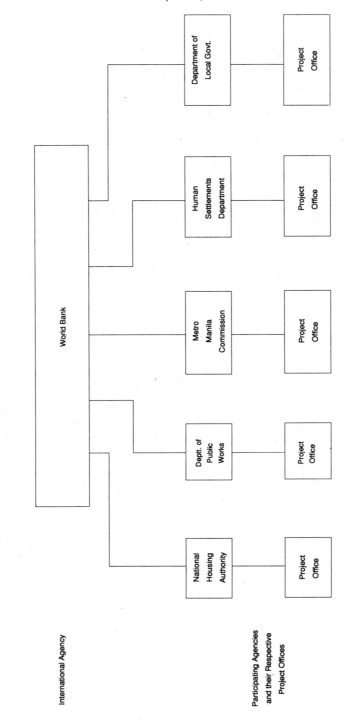

representatives from five national agencies — Department of Public Works and Highways, Finance, Budget and Management, Local Governments and Economic planning or National Economic and Development Authority (NEDA). The members of the Project Steering Committee are no lower than Under-Secretaries and/or Bureau Directors.

The PSC is supported by the Technical Sub-Committee (TSC) consisting of Assistant Secretaries or Bureau Directors. The TSC carries out routine coordination between various agencies, and reviews sub-project appraisal investment packages and lending agreements prior to their submission to the PSC for appraisal.

It is interesting to note that while the committee is created by law, member agencies are bound and committed to each other, not by legislative act but by a memorandum of agreement. On the other hand, the CPO is established through a Department Order of the DPWH as a special project office with accounting, financial and administrative units of its own, separate from the central unit of DPWH. This proves to be a pragmatic arrangement in the sense that the Project Steering Committee can be expanded (as the need arises) by re-drafting the memorandum of agreement and the CPO can be modified and/or expanded by a simple internal office order without going through the long process of amendatory legislation.

At the local level (LGU), a local project office is established as the counterpart direct link for the CPO. The PREMIUMED Local Project Office (PLPO) is composed of technical staff drawn from both Municipal Development Staff and the District Engineer's Office of the Department of Public Works and Highways (DPWH). It is organized to carry out project preparation, implementation, supervision and monitoring.

The main implementating arm for the project components will be the joint City/Municipal Development Staff and the DPWH City/District Engineer's Office, whose directly involved staff and personnel are constituted into joint taskforces. The PLPO, being the overall Municipal PREMIUMED Supervisor/Coordinator, is assisted by a Chief Implementing Officer (CIO) for civil works for day-to-day and regular civil works supervision. Under this, key supervisory staff are Project Engineers who will be the field supervisors for the respective projects, assisted by a pool of Project Inspectors.

The CPO has no approving authority on the plans, designs, work programmes and contracts on all local project components. Such authority will have to be exercised by the authorized official at the city/municipal level. Detailed planning and engineering, bidding and awards of contract, procurement of goods and services (except for international bidding and certain equipment) and construction supervision are delegated to LGUs (cities/municipalities), subject only to review, monitoring and evaluation by the CPO and the World Bank. National project components, however, are the responsibility of the Department of Public Works and Highways (DPWH) and its regional and field engineering offices. However, to ensure that there is a maximum inter-agency coordination of responsibilities and activities, a sub-project agreement is signed between the DPWH-CPO and the LGU (city/municipality) defining the flow of administrative and management responsibilities and levels of decision-making and authority.

However, the CPO evaluates and assesses the performance of the LGU in the execution of PREMIUMED projects. Further, the CPO reviews and evaluates plans, designs, works programmes, bidding and award of contracts as well as project accomplishments. At any stage of the project, the CPO and/or the World Bank may send inspection and evaluation teams to verify and confirm the progress of accomplishments (financial and physical) as reported by the PLPO. The CPO, in the performance of its duties is guided by the policies and directions issued by the Project Steering Committee and the World Bank.

The other key element of PREMIUMED is the pooling of funds from all sources under the Municipal Development Fund (MDF), a revolving fund which has been created for financial assistance to LGUs. Under the PREMIUMED-MDF scheme, all funds from various sources are channelled to or pooled under the MDF and released to participating agencies and the LGUs in accordance with the investment/financial programmes approved by the Steering Committee. World Bank loan proceeds and government agency budgetary allocations are channelled through the MDF.

It has been deemed wise and appropriate to locate the MDF in and under the administrative control of the Department of Finance, and its Treasury Office rather than build it in with the CPO. However, programming, allocation and utilization of the fund are subject to the technical recommendations of the CPO.

In addition, no releases from MDF are made without clearance from and recommendation by the CPO. Upon request of the implementing agencies and LGUs, with clearance from and through the recommendation of the CPO, funds are released directly to the agencies and the local treasurers. Figure 8.3 shows the flow of funds. However, no cash transfer is involved, instead funds are remitted through bank-to-bank transfer, i.e., from the MDF depository bank to the corresponding local depository banks of the cities/municipalities. In the same manner, no World Bank loan proceeds are released and/or replenished to the MDF unless recommended by the CPO. This leads to better coordination of activities and effective implementation of project components.

Figure 8.3: MDF-PREMIUMED Fund Flow Concept

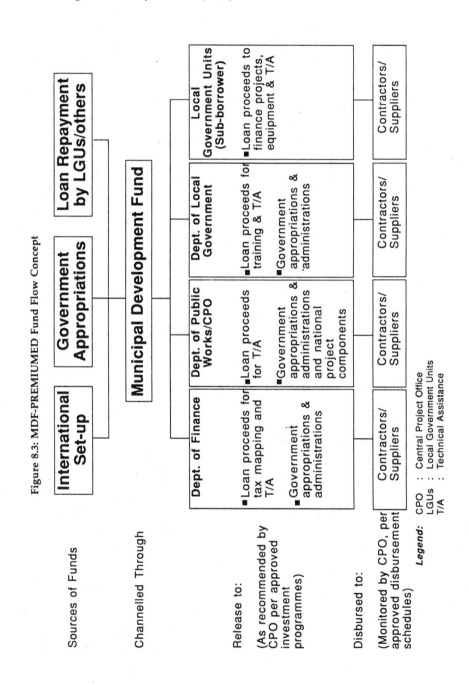

One of the pre-conditions for the release of funds from the MDF is for the city to put up trust accounts for MDF releases, local equity requirement and loan amortization. This ensures that projects are sufficiently funded at the time of implementation, thus avoiding delays, besides assuring loan payment.

Since the MDF is conceived to grow and become self-sustaining in the long-run, amortization made by the LGUs will be retained by the MDF for re-lending to other cities/municipalities. On the other hand, World Bank amortization, including interest charges and commitment fees will be assumed by the national government. While the original concept was that the MDF should service PREMIUMED and the World Bank, the Government in drafting the law creating the MDF deemed it wise to make it applicable to all foreign assistance directed toward urban projects and municipal development in anticipation of the inflow of funds from other non-World Bank sources (i.e., ADB, bilateral assistance, etc).

Concluding Observations

The advantage of the PREMIUMED as compared to the Urban Projects is that it has a greater degree of flexibility. Funds are not tied up to a predetermined city or municipality. Thus, any LGU and/or projects may be discontinued or reduced in scale, and can be replaced by a new LGU and/or projects respectively.

The LGUs are given the full responsibility for the use and disbursements of the funds borrowed from the MDF. The CPO just exercises technical monitoring and provides necessary assistance as requested by the LGUs.

Presently, the LGUs are proving through the PREMIUMED their competence and capabilities in managing urban and municipal finances, including debt servicing. About 90 per cent of the PREMIUMED centres pay the loan authorizations regularly.

The PREMIUMED-MDF concept has generated a positive response from the LGUs and has been demonstrating that the LGUs can be self-reliant and that the regulation of central government's grant to LGUs is workable and feasible.

It has been demonstrated that the decentralization and devolution of more responsibilities to LGUs is highly feasible and can be effected immediately with the intercession and assistance of a technical intermediary. Instead, centralized administration of local projects has led to the lack of interest of LGUs and unnecessary delays.

The MDF or the "fund pool" concept is a very effective mechanism for inter-project synchronization aside from being an efficient mode of fund utilization and disbursement.

The PREMIUMED has also been successful in enhancing technical, administrative and financial capabilities of cities and municipalities in packaging and implementing urban infrastructure projects through the appropriate training programmes provided to the LGUs by the Municipal Training Programme (MTP).

Lessons Learned

The factors which brought about the success of the PREMIUMED are: (a) the Central Project Office (CPO) as a technical intermediary and principal liaison with the World Bank; and (b) the Municipal Development Fund (MDF), as LGUs direct access to soft-term financial loan assistance.

The success of the programme is also attributed to: (a) the strong commitment of the Project Steering and Policy Governing Board Committee members to the project in general and to the CPO in particular; (b) the earnest effort of the national government to decentralize and devolve responsibilities to the LGUs from planning to project identification up to implementation and post- implementation stages; and (c) the full commitment of the local officials to undertake their responsibilities particularly as regards municipal finances, fiscal reforms and urban services administration (Government of the Philippines, 1985; World Bank, 1984, 1992).

The bottom-up self-selection process of the PREMIUMED introduced an element of competition among LGUs for funds which allow the CPO to evaluate cities and municipalities which are capable to undertake projects, provide counterpart funds and to make necessary policy changes and requirements. The PREMIUMED has demonstrated the importance of beneficiary participation in the design of investments. The participating LGUs are required to pass resolutions through their legislative body approving increase of market rental charges after public hearing and consultation with the market vendors before construction of the market is started.

Thus, PREMIUMED has achieved the integration of urban and municipal services through setting up the CPO which has a direct link to the funding institution (the World Bank and MDF) and the LGU as beneficiaries and implementing units.

BIBLIOGRAPHY

Jucaban, A.C. (1987a), 'The Integrated Urban Development The Philippines Experience', Paper presented to 7th International NHA-IHS-ATI Seminar on Integrated Urban Development Programme: A Support Strategy for Housing Development, Asian Institute of Technology (ATI), Bangkok, 11–15 May (unpublished).

Jucaban, A.C. (1987b), 'Case Study on PREMIUMED Project', Paper presented to the EDI Course on Urban Finance, Kuala Lumpur, September (unpublished).

Ramos, J. M. and Jucaban, A.C. *et al.* (1987), 'Urban Development in the Philippines', Country Paper presented to the ADB-UNCRD Regional Seminar on National Urban Policy Issues, Manila, 2–8 February (unpublished).

Government of the Philippines (1985), 'Urban Development Assistance in The Philippines', Country Paper presented at 10th Conference on World Bank Urban Assistance on Accomplishments, Issues and Lessons for the Future, Washington, D.C., 2–6 December (unpublished).

World Bank (1984), *Municipal Development Project, Staff Appraisal Report*, World Bank, Washington, D.C., 10 May.

World Bank (1992), *Municipal Development Project, Staff Appraisal Report*, World Bank, Washington, D.C., 27 February.

9

THE REGIONAL CITIES DEVELOPMENT PROGRAMME IN THAILAND: DEVELOPING URBAN INFRASTRUCTURE

Banasopit Mekvichai and C. Ridhiprasart

Formulation of the Regional Cities Development Project

The purpose of this paper is to discuss the formulation and implementation of the Regional Cities Development Programme (RCDP) in Thailand. Lessons from the RCDP could well be useful for those attempting similar programmes elsewhere.

The concept of regional "growth poles" as a means to diffuse economic growth to less developed areas of a country was an innovation in development theory in the late 1960s. It was soon adapted for use in the national socio-economic development plans for Thailand in the 1970s and 1980s. In addition to spurring economic development in the regions, these "growth poles" were expected to divert migration from Bangkok, the capital city, the main urban area, and centre of most non-agricultural economic activity in the country. The National Economic and Social Development Board (NESDB) has continued to stress the "growth poles" as growth hubs as well as service centres and employment sources for the outlying areas of the country.

Nearly all the cities chosen as "growth poles" were already the main market or urban areas in the regions. They were also selected to be sufficiently distributed throughout the country so that economic growth and social services could be as widely dispersed as possible. Initially, only one centre was chosen for each region (Chiang Mai in the north, Songkhla-Hat Yai in the south and Khon Kaen in the northeast), with regional development activities concentrated in these or nearby sites. The first regional universities had been set up in these cities, and most regional offices were located in or near them.[1] It soon became apparent that many other cities throughout the country needed to be included as growth centres if the effects of regional development and the diffusion of social and economic benefits were to be as widespread as possible.

As a result of this urban development policy, the major cities in different regions of the country were designated as "regional urban growth centres". These were ranked in three tiers, according to commercial, transport, and political importance. The most important were ranked as **regional urban growth centres.** Others considered nearly as important was designated **second-generation regional urban growth centres.** A third group of cities has since been added and designated as **other regional growth centres.** Figure 9.1 shows the location and rank of these various "growth poles".

A crucial element in the development of these regional urban growth centres needs to be the provision of adequate infrastructure to support the economic growth and population increases. In pursuit of this policy, the Regional Cities Development Project was formulated. The Ministry of Interior was the responsible agency for this project. It was divided into two phases, with the first phase of the project approved by the Cabinet in 1985 and expanded in 1988 to provide the infrastructure for four cities: Chiang Mai, Khon Kaen, Nakhon Ratchasima, and Songkhla. Nearly all of the activities under this phase have been completed. The second phase of the project is currently being implemented, to help develop the infrastructure in another eight cities (Office of the National Economic and Social Development Board, 1993).

The Context of the Regional Cities Development Project

The Regional Cities Development Project has the following objectives, guidelines and development measures:[2]

Objectives

1. To reduce economic and social disparities between the Bangkok Metropolitan Area (BMA) and other cities.[3]

---

[1] The Bank of Thailand, for example, set up its southern branch in Hat Yai and its northeastern branch in Khon Kaen, but its northern branch in Lampang (primarily because Lampang was then the transportation centre of the region, with roads to most nearby provinces leading from it rather than from Chiang Mai).

[2] These objectives, goals and development measures were derived from various documents for the planning and and the monitoring of the RCDP.

[3] The Bangkok Metropolitan Area (BMA) consists of Bangkok and Thonburi. The Bangkok Metropolitan Region consists of the BMA and the surrounding provinces where urban growth from Bangkok has quickly spread.

Figure 9.1: Location of Regional Urban Growth Centres, by Rank

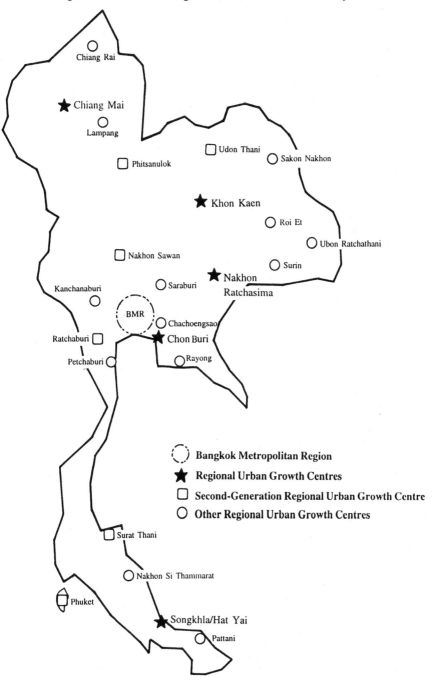

2. To create economic and social centres in the regions to remedy problems of poverty and migration to Bangkok.
3. To develop the urban growth centres to be efficient medium-size cities.

Policy Guidelines

1. The industrial base in the regional cities is to be strengthened in order to generate more employment.
2. Social services of the regional cities will be expanded to meet growing demand.
3. Unique social and cultural characteristics of the regions will be promoted so the residents in each area will be proud of their heritage.
4. Basic public utilities in regional cities will receive high priority in urban development.
5. More efficient land-use control will be provided, and the boundaries of the municipalities will be redrawn to incorporate expanding economic activities.
6. Local finance and administration will be improved in regional cities.

Development Measures

1. Export-oriented processing industries, commercial activities and other small-scale service industries will be assisted actively.
2. Industrial estates will be set up in regional cities expeditiously.
3. Medium- and long-term credit schemes will be devised for industries in regional cities. This will be supported by establishing "regional banks" in the main regional urban centres.
4. Technical advisory services, including marketing and management, will be provided to the regional businesses.
5. The granting of privileges for investment in the Bangkok Metropolitan Region will cease.
6. Tourism will be promoted in regional cities. Tourist-related businesses and services will be promoted, and tourist-related facilities will be improved.
7. Slums and depressed areas will be improved in regional cities.
8. Vocational and non-formal education will be stressed to meet demands of the labour market.
9. The local cultural heritage of each region must be preserved carefully.

10. Regional cities will serve as government administrative centres.

11. Local government units will be encouraged to maintain their independent roles.

12. National and international conferences will be held more frequently in the regional cities.

13. The transportation systems in the regional cities will be improved. This is to include the development of a deep-sea port at Songkhla.

14. Water supply services in the regional cities will be improved, and the service charges will be set at a realistic rate.

15. Telecommunications systems will be expanded throughout the regions.

16. Water drainage systems, including waste disposal systems, will be developed for the regional cities.

17. The private sector will be encouraged to share in infrastructure investment.

18. Efforts will be made to require the enforcement of comprehensive town plans, so that land-use control will be regulated in the regional cities.

19. Municipal boundaries of the regional cities will be redrawn.

20. The tax collection system of rent and land development taxes will be modified to become a property tax.

21. Systematic mapping and tax accounting will be used for property valuation.

22. The government will allocate special funds and loans for the regional municipalities, to enable them to expand basic infrastructure facilities.

23. Technical and planning capabilities of the municipalities will be strengthened.

Scope of the Project

The Regional Cities Development Project consists of numerous infrastructure and urban development projects. These were divided into two phases: the first phase from 1985 to 1991, and the second phase starting in 1992 and expected to continue until 1999. There were 52 projects in the first phase. Another 44 projects were added in the second phase. The various types of projects consist of:

- Improvement of road network, road drainage and bridges;
- solid waste disposal systems;
- flood control and drainage systems;
- waste water management systems;

- water supply systems;
- slum improvement projects; and
- various other development projects including fishing ports and riverside development.

The location of the different types of projects in the cities is shown in Table 9.1.

Administrative Organization of the Project

As already mentioned, the Ministry of Interior is the main organization responsible for the infrastructure development of these cities. The project has been carried out under the general guidance of the Regional Cities Development Programme Steering Committee, established by Cabinet resolution in 1979. The Steering Committee, chaired by the Permanent Secretary of the Ministry of Interior, oversees the project, directs project policy, and helps coordinate activities with the various agencies involved in implementation. The Project Director is the Director-General of the Department of Local Administration. Three key sub-committees of the Steering Committee help coordinate work of the key project components.

The Deputy Project Director is a Deputy Director-General of the Public Works Department. A Project Management Unit was set up under the Local Government Development Affairs (LGDA) Division of the Department of Local Administration, with the Director of LGDA as Project Manager. The basic organization of the project is presented in Figure 9.2.

Coordination of the project is conducted through the sub-committees, which consist of representatives of all the agencies involved in the particular area of responsibility, including representatives from the municipalities where the various infrastructure development projects are being implemented. The administrative organization remains fundamentally the same in Phase II of the project, though more agencies have been included as necessary for the various projects.

Other *ad hoc* committees are also assigned as necessary to deal with special tasks. These have included committees to evaluate and accept bids for contracts, committees to review contracts for the purchase and supply of equipment, and committees to supervise and inspect construction. Though these responsibilities officially lie with the particular agencies involved in the project, the agencies find it more appropriate to coordinate with other agencies by delegating those responsibilities to

Table 9.1: Types of Urban Development Projects by Regional Growth City

Type of Project	1	2	3	4	5	6	7	8	9	10	11	12
Road/bridge improvement	•	•	•	•	•	•	•	•	•	•	•	•
Solid waste disposal		•	•			•	•	•	•	•	•	•
Flood control/drainage	•	•	•	•	•	•	•		•	•		•
Waste water management	•	•	•		•	•	•					•
Water supply												
Slum improvement	•	•				•	•	•			•	
Other projects				•								

1 = Chiang Mai
2 = Nakhon Ratchasima
3 = Khon Kaen
4 = Songkhla
5 = Udon Thani
6 = Phitsanulok
7 = Nakhon Sawan
8 = Ratchaburi
9 = Chonburi
10 = Surat Thani
11 = Phuket
12 = Hat Yai

Figure 9.2: Administrative Organization of the Regional Cities Development Programme Project

Direct Organizational Authority

Indirect Links/Coordination

the *ad hoc* committees that consist of representatives from all the agencies and offices involved in the particular activity.

Procedure for Project Design and Implementation

There were three main stages of project design and implementation. The first was project preparation, the second project approval, and the last has been the actual implementation. The process has had to be carried out for both phases of the project.

Preparation and approval: It is not the purpose of this paper to discuss in detail the procedure of project preparation and approval, since the format and content of feasibility studies, other preparatory reports and planning and the process for approval depend upon the requirements of the government, the agencies to carry out the project, and donors (if any). In this case, the identification of the required infrastructure, the investment plans, and other preparatory reports for phase 1 of the project were funded by the International Bank for Regional Development (IBRD), or the World Bank. The IBRD also funded 60 per cent of total project implementation costs. Preparation of a large project such as RCDP required involvement of the Ministry of Finance and the Budget Bureau of the Prime Minister's Office in addition to the implementing agency, the Ministry of Interior, in project preparation.

The main consideration for these first two stages of the procedure is the length of time required for project preparation and approval. The feasibility study for the first phase of RCDP began in 1981, with the final report of the study published in 1982 for the United National Development Programme (Sinclair Knight and Partners, 1982). It took another three years of negotiations among the various government agencies—in particular offices in the Ministry of Interior and the Ministry of Finance—and the IBRD, and approval at the Ministerial and Cabinet levels, before the project was ready for implementation. Project preparation also involved fitting the staff, material and financial needs of the project in the annual work plans and budgets of the key government agencies. The project began in 1985, four years after the feasibility study was conducted.

Similarly, the feasibility studies for phase II of the project began in 1988, with approval by the Cabinet in early 1992. The implementation of phase II started in late 1992.

Implementation: The procedure for the implementation of the RCDP is rather complicated, but necessarily so because of the nature of the Thai bureaucracy and the administrative and legal status of municipalities.

Municipalities and their boundaries are created by Royal Decree, in accordance with the Municipality Act of 1953. As urban areas expand, the municipality boundaries are changed by amending the Royal Decree. Municipalities are governed by a legislative body, a Municipal Assembly (the size of which depends on the size and type of municipality) and an administrative body, the Municipal Executive Council. The Executive Council consists of a Mayor and Councillor, selected by the Provincial Governor from among the members of the Municipal Assembly. The Provincial Governor, the highest administrative official in the province, is an appointed civil servant from the Department of Local Administration of the Ministry of Interior. The Governor has the power of veto over key affairs of the municipality, in particular the annual budget.

Although somewhat autonomous, municipality administration remains under the jurisdiction of the Ministry of Interior. Most full-time staff of municipalities are civil servants appointed from the Ministry of Interior. These include the Municipal Clerk and others who administer the day-to-day affairs of the cities. Although municipalities have the power to raise some of their own revenues, most of the annual budget comes through the Ministry of Interior from central government funds.

The main responsibilities of Thai municipalities are similar to those in other countries. These include maintenance of roads and waterways, solid and liquid waste disposal, fire fighting, provision of clean water, and other public health, education and infrastructure services. These services can be provided only within the administrative boundaries of the municipality, even if the area of urban growth has spread beyond the official boundaries.

Though the work of the project was for the benefit of regional cities, the bulk of project planning and management has been the responsibility of central government offices of the Ministry of Interior. Project policy and the selection and appointment of outside consultants for engineering and construction management are the responsibility of the Steering Committee (refer again to Figure 9.2). Preparation of infrastructure designs, the management of all aspects of the project (physical and financial), and monitoring and evaluation (including preparation of reports) were the responsibility of the Technical Sub-Committee, the Project Management Unit, the secretariat to the Steering Committee in the Local Government Development Affairs Division in Department of Local Administration of the Ministry of Interior, and the secretariat to the Technical Sub-Committee in the Technical Office for City Development in the Public Works Department, also of the Ministry of Interior. Coordination with project donors, both international and domestic, was through the Local Government Affairs Division. Monitoring of construction consultants and overall construction supervision were the responsibility of the Technical Office for City Development.

Although the work was conducted in and for the benefit of the Municipalities, the Municipal administrations had direct responsibility only for land acquisition and property compensation, and for the inspection and monitoring of the progress of the project(s) within their boundaries. The municipalities participated in, but were not directly responsible for, the project designs. The rationale is that the municipal staff do not yet have sufficient skills to undertake the designs themselves: their participation in the physical design by the central government agencies was seen as a training exercise. The municipalities were also expected to monitor expenditures and to submit accounting and financial reports, using the reporting system set up by the central project offices. Actual construction has been done by private contractors.

Project Finances

The RCDP project was considered economically viable, because improved infrastructure of the regional cities is expected to provide incentive for more businesses to invest in those cities. However, despite the economic advantages of improved infrastructure, neither the municipalities nor the central government had sufficient funds to cover all the construction costs. For phase I of the RCDP, the IBRD provided funds for the investment plans, including the identification of the required infrastructure. The IBRD also provided a loan, covering 60 per cent of the cost of project implementation. The loan was made to the central government (through the Ministry of Finance), which bears full responsibility to repay the IBRD.

The Ministry of Finance arranged the mechanism to pass on the loans on a grant basis to the four cities included in the first phase of RCDP (Chiang Mai, Khon Kaen, Nakhon Ratchasima and Songkhla). The Ministry of Interior was required to ensure that the cities repay their debts on time.

The remaining 40 per cent of the project implementation funds were divided between the municipalities and the central government, with the municipalities expected to provide 28 per cent of the total project implementation costs and the central government responsible for the remaining 12 per cent. The central government funds were dispersed to the four municipalities through grants.

The funds for which the municipalities were responsible are further divided into two sources: funds from the municipal development budgets, and funds borrowed from sources arranged by the Ministry of Interior and the Ministry of Finance. The funds from the municipal development budgets accounted for 39 per cent of the municipalities' contribution (or about 11 per cent of the total implementation costs). The funds borrowed from a Municipal Development Fund, a Sanitary Development Fund, and the Krung Thai Bank (owned by the government) accounted for 61 per cent of the municipalities' contribution (or about 17 per cent of the total implementation costs). The funding sources varied somewhat from city to city, as is evident in Table 9.2.

The main difference in funding between phase II and phase I is that the level of government funding is not as rigid as it was in phase I. Government funding depends upon the expected benefits of the project to the population, as determined by criteria set by the Steering Committee. Thus, direct government funds may be higher if the expected results of the project are deemed sufficiently beneficial to the municipal residents.

Table 9.2: Project Investment Funds, RCDP Phase I

Cities	Total Investment	IBRD loan		Central govt. grant		Municipality' srevenue		Loans to municipality	
	mil. ฿	mil. ฿	%	mil. ฿	%	mil. ฿	%	mil. ฿	%
Chiang Mai	320.4	157.6	49	58.2	18	28.7	9	75.9	24
Khon Kaen	185.6	117.2	63	15.8	9	9.4	5	43.2	23
Nakhon Ratchasima	260.9	195.7	75	6.1	2	12.4	5	46.7	18
Songkhla	475.7	272.7	57	71.4	15	85.8	18	46.3	10
Total	1,242.6	742.7	60	151.5	12	136.3	11	212.1	17

Status of the Project

Phase I of the RCDP was completed by March 1994. This phase of the project consisted of three main components. By far the largest was the infrastructure development component, which consisted of 46 sub-projects, including equipment procurement, in the four targeted regional cities. The second component was a revenue generating sub-project, which was the development of the Songkhla fishport and industrial estate. The third component was to strengthen the institutional capacity of the Local Government Development Affairs Division of the Department of Local Administration, and of the municipal staff of the four targeted regional cities. This last component included efforts to initiate a municipal development planning system.

Phase II of the RCDP started in 1992, with the selection and design of infrastructure projects. This second phase of the project is being implemented in eight cities: Udon Thani, Phitsanulok, Nakhon Sawan, Ratchaburi, Chonburi, Surat Thani, Phuket and Hat Yai. Despite the preparation of manuals and other materials for a municipal development planning system, to be undertaken by the municipal authorities, the Local Government Affairs Division continues to serve as the main implementing agency, including provision of sub-project preparation and design. An additional 61 sub-projects are included. in this new phase of the project, which is expected to continue until 1999.

Evaluation of the Project by the National Economic and Social Development Board

Following a Cabinet Resolution, an evaluation of the RCDP was conducted between September 1992 and February 1993 by the National Economic and Social Development Board (NESDB), with the cooperation of the main implementing agencies, Department of Local Administration and the Department of Public Works of the Ministry of Interior.

The NESDB evaluation had the following results:

Project Impacts on Urban Infrastructure and Basic Services

Roads, bridges and drainage: Almost 90 per cent of the construction in this category was to improve the existing main trunk roads. The purpose of these sub-projects was to relieve traffic congestion in central business areas. The improvement of drainage systems together with the improvement of main roads also appears to have been successful, since there have been no serious floods in Chiang Mai,

Khon Kaen and Songkhla because of inadequate drainage following construction.[4]

Wastewater treatment: Wastewater treatment systems were installed in Khon Kaen and Nakhon Ratchasima. Both are stabilization ponds of 450 rai (72 ha.). After construction, from 50 to 70 per cent of wastewater in these two cities can be treated. This has helped improve the main water resources of both cities considerably.

Solid waste management: Sanitary landfills were built in Songkhla, Khon Kaen and Nakhon Ratchasima to help with the solid waste management systems of those cities. Collection and disposal coverage in each of these cities is now up to about 60 to 75 per cent. Although still not as efficient as desired, these new solid waste systems have helped reduce pollution considerably in all three cities. With less solid waste left in the streets, public health has also improved.

Slum settlements development: A key activity was the improvement of infrastructure in slum developments, including the provision of walkways, drainage, water supply and power supply. These activities were implemented in Chiang Mai, Songkhla and Nakhon Ratchasima. A new settlement of 350 households was built in Songkhla, about 3 kilometres from the original site of the Kao Seng slum. In addition to provision of roads and the other previously mentioned infrastructure, the Kao Seng community included provision of a waste collection service. A major obstacle has been faced with this sub-project, however. The families being relocated are expected to pay for their new housing, but it costs considerably more than their previous housing. Many who were expected to move have not yet done so, insisting that they first be provided with sufficiently low-cost housing.

Songkhla Fishing Port: Songkhla is one of the country's main fishing ports. The main wharf was operated by the Fish Marketing Organization (FMO). It faced several serious problems. First, access to this wharf was through the central business district. This caused traffic problems as well as serious pollution. Garbage accumulated in the area, much of it was fish-based and quite smelly. Several types of less-economical fish were also not iced and were kept several days before being removed. Crowding and problems of access led many fishermen to use other, privately-operated wharfs.

---

[4] Serious flooding occurred this year in Chiang Mai, but that was due to the extremely high level of the river flowing through the city and not because of inadequate drainage.

A feasibility study recommended relocation of the FMO-operated wharf to a site 2 kilometres upstream from the old port. Construction included a reclamation area extending from the shore toward the existing channel. This allowed the wharf to accommodate medium-sized vessels in addition to the smaller boats that were the only vessels that had been able to reach the old wharf.

The FMO operates this new wharf under a franchise from the municipality. The Songkhla Municipality earns 9.5 million Baht per year from the franchise, including 8.3 million Baht earned from leasing a commercial building behind the port. The municipality is thus able to repay easily the loans it took out to build the wharf. It also has improved its capacity to develop the municipal area, with a regular and substantial source of revenue.

Impacts of municipal capacity on urban development: Because the municipalities were responsible for providing funds for all land acquisition under the project, they did not have sufficient financial resources to meet even the projected 28 per cent of implementation costs. Thus, the proportion of the contribution from municipalities for construction of their infrastructure was reduced to 186.1 million Baht, or 23.8 per cent of the total 785.86 million Baht eventually expended for construction. This the NESDB evaluation found to be quite low, considering the cities should be able to provide most of the funds for any future infrastructure development and improvement.

Critique and Recommendations

In its evaluation of the project, the NESDB had several key criticisms. One was that the main objective of the Regional Cities Development Programme was to strengthen capacity of the regional cities to allow them to become true regional growth centres. However, the scope of the project primarily emphasized improvement of infrastructure. Other facets of regional development, such as industrial development or tourism development, were not covered by the project.

Another criticism was that the financial capacity of the municipalities was inadequate: the cities were not able to provide their expected share of the costs of construction implementation, even though it came to only 28 per cent of total costs. In the end, the cities could provide only a bit less than a quarter of the total implementation costs. These expenses, it should be pointed out, did not include the costs of project preparation, planning or design.

The NESDB also found that nearly all the sub-projects could not earn revenue. Although improvement of the facilities were expected to increase business investment and spur economic growth, there was no firm evidence that this was occurring in most cases. At the same time, the new facilities had to be maintained, and the costs of maintenance were expected to come from the cities, which were not able to gain any additional revenues from the new infrastructure.

For administrative reasons, the provision of infrastructure was limited only to areas within municipal boundaries. Thus, new urban settlements on the outskirts of the cities, the areas where the most rapid growth is occurring and where most of the larger factories are located, could not be served by the improved or new infrastructure under the project.

Given this critique, several key recommendations are made to help plan and implement similar projects.

First, the financial capacity of regional cities should be strengthened so they can provide an adequate share of the costs of infrastructure development and operation and maintenance of facilities.

Second, the system of municipal management needs to be strengthened to cope with the rapid urbanization and industrialization of the regional municipal areas.

Third, industrial development should be implemented together with infrastructure development, so the two can complement each other. Provision of infrastructure should not be limited to the area of municipal boundaries, but should be extended to include areas where the cities are expanding. This can be done by expanding the area under the administration of municipalities to include sites where industrial or other urban development are planned or anticipated.

Fourth, planning for new or improved infrastructure and for other urban development should be done in accordance with the city plans prepared by the Department of Town and Country Planning. This will ensure that the infrastructure plans fit with other aspects of urban development, as approved by the municipal, provincial, and national authorities.

Fifth, even if the RCDP continues to emphasize infrastructure development, it is necessary to show clearly how this work can benefit broader urban development. The role of infrastructure is crucial to economic development, but roads, water supply, etc., do not necessarily provide direct sources of revenue. Thus, a proper perspective is needed by project planners, monitors and evaluators to understand how the development of infrastructure is linked to other elements of urban and regional development.

Finally, since the infrastructure and facilities usually do not provide direct sources of revenue for the municipalities, mechanisms are needed to allow the municipalities to raise sufficient revenue to operate and maintain the infrastructure and facilities.

BIBLIOGRAPHY

Office of National Economic and Social Development Board (1993), *Report of Monitoring and Evaluation (RCDP I, II) (1992-1993)*, Urban Development Co-ordination Division, Bangkok.
Sinclair Knight and Partners Pvt. Ltd., (1982), *Feasibility Studies for REGIONAL Cities Development*, UNDP, Bangkok.

10

SONGKHLA FISHPORT: STRUCTURING AND IMPLEMENTING A PUBLIC–PRIVATE PARTNERSHIP PROJECT

Michael Lindfield

The case of the Songkhla Fishport in Thailand is interesting because it illustrates how a relatively small-scale, but complex, infrastructure project can be implemented more effectively using private participation. It also illustrates how such a project, implemented within an integrated urban development project, requires new dimensions of integration—integration of marketing, financial structuring and design.

As described in more appropriate detail elsewhere (Sinclair Knight and Partners, 1983), the Songkhla Fishport project was undertaken as part of the Regional Cities Development Project (RCDP). The city of Songkhla is on the coast of the Gulf of Thailand in the south of the country. The "fishport project", in reality, consisted of: a new fishport for fishing vessels and a market for their produce, which occupied approximately one-third of the site (3.8 hectares); a medium-sized industrial estate (8.7 hectares); and the redevelopment of the existing port site (0.4 hectares). The first two components of the project are located immediately to the west of the Songkhla Central Business District (CBD) on land reclaimed from Songkhla Lake and are an extension of the CBD. The existing port was located in the CBD.

The Decision to Use Public–Private Partnership

The project was identified as a high priority one by Songkhla Municipality as the existing fishport, originally on the periphery of the city, was, as a result of the expansion in 1985, then in the heart of the city. The port used the land inappropriately and occupied valuable land. It was also overcrowded. However, the size of the proposed fishport project—some US$ 8.6 million—was disproportionate to the financial resources and management capacity of the Songkhla Municipality—with total yearly revenues (including central government subsidies constituting almost 50 per cent) (Sinclair Knight and Partners, 1986a) of US$ 12.3 million—almost all of which was committed recurrent expenditure. In order to ensure that the project would be sustainable in the long term, the World Bank, which was financing construction, requested the Australian International Development Assistance Bureau (AIDAB) to fund a study on the management and marketing of such a port as part of its preparatory financing. The study identified three options:

— Central government (Industrial Estates Authority of Thailand) development and operation;
— Municipal development of the new port using a separate entity within the municipality to manage the development; and
— Municipal development of the port and sale to the private sector.

As the structuring of the project progressed, it became apparent that legal constraints would prevent the municipality from selling the development—the reclaimed land was "owned" by the Royal Thai Government (RTG) and would only be leased to the Municipality which could not, as a consequence, "sell" the land or anything built on it, in the sense that the buyer would receive freehold title. Thus a fourth option was developed:

— Private sector tender for operation of the fishing port and development of the existing port site and the industrial estate on leased land.

It was considered that the most efficient option would be to tender the construction of the fishport and the infrastructure for the industrial estate together under the RCDP, development of the land being the responsibility of the private developer who would pay a commercial rate for the lease of the developed land.

The latter course of action was chosen as it was felt that:

— It was not the role of the central government to undertake the management of infrastructure development in the Regional Cities, where this could be done by other (local) organizations; and
— The municipality had neither the institutional capacity to manage the development process and the completed development nor was it considered by the RTG a task that a municipality should adopt.

This course of action being chosen, the institutional context for its implementation had to be designed.

Organizational Context

The design of this institutional context was focussed on determining the market for the fishport project; designing the regulatory, implementation and operating organizational structures; and devising a management and marketing strategy for these organizations (Sinclair Knight and Partners, 1986b). The market for the project, structured by organizations/ groups on both supply and demand sides, will be analysed in this section.

Supply side: "Supply side" is defined in this context to mean all the organizations potentially involved in implementing the fishport project.

Office of Urban Development (OUD), Ministry of the Interior (MOI): This was given the charge to support strengthening of all secondary cities in Thailand in general and to oversee the Regional Cities Development Project in particular. This agency had to approve the institutional arrangements for the implementation of the new fishport and to oversee and coordinate the implementation of the fishport as a component of the RCDP.

In particular, once the decision to implement through the private sector was taken, OUD had the responsibility for formulating and undertaking the tendering process to identify the operators/ developers. For this task, OUD required temporary consultant advice—the agency not being in the business of structuring such activity, even though it was routinely running tenders for infrastructure works under the RCDP and, indeed, coordinated the tender for the fishport infrastructure under the International Competitive Bidding procedures of the World Bank.

In addition, OUD had the responsibility of monitoring that proportion of funds (approximately US$ 1.1 million or 14 per cent of the total) which would be on-lent to the municipality from the proceeds of the World Bank loan for the purposes of construction of the fishport, the payment of the municipality's cash contribution (approximately US$100,000) and the repayment of the loan.

Songkhla Municipality: As the administrator of the "land" (see below) and the responsible local authority, the municipality was centrally involved in the process. After the development was tendered and construction completed, the municipality would assume the ownership of the infrastructure and the responsibility for operation and maintenance of the roads, drainage, solid waste collection, sewerage network and sewerage treatment system. For this role, the municipal service departments were strengthened in terms of improved systems and equipment. Cost recovery on these services required improved billing and collection systems. Technical assistance in these fields was provided by AIDAB and equipment was procured under the RCDP loan.

In addition, the municipality would have the responsibility of marketing the project before the tender and would continue to be involved in the project as:

— A monitor of development and collector of staged payment for land; and

— A liaison with the end-users of the areas of the developed areas over service provision, etc.

The administration of these activities required the establishment of a small unit — the Development Management Unit — within the Municipality.

The Fish Marketing Organization (FMO): A Statutory Authority with a monopoly position in the provision of (legal) port facilities in the city. This authority considered that it should have automatic right of operation of the new fishport. It also considered that it was entitled to compensation of the order of Baht 10.5 million (US$ 0.4 million) for the existing fishport site.

The Fishermen's Association: An association of fishing boat-owners, based in Songkhla, ranging in wealth of the owners of small (3-metre) inshore vessels to the owners of several large (20- metre) deep-sea trawlers. The association was politically influential in Songkhla and was dominated by the wealthier owners. Nevertheless, the association provided facilities for all its members in the form of an illegal fishport which was almost as busy as the main port and which was much used by the smaller boats. The association had a rudimentary administrative apparatus.

Private developers: Two types of developers were interested in the fishport project—the large, Bangkok-based conglomerates and the local developers who knew the local market. Several private developers operated in Songkhla and were interested in the development of the industrial estate and, unusually enough, in the running of the fishport. These developers had significant resources and were able to prepare tenders.

Demand side: "Demand side" is defined in this context to mean all the groups potentially using the fishport project or impacted by the project.

Fishermen: "Big" fishermen, meaning the owners of deep-sea trawlers, had several very important reasons for wanting a new port. In the first instance they could unload their boats more quickly — waiting time at the existing ports was long, sometimes several hours, and this wait, in turn, sometimes meant that good fish became "trash fish". In addition, because their Association was offered a chance to bid for the port operation, they saw it as a chance to:

— Legitimize their port operations (before enforcement became stricter after the excuse of lack of capacity in the existing port had ceased to be valid); and

— Reduce the cost of doing business (both official and unofficial) at the existing port.

— "Small" fishermen, meaning the owners of small coastal boats and those boats which operated in the lake. With a jetty designed especially for small boats, these owners stood to benefit proportionately more in terms of access and were also likely to benefit from reduced costs.

House and shop buyers: In concept design, this development offered little housing - some 300 shophouses were included to service the industrial estate. As the name implies, shophouses are designed to incorporate a house and a shop and is the archetypical South-East Asian commercial building. In Thailand, however, many such units are used exclusively for housing. Given the position of the proposed development, adjacent to the CBD, significant interest in any new shophouses, both as commercial property and as dwellings, could be envisaged. Latent demand for housing was calculated as part of the development of a marketing strategy.

Based on projected population increase matched to projected supply of housing, it was found that there would be a substantial demand for a development which supplied housing in this location. This is particularly the case as Songkhla is situated on a peninsula between the lake and the sea and no more land is available. When the municipality surveyed only those businesses located near the existing fishport, valid applications received amounted to more land than was available in the estate.

Industries and commercial enterprises: This includes the following subgroups:

— Fishing-related Industries: These industries commenced operations in the vicinity of the existing fishport, processing fish for local consumption in one or two shophouses. As the scale of operations expanded over time and as more of the catch was destined to be processed for export, these industries moved out of the city centre to peripheral areas where more, cheaper land was available for facilities and for waste treatment ponds. These industries produce waste material of high "Biochemical Oxygen Demand" (BOD) load which requires extensive treatment. Treated wastewater was to be discharged into the lake—an environmentally sensitive area. In order to keep open the option for establishment of such industries in the industrial estate, the waste treatment facilities of the estate had to be able to handle the waste of such industries. The cost of such treatment increased the cost of the infrastructure and the continuing treatment charges. The cost of land in the estate had, however, to be competitive with peripheral land.

These potentially conflicting conditions could be reconciled for some fishing-related industries. From the municipal survey, a number of enterprises were interested in locating in the estate (at the likely lease terms), but demand was not sufficient to justify the original design concept of an exclusively fishing-oriented industrial estate. Flexibility in terms of land-use was thus required in the tender process. Subsequent tenders for estate land have borne out this judgement.

— Other Industries: Heavy and polluting industries, mostly producing goods for export or for further processing in Bangkok, were not, allowed to be located around Songkhla, but in the vicinity of the new "deep-sea" port, some distance to the north of the city. Most other industries likely to be located in the vicinity of Songkhla could utilize the facilities of the estate subject only to the constraint of keeping land prices down to levels competitive with peripheral land. In the effective absence of zoning controls for such light industry, the estate had to compete on price and facilities alone.

— Traders, etc: The demand for estate space from traders was indistinguishable from the demand for housing discussed earlier. The position of the development adjacent the CBD gave the estate great value for the these businessmen.

Users of the lake: Songkhla Lake was already under some environmental pressure as development around its shore, both on the shore (causing siltation and pollution from urban runoff/wastewater discharge) and in the lake (fish farms) threatened the marine life of the lake. It was thus important that the port did not further make an adverse impact on the lake. To this end the construction of the port was designed in such a manner as to minimize siltation and the major impact from operation, the outflow from the waste-water plant, was minimized by the design of the plant—which was of high capacity (capable of handling the "worst scenario" loads of fish processing plants).

Squatters: About 80 families of squatters lived on the site. In accordance with the practice of the Thai government, and before the current World Bank Relocation Policy came into effect, these families were moved to a site on the periphery of the city by the municipality. The procedure would be somewhat more complicated if it were carried out today, but would not constitute a major impediment for the development.

Structure of Funding

Financing of the supply-side organizations will be the main focus of this section. As the project implementation was structured through local government and not by means of an independent company, only debt financing (to the RTG and to the municipality) was used—this being a "World Bank" project. However, it should be noted that demand-side financing may also need attention where the outlay is large relative to income (such as a house purchase) and/or where the financial institutions are not as developed and entrepreneurial as they are in Thailand. This issue does arise in the financing of small-scale enterprises (see the section on "Private Developers" cater).

Office of Urban Development (OUD), Ministry of the Interior: Crucially, financing of institutional strengthening efforts designed to enable OUD to implement such a project was supplied by bilateral assistance, most importantly AIDAB. In addition, USAID funded a re-design of the Municipal Finance System which enabled the municipality to keep tighter control over revenue-raising activities and of expenditures which were required to implement the project successfully.

The regulatory agency thus had the capacity and systems to implement and monitor the project.

Songkhla Municipality: The municipality had some funds of its own (US$ 100,000) which were available as its "equity" in the project. Funded by the World Bank loan for the RCDP, 14 per cent of the capital funds (US$ 1.1 million) were on-lent from the Ministry of Finance in the form of a fixed interest loans, mainly at 10 per cent interest, with a term of 15 years. The remainder of the capital funds were given as an RTG grant.

An alternative formulation—that of funding this and other infra-structure projects using the existing Municipal Development Fund which would be capitalized by the World Bank loan—was not implemented despite significant benefits for the strengthening of the infrastructure financing system as a whole. This was due to the perception of the local governments, which had effective control over the disbursement from the fund, that such a capital injection would lead to tighter MOI control of lending procedures—which it would have—and consequently that they would lose control over the allocation of funds.

The repayment capacity of the municipality was calculated based on the net revenues from the fishport development alone. The debt service capacity of the municipality based on its revenues from property taxa-tion and other taxes was not considered as these sources were fully committed to funding other components of the RCDP.

Cost recovery for the services provided had also to be considered. Any shortfall in cost recovery would impact on the municipality's abil-ity to service debt. The requirements and systems for fee-setting were detailed under the management and marketing plan for monitoring by OUD.

The Fish Marketing Organization (FMO): As a Statutory Authority, the FMO was in a position to raise funds from the banking system—with a government guarantee and therefore at lower cost than private competitors. It also, apparently, had significant cash reserves.

The Fishermen's Association: The Fisherman's Association, as such, had little capacity to raise funds from the banking system; indeed the Association was not constituted as a company in a way which would make this possible. However, several important officers of the Associa-tion were personally very wealthy and the Association had significant income from selling ice, and from renting space on its illegal wharf. Properly constituted as a company, therefore, it had significant capacity to borrow, either from formal sector organizations or from its own members.

Private developers: The private developers interested in the project were relatively wealthy individuals who could access funds from the formal banking system, although most of the Songkhla-based developers were hard pressed to raise collateral for the scale of bridging finance required by the development of the industrial estate section of the fishport project. To alleviate this problem, the municipality had to agree in writing that the successful tenderer would be awarded a 30-year head lease on the property of the port which could be used as security by the developer.

In addition, it was proposed to cut up the development into several packages which were more "digestible" for the local development industry.

As it was envisaged that the marketing of the development of the industrial estate and the existing fishport would mainly be focussed on private developers, it was also important to consider potential finance for those who would sub-lease from the developers. This was particularly important for the smaller developers. Thus, an important role for the Development Management Unit of the Municipality was to assist potential occupants of the estate obtain access to the numerous sources of finance and incentives for investment available in Thailand.

The Tender Process

The marketing and financing strategies had to be realized, in large part, through the structuring and conduct of a tender process designed to attract appropriate developers. This section discusses the major issues in the design of that process (Sinclair Knight and Partners, 1986a and 1986b).

The existing lease: The FMO, it will be recalled, was claiming compensation for the closure of its present port. This claim was based on an estimate of the value of the infrastructure and facilities which existed, even though they had been fully written off and were of no residual value as they would have to be demolished in order to develop the site. The land belonged to the Royal Thai Government.

The claim, if paid at the beginning of the project, would have wiped out Songkhla Municipality's reserves which were destined to be used as its contribution to the project. Given that Songkhla's debt service capacity from port revenues was already fully used, especially in the early years, to finance the project, the claim thus threatened the project's financial viability.

The problem was solved by the simple expedient of someone getting and reading the FMO's lease on the land. In it, there was a clause which clearly stated that no compensation was due if the government (including for this purpose the municipality as represented by the MOI) wanted the land for government use. As the land was not going to be sold and the municipality was going to be the beneficiary, the project constituted "government use" and this matter was resolved in the favour of the municipality. Nevertheless, as a contingency measure, compensation to the FMO was allowed for in the cashflow, paid in installments over the implementation of the project.

The structure of the tender: As the fishport component of the project would be completed some 18 months before the completion of the industrial estate component, and the tendering of the fishport would be a significant income for the municipality, it was decided to split the tendering process into two parts—the first for the fishport and the second for the various parts of the industrial estate. The reason for structuring the tender in this way was to provide cash inflow from the fishport at the earliest possible time.

Another issue to be addressed was the structuring of the payment system. This decision had significant implications for cashflow. This was because of the interesting payment system usually used for paying for leased land in Thailand. It is customary to divide the payment into two parts—a premium which constitutes a large upfront payment representing most of the present value of the usage of the property (1.25 times the development costs) and a yearly payment which is a relatively low ground rent. However, this is a disincentive to invest for many smaller enterprises and, in the light of the objectives set out below, lease payments were structured as constant payments indexed to inflation. This decision, depriving the municipality of the large upfront payment, made consideration of cash inflow very important.

This decision also had some design and construction programming consequences. The design of the project had to be such that the port could operate effectively while construction activity (particularly traffic) was on-going first on the infrastructure for the estate and second on the buildings constructed by the developer(s).

The lease documents: Owing to the fact that both sites—the existing fishport and the new port site—were "owned" by the Royal Thai Government (RTG), the project land titles had to be structured around a "base lease" of the land by the RTG to Songkhla Municipality. First, however, the new port, then water, had to be recognized as "land". This required the Marine Department to give its approval—which was done efficiently. Then the Crown Property Board could frame a lease in favour of the Municipality. This lease was important for what it **should not** say. It should not, and in the event did not, encumber the municipality from sub-leasing the property or in any way deriving benefit from the property.

The municipality had then to frame head leases—different leases for the fishport operators and for the developers of the industrial estate. The latter had to be written in a way which expressly recognized that they (the leases) would be used as security for development finance and that there would be sub-leases for the properties developed.

The "development leases", as they were termed, had to be for as long a term as possible (30 years, the timespan of the municipality's lease) and be as little encumbered as possible in order not to restrict the freedom of design of the developers and consequent narrowing of their ability to cater to demand as they perceived it.

In addition, it was important to consider the procedure to be followed in the event of the bankruptcy of a developer. While the premium system minimizes the impact of this eventuality on cashflow, the method chosen exposes the municipality to problems should a developer default and significant consequences for the municipality could ensue, depending on the stage of construction achieved and the number of sub-leases sold.

In order to provide sufficient information for the tenderers, acceptable forms of sub-lease documents—those leases between the developer and the "buyers" (sub-leasees) of the properties that the developer constructs—also had to be drafted and included for information in the tender documents.

Pre-qualification, tender document and tender: Pre-qualification of tenderers was a well-established concept and procedure within OUD. The fishport itself was the subject of an International Competitive Bidding (ICB) process which was undertaken and evaluated by OUD with some technical assistance funded by AIDAB. The development pre-qualifications were structured according to the "split" structure of the tendering—one for the port operator and another for the developer(s) of the industrial estate and existing fishport.

The pre-qualification document asked information concerning the tenderers':

— Experience and past performance;
— Technical capabilities;
— Financial capabilities;
— Other administrative issues; and
— Design of proposed development.

The difference in approach between a normal construction pre-qualification and the pre-qualification for the development of the fishport project is that the latter involves the need to appraise a design from which the party calling the tender will derive benefit. In a normal construction tender, the party calling the tender will pay and it is only necessary to determine the technical capacity of the contractor and his ability to finance construction between progress payments. In a development tender, given clear definition of the parameters defining the limits of acceptable development, the winner will be the developer who promises to pay the municipality the most. This promise must be based on a sound technical and financial base—which is much more difficult to determine than in respect of a contractor.

The pre-qualification process sought to:

— Identify a range of potential tenderers in order to encourage competition and thus achieve the maximum net return for the municipality;
— Identify potential tenderers with the financial and technical resources to execute the project quickly and efficiently; and
— Allow the participation of local (Songkhla-based) enterprises.

In order to achieve this, the pre-qualification exercise had to:

— Be formulated as simply as possible and allow the participation of companies of modest experience/financial means in order not to dissuade small enterprises and/or NGOs from participating;
— Clearly state the primary criteria on which the tender will be evaluated and the return to the municipality; and
— Clearly set out the parameters within which the tenderer had freedom to determine the design of the proposed development.

It goes without saying that the documentation had to be prepared in Thai.

For the last of the above requirements, the concept of "performance standards" was used where feasible. These standards define the result of a design solution rather than determine the physical design. For example, the maximum impact on the main sewers was defined in terms of a "peaking factor" and it was left to the developer's engineers to design a sewerage system which would not exceed this parameter. Elsewhere it was necessary to be prescriptive—"all sidewalks should slope to the road", for example.

Breaking up the development of the industrial estate into five components—one developer could tender on all if he wanted—also encouraged small (local) companies to participate.

Tender period of three months was deemed to be appropriate to the organizations targeted and to the task as development tenders had to include a fairly detailed design.

Tender evaluation and result: The difficulty was to set the pre-qualification "pass mark" low enough in the measures of technical and financial capacity so as not to eliminate viable offers from small local companies and high enough to ensure that they would, after all, perform if awarded the tender. For example, in the case of the fishport operator:

— Years of company experience was not important—and the "pass mark" would be set correspondingly low—if the company was a newly established company of the Fishermen's Association which had been running an illegal port for many years;

— Company profitability was not important—and again the minimum standard required for pre-qualification would be low—if the newly established Fisherman's Association company did not account for revenue from the shops and ice sales in its existing (illegal) port lest it attract the tax man; and

— Expertise of staff was important as operating the port efficiently was a consideration.

Once the tender had been "passed" on these measures, the results would depend on the price offered to the municipality.

In the case of the fishport operator, the result of the tender process was that the Fishermen's Association tendered over Baht 11 million yearly rent, the private developer, Baht 8 million and the FMO, Baht 4.5 million, against an estimated minimum of Baht 5 million.

One complicating issue was that developers were allowed to offer for one or all packages of the industrial estate and the existing fishport site. This made the evaluation more difficult. Not to allow the possibility of tendering on all packages would deny the possibility of economies of scale. To tender all the development together would eliminate all but the biggest developers. Thus, the tenderers were made aware that their tender would be compared against other tenders on each component. This may result in losing the benefit of returns to scale as, for example, a tenderer tendering on all components will have to spread the benefits of scale economies over all components and may be outbid on a particular component, **but** may provide the municipality with the maximum return overall (when the next-best offers on the other components are added to the higher tender for that one component). In this case, the higher overall offer would prevail.

The process suggested also consisted of two stages—with the highest bidder on conceptual plans (complying with the performance standards set out in the tender documents) being subject to technical evaluation and revision of bid if necessary. If negotiations failed, the second bidder would be called.

Institutional and Regulatory Issues

The organizational structure for implementation and operation had to be considered carefully. Several major issues were involved.

First, the issue of regulating the developers was important as they are likely to be in a monopoly position in respect of prospective tenants. It is thus important that the rights and interests of the sub-leasees are protected and this was achieved by the creation of a tenants liaison committee which would have a direct link ·to the municipality Development Management Unit (DMU).

The enforcement of standards of construction, health and service provision was also to be coordinated by the DMU, both in respect of design and operation.

Second, the issue of which organization was to monitor the DMU and the municipality in the implementation and management of the development had to be addressed. In this role OUD had to perform the primary tasks of monitoring of cashflows and loan repayments and of physical progress of construction. In addition, it is important that the new organizational structures within the municipality be designed so as to help maintain transparency and accountability. Such details as routing the flow of funds from the developers through the municipal finance section rather than through the DMU are important in this respect.

In addition, it was important that there be a higher level organization to assist in policy direction in the event of unforeseen circumstances, such as possible slow rates of "take up" by developers, or low tender prices. Again, OUD with its trained personnel and additional influence on RTG agencies would be required to take this role.

Conclusion

The integration achieved by the Songkhla fishport project was achieved in dimensions not usually considered when "integration" is discussed— physical, financial and institutional design (see Figure 10.1). This integration was the result of a process which proceeded from a basic understanding of community needs—at least the needs of an economically and socially important part of the community—which were given a concrete form in the planning of a new fishport.

The recognition that this investment could be undertaken—could better be undertaken—by the private sector required an open approach on the part of regulators.

**Figure 10.1: The Project Process of the Songkhla
Fishport Development**

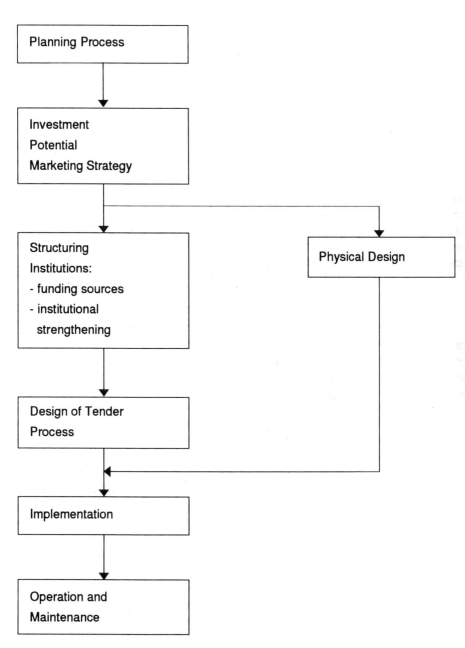

That approach enabled the design of a tender process which:

— Structured the organizations involved and the marketing strategies to enable them to tap potential demand;

— Determined the physical design parameters which in turn determined the limits of flexibility in the tender design proposals; and

— Structured the funding mechanisms involved in order to maximize demand and return to the implementing organization.

As part of this process, the implementation and operational requirements of the project were integrated into the physical, institutional and financial design. Appropriate strengthening measures were also formulated in order to ensure that these requirements were met — including measures to strengthen regulatory agencies.

BIBLIOGRAPHY

Sinclair Knight and Partners Pvt. Ltd. (1983), *Feasibility Studies for the Regional Cities Development Project, Songkhla*, Vol. 6, April, Ministry of Interior, Bangkok.

Sinclair Knight and Partners Pvt. Ltd. (1986a), *Financing Regional Centres Infrastructure*, February, National Economic & Social Development Board, Bangkok.

Sinclair Knight & Partners Pvt. Ltd. (1986b), *Songkhla Fishport and Industrial Estate Development: Management and Marketing Plan*, January, Ministry of the Interior, Bangkok.

11

INTEGRATED ACTION PLANNING: THE EXPERIENCE IN NEPAL

David M. Irwin and Jibgar Joshi

Introduction

Context: At present there are 36 municipalities in Nepal. Although Nepal is still predominantly rural, with only about 8 per cent unit urban population, the rate of urbanization is conspicuously high, the recent estimate being 7.2 per cent per annum. Urban areas have acute deficiencies in infrastructure and service provision, and there is a severe financial resource constraint to resolve this.

Lack of coordination between the private and the public sector, as well as among the sectoral line agencies, in the implementation of urban projects is a major problem. Technical competence for implementing the municipal projects is also severely lacking.

In this context, planning must provide an appropriate framework for programming development activities, annual budgeting and ensuring planned development.

Past experience: The conventional planning approach had been master planning. This approach, based on the traditional paradigm of "survey-analysis-evaluation-plan implementation" was evolved in a context where technocratic solutions led to a highly analytical form of planning which was time-consuming, rigid and geared to a single, long-range outcome. Master plans attempt to pre-determine the physical development of an area, which can include the total municipality or part of it. The master plan describes the proposed future land use and infrastructure pattern for a city 15 to 20 years in the future. The underlying principle of this approach was that the investment programme should be determined by the physical development plan.

At the municipal level, master plans seldom get implemented mainly because future events and circumstances cannot be predicted well and the plan becomes obsolete when things change rapidly. Another difficulty is that the implementing agency does not have the ability to determine the nature of land use in accordance with plan designations, as assumed during the planning phase. Since the majority of urban development activities are undertaken by institutions not under the control of the municipality (or the planning department of the government) its realization is very unlikely. As a result master plans are justly criticized for being unrealistic.

As an alternative to master planning, structure plans were prepared between 1988 and 1991 for all the municipalities by the Department of Housing and Urban Development (DHUD), with the support of a UNDP/World Bank project called Management Support for Urban Development (MSUD). The intention was that structure plans would overcome the shortcomings of the master plan approach, but these were not altogether adequate as their content was limited to general policy statements, and details were not worked out. Moreover, the approach continued to be physically biased, and hence unrealistic, as they were conceived as physical plans that did not take into account financial, institutional and other dimensions affecting municipal activities, although these shortcomings could have been overcome as part of the implementing strategy (UNCHS, 1989; Peterson *et al.*, 1989).

Integrated action planning: As an alternative to either of these conventional approaches, integrated action planning (IAP) is gaining much popularity in Nepal. Although IAP is an action-oriented approach, it can still include strategic elements. In a realistic way, IAP attempts to translate and then implement the goals of strategic planning as applied within a shorter time frame during which progress can be monitored more closely. In this way, IAP tries to replace master planning and eliminate the physical bias of structure plans. As such, it provides a general planning and budgeting framework for making detailed local area plans or even ward-level plans (Joshi, 1991).

In IAP, the word *"integrated"* is used to denote incorporation of all the relevant sectors and combinations of physical elements within financial and management planning. It also:

— Utilizes the collaborative participation of public, private, household and informal sectors in an attempt to better understand and exploit the complex linkages among all the various interests operating within the municipality;

— Encompasses vertical integration, fostering a healthy partnership between the national and municipal governments; and

— Covers spatial integration, establishing viable urban-rural linkages, dealing at the same time with the "ecological footprints" of the urban settlement.

"*Action*" in IAP refers to an early implementation of projects which:

— Have strong support; and

— Require comparatively less resources for identification and design, and form an overall plan based on promotion and facilitation, rather than control of development (Heinrichs, 1993).

The Integrated Action Planning Approach (IAP)

Application and Characteristics of IAP

IAP is appropriate where:

— Urban centres are undergoing rapid growth and change;

— There are severe resource limitations and inadequate institutional capacities; and

— The planning process needs to be simplified, reduced in time and focussed on actual development opportunities rather than on the optimum long-term physical form of the overall town or city.

In relative terms, the IAP takes less time. Data collection and analysis are done rapidly as a flexible and dynamic exercise. The approach is more realistic and attempts to cover all the developmental aspects, not just those that correspond to physical planning.

The main characteristics which make IAP appropriate are:

— A thorough investigation of problems as perceived by the users (whether as households or collectively as small community groups), and by the private commercial sector, the municipalities, the public sector agencies and by political parties;

— An analysis of existing, available and readily mobilized financial, human and natural resources, and of the implementation mechanisms within and across institutions;

— Rapid systems of data collection and processing, avoiding time-consuming complex techniques, and ensuring that surveys and studies are directly related to problem-solving;

— The early implementation of projects for which there is political and popular support, with assured resource commitments providing a rapid feedback, shaping future town-wide plans, rather than waiting for formal adoption of a comprehensive plan before any action can take place; and

— The combination of micro-planning techniques at the individual project level with strategic planning for the town as a whole (Joshi and Lojewski, 1993).

Outputs of IAP: The outputs of IAP at the current stage in its development in Nepal are :

— A package of mutually supportive projects, with preliminary designs and cost estimates;

— A Multi-sectoral Investment Programme (MSIP) for a period not exceeding five years, incorporating the detailed formulation of the municipal budget for the first year;

— A Physical and Environmental Development Plan (PEDP) communicated in the form of maps and additional explanations;

— Financial management and organizational development provisions to support projects, MSIP and PEDP, and to improve the general administration of the municipality; and

— Recommendations for the introduction of planning bye-laws and regulations for implementation and enforcement of the PEDP.

The IAP process is shown in the flow chart presented as Figure 11.1. The process is interactive, the main steps of which are described below.

IAP Steps

Community consultations: At the beginning of any planning process it is necessary to establish channels of communication with individuals, organizations and institutions who will be involved. It is recommended that the following public meetings in every ward, contact groups are formed. A steering committee should also be formed, to include elected representatives, line agencies, Non-Governmental Organizations (NGOs), private sector, associations and local experts.

The objective of consultations is to identify the main problems experienced within the municipality, from the community perspective to a town-wide perspective. Meetings and discussions are guided by constraints to solving problems, the most typical of which is of course finance. It is therefore important that problems are identified in a realistic way, and that people's expectations are not raised beyond what can be achieved.

Experience has shown that people can be very insular in their appreciation of what constitutes a problem and can misinterpret the IAP process as merely an opportunity to enlarge their share of the

Figure 11.1 Integrated Action Planning Approach

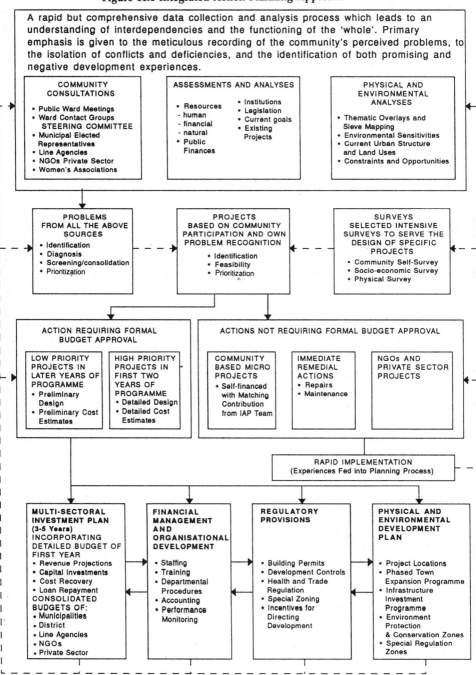

municipalities development budget with little regard to needs of the town as a whole. A further danger is that people may not always perceive or recognize that problems exist, for example, community consultations in a recent IAP in Bharatpur, Nepal, failed to identify that the current practice of disposing of solid waste in the river (upstream of the National Park) is a problem.

Assessment and analyses: In parallel with community participation, various assessments should be conducted to determine and evaluate the opportunities and constraints that may exist within the municipality. In particular, attention should focus on:

— *Resources*: What are the staff resources of the municipality to prepare and implement a plan? What is the development budget for the current year, and could it be increased through better generation of local revenues, grants or loans? Is there any possibility to increase the community's contribution (in cash or kind)?

— *Institutions*: Do the necessary institutions exist to operate/implement plan proposals, and if yes, are they sufficiently equipped with human and material resources?

— *Legislation*: Do the necessary laws, regulations, etc., exist to control activities in a planned manner?

— *Existing Projects*: What projects are under implementation, committed or in the pipeline? How do these relate to problems that have been identified by community consultations? Are the necessary institutional, legal and financial resources available to implement and operate the existing or committed projects?

It is often useful to undertake the assessment at the same time as community consultations, if not in advance, since the conclusions are more often constraints than opportunities.

The experience of IAP in Nepal has focussed on small towns with populations of less than 50,000. However IAP is now being applied to larger towns, such as Patan (Nepal's second city, with a population of 140,000) and in this regard assessment and analyses are realized to be important steps to be completed in advance of community consultations. In the case of Patan a strategy review was conducted, which covered the aspects summarized earlier (and in the next section) in order to give a broad-based context/framework in which community consultations could be carried out.

Physical and environmental analysis: These analyses should also be done at an early stage, in parallel with community consultations, and provide an opportunity to identify problems at a town level. Problems identified at ward levels are often a manifestation of a larger problem which needs to be considered at the municipal level. In addition, these analyses can help the IAP team to identify problems which have been missed or overlooked during community consultations.

The analyses should also seek to determine opportunities, as well as problems, particularly physical and environmental characteristics with implications on the community.

The activities may be summarized as follows: ·

— Prepare a reasonably accurate base map of the municipal area (at a suitable scale), showing all physical and built features;
— Assess the characteristics of the municipal area in terms of its land use, terrain, environment, etc.;
— Identification of development trends (conversion of agricultural land to urban use) by collecting historical data, for example, building permits, which when plotted ward-wise will reveal the direction and location of recent built development. The cadastral map will reveal areas where land ownership sub-division has been active, which is usually an indication of where built development may occur in future; and
— Population and population density at the ward and town levels, analysis of which can help predict the future growth of the overall town and the spatial distribution of its population.

Constraints may occur in a variety of forms, but typically include:

— Land which is unsuitable for built development due to reasons such as steep slope, flooding, inadequate infrastructure (especially water supply) and proximity to unpleasant/hazardous activities, etc.; and
— Land with better alternative uses, such as agriculture, forestry, nature reserves, etc.

Opportunities may also vary but are typically as follows:

— Gently sloping, well-drained land that is easily accessed by existing infrastructure (especially roads and water) or by simple extension of existing infrastructure. Such land is ideal for urban development provided it is not better suited for some other activity (e.g., irrigated agricultural land); and
— Land which by virtue of its scenic, environmental or ecological value, should be promoted as a national/international place of scientific, recreation or tourist interest.

Identification and prioritization of problems: The procedure for problem identification should involve surveys, investigations and inquiries in accordance with the steps recommended above. Of these, community consultations deserve emphasis as this has hitherto been neglected and resulted in a top-down approach (everything is decided at a top level and imposed upon the community) with little support from the people. Criteria should be determined for assessing and prioritizing problems. Some issues help to determine the criteria. For instance, the problem should be solvable; how critical is the problem, what could happen if the problem is not solved, can we wait to solve the problem, and so on. Problems may overlap within one area/ward, or occur again in a number of adjacent areas/wards. In such cases the problems should be diagnosed to determine whether they can be consolidated into a single problem, or they lead to other problems. The geographic distribution of problems should be identified and compared against the socio-economic characteristics of the community, and their welfare needs to see if the nature and severity of problems have any particular incidence in any group or area. The responsibility for solving problems needs to be determined. Problems not falling under the responsibility of the municipality should also be identified and brought to the attention of the concerned agency.

It should be stressed that in many cases, problems or their solutions, have a bearing on the physical (spatial) planning of a municipal area. The output of analyses conducted into physical and environmental characteristics, in particular existing and future opportunities and constraints, should be used to determine the priority of problems. More specifically, any problem, the resolution of which enhances opportunities, should be given a higher priority than one that does not. This kind of judgement needs to be taken from a town-wide perspective rather than a ward-level perspective.

Project formulation: Projects assume a critical position in the IAP process. They are identified considering all the steps mentioned above, and their implementation leads to the realization of the PEDP. Projects should be formulated to solve only those problems which meet the criteria discussed above, and with special attention to high priority problems.

As a first step, projects should be formulated quickly to an approximate level of detail (tentative design) in order to identify their broad parameters, including cost. This is important in order to assess whether or not the project is within the financial capacity of the municipality. It will also enable an approximate assessment of whether the project is technically feasible, and effective in terms of solving the problem.

Projects satisfying these assessments may proceed to the next formulation step, which is to prepare the projects in more detail to a level of preliminary design. For this purpose it will be necessary to carry out selected and sometimes intensive surveys to provide the necessary information for design. This will depend on the nature of the project and may include topographic surveys, socio-economic surveys and other methods of data collection as may be necessary. Wherever possible the participation of the community is desirable.

Project feasibility: For examining the technical feasibility, the project must solve the problem within the limits of existing levels of available technology, technical know-how, equipment and management capability. For ascertaining financial feasibility, cost estimates, affordability and cost recovery need to be examined to ensure that the project is not beyond the financial capability of the municipality. In order to ensure socio-economic feasibility some questions must be answered. Does the project help disadvantaged sections of the community? Is the cost-benefit analysis of the project favourable and are the need and affordability criteria satisfied ? Does the project have benefits in terms of health and welfare of the community? Does it generate employment, etc.? For examining environmental feasibility, especially relevant in the present context of Nepal's deteriorating urban environment, the project should be examined for any negative consequences or impact. In other words, the impact on the environment needs to be assessed. Finally, projects should be sustainable in terms of their maintenance requirement, a factor which is often neglected in Nepal.

Project prioritization: Prioritization of projects is the most difficult and politically sensitive part of any planning and programming exercise. The first criterion for priority must be the gravity of the problem, together with some judgement concerning "value for money". For example, a few people may experience a serious problem which can only be resolved at great expense. Such a project should not be given a higher priority than another similar project which at the same cost can solve an equally serious problem affecting many people.

A second criterion for priority should be the extent to which the project supports the proposals contained in the Physical and Environmental Development Plan (PEDP). As will be discussed later, the PEDP should attempt to encourage urban development in certain areas and discourage it in other areas. Any project that corresponds to or reinforces PEDP proposals should be given a high priority. For example, a project which involves the construction of a new road into an area where urban development or expansion is identified should be given a high priority.

At a detailed cost-benefit analysis can be conducted, the essential purpose being to prepare a systematic comparison of the positive and negative aspects of the projects in order to determine which of them has the greatest cost-benefit.

The experience in Nepal has established this step to be the crux of the IAP process because the geographic distribution of high priority projects necessarily determines the allocation of the municipality's development budget by wards. Political pressure tries to ensure that all wards receive a proportionate share of the budget, irrespective of needs and prioritized projects. Some flexibility in the application of the IAP is rather imperative.

Project programming: The first step in the formulation of programmes is to categorize high priority projects into those which require formal budget approval and those which do not. The latter are likely to include projects which cost little and can be approved by the mayor without reference to the town council. Other projects may include those which are to be financed and implemented by NGOs and the private sector. Projects which fall into these categories may proceed immediately, provided funds are available.

For the remaining projects it will be necessary to assess their cost (over the determined implementation period) against the financial resources of the municipality, in particular the forecast development budget for each year over the next five years. For those projects which incorporate cost recovery, the revenue generated should also be added to forecast municipal accounts. Based on their relative priority, sequential combinations of projects can be matched against anticipated financial resources to achieve a five-year development programme that is affordable. Preparation of the five-year programme should precede the preparation of the annual programme for the first year. This enables municipalities to formulate development objectives in a rational and affordable manner, and takes account of the fact that very few projects can be designed and implemented within a single year. Moreover, the five-year programme should be reviewed annually, so that it always remains valid for a five-year period. In this way the five-year programme is continually moving forward and is called a "rolling" programme.

Multi-sectoral Investment Programme (MSIP): This represents the final step in the preparation of annual and five-year programmes. As the name suggests, the programmes of all organizations and agencies involved in development within the municipal area are consolidated into a single programme which covers all sectors. This is necessary to ensure that projects planned by others do not conflict with those of the municipality, or with each other. Moreover, the overall consolidated programme inter-relates projects of different agencies in such a way that individual projects can complement each other and thereby be more effective using the concept of synergy. This is particularly true where projects of different agencies are focussed in one area. In such cases the consolidated programme enables projects to be implemented as single integrated project.

The preparation of MSIP should take into account revenues, loans and grants that may become available as a result of the projects selected. Revenues may accrue if the project incorporates a cost recovery component. This will apply if project beneficiaries are required to make a financial contribution towards the capital cost, or the recurrent costs of the project. Payment can be made at the beginning of the project, or in installments (monthly, quarterly or annually) for a pre-determined period after project completion.

An example of an MSIP is shown in Table 11.1, taken from the IAP prepared for Dhulikhel municipality.

Physical and Environmental Development Plan (PEDP): An important component of the IAP process is the resulting physical and environmental development plan. The physical components of the plan may include:

— All existing features, natural and man-made.
— Designation of areas where no development should occur due to physical or land-use constraints/considerations, for example, steep slopes and flood-prone areas. It should be noted that agricultural land (even the best grade) is seldom accepted as a viable constraint.
— A simple land-use zoning system, based on predominant (primary) land use, together with a range of permitted, secondary land uses.
— Areas where urban expansion is to be encouraged (or discouraged).
— A simple phased programme for the urban expansion of the town that relates to realistic and logical programmes for the extension and improvement of infrastructure services (especially roads, water, electricity and telephone).
— Areas where policies for controlling the nature of activity or type/scale of buildings are to be applied and proposed projects.

The environmental component of the plan may include:

Table 11.1: Multi-sector Investment Programme for Dhulikhel (Rs.1,000s)

SECTORS / PROJECTS	Ward No.	Project Implementation Schedule					Approximate Total Cost	Investment Agencies for Implementation			
		F.Y. 51/52 94/95	F.Y. 52/53 95/96	F.Y. 53/54 96/97	F.Y. 54/55 97/98	F.Y. 55/56 98/99		Muni-cipality	(1) Grant Funded	P.P.	Other Agency
Other Agency											
1 WATER SUPPLY											
1.1 New Water Supply Project	1,6						2,248	569	—	220	1,459
	1						451	451	—	—	—
	1						134	134	—	—	—
	1,9						302	302	—	—	—
1.2 Extension, Repair & Maintenance of Existing Water Supply Projects	1,5,7,8,9						841	841	—	—	—
	1,6,8,9						529	329	—	—	200
	1,6,7,8,9						632	432	—	—	200
	6,8,9						472	472	—	—	—
	1						50	50	—	—	—
1.3 Repair, Maintenance & Conservation of Existing Tank	1,6,7,8,9						132	117	—	15	—
	1,3,4,5,7,8,9						343	276	—	67	—
	2,3,4,5,7,8,9						289	265	—	24	—
	2,3,4,5,7,8,9						369	323	—	46	—
1.4 Feasibility Study of Water Supply (Long Term)	7						150	50	—	—	100
	7,8,9,1,6						150	150	—	—	—

Note: (1) Grant funding from TDFB or any other donor/agency

(Table 11.1 contd.)

SECTORS PROJECTS	Ward No.	Project Implementation Schedule					Approximate Total Cost	Investment Agencies for Implementation			
		F.Y. 51/52 94/95	F.Y. 52/53 95/96	F.Y. 53/54 96/97	F.Y. 54/55 97/98	F.Y. 55/56 98/99		Muni-cipality	(1) Grant Funded	P.P.	Other Agency
16 TOURISM											
16.1 Recreational Parts (1st Phase)	2						2,750	—	2,750	—	—
	2						303	303	—	—	—
16.2 View Shed	1						85	85	—	—	—
	1						85	85	—	—	—
	1						85	85	—	—	—
16.3 Tourism Development-Feasibility Study	All						150	—	—	—	150
17 BUS PARK											
17.1 Feasibility Study (For Long & Short Term)	—						250	25	225	—	—
18 MISCELLANEOUS											
18.1 Bus Stand Shed	7						40	40	—	—	—
18.2 Fire Hydrant	4,5						60	60	—	—	—
Establishment & Operation	4,5						90	90	—	—	—
	4,5						60	60	—	—	—

Note: (1) Grant funding from TDFB or any other donor/agency
Source: IAP for Dhulikhel

— Designation of areas with special environmental characteristics, the conservation or enhancement of which requires special policies/regulation to restrict or control land use and development. These may include areas of special ecological value, wildlife reserves, areas prone to environmental damage or soil erosion (steep slopes), forest resources, etc. Such areas may be termed **conservation areas.**

— Designation of special areas where land use or built development should be controlled for reasons of health, safety or resource conservation. These might include buffer areas adjacent to sewage treatment works or solid waste disposal sites. Another example is a watershed management area, where the continued supply of surface water for portable purposes is dependent upon protecting vegetation and restricting development. Such areas may be termed as **protection areas.**

— Policies to enhance the environment, some of which may have a spatial dimension. These may include a range of intentions such as green belts, park land, etc. Such areas may be termed **green areas.**

When designating conservation, protection or environmental policy areas it must be borne in mind that the rights of affected landowners are infringed, and in most cases denied. For this to be accepted the justification must be understood and reasonable. If not, the municipality will have difficulty to enforce policies and ultimately may have to consider compensation payments to landowners.

One way of resolving this difficulty is to introduce a policy that the entire cost of providing infrastructure to any new building or house must be paid by the owner. Exceptions to this policy would only be granted where the building or house is within an area that is already deemed urban, or is identified for urban expansion.

This policy can be linked with efforts to plan urban expansion areas using Guided Land Development or Land Pooling approaches. For such a policy to operate, care must be exercised when selecting/prioritizing projects, especially those which involve the extension of infrastructure, in particular roads and water pipelines. In this regard any extension of infrastructure networks should be within designated urban expansion areas.

Monitoring

The strength of IAP is to facilitate and promote an on-going development process. To this end, the process must involve a continual review of the success or otherwise of projects, both individually and as an overall programme. Particular attention should be given to the success of projects that support the PEDP.

If it is recognized that policies in the PEDP are not satisfactory, corrective actions should be sought immediately. It is possible that enforcement of planning bye-laws and related policies is not effective due to understaffing or undesirable practices. This can be remedied by appropriate actions. On the other hand, bye-laws and policies that do not have a majority acceptance will be difficult to implement, even with very strong enforcement. In such cases it may be prudent to revise the PEDP.

IAP Practice in NEPAL

Achievements: The method of IAP described above, as currently practiced in Nepal, has evolved through continuous application and by a process of "learning by doing". The method is still being refined since its first application in 1989.

At the outset, a production-oriented training workshop was conducted in Dhading, a small urban centre about 130 km. from Kathmandu. After running three workshops between 1989 and 1992, it was applied at an operational level in two municipalities, Vyas and Banepa, and later in two further municipalities, Dharan and Tulsipur. Then another workshop-cum-operational IAP was carried out in Damak municipality in 1994, bringing the total of engineers and architects trained in IAP to more than 100. In 1994, IAPs were completed in three more municipalities, Ilam, Birendranagar and Dhulikhel (Department of Housing and Urban Development, 1994b). The location of the municipalities and small towns covered so far are indicated in Figure 11.2. As of mid-1995, IAPs are on-going in three more municipalities, Bharatpur, Mahendranagar and Patan, bringing the total number of IAPs to 11.

Operational procedure: Three teams work more or less simultaneously on three IAPs, although their programme maybe staggered by a week or so due to logistic at constraints.

"Reconnaissance: For each town there is a separate reconnaissance visit, of two or three days, during which some activities are carried out, including:

— The reconnaissance team rapidly assesses the scope and complexity of the situation facing the municipality;

Fig. 11.2: Location of Municipalities that have Received IAP in Nepal

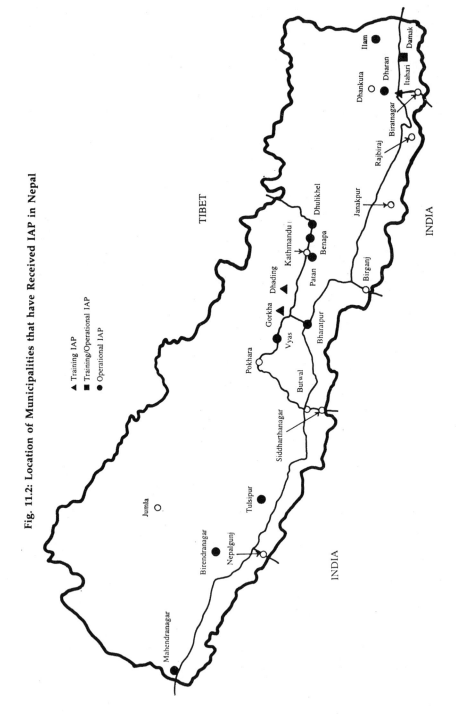

— Officials are provided detailed briefings about the nature, scope and procedure of IAP;

— Questionnaires are distributed to line agencies, NGOs and ward members;

— Additional specific requests for advance data collection are made; and

— Arrangements are confirmed about the timing of activities, logistics, staff accommodation and work space, etc.

Orientation, preparation and training: The reconnaissance is immediately followed by a joint training period for all three teams. This comprises lectures and presentations about IAP; group work and exercises; and familiarization with the IAP Training Manual in the context of the IAP Operational Guidelines. The outcome of this activity is a detailed work plan with individual task assignments. The workplan is prepared in consultation with key actors involved, for example, elected municipal representatives, line agency officials, NGOs and community groups who are requested to attend one day of the training (Department of Housing and Urban Development, 1994a).

Field study: The teams then depart to their respective towns to conduct an eight-week long intensive programme. Out of these eight weeks, two-and-a-half weeks are allocated for: initial structured community consultations; rapid data collection and analysis; assessment of present conditions and issues, leading to a broad multi-sectoral overview, concentrating on a comprehensive coverage, rather than in-depth statistical analyses; and preliminary concepts for the PEDP.

Towards the end of this period, sufficient information is gathered and synthesized to allow problems to be identified, diagnosed and prioritized. Three-and-a-half weeks are then devoted to translation of problems into action projects; completion of selected detailed surveys in response to the specific requirements of priority projects; the development of identified projects into a prioritized three to five years programme (MSIP) commencing with a reliable first year budget; and refinement of the PEDP.

This package of action projects is then assessed to determine the requirements for regulatory provisions and the practicality of such controls. Finally, the remaining two weeks are allocated for the consolidation of the total work into the plan components including: problem overview and project description; MSIP and financial management; a broad institutional framework; and the PEDP and related regulations.

Presentations: The teams then present the draft conclusion of the study to the steering committee and modify the recommendations as necessary prior to a final presentation to the municipality board.

Reporting: The teams return to Kathmandu to write the reports. These comprise two volumes: Report A—the recommended IAP; and Report B—details of the projects. The draft reports are submitted for the approval and comment of the board. Revisions are made as necessary prior to the final report being published.

Follow-up: Key members of the planning teams continue to take an interest in the IAP for a period of at least one year following the submission of the final report. They are available to assist the municipality in the interpretation and implementation of the IAP and in any revisions. Generally, follow-up teams visit the municipality at least twice a year.

Conclusions

The government of Nepal is committed towards local ennoblement, decentralized government action and institutional strengthening of the municipalities. The major problems for implementing this strategy are resource constraints and a very weak institutional base of the newly elected municipalities (two years old). Most municipalities find it difficult to implement urban projects as there is a severe lack of manpower, resources and urban awareness.

The principal outputs of the IAP are the tools for municipalities to implement decentralized government actions, and strengthen their technical competence. These outputs are the minimum required for any municipality to implement their own projects. Thus IAP is highly responsive to local needs and has a good chance of success. Moreover, as at least half of the identified projects will be executed, the IAP approach facilitates the on-going development process, thereby satisfying the needs for smooth functioning of municipal affairs. This perhaps explains why there is a growing interest and overwhelming demand for IAP amongst municipalities in Nepal.

IAP is highly recommended for municipalities in Nepal and perhaps elsewhere. It is planned to improve the methodology as a part of a programme to cover all the 36 municipalities within the next four years, after which the programme will commence again. After completing an IAP, it is believed that the municipality will have the in-house capability to manage better their own affairs, thereby replacing the current tendency for centre-driven planning and development.

BIBLIOGRAPHY

Department of Housing and Urban Development, HMG (1993), 'Nepal and Urban Development through Local Efforts (*udle*)', Gesellschaft für Technische Zusammenarbeit (GTZ) (eds.), *IAP Training Manual*, Kathmandu.
Department of Housing and Urban Development, HMG (1994a), 'Nepal and Urban Development through Local Efforts (*udle*)', Gesellschaft für Technische Zusammenarbeit (GTZ) (eds.), *IAP Operational Guidelines*, Kathmandu.
Department of Housing and Urban Development, HMG (1994b), 'Nepal and Urban Development through Local Efforts (*udle*)', Gesellschaft für Technische Zusammenarbeit (GTZ) (eds.) (1994b), *IAP Dhulikhel (Draft Report)*, Kathmandu.
Heinrichs, B. (1993), 'Urban Planning Methods in Nepal I : The first application of IAP in Nepal *Trialog* Darmstadt, 39.
Joshi, J. (1991), 'Planning Approaches to Urban Development in Nepal', *Vikas*, (Kathmandu), 2:3.
Joshi, J. and Lojewski, H.V. (1993), 'Urban Planning Methods in Nepal II : Further Experiences with the Integrated Action Planning Approach (IAP) in Nepal', *Trialog*, (Darmstadt), 39.
Peterson, G.E. *et al.* (1989), *Multisectoral Investment Planning*, Discussion paper prepared for UNCHS, Urban Management Group, September, Nairobi.
UNCHS (1989), *Integrated Action Planning : Analysis and Synthesis Report*, First Draft, May, Nairobi.

THE INTEGRATED DEVELOPMENT OF SMALL AND MEDIUM TOWNS PROGRAMME IN INDIA

K. Dharmarajan

Indians are not compulsory movers. Given a choice, most people would like to remain in the place where they grew up, be it a village or small town. But Census statistics show that over 40 million people have moved into larger settlements. Over the last 30 years, what started as a trickle shows signs of assuming a greater volume—though the distribution of urban population spatially is not as skewed as in many other countries in the South East Asian region. However there has been a significant shift towards larger towns.

In India, our commitment to promoting the growth and management of small- and medium-sized towns was formally made in December 1979 with the scheme of Integrated Development of Small and Medium Towns (IDSMT), so that these towns could serve as growth and service centres for the rural hinterland. This paper gives an overview of the IDSMT scheme (Government of India, 1977).

A Gradual Urban Transition

India is still predominantly a rural country with nearly 74 per cent of its 900 million population living in villages and two-thirds of its workforce engaged in agricultural and allied activities. However there has been a significant structural shift in the economy with the share of the primary sector in economic output declining to around one-third. The urban population has been rising gradually with:

— An annual growth rate of 3.1 per cent (in the 81–91 period);
— A doubling of population in the two decades 1971 to 1991;

— Reaching 217 million in 1991;

— Spread over 3,700 urban centres;

— Share in urban population of '100,000 plus' towns increasing from 52 per cent to 65 per cent between 1961 and 1991;

— Share of 'less than 50,000' towns declined from 37 per cent to 24 per cent in that period;

— 23 'one-million-plus' cities accounting for a third of the urban population in 1991.

Why Do People Migrate ?

What is the attraction of towns and metropolises, despite these centres bustling with people, with more congestion, pollution and lack of basic sanitation than most villages? May be the answer lies in what metropolitans seem to promise—a chance to make dreams come true. Often what drives the villager to metropolises is just a small desire to have a decent life, free of as much care as possible, with employment opportunities, a better living environment, good schooling for children, proper medical services for the family and recreation and entertainment opportunities.

It is often argued that, if basic infrastructural facilities can be provided in villages, or small and medium towns, most families may not migrate. The IDSMT scheme was formulated with this premise at its heart (Government of India, 1989). It is believed by many that the role of government is more than being a mere provider of services. It is to make life as easy and fruitful as possible for the common man. This, unfortunately, is not one of the explicit objectives of any development scheme.

What was the Original Vision behind IDSMT?

The idea behind IDSMT was to pump in more investments into urban infrastructure and essential facilities in several towns below 100,000 population. It was envisaged that by this one could:

— Reduce the rate of migration from the rural to urban areas (especially large cities);

— Provide more employment opportunities in smaller towns and thereby promote an even and balanced dispersal of population;

— Develop the town to act as counter-magnets to the metropolitan areas and subserve rural development; and

— Tackle the problem of slums on a more enduring basis (National Institute of Urban Affairs, 1990; Town and Country Planning Organization, 1990).

Evaluation of Policy for Development of Small and Medium Towns

The issues relating to balanced regional development and urban/rural planning were first raised in the *Third Five Year Plan (1961–66)*. Urbanization was discussed in the context of the industrial location policy. However little attention was paid to the dynamics of town/city development and the discussions on town planning were dominated by issues relating to housing.

In the *Fifth Plan* period (1974–79) there was a greater focus on balanced regional development and urbanization when the idea of partial dispersal of industries for balanced regional development took shape.

The Integrated Urban Development Programme (IUDP) scheme was initiated by the Government of India providing financial assistance to state governments for urban development projects. By 1978–79 the scheme had covered 31 cities and towns in 11 states with a total government outlay of Rs.136 crores. Of these, as many as 17 were big cities, out of which 9 cities received 78 per cent of the total outlay. The scheme was discontinued by the end of 1978–79.

In 1975, the Ministry of Works and Housing (subsequently called the Ministry of Urban Development) appointed a *Task Force* to assess the situation of small and medium towns and cities and suggest possible solutions to improve the quality of life in them so that they could act as a counter-magnets to the metropolises.

The Task Force, which submitted its report in 1977 noted that the small and medium towns had been neglected when in reality it was possible for them to assume an active and positive role. The report concluded that it was necessary to initiate urbanization as a process through a system of human settlements in the context of the whole country and for all activities so that each human settlement may play its own role for development, self-sustaining and yet inter-relating to other settlements.

The *Sixth Five Year Plan* (1980–85) led to the formulation of a definite policy for the development of small and medium towns. The Sixth Plan document stated that urban development should be viewed in the context of its relationship with rural development in the region. It was felt that the neglect of infrastructure provision in small, medium and intermediate cities may have restricted their role as dynamic growth centres. Hence it was proposed that increased investment on infrastructural and other essential facilities be made in such towns in the coming decade to enable them to serve as growth and service centres for the rural hinterland. This led to the intensification of the scheme of IDSMT that was launched in December 1979.

Apart from providing enhanced outlays for the IDSMT scheme the Sixth Plan envisaged that the some policy initiatives should also be pursued including:

— Tax incentives for inducing new industries and other commercial and professional establishments to locate in these towns; and

— Appropriate concessions in respect of capital expenditure on housing, schools, entertainment facilities, power, water supply, sanitation and drainage.

An Overview of the IDSMT

Selection of towns: The selection of the towns was left to the state governments. The selection was to be done keeping in mind that the towns should help in checking the migration of the rural population to larger cities and perform the role of market and service centres to the rural hinterland.

The criteria for selection of the towns were:

— Administrative base; with preference being given to the district headquarter town; the sub-divisional town; the *mandi* (i.e., temple) town; and then to other important growth centres.
— Location between large cities and rural areas.
— Potentiality to act as a service and market centre for the rural hinterland.
— Demographic growth rate.
— Potentiality for generating employment.
— Institutional capacity.

Pattern of assistance: Central assistance is given in the form of a soft loan. The details of this are given in Table 12.1.

IDSMT project components: The components prepared for implementation under an IDSMT project which would qualify for financial

Table 12.1: Project Costs

	VI Plan (1980–85)	VII Plan (1985–90)
Low-cost sanitation (LCS) component	Rs 15 lakhs	Rs.52(+8 for LCS) lakhs
Sharing	50:50 Centre : State	24 lakhs (compulsory)
Maximum assistance from Government of India (GOI)	Rs 40 lakhs (later 46)	18 lakhs (optional)
Interest rate	5.5%	9.25%

Note: 1 lakh = 100,000, 1 crore = 10 million

assistance from the central and state governments were in two parts: Part A components were to generate employment opportunities in the target towns and Part B components were to improve the physical environment of the towns.

Part A: Components eligible for central assistance on a matching basis were:

— Land acquisition and development, residential schemes which included sites and services with or without core housing;

— Traffic and transportation to serve residential and employment areas —projects could include construction of roads and improvement or upgradation of existing roads but could not include the purchase of motor vehicles;

— Development of *mandis* and markets;

— Development of industrial estates;

— Provision of other services and processing facilities for the benefit of agricultural and rural development in the hinterland; and

— Construction of municipal slaughter houses.

Part B: Components for which funds were to be found from the resources of the state governments or implementing agencies but which were to form part of the integral scheme were:

— Slum improvement and upgradation, urban renewal;

— Measures for generation of small-scale employment;

— Low-cost schemes of water supply, sewerage, drainage and sanitation;

— Preventive medical facilities/health care;

— Parks and playgrounds; and

— Assistance for the purpose of making modifications, wherever necessary, in city master plans to permit mixed land use.

Integrated development plans: Guidelines were issued to the states and union territories for the preparation of integrated development plans for small and medium towns. The methodology for the preparation of IDSMT programmes as spelt out in these guidelines is now enumerated.

— Identification of development priorities and the needs of the specific towns selected for integrated development, its functions, and the gaps and inadequacies in the existing services.
— Ensuring the conformity of the integrated development plan for the town with the general development plan of the area.
— The formulation of the integrated development plan in consultation with the urban local body.
— Costing of item-wise projects keeping in view the economic viability of the project and affordability.
— Giving preference to those projects for which land was readily available.
— Financial estimates to take into account the cost escalation of the project.

Table 12.2 outlines the organizational structure of IDSMT scheme.

Release of Central Assistance: The total release of central assistance under IDSMT amounted to Rs. 207.27 crores for 645 towns till the end of March 1994. The plan-wise break-up is given in Table 12.3.

Overall progress of the project in the Sixth Plan period: The approved programme during the Sixth Plan period amounted to Rs. 224 crores. The actual expenditure during this period was Rs.93.81 crores which was 73.8 per cent of the total central assistance plus the matching share

Table 12.2: Organizational Set-Up of IDSMT

Approval of Projects Release of GOI Assistance	Ministry of Urban Development
Processing of Project Reports Monitoring	Town and Country Planning Organization
Coordination at State Level	Housing or Urban Development Department
Implementation	Town governments and various state-level agencies

Table 12.3: Release of Central Assistance to IDSMT

Plan Period	No. of Towns	Amount (Rs. in crores)
VI Plan 1980–85	235	63.57
VII Plan 1985–90	145	80.06
Annual Plan 90–91	77	19.10
Annual Plan 91–92	60	13.44
VIIIth Plan (1991–97)		
VIIIth Plan 1992–93	44	11.60
VIIIth Plan 1993–94	84	19.50
Total	645	207.27

Note: 1 crore = 10 million

of the states. The comparative break-up between various components is given in Table 12.4.

Physical achievements to the credit of the scheme reported by the Town and Country Planning Organization (TCPO) were:

— An estimated 110 lakh mandays of employment generated.
— Residential area development scheme: Out of a proposed 2,854 ha of land, 1,649 ha were fully developed.
— Commercial area component: Out of a proposed development of 284 ha of land, 227 ha (80 per cent) were developed.
— Institutional area: Out of a proposed 3120 ha, 139 ha (45 per cent) were developed.
— Roads: Out of a proposed 361 km, 179 km (49.4 per cent) were constructed.
— Low-cost sanitation: 94,181 new units were constructed 103,544 units were converted and 5,018 public latrines were constructed.

Table 12.4: IDSMT Components

	Percentage in the	
	Approved Outlay	Actual Expenditure
Sites and services	32.6	31.4
Markets and *mandis*	30.6	35.4
Roads	15.3	18.6
Bus stands and terminals	9.2	18.8
Low-cost sanitation	7.8	18.8
Industrial areas	3.4	2.6
Slaughterhouse	1.1	1.2

A Review of IDSMT and New Guidelines

A number of evaluation studies have been carried out from time to time. Among these are those of the Town and Country Planning Organization (1985), All India Institute of Local Government (1986), Prasad et al. (1988), the Government of India (1989) and the National Institute of Urban Affairs (1990).

It is clear from these studies that while there was improvement in the physical infrastructure in many of the IDSMT towns, their impact as growth centres to prevent migration and support rural development was not adequate.

Some deficiencies in the implementation of the scheme that have been brought in these studies include:

— Inappropriate selection of towns without adequate consideration of their function in the regional context and their growth potential (sometimes selection was purely on political considerations).

— The dominant functions of the selected towns were not identified and taken note of with the result that the programme could not be tailored to the needs of the individual towns.

— Linkages between the town and the hinterland were not planned explicitly and provided for.

— In many cases there was an absence of pre-project planning modalities such as demand surveys and feasibility studies.

— Inadequate attention was given to the steps involved in the identification of schemes and location of sites.

— Non-availability of land for projects and considerable delays in land acquisition.

— Mismatch between the scale of land acquisition and the actual requirements for housing and infrastructural development.

— Absence of proposals for the development of industrial sheds and small-scale enterprises best suited to the economy and functional needs of the town to strengthen the economic base of the town.

— A lack of suitable institutional mechanism to ensure proper inter-agency coordination at the field level.

— Inadequacy of technically qualified and trained personnel at the city level and the inability of personnel at the state and central town planning agencies to provide the needed technical support.

— Inadequate attention to issues relating to urban land and a lack of planned effort to use land as a resource.

— Reluctance or inability on the part of state governments to give their matching share of funds.

— Absence of an integrated plan for the towns with more emphasis being given to remunerative components like markets, sites and services, etc., and less to basic infrastructural facilities.
— Insufficient attention to the needs of the lower income groups and slum settlements.
— Inadequacy of financial allocation under the programme resulting in the available resources being spread rather thinly.
— Inadequate feedback, evaluation and monitoring mechanisms.

Revised Guidelines

For the Eighth Plan (1992-97) the Government of India issued revised guidelines for processing of IDSMT project proposals. The main changes that were incorporated were:

1. *Urban Strategy Paper*: Each state was required to prepare an urbanization strategy paper covering a 10-year period which was to look at past urbanization trends and the future of urban growth in the state in the light of various sectoral policies and investments of the central and state governments. This paper was to bring out the growth potential and functional role of the different urban settlements in the content of the projected socio-economic development of the state.

2. *Selection of Towns*: The selection of towns and intense prioritization was to be done on a rational basis considering the importance of the town in the regional context as brought out in the urban strategy paper. (Towns up to a population of 300,000 were eligible). Preference was to be given to headquarters of districts having rural population more than 90 per cent, *mandi* (agricultural market) towns, industrial growth centres, tourist centres, pilgrim centres, etc.

3. *Financial Assistance*: The total quantum of financial assistance was stepped up substantially by increasing the central sector budgetary outlay and also by dovetailing resource from infrastructure-financing institutions like HUDCO. The sharing between the central and state government was changed from 50:50 to 60:40

Towns were categorized into the groups for the purpose of assistance under IDSMT. Table 12.5 lists this categorization.

The quantum and pattern of financing was dependent on the category of the town (see Table 12.6).

Table 12.5: Categories of IDSMT Towns

Population	Category
Less than 20,000	A
20,000 – 50,000	B
50,000 – 100,000	C
100,000 – 300,000	D

Table 12.6: IDSMT Financing Patterns

(in Rs. lakhs)

Category	Project cost (maximum)	Central assistance (loan) institution	State share	Loan from HUDCO/other financing institution
A	100	36	24	40
B	200	72	48	80
C	500	120	80	300
D	1000	180	120	700

The central assistance is in the form of a soft loan repayable in 25 years and carrying a rate of interest as decided by the Government of India from time to time. Presently the rate of interest is 12 per cent.

In addition central assistance in the form of grant is available for the preparation of the development plan/feasibility study/project reports to the extent of 2 per cent of the project costs subject to maximum of Rs. 2 lakhs.

4. *Components*: The components eligible for assistance were enlarged and made flexible. These now include:

— Strengthening of link road facilities.
— Provision of bus terminals.
— Construction/upgradation of roads and side drains.
— Development of shopping centres.
— Provision of tourist facilities.
— Localized drainage works.
— Street lighting.
— Slaughterhouses.
— Cycle/rickshaw stand.
— Development of parks and play grounds.
— Traffic management schemes and social amenities.

— Construction of retaining walls and slope stability measures in hill station towns.
— Water supply and sanitation schemes (to be financed by institutional finance or under other central sector schemes).

States are expected to adopt a "basket approach" in selecting schemes with a judicious mix between remunerative and non-remunerative schemes.

5. *Town Project Report*: A multi-sectoral integrated development plan is to be prepared based on the long-term master plan. The report had to clearly identify the infrastructural gaps keeping in mind the projected growth profile and functional activities of the town. A cost-benefit analysis was required to be made for each scheme. Besides, the report was to include an action plan for improvements in the finances and administration of the local body so that over a period of time they would become self-sufficient.

6. *Sanction Process*: The modal agency continues to be the TCPO. It is required to ensure that the project is consistent with the central guidelines, the state urban strategy paper and priority list and the master plan/development plan of the town. The technical appraisal by HUDCO is a new element. Hopefully this would introduce a greater financial/technical vigour in the examination of the project proposals. HUDCO is to advise on the suitability of technology and financial viability.

The proposals are considered by a Sanctioning Committee headed by a Additional Secretary in the Ministry of Urban Development.

A Revision in the Nineties

While formulating the Eighth Plan a review of the scheme was undertaken. The review concluded that while the scheme had succeeded in creating *some* infrastructure in these towns there were many inadequacies, including:

— Development has been compartmentalized.
— There was no discernible impact on the hinterland.
— The selection of towns was not linked to a proper urbanization strategy for the state.
— Investments were at a sub-optimal level.

Although the scheme was revamped for the Eighth Plan (1992-97), the basic objectives remained more or less unchanged. But budgetary support in this five-year period was increased from Rs.88 crores to Rs 145 crores. There were other major changes, also:

— Each state had to prepare an urban strategy paper. This would be the basis for selection of towns and their prioritization.
— Central share was increased to 60 per cent.
— Institutional finance was also to be tapped.
— Quantum and pattern of assistance was dependent on size category of the town.
— Components eligible for assistance were enlarged and made flexible.
— An integrated town development plan was to be prepared.
— An action plan was required for improvement of the town management and finances;.
— The appraisal process was made more rigorous (Town and Country Planning Organization, 1994, Government of India, 1994).

What Has Been Achieved?

In terms of numbers the achievement is impressive—645 towns covered under the programme and over Rs 200 crores released as financial assistance by the Government of India. There is no doubt that this provided funds to some resource-starved urban centres for infrastructure development. In some towns the income from the remunerative schemes implemented under IDSMT has enabled them to at least pay salaries to their staff regularly.

The IDSMT programme in India is now more than a decade old. One would have expected that by now the programme should have had some impact in accelerating the growth of the small and medium towns. But the Census figures of 1991 do not reveal any such trend. In fact, a detailed analysis of growth rates of IDSMT towns shows that to the contrary, in a majority of cases there has been a fall in the decadal growth rate compared to the previous decade.

And as far as the goal of improving the lives of people in rural areas and small towns is concerned, the programme has been a failure.

What Went Wrong?

Policy statements by government or mere plan outlays will not make things happen. Government has to be committed to the basic philosophy behind the programme which puts people first. If we are serious, every action of the government should be governed by this commitment. Otherwise many other policies or activities of government may run counter to the programme.

In the present context, in India, for example, the industrial liberalization policy and export orientation would lead to fast growth of metropolises, counter to the policy of promoting small town development. The structural readjustment will also, at least in the medium term, increase poverty. So, government should have actually come up with a safety net programme for these smaller towns and the poor. Just the reverse has happened. Allocations for urban poverty programmes have been drastically reduced.

Within the programme of the Ministry of Urban Development contradictions have developed. Under the proposed mega-city scheme nearly Rs.2,000 crores are to be invested in five metropolises. Compare this with only Rs.400 crores sought to be invested in 200 to 300 towns under the IDSMT scheme. In terms of per capita outlays government would be investing four times more in the mega-cities as compared to the IDSMT towns. If one takes into account the public investments by way of telecommunications, power, rails, roads, schools, colleges, hospitals, etc., the disparity would be far wider. In this situation how can the small towns compete with the pull of mega cities?

For the development of a town to become self-sustaining, a certain critical level of investments is needed. Investment in government programmes are often spread thinly. In the IDSMT scheme, for example, the limited resources from the budget have been spread over a large number of towns. This is more a game of numbers to make plan documents look impressive.

In the present reality where government resources are limited, and financial resources available for IDSMT will continue to be lower than what is needed, we need to be more creative. It is not as if we need extra funds to tackle these problems. There are many on-going programmes of various ministries/departments of government, both the central and state. What is needed is to take advantage of these programmes.

Many opportunities have been missed. Administrators find that it is easy to forget the woods for the trees; to forget that urban planning and development has to do with human settlements; that the focus of any plan or project has to be centred on the people who live in these urban centres. Many civil servants are caught up in day-to-day pressures and often daily routine of meetings, briefings and "starred questions" leave little time to reflect.

Development is Not Just Water, Roads and Drains

It is not sufficient to merely think of urban infrastructure in the narrow sense of having enough money to lay roads and sewerage, give electricity and make big town-planning blueprints. One has to look at the total needs of the people. Looking around one will find poverty in villages and small towns; child labour which drives adults into unemployment and families into greater poverty; Lack of schooling facilities that bolster traditional practices like not sending girls to school; or allowing a family to go through needless worries and sorrow through diseases that can so easily be prevented or cured. People migrate looking for small comforts of life and end up living in the degraded, degrading environments of urban and small town slums.

Proper planning should also mean the development of proper commercial centres. For example, Chandigarh or any of the larger cities have well-planned shopping centres. But one does not find these in smaller towns. Why?

Big hotels have business centres. But even Tirupur, a place that does a multi-billion dollar business in exports the government has not facilitated the development of a business centre. Why can't money be invested in such well-thought-out exercises that will facilitate rapid and sustained upward mobility in communities?

Most small towns do not have proper and well-equipped colleges; just as most villages do not have proper schools. And hospitals are a far cry for most small towns.

An IDSMT scheme that sees only spatial planning but does not see a role for itself in cooperating with other government departments, that does not build up capacities in urban developers to share the pie more equitably, must be termed deficient.

Infrastructure is Not Just "Urban" Infrastructure

One of the main drawbacks in the earlier IDSMT Scheme, and one that has been carried on into the current guidelines is that integration is envisaged between components that comprise "urban" infrastructure. But a town needs power, it needs a good telecommunication system, it needs good schools, colleges and hospitals.

On the other hand, however, many of these facilities or investments are not under the control of the urban development department. Therefore we need to bring in other sectors like telecommunications, public works (roads), ports, industries, education, health, agriculture, etc. We need to draw upon the resources of these sectors.

As part of the IDSMT planning exercise, discussions were initiated with the Tourism Department. What were they projecting as tourist towns? What tourist traffic was expected. The tourist town maps were compared with the IDSMT map. We found mismatches. Then started a series of dialogues, and the IDSMT benefited as it could try and take advantage of the Tourism budget. Tourism development gained as the IDSMT was to ensure a better urban environment for the tourists. A similar exercise was done with the agricultural ministry, looking at *mandis*. They could pick up the tab on the marketing yards; and rural development picked up the tab on link roads. So the IDSMT kitty had expanded. And no extra funds came from the budget.

An Alternate Approach

One would like to suggest an alternate strategy for sustainable development that makes people central to development, and where the Ministry of Urban Affairs and Employment (MOUA&E) is only a catalyst and mobilizer of the resources, ideas and abilities or strengths resident in other partners like the Government of India's various ministries, the states, municipalities, business and other interest groups.

Formulating an urban strategy: When choosing IDSMT towns, one needs to look at the development potential of each town and the functions it performs in the regional/national context. One cannot see the growth of the town in isolation. One has to look at it in the perspective of urban growth in the state and in the regional context. Hence, each state must draw up an urban strategy. For this they need to know:

— What sectors apart from the urban development sector are planning?
— What will be the impact of these developments/policies on different human settlements?
— How can different towns benefit from that development?

When the MOUA&E revised the guidelines for the scheme it required the state to apply its minds on these issues. All states completed their exercise. But most of the documents lacked even the basic information, maybe because the education and in-service training that was given to the town planners only gave them the ability to look at spatial issues.

The town chiefs also have an interest: The presidents and councillors in the elected body of the town governments have to be involved in the development process right from the beginning. There are many elected representatives who have a genuine interest and commitment towards development of a town, but they may not have the broader vision or technical skills of a professional urban planner or manager. Given proper technical support when needed, such committed political leadership would be able to perform wonders in the town.

Build capacities in planners: Urban planning needs a multi-disciplinary approach. We need to look at social, economic and financial aspects. It is clear that we need to undertake a capacity-building exercise in our town planning departments. It is perhaps premature to call for urban strategy papers before re-orienting our planners and upgrading their skills.

It is not sufficient to think narrowly in terms of just urban development departments or just in terms of annual plans and budgets. If a change is required one must first be bold enough to dream. There is no use that all planners be dreamers nor is this a hierarchical quality. There is an urgent need to develop debate and discussion within a department or organization, and to facilitate and foster a free exchange of ideas from all levels in the hierarchy.

Support initiatives in the bureaucracy: The general feeling is that bureaucrats are not committed. But take the city of Nasik, for example. The Director of the Urban Basic Services (UBS) programme is a retired civil servant, but he belongs to Nasik and is committed to making a difference to the lives of the slum-dwellers. He has with him a team of dedicated community organizers, many of them post-graduates, working on the project at low salaries. When asked what made them stay for two years, most of them said it was because of the satisfaction they derive from the job while working with the poor. Here, a committed bureaucrat has been able to systematize and operationalize the process of planning at the slum-community level and incorporate it into a city plan.

Or take the city of Alleppey, where a bureaucrat, again, has turned the Urban Basic Services for the Poor (UBSP) programme into a groundswell for women's empowerment. The fact that the National Bank for Rural Development (NABARD), that had never funded an urban programme before, gave over two crore rupees for increasing employment opportunities for women of Alleppey, or the fact that 10,000 poor women, members of a Community Development Society, were able to meet the state political leadership in a conference proves conclusively not only that one person can make a difference but that such initiatives can spread. The Alleppey model is being adopted by 58 other towns in Kerala.

And these are not isolated incidents. There are many such mavericks in government. If it is possible for such committed people to work on programmes it can make a significant difference. It must be government's responsibility to look around for such people and give them the necessary support to make things happen. And once it happens it can catch on like wildfire.

Ownership: Whenever a programme is seen as centrally sponsored, citizens and even town governments, shrug their shoulders and allow the madness planned in Delhi or state headquarters to be put through by the powers that be. For the people in a town to own the project, they must see a definite gain for themselves, either in measurable terms like a better schooling system, better entertainment opportunities, better employment, sometimes, even something that is immediately invisible, like a better environment. Only this can make people pledge their support to a programme.

It is the people that make up a town. We must know how the denizens of a small town see their hometown growing, what do they see as its strength and weakness, what do they want from the place where they live, and what are their priorities. So people have to be involved right from the planning stage. Only then will they feel that it is their programme and that they have a stake in it.

This is an aspect which unfortunately the MOUA&E does not touch upon at all in its revised guidelines. It should have clearly spelt out the need for such citizen involvement. It should also have spelt out the process of going about this.

A public debate on development issues can help to bring in different perspectives and different skills into the thinking process and may help in drawing up a better strategy plan for development that takes care of different interest groups.

After this, of course, it should be a citizens' council that puts the plan into action. Hence, the problems are also jointly addressed by them, and solutions do not become the prerogative of a handful of bureaucrats. This way also, in case a plan does not materialize or there is no follow-up action, the blame would not come to roost in government offices.

Government as a partner in development: Government funds should be used as seed money rather than as the only means of funding a scheme. Maybe the answer to proper and systematic and sustained development lies in seeing budget funds as mere catalysts for action from other and more important actors in the town — the community, the business and the private sector, other sectoral agencies.

Government has to shed the attitude of being the boss and become one of the partners, albeit a key one, in the development process of the town. There are no doubt certain skills and resources that government alone can bring into this partnership. But there are other resources that various interest groups can contribute. So the formulation of town development plan needs to involve these groups right from the initial stage so that it is seen as a partnership programme. Our endeavour should be to mobilize hitherto underutilized or untapped resources.

Mobilizing local resources: Can citizens be helped to ask how can they, individually or as a group, contribute to its development? The contribution could be by way of investments, but it can also be, say, in terms of management skills or adoption of different programmes. For example, in the city of Anand several projects under the town planning scheme have been implemented but still one sees haphazard development. Right adjoining the town is the Institute of Rural Management, Anand, as also the National Dairy Development Board (NDDB) - two centres which have very competent professionals and managers. Now it strikes me that maybe we could have encouraged these people to have got involved in the planning and management of this medium town. Now, that would have been a model for IDSMT programming.

India can proudly showcase many excellent examples of citizen interest and initiative in other development programmes. In the city of Baroda, a fired-up group of citizens is contributing to slum improvement and in keeping the town clean. Active interest has been taken by several industries in the locality who have helped in forming a voluntary organization called Baroda Citizens' Council, which is working in close partnership with the city government.

A similar experiment has been extremely successful in Madras also, the only difference being that the exnora solid waste collection scheme, which started as a small community initiative under the stewardship of a bank manager, has caught on in several neighbourhoods today.

In Anand, there is the same excitement in a major urban renewal programme that has mobilized funds for itself through land re-adjustment. Here, the leadership had come from the elected president of the municipality.

A slum project in Gillbert Hill, Bombay, shows how young students and faculty from SNDT, an academic institution, could be involved in a community development and empowerment programme.

If one is to believe what Rupert Sheldrake says about morphology (where he argues a case for the fact that when one mouse breaks a maze it creates a field making it easier for other mice to do the same thing more easily), then such isolated incidents must have created the right atmosphere for the right kind of enthusiasm and sustainable development to take place.

The main question then should be: how can we induce the people in a town or its business or its industry to take interest and pride in its development. If we can give them the feeling that their contribution can make a positive impact in the social and economic life of people in town, they may derive a great satisfaction in taking interest in the developmental activities of their town and contribute positively towards such development.

Self-propelled Towns

In the final analysis the objective of any support programme like IDSMT should be to build up the capacity of the town so that it can go ahead with development on its own. Town governments need strengthening both administratively and financially if development has to be sustained. City governments have to become self-reliant in terms of finances. Hence an institutional development plan or resources improvement plan for the town needs to be drawn up and implemented as part of the development process.

Development is a Process

Development is not merely a string of projects in which investments are made. It is the process which is important, the process of planning, the process of involving the people for whom the town matters, the process of bringing about a synergy between the various agencies and interested parties. This is a slow process and we need to give it time. We cannot expect full achievement of physical targets at the end of the annual plan. And for this orchestration to take place we need to have a conductor (leader) who has the commitment to the town. We need to select proper persons to work on the team. Skills needs to be endowed on them.

Having done this, they need to be on the job long enough for them to perform and make the dreams of the town and its people come true.

BIBLIOGRAPHY

Government of India (1977), *Report of the Task Force on Planning and Development of Small and Medium Towns and Cities*, Ministry of Works and Housing, February, New Delhi.

Government of India (1989), *Report of the Comptroller and Auditor General of India*, Report No. 12 of 1989, CAT, New Delhi.

Government of India (1994), *Draft Revised Guidelines - IDSMT*, Ministry of Urban Development, July, New Delhi.

National Institute of Urban Affairs (1990), *Integrated Development of Small and Medium Towns (IDSMT) - An Evaluation Study*, National Institute of Urban Affairs, January, New Delhi.

Prasad, D.R. et al. (1988): *Integrated Development of Small and Medium Towns in Karnataka and Tamil Nadu - An Evaluation*, Regional Centre for Urban and Environmental Studies (RCUES), Osmania University, Hyderabad.

Town and Country Planning Organization, Ministry of Urban Development (1990), *Indian Programme on the Management of Urban Development*, January, New Delhi.

Town and Country Planning Organization, Ministry of Urban Development (1994), *IDSMT: At a Glance*, New Delhi.

THE INTEGRATED DEVELOPMENT OF SMALL AND MEDIUM TOWNS IN THE PUNJAB

Gopal Krishan

With a serious concern for stagnation of small and medium towns, concurrent with an explosive growth of big cities, the Government of India launched the Integrated Development of Small and Medium Towns (IDSMT) programme in 1979. Subsequently the programme was incorporated in the body structure of the Sixth Plan (1980–85). This was a sequel to the earlier Integrated Urban Development (IUD) programme which covered 31 cities and towns under the Fifth Five Year Plan (1974–79).

The overall assessment was that it were the small and medium towns rather than the cities which called for special attention. An improvement in their living conditions, job potential and rural linkages was expected to check migration to cities. It was envisaged that the strengthening of infrastructure in small and medium towns would generate additional employment at local level, thereby allowing them to act as growth centres for their surrounding countryside and as mini-counter-magnets in respect of migration to big cities. A more dispersed pattern of urbanization was visualized in the process (National Institute of Urban Affairs, 1990).

The Census of India defines a small town as the one having a population of 20,000 and a medium town as having a population between 20,000 and 100,000. The IDSMT guidelines, however, recommend that normally a town smaller than 20,000 should not covered for being more rural in character and the population range for medium towns be taken up to 300,000.

In practice, four population categories of towns are distinguished for the purpose of the programme: (i) less than 20,000; (ii) 20,000 to 50,000; (iii) 50,000 to 100,000; and (iv) 100,000 to 300,000. This is done for determining the quantum and pattern of financing the programme. The stipulations are that the maximum project cost could be Rs.1 crore

(10 million) in the case of A category, Rs. 2 crores in B category, Rs.5 crores in C category, and Rs.10 crores in D category towns. The Housing and Urban Development Corporation (HUDCO) and other financial institutions would give loans to the extent of 40 per cent of the project cost to A category, 40 per cent to B category, 60 per cent to C category, and 70 per cent to D category towns.

The programme covered 235 small and medium towns under the Sixth Five Year Plan (1980–85). Another 145 towns were added during the Seventh Five Year Plan (1985–90). During the Annual Plans (1990–92), 147 additional towns were brought under the programme. Most of them were the potential Generators of Economic Momentum (GEM) towns, as identified by the National Commission on Urbanization (Government of India, 1988, p.44).

Till 31 March 1994, a total of 645 towns in various states and union territories had been incorporated (Government of India, 1994, p.1). The programme is continuing in the Eighth Five Year Plan (1990–97). Now the thrust is upon infrastructure in which loaning from HUDCO is to play a crucial role.

Here we are led to frame some questions:

1. What are the basic parameters of the IDSMT Programme?
2. To what extent did the programme lead to the development of integrated urban infrastructure?
3. What has been the experience of the Punjab in this regard?

This paper addresses itself to these posers. A brief note on the Punjab will be in order here before taking up the discussion on these points.

The State of Punjab

Located in the northwestern part of India, Punjab is one of the relatively smaller states of India. It covers an area of 50,360 km. As per the 1991 Census, it has a population of 20 million. The state ranks first in per capita income in the country. Geographically the Punjab is mainly a flat, featureless plain. As much as 90 per cent of it lies at an elevation of 300 m in the northeast to 180 m in the southwest. The Sivalik hills, 300 to 1000 m, make a distinct appearance all along its northeastern border. Sand dunes are sporadically distributed in the southwest. The Ravi, the Beas and the Satluj are the perennial streams. Their waters are critical to agriculture in the Punjab. The Bhakra-Nangal project for irrigation and power on the Satluj transformed the economy not only of this state but also of the adjoining ones. The Rajasthan canal, one of the longest in the world, has been taken out from the Beas-Satluj confluence at Harike. Cultivated area accounts for 85 per cent of the total. Due to the continental semi-arid to sub-humid climate, irrigation is indispensable for good agriculture. Almost 90 per cent of the cultivated area is irrigated, the highest percentage for any Indian state. Wheat is the king crop sharing 40 per cent of the cropped area. Rice accounts for 25 per cent. Cotton is grown over 10 per cent of the cropped area. Vegetables, mainly potato and onion, occupy 5 per cent.

The Punjab is distinguished for its glorious Green Revolution. Agriculture is highly commercialized and relatively more prosperous. The state makes the largest contribution to the national pool of wheat and rice procured for the public distribution system. Most of the industry in the state is agro-based, processing agricultural raw materials, or agro-oriented, producing agricultural inputs, or agro-income beneficiary, responding to a lucrative rural market. Food products, textiles, sugar, fertilizers, agricultural implements, re-rolled steel, machine tools, sports goods, furniture, transport vehicles, and electronics find a high place in the inventory of industrial products. Most of the important industrial centres are located on the Amritsar-Delhi railway line. Ludhiana is the biggest industrial concentration, followed by Amritsar and Jalandhar. Mohali near Chandigarh is coming up as an important electronics city of India. The state is heading toward a sound agro-industrial economy. Rural-urban linkages are strong. Practically every village is connected with a metalled road and is electrified. Several central villages have acquired urban functions including agricultural market site, health centre and degree college. Towns and cities are closely spaced and rural-urban commuting is noted for high frequency. Almost 30 per cent of the total population is urban. It is distributed amongst 120 towns/urban agglomerations. Ten among these are cities with a population of 100,000 each; 43 have a population of 20,000 to 50,000; and 67 of less than 20,000. Population of three cities, Ludhiana (1,042,740), Amritsar (708,835) and Jalandhar (509,510) exceeds 300,000. It signifies that all but three urban places in the Punjab are eligible for being covered under the programme.

The IDSMT Programme

In the spirit of its nomenclature, the programme envisioned three kinds of integration:

1. Administrative, seeking a collaborative effort on the part of the central, state and local governments;

2. Functional, linking different components of the programme with the town's existing infrastructure, especially by way of filling the gaps; and

3. Territorial, promoting linkages between the towns and its rural surroundings.

Preference was given to the district and sub-divisional headquarters as also to the *mandi* (market) centres in adoption of towns. The most critical consideration was their growth potential. Another crucial point to be kept in view was the capacity of the local body to implement the programme effectively. The 1971 Census data was to be used for identifying the small and medium towns (Government of India, 1979, p.1).

The programme had two project components:

1. Those eligible for the assistance from the centre on a matching basis;

2. Those for which funds were to be found from the state plans. The former included land acquisition and development, traffic and transportation, development of market sites, industrial estates, service and processing facilities for the rural hinterland, and construction of abattoirs. The latter covered slum improvement, low-cost schemes of water supply, sewerage, drainage and sanitation, preventive medical facilities, playgrounds and land-use plans. Under fresh guidelines, transport, tourist and other infrastructure facilities are to be accorded higher priority than land development. It was noted that generally the state sector components, such as slum improvement, water supply and sewerage, and preventive medical facilities were not taken up. Pre-project modalities, such as the demand surveys and feasibility studies, were not carried out. The necessary coordination between the participating agencies was found wanting. Above all, the selection of many towns did not conform to the criteria laid down.

The Government of India (1994, p.1) had a somewhat different assessment. It opined that the IDSMT programme did serve its objective and was successful in creating sufficient infrastructure in small and medium towns. A continuation of the programme, with necessary modifications, was favoured under the Eighth Plan. A prior land acquisition has been recommended as a condition for selection of an IDSMT town. Flexibility in identification of projects in the light of local needs and feasibility considerations was also granted.

The Case Study

What is the Punjab story? Which are the basic tasks involved in the development of its small and medium towns? To what extent is the programme relevant to the state? Did it address the right kind of issues? We now attempt to answer these questions.

Notably Punjab had pre-empted the programme. The state's development strategy had already imbibed its spirit and purpose. The New Mandi Township Development and Regulation Act (1960) was legislated to provide developed sites for marketing agricultural produce as also for residential and other purposes. Now there are 144 places with a regulated agricultural marketing site each: 95 urban and 49 rural.

The process got a further boost from the Crash Programme for Construction of Rural Link Roads initiated in 1968. Every village in the state was connected with a metalled road. Later in 1977, the 'Focal Point' Programme was undertaken to provide a package of agro-services at central villages.

This thrust on agricultural development provided a stimulus to a sustained growth of small and medium towns by way of promoting trade, general services and agro-based industrial activities. Urban-rural interaction become distinctly strong and the urban-rural gap narrowed visibly (Krishan, 1991; and Gosal and Krishan, 1984). The average assets per household in rural areas were recorded as nearly two times of those in urban places: Rs. 96,631 and Rs. 54,822 respectively (Reserve Bank of India, 1986, p. 439). The percentage of people living below the poverty line in rural areas is half of that in urban areas, being 11 and 21 per cent respectively (National Institute of Urban Affairs, 1990, p. 65).

Urban-rural integration manifests in several ways: disposal of the produce at the regulated agricultural market; purchase of daily use items; repair of agricultural machinery, electricals and electronics; and commuting for work, education and medical aid. Work opportunities for the rural job seekers are mainly as labourers in the regulated agricultural market as also at the construction and brick-kiln sites; as semi-skilled mechanics at the repair shops; and as employees in government institutions, including offices, schools and hospitals.

Rural-urban transfer of population is also picking up. This is more popular among those who are in a regular job at urban places. Ex-servicemen, with rural background, normally prefer to settle in a town after retirement. All such persons maintain a regular link with their native villages. As a result, a class of people is emerging whose economic interests are partly rural and partly urban.

Small and medium towns are also expanding physically. Transformation of their morphology has become necessary for meeting the space demand of new land uses, especially for relocation of facility points to new sites and for coping up with the fast increasing use of motor vehicles. The response is visible in the emergence of new residential colonies, re-siting of old grain markets and bus-stands, and construction of bypasses to divert the inter-town traffic. Much of this development is haphazard. There is frequent encroachment on public land by not only slum-dwellers but also influential citizenry. Corridor development along the roads connecting the big cities, such as Ludhiana, Amritsar and Jalandhar, is most conspicuous. Linear physical growth of small and medium towns is a part of this process. This is posing problems in respect of provision of urban services and movement of traffic. Level railway crossings are common to several small and medium towns. This aggravates the traffic problem. Places like Rajpura, Dhuri and Kot Kapura illustrate the point. Above all, the level of services in small and medium towns does not match with their functional dynamism. This refers particularly to sanitation, drainage and road maintenance. Electricity shutdowns and breakdowns are not uncommon. Supply of some items in the chain of public distribution system, such as cooking gas, kerosene and petrol/diesel, requires to be streamlined on assured lines. It follows that small and medium towns in the Punjab are strong on their economic base and in respect of their links with the surrounding countryside but are relatively weak on their infrastructural base and land-use planning.

The IDSMT Programme in the Punjab

As a successor to the IUD programme under which Punjab's three cities of Ludhiana, Amritsar and Jalandhar were covered during the Fifth Plan, the IDSMT Programme in the Sixth Plan embraced eight small and medium towns of Bhatinda, Pathankot, Hoshiarpur, Moga, Batala, Phagwara, Khanna and Sangrur (Table 13.1). During the Seventh Plan, seven additional towns of Patiala, Barnala, Kapurthala, Gurdaspur, Nabha, Gobindgarh and Ropar joined the list. The Annual Plans period saw the inclusion of Firozpur. The programme has been extended to Malerkotla, Rajpura and Faridkot under the Eighth Plan. The beneficiary towns now total up to 19. In other words, one in every six among the small and medium towns in the state is now covered under the programme.

The selection of towns has been in conformity with the guidelines. As stipulated, district and sub-divisional headquarters as also the dynamic market centres received the priority. A profile of 19 towns shows that nine of these are district headquarters, eight sub-divisional headquarters, and two towns without any administrative status (Table 13.2).

All towns, with the solitary exception of Patiala, had a population of less than 100,000 in 1971 (Table 13.1). In 1991, six of these had a city status (population 100,000+ above). As many as 12 towns are located in the Malwa, three in the Bist Doab and four in the Majha region of Punjab (Table 13.2). The regional distribution of the towns tilts slightly

Table 13.1: Towns covered under the IDSMT Programme up to September 1994 in the Punjab

Towns	Population			Growth rate (in percentage) during	
	1971	1981	1991	1971–81	1981–91
Sixth Plan (1980–85)					
1. Bathinda	65,318	127,363	159,042	95.0	24.9
2. Pathankot	78,192	110,039	128,198	40.7	16.5
3. Hoshiarpur	57,691	85,648	122,705	48.5	43.3
4. Moga	61,625	80,272	110,958	30.3	38.3
5. Batala	76,488	101,966	103,367	33.3	1.4
6. Phagwara	55,012	75,981	88,316	38.1	16.3
7. Khanna	34,820	53,761	71,990	54.4	33.9
8. Sangrur	,105	45,220	56,419	32.9	24.8
Seventh Plan (1985–90)					
9. Patiala	151,041	206,254	253,706	36.6	23.0
10. Barnala	31,847	43,680	75,430	37.2	72.7
11. Kapurthala	35,482	50,300	64,567	41.8	28.4
12. Gurdaspur	32,064	39,529	54,733	23.3	38.5
13. Nabha	34,761	45,921	54,421	32.1	18.5
14. Gobindgarh	9,387	26,637	42,063	183.8	57.9
15. Ropar	16,454	25,165	37,996	52.9	51.0
Annual Plans (1990–92)					
16. Firozpur	51,090	61,162	78,738	9.0	28.7
Eighth Plan (1992–97)					
17. Malerkotla	48,859	65,756	88,600	34.6	34.7
18. Rajpura	14,840	58,645	70,983	45.8	21.0
19. Faridkot	27,725	42,423	58,625	53.0	38.2

Source: Census of India, Punjab , 1981 and 1991, and Town and Country Planning Department, Punjab

Table 13.2: Profile of the Towns covered under the IDSMT Programme in the Punjab

Population size 100,000+ to 100,00	50,000 to 50,000	20,000 20,000	Less than	Total
1991 6	11	2	-	19
1971 1	7	9	2	19

Administrative Status	District headquarters	Subdivisional headquarters	Others	Total

Regional distribution	Majha	Doaba	Malwa	Total
Number	3	4	12	19
Percentage in IDSMT Programme towns	15.8	21.0	63.2	100
Percentage in the state's small and medium towns (up to 300,000 population)	17.9	21.4	60.7	100

Note: Number of towns = 19.

in favour of the Malwa. In a way, this corrects an imbalance wherein urban development in this part of the state has been of a lower order.

Judged by the criterion of utilization rate of funds released by the central and state governments, and contribution made by the local bodies, the programme could be rated as a success in the Punjab. Contrary to the experience in some other states, the Punjab government showed a great earnestness by way of releasing their share of funds in full. Most impressive was the sizable mobilization of resources at the local level (Singh, 1989, p.9).

In terms of its components, the programme remained largely confined to land development, road construction and low-cost sanitation. This pattern was common to virtually all towns. Here one could infer that no special effort was made to identify the specific needs of different places.

What was the outcome of projects undertaken under this programme? The success was of lower order than expected and was feasible. The programme should have accelerated the growth rate of beneficiary towns. This did not happen in most cases. Among the 19 concerned towns only four—Moga, Barnala, Gurdaspur and Firozpur—were noted for a higher growth rate during 1981-91 as compared to that during 1971–81. All others slowed down in their growth (Table 13.1).

Why did the programme meet with only a partial success? Discussions with the concerned functionaries revealed that it suffered from at least four major constraints. These were:

1. The job of implementing the programme was entrusted to the Director, Local Government, a bureaucrat, rather than to the Chief Town Planner, a technocrat. Planners did the actual work on behalf of the Director but this was a situation of responsibility without power to deal effectively with the personnel at the local level. Things would have worked much better if the job was assigned directly to the technocrats.

2. Some agencies, such as the Agricultural Marketing Board, with enormous funds at their disposal, did not participate in the programme. Perhaps the existing rules stood in the way. Such bodies, though located mostly in the town precincts, are meant to serve the countryside exclusively. Necessary modifications of rules would have helped.

3. Projects under the programme could not be dovetailed fully to capital works undertaken by other state departments, such as education, health and transport. For example, in some residential colonies developed under the programme, the sites left for the schools and health centres were not taken up promptly by other concerned departments. Nor were such colonies given the necessary local bus service on a priority basis.

4. Above all, Punjab does not have an integrating agency, such as some urban authority, to carry out jobs of this nature. A special institutional arrangement is a pre-requisite for any programme seeking integration. This was not provided for in Punjab.

Concluding Remarks

The IDSMT programme had a limited role to play in Punjab. Its relevance for promoting urban-rural linkages or for stimulating the growth of small and medium towns was pre-empted. The most crucial task left for it was to upgrade the level and quality of urban services.Quality of life in Punjab towns must reflect the material prosperity the state has achieved.

Integration envisaged under the programme proved difficult to achieve. Institutional integration was lacking because Punjab did not have any integrative agency, such as an urban development authority, to coordinate the diverse activities under the programme. Functional integration was missing because the schemes under the programme did not get satisfactory support from other sister departments. Territorial integration was not additionally strengthened because hardly any conscious effort was made to build infrastructure that catered directly to the needs of the countryside.

Indeed the programme's twin objectives of strengthening the urban-rural linkages and checking migration to cities are not easy to reconcile with each other. The first objective calls for preference to towns located in backward areas for coverage while the second objective is best served if these towns are adopted among those which are located close to cities, particularly along the urban corridors. The choice is obviously difficult.

BIBLIOGRAPHY

Gosal, G.S. and Krishan, G. (1984), *Regional Disparities in the Levels of Socio-Economic Development in Punjab*, Vishal, Kurukshetra.

Government of India (1979), *Guidelines for the Centrally Sponsored Scheme for Integrated Development of Small and Medium Towns*, Ministry of Works and Housing, New Delhi.

Government of India (1988), *National Commission of Urbanization—Main Report*, Ministry of Urban Development, New Delhi.

Government of India (1991), Census of India 1991, Ministry of Home Affairs, New Delhi.

Government of India (1994), *Integrated Development of Small and Medium Towns: Revised Guidelines*, Ministry of Urban Development, New Delhi.

Krishan, G. (1991), 'Urban-rural relations in India: A critique', *Indian Association of Social Sciences Institutions Quarterly*, 10: 1, 92–104.

National Institute of Urban Affairs (1988), *State of India's Urbanization*, NIUA, New Delhi.

National Institute of Urban Affairs (1990), *Integrated Development of Small and Medium Towns: An Evaluation Study*, NIUA, New Delhi.

Reserve Bank of India (1986), *Bulletin*, June, New Delhi.

Singh, G. (1989), *Integrated Development of Cities and Towns in Punjab*, Department of Towns and Country Planning, Chandigarh.

14

THE MUNICIPAL URBAN DEVELOPMENT FUND OF TAMIL NADU: OPERATIONS AND EXPERIENCES

R. Sundararajan and K. Mukundan

Background

Tamil Nadu is one of the most urbanized states in India, with a level of urbanization of 34.25 per cent as against a national average of 26.13 per cent. The total population of Tamil Nadu as per 1991 Census is 558.58 lakhs, (one lakh = 100,000) and the rate of decadal growth of total and urban population has been 15.39 per cent and 19.59 per cent respectively. The growth of economic activity has a direct bearing on the levels of urbanization and efforts at reorganizing production facilities have not yielded much results. This has led to a thought that the most important actions need to strengthen institutions to support and manage the economy, and improve the quality of living in urban areas. Considering the need to improve institutions and civic services, the Government of Tamil Nadu (GTN) implemented one of the first integrated urban development projects, for one of the largest cities, Madras, in 1976. This project focussed on providing access for the poor to shelter, economic activity, transport as well as strengthening other basic services. This was followed by a second urban development project for Madras. The success of implementing the projects in Madras, and the thrust of the state's development policy towards secondary centres as well as medium towns in terms of industrial investments, prompted GTN to reorient its policies of urban service investment to these centres. This formed the basis for the Tamil Nadu Urban Development Project (TNUDP). This project is a multi-sectoral project with participation from all agencies related to urban development including the highways. A major feature of this project is the creation of a Municipal Urban Development Fund (MUDF), a window to facilitate local bodies to access funds for investments in core services. The outlay for TNUDP is Rs.6,326 lakhs and the allocation for MUDF is Rs.1,672 lakhs. This constitutes 26.43 per cent of the project outlay. It needs mention that most other sectoral investments are complementary to municipal investments in project areas.

The Municipal Urban Development Fund

The Fund was established in 1988 to finance equipment and civil works for the maintenance and delivery of services and remunerative enterprises such as bus terminals and markets, primarily in 60 municipalities in the 10 largest urban agglomerations. Demands on the fund are mainly for roads, street lighting, storm-water drains, conservancy and remunerative enterprises. The size of the fund is Rs.1,672 lakhs, and at the time of formulation, the fund was conceived to be self-sustaining by generating cash surplus for its lending programmes:

— The spread between its average borrowing rate on grants and loans from GTN and its average lending rate to municipalities is 2 per cent. Currently on-lending rates to local bodies are at 14 per cent, repayable in 10 to 15 years depending on the type of project.

— Projects are financed as a loan/grant mix varying from 100 per cent loan up to 25 per cent loan and the mix is dependent on the resource base, resource-generation effort and service needs of each municipality. Of the fund, 67 per cent and 33 per cent are expected to be issued as loan and grant respectively which the fund would receive a loan-grant mix of 60:40 from GTN.

— The sources to the fund bears a moratorium of five years for the loan portion from GTN, and the on-lending to municipalities has no moratorium except a gestation period of one year from the date of drawal.

The initial size of the fund was based on input studies conducted on assessment of fiscal capabilities, levels of services and institutional systems. These were carried out for Madras, four secondary centres and 10 small and medium towns. The major outcome of the study revealed a wide gap in services, limited revenue surpluses for capital investments and a very high investment need to fill the gaps. It became apparent that most local bodies did not posses the capabilities to make investments on a 100 per cent loan basis in order to provide acceptable levels of services. This prompted the World Bank, the Madras Metropolitan Development Authority (MMDA), the nodal agency and the consultants to generate a plan using a computer-simulated module to identify the quantum of investment the local entities could sustain under alternate assumptions of acceptable service requirements and loan-grant mix. The outcome of this was the preparation of Financial and Operating Plans (FOPs) (Kumar, Mukundan and Vaidya, 1988). These are medium-term plans which indicate the maximum possible investment under a resources-generation scenario or *vice versa*. The Operating Plan prepared under various financing options for Madras Corporation, four secondary centres and the outer municipalities formed the basis of the fund size, and the FOP became the base document to assess the capability as well as to decide on financing options.

Operating Principles

The basic lending principle of the fund is to support local bodies with the capability to sustain investments in terms of ability to service the debt as well as maintain assets created. The fund is operated within a framework of rules and procedures imposing strict financial discipline which require municipalities to set acceptable revenue performance targets, select service standards and technologies consistent with their priority needs and financial resources, and to substantiate requests for project funding with adequate feasibility studies. To access the MUDF, the local body will have to indicate to the Director of Municipal Administration, who in turn forwards the request to the Project Management Group (PMG). PMG in turn nominates a consultant to assist the local body in preparation of feasibility reports (Figure 14.1). The feasibility studies conducted with support from consultants are funded as a grant by MUDF. The scale of projects that a local body could apply for funding assistance for capital projects is in the range of Rs. 5 lakhs to 1,000 lakhs but without restriction as to the type of project. Financial assistance to local bodies normally has greater emphasis on service projects particularly from those municipalities coming back to the fund for the second time. It is contrary to the principles of the fund for the Fund Committee to impose quotas or limits on borrowing capabilities of particular municipalities or groups. But the proposal should be accompanied by a FOP. This FOP as a medium-term multi-sectoral investment plan outlines:

— The performance of a local body on the current and revenue account for five past years.
— The likely revenues given alternative assumptions of revenue collection performances and revisions in base or basis of levy of taxes, charges and rates.

— Expenses for current levels of services and debt-servicing commitments.

— Proposed investments in various services sectors, under alternate technology and population coverage options for a horizon of five to seven years.

— Annual burden due to new investments in terms of debt-servicing, and operation and maintenance.

The generation of a FOP is an iterative exercise and this computer-based tool offers enough flexibility to alter any variable affecting municipal budgets (Kumar, Mukundan and Vaidya, 1988). This Operating Plan, apart from being the basis for assessing the municipal capability, is also used to decide on the loan-grant mix. The principle in assessing the mix is as follows.

The starting point for access to MUDF is 100 per cent loan basis and the only exception for grant will be a good case made on the basis of poverty. When PMG presents briefing material to the Fund Committee for a municipal application for access to funds, it needs to be satisfied on the above issues. These can be formalized as a set of questions in a decision-tree, for example:

— With a 100 per cent loan, is the municipality going to have a surplus? If yes, advise only 100 per cent loan.

— If the answer to this question is "no", then have all steps been taken to raise revenues? (Inspection is made of Annual Rateable Value (ARVs), property tax rates, revisions and their effects and collections performance).

— Also, have all steps been taken to reduce service delivery costs and to achieve efficient solutions? If "no" to either question, then rework the FOP.

— If the answer to question 3 is "yes" advise the Fund Committee that only a 100 per cent loan is in order, but for the reduced size of the programme of projects.

Fund Organization and Management

The Project Management Group (PMG) is responsible for the day-to-day management of fund policy. The Commissioner or Director of Municipal Administration disburses the funds, receives payments of interest and principal from municipalities and is responsible and accountable for all other transactions. The project report prepared by the consultant and the local body after being vetted by the Regional Director of Municipal

Administration is forwarded to the City Management Committee (CMC) headed by the District Collector, who also heads the Tender Committee. On approval by CMC, the project report is forwarded to PMG for consideration, which in turns is placed before the Empowered Committee for sanction (see Figure 14.1).

Performance

As of date MUDF has been in a position to cater to the needs of 75 of the 114 local bodies in the state. Till today PMG has prepared operating plans for 87 local bodies, but 12 were not provided with funds due to their inability to sustain investment even at a higher grant level. The disbursements as on February 1995 was Rs.10,795.11 lakhs of which the extent of grant is Rs.927.92 lakhs (8.60 per cent). The target achieved against disbursements was 69 per cent, and the funds have been released for 545 schemes spread over 75 urban local entities. Of the total works 239 have been completed and 117 are in progress. Most other schemes are in the design and estimation stage.

In terms of mix of schemes the funding for service schemes is 81 per cent, 18 per cent for remunerative schemes and approximately 1 per cent towards equipment. The thrust in service investments has been towards roads, drains, lighting and solid waste management, especially for purchase of vehicles.

Institutional and Management Experience

The first and foremost contribution of MUDF has been in institutional reform. It has been in a position to introduce fiscal discipline among local bodies, awareness of multi-year and multi-sectoral investment planning, and in utilizing the Financial and Operating Plan (FOP) as a management tool. Given its approach of capability-based lending and performance-based subsidy, the MUDF has been able to bring about this change in attitude of municipal managers. This has been partly due to the fact that the MUDF was ready to offer recurring assistance despite the risks involved in financing municipalities, the on-line process of educating borrowers on the utility of FOP, and many a time its function as an advisor to local bodies directly from the apex body (PMG) and through local coordinating arms of PMG, the City Management Committee. Another feature of MUDF is that despite a mandate to recover dues from other transfers from the state to the local body MUDF has not used this channel to recover its dues, and has been in a position to maintain

Figure 14.1: MUDF - Flow Chart Showing Fund Flow

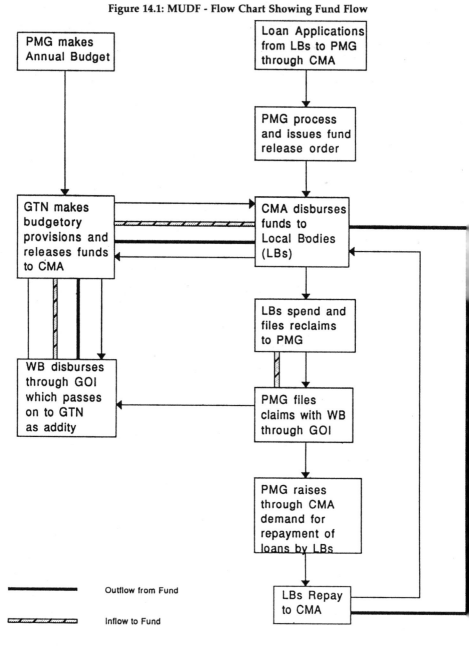

over 85 per cent collection levels. The default has been generally due to the inability of local bodies to raise revenues as anticipated in the preliminary analysis of the operating plan.

Effectiveness of FOP

The Operating Plan as such is based on tested assumptions and also based on the historical performance of the local body. Generally the variation between forecasts and actual is within the range of 10 per cent. (Tables 14.1 to 14.6). The variations at the smaller local body level have been moderate, as in most cases the actual revenues have been higher than the forecasts and expenditures have been within the estimated limits. The only major deviation is that the local bodies have been 5 to 10 per cent short in property tax collection performance. This analysis is

Table 14.1: TNUDP Cost Estimates

(Rs. in lakhs)

Component	Costs	Per cent
Sites and Services (LAND)	24,640	38.90
Guided Urban Development (GUD)	350	2.13
Slum Improvement Programme (SIP)	4,640	7.30
Traffic Management and Transport (TRAMP)	10,030	15.85
Bus - Pallavan Transport Corporation (PTC)	5,880	9.29
Municipal Urban Development Fund (MUDF)	16,720	26.43
Technical Assistance	1,370	0.10
Total Cost	63,260	100.00

Source: Project Management Group (PMG) (1992–94).

Table 14.2: Disbursements from the Fund

(Rs. in lakhs)

Year	Target	Achievement	Per cent
1989–90	1000	248	24.80
1990–91	2000	1365	69.49
1991–92	2500	2199	87.96
1992–93	3000	2186	72.86
1993–94	4000	3124	78.10
1994–95	3044	1670	54.80
Upto Feb.95*	14000	12553	89.50

Note: The disbursements by the Commissioner of Municipal Administration till February 1995 were Rs. 10,795 lakhs.

Source: Project Management Group, 1995.

Table 14.3: Disbursements by Sector

Sector	Release (Rs. in lakhs)	Distribution (in per cent)	Distribution within sector (in per cent)
Service Schemes			
Solid waste management	1,288.35	9.28	11.43
Storm-water drainage	1,519.81	10.94	13.48
Roads	5,320.25	38.31	47.19
Burial grounds	226.74	1.63	2.01
Pay and use toilets	93.46	0.67	0.83
Bus stand	676.32	4.87	6.00
Street lighting	1,707.02	12.29	15.14
Maternity homes	5.00	0.04	0.04
Water supply	409.92	2.95	3.64
Play grounds	27.35	0.20	0.24
Sub-total Services	**11274.22**	**81.19**	**100.00**
Remunerative Schemes			
Truck terminal	146.75	1.06	5.90
Shops	1,039.47	7.49	41.77
Markets	441.36	3.18	17.74
Office complex	299.20	2.15	12.02
Marriage halls	196.51	1.42	7.90
Cattle shanty	43.05	0.31	1.73
Commercial complexes	322.16	2.32	12.95
Sub-total Remunerative	**2,488.50**	**17.92**	**100.00**
Equipments			
Road rollers	25.58	0.18	20.62
Computers	29.00	0.21	23.37
Others	69.49	0.50	56.01
Sub-total equipment's	124.07	0.89	100.00
Total	13,886.79	100.00	

Source : Project Management Group, unpublished data, 1995.

Table 14.4: Recovery of Debts

	(Rs. in lakhs)
Demand	2133.40
Collection	1833.45
Balance	299.95
Collection Percentage(%)	85.94

Note: As February 1995.
Source: Project Management Group, 1995.

Table 14.5: Madras Corporation Forecasts versus Actuals

(Rs. in lakhs)

	Forecast		Actuals		Deviation	
	1992–93	1993–94	1992–93	1993–94	1992–93	1993–94
Income	11462.9	16232.5	12499.0	17899.2	−2123.9	1666.7
Expenditure	8647.5	9380.5	8338.0	9521.4	−309.5	140.90

Table 14.6: Forecast versus Actual—Smaller Municipalities

(Rs. in lakhs)

	Forecast		Actuals		Deviation	
	1990–91	1991–92	1990–91	1991–92	1990–91	1991–92
Erode						
Revenue	387.18	429.31	457.49	485.90	70.31	56.59
Expenditure	355.45	390.99	307.92	354.29	−47.53	−36.70
Status	31.73	38.32	149.57	131.61	117.84	93.29
Current collection of property tax %	85	85	73	71	−12	−14
Tiruppur						
Revenue	422.81	465.050	479.50 ·	585.22	56.69	120.17
Expenditure	338.53	373.39	397.86	443.18	59.33	69.79
Status	84.28	91.66	81.64	142.04	−2.64	50.38
Current collection of property tax %	85	85	62	73	−23	−13
Sivakasi						
Revenue	132.33	157.70	107.7	116.16	−24.63	−41.54
Expenditure	95.76	108.44	78.71	83.32	−17.05	−25.12
Status	36.57	49.26	28.99	32.84	−7.58	−16.42
Current collection of property tax %	95	95	92.5	83.4	−2.5	−11.6

Source: Local Accounts Status and Expenditure Excluding Debt.

carried out whenever a local body comes to the fund for the subsequent round. The variations in the case of Madras Corporation was to the extent of 10 per cent as regards to revenues in 1992–93 and 1993-94, whereas the variation as regard to expenditure was within 5 per cent. The major reason for a slightly higher variation in 1992–93 was due to a focus on collection of arrears towards property tax. This in turn affected the reassessment of properties, which was completed in 1993–94 and effected in 1994–95. Similarly, in the year 1992–93, the actual transfers of surcharge on sales tax was Rs.3,900 lakhs as against an anticipated transfer of Rs.6,000 lakhs. The lower variation in 1993–94 as compared to 1992–93 is due to compensation of additional transfer of surcharge. As per the FOP of 1994–95, the Corporation proposed to increase its revenue from property tax alone by Rs. 2,789 lakhs in 1993–94 to Rs. 5,100 lakhs.

Krishangiri Municipality in the first instance refused to access MUDF unless an element of grant was offered. During a review it was indicated that the local body was collecting only 40 per cent of the demand from property tax, and the Fund assured grant if it was able to improve its collection to over 75 per cent. The Commissioner worked on his collection machinery, reworked his FOP and came back to PMG, stating that he had adequate surplus and therefore did not need any grant.

Madras Corporation had been insisting on a similar subsidy which was turned down on the grounds that Madras has not tapped its potential in terms of raising its resources by objective assessments as well as in tax collection performance. This impact of better performance and revisions were demonstrated using the FOP. Subsequently, the Corporation through marginal adjustments to the assessments and increasing collections was in a position to raise its revenue from property tax by Rs.1,000 lakhs in the year 1993–94. But after a reformulation of the FOP, especially on the effect of revision in 1994–95, it was explicit that it would be left with enough surplus. The Corporation, assuming additional revenues, repaid part of an earlier loan taken from MUDF.

Madras, apart from using this tool to take financial decisions, has also been using this as a document supporting the budget. This is due to the fact that the FOP document details all assumptions used for financial forecast as well as the physical parameters of projects. The role of MUDF in project financing is relevant from the fact that most local bodies have been in a position to invest in basic services. Till 1991–92, the average annual capital investments of Madras Corporation were around Rs.2,200 lakhs. With Madras being allowed to borrow from MUDF, after an initial restriction, the capital outlay increased to a level of Rs.4,233 lakhs in 1992–93, to an outlay of Rs.9,950 lakhs in 1993–94 and Rs.11,000 lakhs in 1994-95. Investments through assistance from MUDF contribute around 34 per cent of the average annual capital outlay.

Coimbatore Corporation, as part of the World Bank-aided Tamil Nadu Water Supply and Sanitation Project, had initiated a Rs.5,200 lakhs water supply augmentation project. At the time of conceiving it was indicated that the existing distribution system would handle the additional yield. With a slight delay in completion it was found that additional storage and distribution was necessary to serve the newer layouts and extended areas. In the year 1994–95, the Corporation requested MUDF to finance the Rs. 2,000 lakhs distribution system project. Due to the limit on the project funding of a maximum of Rs. 1,000 lakhs, PMG requested Coimbatore to undertake part of the project from own funds. Coimbatore in the meanwhile decided to raise resources by:

— Increasing new connection fees from a level of Rs. 500 to a level of Rs. 2,500 for domestic and Rs. 5,000 for non-domestic users;
— Introduced a progressive tariff mechanism on water supplied to commercial sector, which till then was charged at domestic rates. This was due to certain agreements reached at the time of water sharing with a neighbouring state.
— Doubled its current demand from property tax as a result of 100 per cent revision of the base. The water account of Coimbatore sustains on transfers of Water and Drainage Tax collected as part of the property tax, water charges and connection fees and fines.

Coimbatore Corporation while framing its budget for 1995–96, used the FOP and the assumptions as a base document; in fact the same consultants were involved at the time of finalization of the budget. The city also utilized the services of consultants to formulate tariff booklets to overcome delay in revenue loss as a result of the delay in reading meters. This delayed reading was due to limited staff to read meters and raise bills.

Project Formulation and Appraisal

A major impact of MUDF is the rigid appraisal of projects, which most municipal officers agreed to. There have been adequate successes in implementation, as well as setbacks. Setbacks have been largely with respect to commercial projects, wherein local syndicates have been restricting the levy of the minimum rental level arrived at the time of economic appraisal of projects.

A major impact of this appraisal mechanism is the ability of the engineers to understand the processes involved in appraisal as well as feeding the consultants with required information. The project identification and appraisal, apart from looking at the need and feasibility, also involved prioritization. At the time of appraisal Madras and Madurai Corporations and quite a few smaller local bodies presented an integrated package of bus routes and major roads, drain and lighting projects wherever possible, and started working on a list of projects prioritized on low or inadequate facilities. For example, roads without drain or lighting were provided these facilities on a priority basis. Similarly, in the case of Madras, roads with high volume and poor surface condition were taken up for strengthening. In case of solid waste management, there have been considerable improvements in the levels of collection. In most towns the collection prior to MUDF investments in vehicles was at around 50 per cent. This has increased to between 75 and 80 per cent.

Remunerative projects were funded with the objective of enabling local bodies in raising resources in the long run. While there have been a few setbacks, most facilities have been put to use and some have yielded better returns than those suggested as a minimum level during appraisal (Table 14.7). This is a major achievement considering the low yields from most such schemes.

Issues and Prospects

MUDF at the time of conceptualization, was designed as a recurring source for urban service investment with unlimited access to local bodies subject to its rules (Figure 14.2). The design of the terms of inflow into the fund and outflow was basically to see that MUDF lives beyond the scope of TNUDP. Though the mandate of MUDF indicates that it would be the first port of call for urban local bodies, but this has not been enforced in the strictest sense, as there have been other windows offering assistance. It is generally agreed that larger the number of windows, greater the flexibility in borrowing. But the basic issue that need to be addressed is:

— Will the lending institution enforce necessary fiscal discipline and assess the real capabilities?
— How effective will they be in inducing policy changes at the municipal level?
— Will subsidies be capability, performance and need based?

An illustrative case is that under the MUDF, most local bodies are eligible for assistance on a 100 per cent loan basis. This is more due to their resource base and potential. Whereas under a project-specific lending programme for strengthening mega-cities, the service schemes of local agencies within metro region are eligible for a subsidy of 10 per cent.

MUDF has been in a position to enforce fiscal discipline among local bodies, a fact which other project-specific lending has not been in a position to achieve. While this programme has been successful in terms of set goals of inducing investments and strengthening local institutions and capabilities, most other programmes have focused on lending than larger institutional and fiscal issues. This is despite the broader

Figure 14.2: Implementation of MUDF

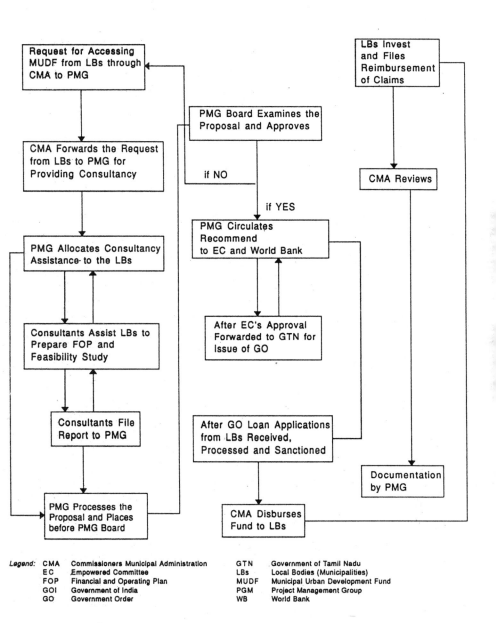

Legend: CMA   Commissioners Municipal Administration   GTN   Government of Tamil Nadu
          EC   Empowered Committee   LBs   Local Bodies (Municipalities)
          FOP   Financial and Operating Plan   MUDF Municipal Urban Development Fund
          GOI   Government of India   PGM   Project Management Group
          GO   Government Order   WB   World Bank

Table 14.7: Performance of Selected Remunerative Schemes

Town / Scheme	Unit	Estimated	Actuals
Tiruppur			
Shops at Selambarankuttai market	Rs./shop/day	15	10
Shopping complex at Kamaraj Road	Rs./sq m	60	130
Sivakasi			
Daily market-	Rs.lakhs/year	1.10	4.57
Stalls	Rs./sq m	15	15
Shops	Rs./sq m	16	27
Bus stand	Rs.lakhs/year	0.77	3.01
Shops at Kamaraj Road	Rs.lakhs/year	1.01	2.03
Erode			
Shopping complex at bus stand			
Shops A	Rs./sq m	34	273
Shops B	Rs./sq m	51	140
Shops at weekly market	Rs./sq m	34	122
Rajapalayam			
Shopping complex with basement cycle stand	Rs.lakhs/year	2.21	8.50
Nagercoil			
Shops at new bus stand at Perumalkulam	Rs.lakhs/year	7.20	3.75
Shops in municipal compound	Rs.lakhs/year	2.40	1.98
Palayamkottai			
Marriage hall	Rs.lakhs/year	2.20	2.65
Shopping complex at Maharaj Nagar	Rs.lakhs/year	3.00	3.41
Tirunelveli			
Shops on first floor of bus stand	Rs.lakhs/year	1.75	1.87
Offices over shops on SNH Road	Rs.lakhs/year	1.80	1.66
Tuticorin			
Shops at Conservancy Depot	Rs.lakhs/year	5.80	8.68
Marriage hall at Sevanthakulam Road	Rs.lakhs/year	0.75	2.00

Note: Estimated figure is that indicated at the time of appraisal stage.
Source: Consultants Review, Project Management Group and Report of Banks Inspection.

framework within which they were supposed to operate. This has been one of the strengths of MUDF and PMG. Considering the success of this performance-based lending approach, completion of the TNUDP period and the need to extend MUDF as a permanent body—as a bank or a financial institution—it was felt necessary that integration of all lending windows would be appropriate. There have been discussions on the nature and location of such a window. The options are whether it would be a bank or a financial institution—within or outside the government. The discussions are on at the state level, but still it needs mention that the proposed institution should have the mandate to intervene in fiscal policies, and have a say in disbursement of subsidies for capital works.

This approach of performance-based lending, appraisal of capabilities and medium-term planning is of relevance today in a situation where the local governments have been empowered to decide on their future. This exercise of the Financial and Operating Plan is crucial, especially when the local agencies will have to either go to a financial institution or possibly to the capital market to meet their capital needs. This approach in Tamil Nadu is replicable elsewhere and quite a few neighbouring states have attempted to use this approach in municipal management.

BIBLIOGRAPHY

Kumar, M.V., Mukundan, K. and Vaidya, C. (1988), 'Approach to Financial and Operating Plan', paper presented at International Seminar on Human Setlements, Centre For Human Settlements, Madras.

Madras Metropolitan Development Authority (MMDA)—Operations Research Group (ORG) (1987), *Infrastructure Levels and Establishment of Development Managament Systems for Small and Medium Towns in MMA*, Madras (unpublished).

MMDA-ORG (1987), *Financial and Operating Plans for Urban Areas in Tamil Nadu*, Madras (unpublished).

MMDA-ORG (1987), *Municipal Finance and Project Feasibility for Madurai, Coimbatore, Salem and Tiruchi Towns in Tamil Nadu*, Madras (unpublished).

Project Management Group (PMG), Kirloskar Consultants Limited (1992–94), *Financial and Operating Plans of Madras, Coimbatore, Erode, Tiruppur and Sivakasi Towns*, Madras (unpublished).

Vaidya, C. and Mukundan, K. (1992), 'Approach to Sustainable Investment Planning. *Nagarlok*, Special Issue, Oct.–Dec, New Delhi.

15

INTEGRATED INFRASTRUCTURE PLANNING AND PROGRAMMING: A FIVE-YEAR CAPITAL INVESTMENT MODEL FOR SMALL AND MEDIUM TOWNS

B. Bhaskara Rao and N. Nageshwara Rao

Introduction

Integrated Infrastructure Planning and Programming (IIPP) as a five-year capital investment plan is propagated mainly to fill up the vacuum and bridge the gap between the situation of "no plan and no action programme" at local levels and "non-resource-based long-range master plans" of towns proposed by state-level town planning authorities.

The Urban Local Governments (ULGs) of small town to large cities have the twin problems of (a) increasing demand for services, amenities and facilities, and (b) inelastic revenue and resources. These local authorities have developed neither planning and technical capabilities nor evolved any means and techniques. Due to the non-availability of relevant and adequate data base, development and planning decisions are *ad hoc*, often based on exogenous variables, and lack internal prioritizations of the needs of the town.

With meagre internal resources, adequate funds are not available to ULGs to undertake and implement capital works. External borrowing has become a necessity and a favourable option. In order to avail funds from external sources either as a loan or a grant, the assessment of the extent to which a local authority can sustain this investment becomes imperative. A few attempts made in this direction are in the contexts of:

(i) Integrated Development of Small and Medium Towns (IDSMT),

(ii) Programme under Municipal Urban Development Fund (MUDF) in Tamil Nadu, and

(iii) Infrastructure financing window of the Housing and Urban Development Corporation (HUDCO), coupled with the decentralized training in Karnataka by the Indian Human Settlement Programme (IHSP) (IHSP-STEM, 1993a and 1993b).

Some of these programmes are launched for creating resource-generating ventures, for the provision of sufficient supporting infrastructure facilities and the development of these towns and cities as growth centres for the betterment of the rural hinterland, and for the reduction of migration to bigger cities. Substantial budgetary allocations by national and state governments have been made to improve the small and medium towns with an integrated approach by improving and/or creating a mix of urban services and remunerative enterprises. In recent years, access to institutional finances has also created to overcome the financial constraints from budgetary sources.

It is in this context that the studies on investment and financial operating plans (FOPs) for providing municipal services, amenities and facilities have become vital for the decision-making process by the funding agencies. IIPP with resource mobilization at local levels can be considered as an effective tool.

Scope of IIPP

Most of the towns and cities have their Master Plan, Outline Development Plan (ODP) or Comprehensive Development Plan (CDP) and these are constituted legally under the Town and Country Planning Acts. They are long-term development plans ranging from 10 to 25 years. However, the experience indicates that the implementation of these plans is rarely satisfactory due to many reasons, i.e., financial, technical, elaborate but unrealistic, rigid land use and leasing regulations based on traditional concepts of master plans. The proposed IIPP has in a way not only bridged the long-awaited gap between short- and medium-term plans and long-term master plans, but also emphasizes the immediate infrastructure needs of the citizens instead of waiting to fulfil the long-term goals and targets of the master plan.

Objectives of the Study

The present study proposes a methodology for the development an IIPP technique on scientific and systematic lines through "systems approach". The IIPP technique was developed in the course of preparation of

Infrastructure Development Plans for small and medium towns in Tamil Nadu and Karnataka (STEM, 1989). The technique has reached an operational stage, after being experimented with and successfully implemented in many towns and cities in Tamil Nadu (Project Management Group and STEM, 1993a, 1993b, 1993c, 1993d, 1993e) and is presently being replicated in Karnataka. To illustrate the technique, a case study of Hassan, a medium-sized city in Karnataka, has been taken up and was used for training under the IHSP-sponsored programme. The following sections present briefly the IIPP process and its adoption.

The Purpose and the Process of IIPP

The aim: The two major aims of IIPP as an effective tool and technique are: (a) to generate a sustainable five-year capital investment plan and programme for ULGs for the management of infrastructure; and (b) to increase the participative role of the community as users and planners.

The objective of the IIPP technique: The objectives of the IIPP technique are:

(i) To assess physical and financial carrying capabilities of the ULGs.

(ii) To suggest the *modus operandi* for mobilizing resources—internal and external.

(iii) To make people and decision-makers aware of the levels of municipal services and the state of urban finance.

(iv) To involve the senior citizens and the officials of development organizations and make them participate in the preparation of IIPP.

(v) To prioritize developmental needs through a participative process.

(vi) To create a sustainable and adoptable Financial Operating Plan (FOP).

The process: The major components of the of IIPP process consists of:

(i) Analysis of the financial structure of the ULG, given the cash-based accounting system.

(ii) Identification of gaps and shortcomings in the delivery process of municipal service systems.

(iii) Identification of options for improving the financial status.

(iv) Identification of service and remunerative projects and their appraisal to meet the shortage or gaps of delivery of specific services on priority basis, and to add to or improve financial resources.

(v) Formulation of a five-year development programme to revive the functions of the ULG to operate on its own, on the strength of realistic assumptions.

(vi) Seeking financial support from funding agencies to undertake developmental activities within an acceptable framework.

(vii) Helping the ULGs to achieve active participation in the developmental process at community or local level.

The Analytical Process of IIPP

An outline of the process and analytical flow is explained in the following sections and also indicated in Figure 15.1. The analytical process of IIPP consists of two important simultaneous decision streams with initial objective with inter-linkages and sub-routines: Stream A—physical assessment and planning—and Stream B—financial assessment and planning. Until a "feasible" solution is obtained, the iteration processes A and B with their sub-routines have to be repeated with alternative scenarios.

The Methodology and Major Steps of IIPP

It is most essential and a pre-condition that once the decision is taken to implement IIPP for a town or city, an expert committee has to be formed consisting of professionals, officials, noted citizens and elected representatives. These members should have a good understanding of the objectives, managerial techniques and commitment for the improvement of the town or city through a developmental programme. They should prepare a systematic ground plan and initiate the action of IIPP.

The analytical process involved and the interaction of various activities between and within the groups now elaborated and presented with the help of a comprehensive flow chart (Figure 15.2). Once all the activities and interactions are completed, the final IIPP is ready for approval and execution.

Major Steps

Step 1   : Decision and initialization of IIPP.

Step 2   : Planning for information : contact drive for information—primary, secondary and opinion survey data.

Step 3   : Component analysis : municipal finances—data analysis through designed formats.

Figure 15.1: Analytical Process of IIPP

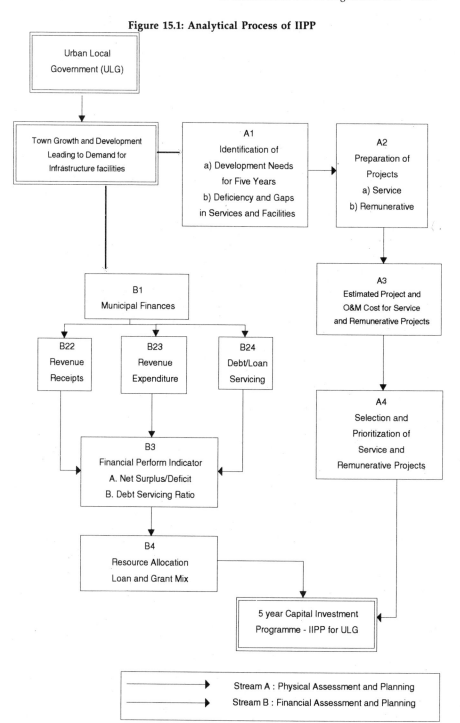

Figure 15.2: Flow Process of IIPP

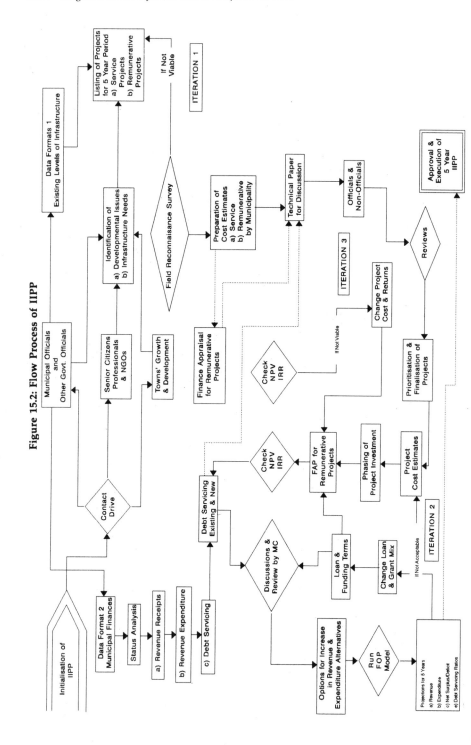

Step 4   :   Component analysis : municipal services—data analysis through designed formats.

Step 5   :   Identification and prioritization of projects—service and remunerative projects.

Step 6   :   Field reconnaissance (iteration sub-routine process-1).

Step 7   :   Financial operating plan (FOP) model (iteration sub-routine process-2).

Step 8   :   Financial appraisal of the project (FAP)—for remunerative projects and prioritization (iteration sub-routine process-3).

Step 9   :   Approval and execution.

It is to be noted that the flow of events and steps are not independent, but are mutually inter-dependent and inter-linked. Different flows start and proceed simultaneously with minor time differences and interact at appropriate stages so that the most appropriate and acceptable solutions are obtained. Hence, the explanations of each event or step in the analytical process of IIPP do not strictly follow the sequential order as presented in the flow chart (Figure 15.2).

Formulation Process

Planning for collection of information: Once a decision is taken to initialize the IIPP for a selected town or city, it is essential to understand the town, its potential, its present problems and its possibilities. The professional team working on IIPP need to (a) undertake a contact drive to establish rapport with officials, citizens and non-governmental organizations, and (b) identify information areas for data collection.

Contact Drive: This consists of:

(a) Meeting with senior citizens, municipal officials, officials of other development agencies to understand their opinions, attitudes, perceptions and priorities;

(b) Reconnaissance of the town or city; and

(c) Study of existing literature.

Data Requirements: Data requirements pertain to:

(a) Municipal services;

(b) Municipal finances;

(c) On-going programmes of other developmental agencies in the town or city; and

(d) Information on general profile, demographic characteristics, historical background and economic base of the town or city.

These are elicited from various secondary sources. For preparing the IIPP, it is essential to have at least data of preceding three to five years to be utilized as information base. Information has to be collected with reference to this base period. The information from "contact drive" provides an avenue for prioritization of the basic requirements of the town or city on the basis of the local community's attitudes, perceptions and their requirements. The information areas serve as basic inputs to the formulation of the IIPP.

Component analysis: Municipal finance resources (internal and external revenues) and functional allocations (expenditures) are analysed in order to define the fiscal capacity of the town or city to undertake developmental activities. The municipal annual budget documents provide a major part of information on revenue, expenditure and loan and debt accounts along with the demand collection balance (DCB) statements. With minor re-classification the overall financial status and capacity of the town or city could be analysed.

Additional resource mobilization: Assessment of revenue-expenditure gaps, estimating the revenue generation potentialities and resource mobilization efforts of ULGs constitute another step in planning for IIPP. Identification of critical areas in revenue generation and additional resource mobilization for sustained development of the town or city require in-depth investigation.

Component analysis—Municipal services: Once the fiscal components and revenue generation and resource mobilization capacities are analysed, these are linked to analyse the corresponding urban service delivery systems and income-generating enterprises undertaken by the ULGs.

From the data collected contact drives and reconnaissance of the town, the present status, service gaps and uses of various municipal services and the desired levels can be analysed.

Based on the proposed and designed developmental activities for each service, it is desirable to plan systematically the approach to achieve the goal. This can be done by designing the flow charts for each activity. Figure 15.3 presents an illustrative flow chart for water supply service development. Similarly, other services such as solid waste management, street lighting, sewerage disposal, parks and playgrounds, roads and footpaths can be prepared.

Figure 15.3: Water Supply Service Development

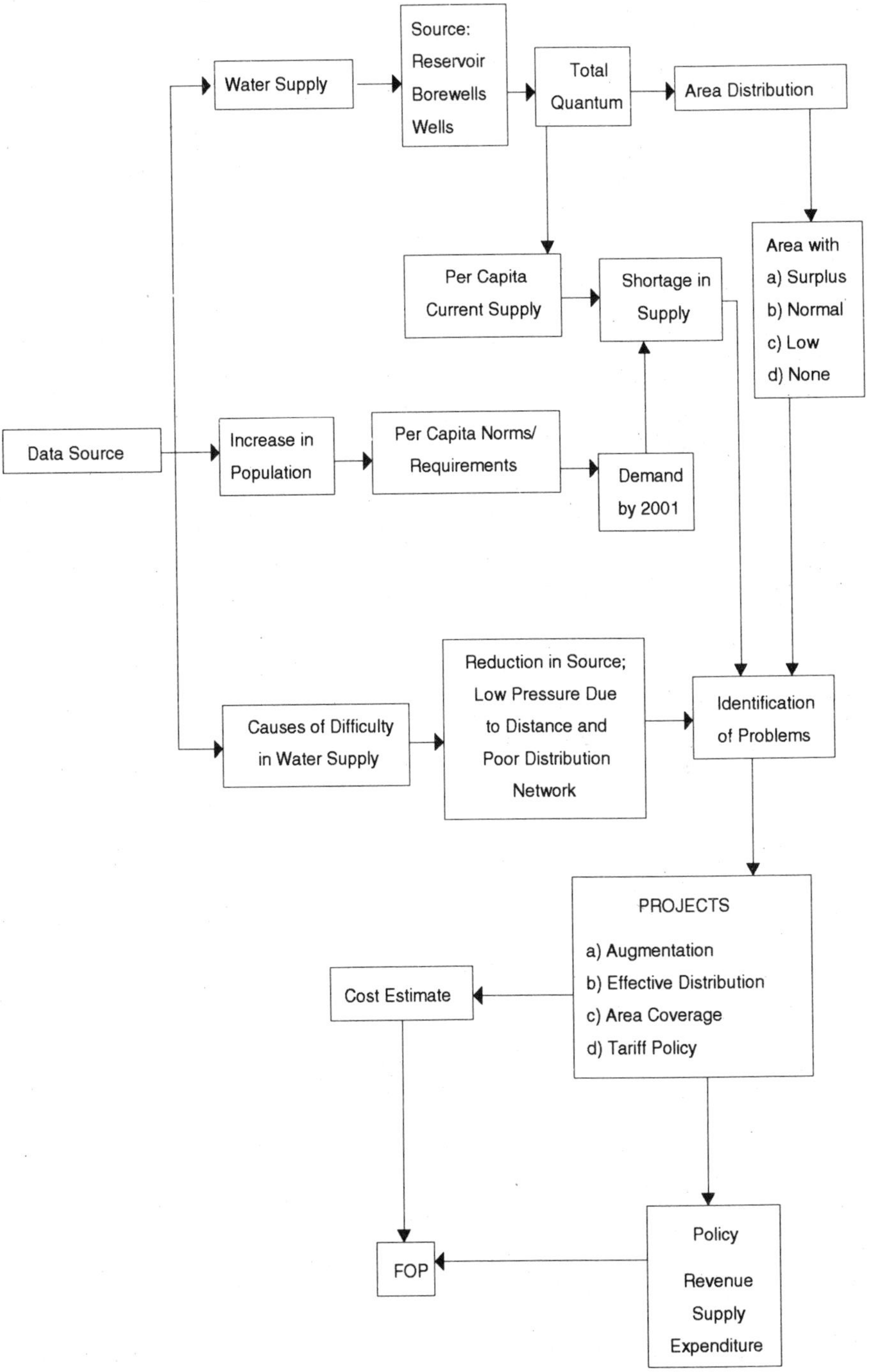

On-going Development Activities

Once the above steps are completed in a mutually coordinated method, an important stage is reached to review the on-going developmental activities of other agencies and departments to identify projects that could be taken up and their financial and physical forecasts and phasing over a five-year period or less.

Review of on-going development activities: The on-going developmental activities by other agencies such as *Nehru Rozgar Yojana* (NRY) a poverty alleviation scheme, projects of State Housing Board, Water Supply Board, and Slum Clearance Board, etc., have to be taken note of and reviewed before identifying the new development of service or remunerative projects.

Project Identification and Phasing

Approach

(i) The "systems approach" is found most appropriate for identifying and assessing the feasibility of different projects needed by the ULG to raise the existing service levels to a desired level within a pre-determined time and financial framework.

(ii) The earlier steps—particularly, contact drive, professional meetings and in-depth discussions with leading citizens and elected representatives—are the main avenues to take into account all relevant issues into considerations. Wherever possible the project proposals may also be discussed with the concerned district authorities.

(iii) The approach adopts "social mapping" of state-of-the-art and "need-based" prioritization of projects for a five-year IIPP of the concerned ULG. This can be achieved through wide participation of concerned people of the locality and local officials.

(iv) It is necessary to arrive at a priority for investment in the different schemes and the projects to be undertaken for raising the level of services to provide maximum benefit. This would also mean that alternative cost-effective approaches for projects should be evaluated before arriving at the most appropriate solutions to the problems on hand. After studying and identifying the problems, the concerned officers are to be involved in the discussions with a view to select the best alternative or combination of projects to match the limited resources and time frame, and arrive at the final IIPP.

Criteria for selecting project package: In the framing of the projects, the following set of criteria have to be applied:

(i) Priorities reflect the need to upgrade the low level of services to meet the basic needs of the general public.

(ii) The projects should also serve the needs of the weaker sections of the population.

(iii) The approaches and specifications adopted should help to lower the cost of projects.

(iv) Cost recovery components have to be built into the project itself to the extent possible, particularly in remunerative projects.

(v) As the gestation period of investments is small (not exceeding 12 to 18 months), the projects have to be phased suitably so that benefits begin to accrue immediately on completion.

(vi) Alternative project mixes are to be evaluated for obtaining maximum socio-economic returns for the investments.

(vii) The implementation capability of the institution, taking into account the strengthening of the organization and simplification of the procedures have to be considered.

Identifications of developmental issues: Details of on-going programmes of other departments, proposed projects and possible lines of development identified in other sectors will indicate the possible alternatives for which the ULG should prepare for. For instance, industrial development in the vicinity, or the programmes of the Tourism Department are indicators of:

(i) Future inflow of population into the town;

(ii) The housing needs; and

(iii) Additional strain on municipal services.

Preparation of Cost Estimates

Once the projects are identified, the next step is to estimate their costs, usually rough estimates with line sketches and the period required for construction.

Phasing of Projects and Investment

(i) Investment planning has to be worked out depending upon the project costs, operative and maintenance expenses and the annual revenue generated and expenditure incurred; and

(ii) The expenditure for implementing the projects should normally be phased over a period of one to three years. This phasing is done depending upon the nature of the project, time required for completion in normal circumstances and generation of resources.

General Profile of the Town or City: A Development Scenario

Keeping in view the constraints of master plans and the need of immediate infrastructure facilities for the town or city, an attempt has to be made to evolve a five-year period growth and development profile scenario for the town. The major steps and parameters involved in the process are :

(i) Projection of population for 5 to 10 years.

(ii) Economic growth of the town and employment generation in primary, secondary and tertiary sectors.

(iii) Identify critical development issues of the town through participative group meetings of citizens, voluntary organizations, developmental agencies of the government and municipal officials.

(iv) Identification of areas to be conserved, preserved and developed, such as (a) open spaces parks, landscape areas, etc.; (b) water bodies—tanks, canals, river fronts, etc.; and (c) architectural and cultural heritage—buildings, historical areas, temples, mosques, churches, etc.

(v) Physical barriers of growth—hills, high embanked railway lines, rivers.

(vi) Arterial roads—major roads of the towns and feeder road networks.

(vii) The areas where (a) growth and development was fast in the past 5–10 years; and (b) the development such as industrial, institutional, residential development is committed by Housing Board, Slum Board, Development Authorities, Industrial Development Boards, and others.

The Financial Operating Plan (FOP)

Approach

While the above steps are being taken up, the stage for the FOP is reached. This 'sub-routine process' involves the following steps:

(i) Reviewing of existing financial status (component analysis : municipal finances).

(ii) Identifying the drawbacks on the basis of the above suggestions made to enhance resource mobilization efforts.

(iii) Using the above, the FOP is generated.

The steps (some are already explained) involved in finding the optimal solution through "FOP Sub-Routine" (through various iterations) are:

(i) Decisions on investment phasing and planning.

(ii) Decision on levels of services.

(iii) Project feasibilities, internal rate of return (IRR) and net present value (NPV).

(iv) Resource mobilization at optimal levels.

(v) Decision on loan and grant mix.

(vi) Phasing of project completion.

(vii) Apportioning of capital costs.

(viii) Fixation of terms of repayment.

The components that go into the sub-routine process are :

(i) Forecast of annual revenue of ULG under different heads with alternative assumptions and scenarios.

(ii) Projection of expenditure of ULG both for existing and proposed levels and service options.

(iii) Estimation of capital expenditure for services at different levels and service options.

(iv) Estimation of operation and maintenance costs of new projects.

(v) Estimation of debt-servicing capacity of local body with alternative scenarios of loan and grant mixture.

Since the formulation of FOPs involves the earlier steps and stages, and these in turn are fed by the solution of each iterative FOP in rotation, it is found ideal to develop a computer software for easy and time-saving operations.

Computer model[1]: The model provides the facility for the iterative process under different scenarios to balance the revenue and expenditure patterns of the ULG in order to obtain desired levels of development

---

[1]   The computer model for FOPs was developed by Centre for Symbiosis of Technology, environment and Management (STEM), Bangalore.

and investment options. It serves the dual purpose of knowing the financial stability and accepted norms of debt repayment and servicing of the ULG for IIPP. The operation of the computer model requires the user-level basic knowledge of municipal finances and a working knowledge of the Lotus 1-2-3 computer software package.

Financial Appraisal of Projects (FAP)

While some services have to be delivered without commercial motives, such as roads and street lights, whose returns have to be generated though taxation and taxes, some services deserve direct returns on a *quid pro quo* basis. Such remunerative projects require examination of financial and economic feasibility and appraisal to evaluate the extent at which the cost could be recovered and its of capacity of self financing. FAP is an appropriate technique to derive such parameters.

Approach to FAP: The cost and returns, estimated after discussions with concerned engineers, are projected for its life period of 10–15 years for which the loan is taken. The Net Present Value (NPV) shows the percentage recovery of the capital cost within its project life period. The Internal Rate of Return (IRR) indicates the percentage returns of the individual projects over a fixed period for a town.

Once the cost estimates are made and the cost of construction is known, the annual returns are assessed. With the capital expenditure, construction period and the returns per annum known, the financial appraisal of the project—including the annuity of loan repayment— is assessed. Depending on the financial viability of the project, it is accepted or rejected. (Since the loan amount, period of repayment, rate of interest, annuity, the returns from the project are known, the IRR and NPV are calculated. IRR should be more than the percentage of interest and NPV should be more than zero if the project is to be selected).

The Basic Assumptions for FAPs

Sensitivity tests: The remunerative projects have to be critically evaluated for determining the financial viability. The viability tests have to be carried out for each of the projects for alternative sets of options relating to project cost and revenues as variable costs.

The market rates and the revenues are to be taken as the basic figures for normal options. For the other options, the sensitivity has to be tested for a pre-determined variation in project cost and revenue.

The IRR and NPV calculations have to be computed and presented along with the sensitivity test results of all the options for each of the project.

The decision process of FAP for a remunerative project can be illustrated through Figure 15.4.

Hassan City—A Case Study

Profile of Hassan town: Hassan is classified as a Class-I town in the 1991 census and has a status of City Municipal Council. It is an

Figure 15.4: Financial Appraisal Process for a Project

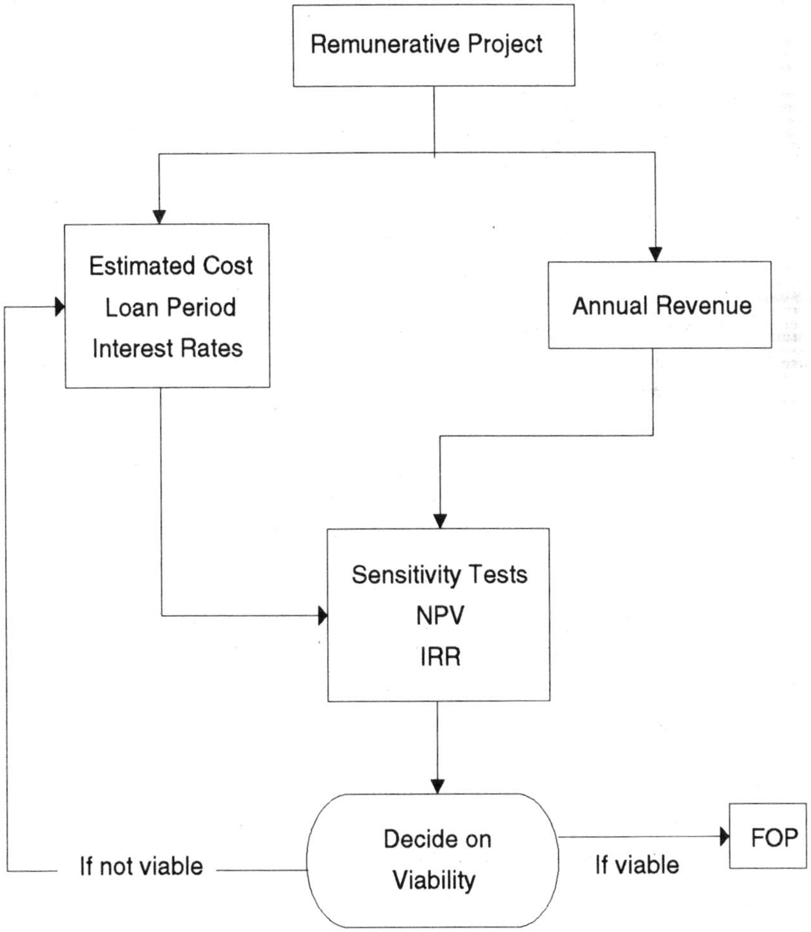

administrative headquarter for the district named after it. The town is located midway between Bangalore and Mangalore and geographically in semi-Malnad region (between plains and mountains) with continuous rainfall for nearly four to five months in a year.

Its population has doubled since 1971 and reached 1.08 lakhs in 1991. It is likely to cross 1.5 lakhs by AD 2001. About 84 per cent of Hassan Urban Agglomeration population lives in municipal area of 7.6 sq km.

The town has developed on the northern side of the national highway and has become an educational centre also. The workers' participation rate has increased from 26 per cent in 1981 to 30 per cent in 1991. About 73 per cent of the population in Hassan town is literate. The slum population is about 19 per cent of the total population of the town.

The approach to IIPP for Hassan town: Hassan town in Karnataka state was chosen as a model town for taking up such an exercise. IIPP for Hassan, through its local body, i.e., the municipality, was a well-knit package of many programmes—services and remunerative—integrated into one cohesive unit, instead of disjointed projects planned without any inter-relations among them.

The exercise was to find ways and means of increasing the local internal resources of Hassan Municipality while at the same time looking to lending agencies for financial assistance towards schemes for the provision of infrastructure facilities and other remunerative schemes designed for resource augmentation and asset creation.

It was proposed to support the municipal officials in making a study of existing service levels and finances, identifying the gaps, exploring the possibilities of increasing the revenue and reducing the expenditure to bolster up the savings. The next step was to estimate the funds required to take up the service and remunerative projects and assess the capability of the municipality to borrow and finally prioritize the schemes to meet its purpose.

The process: After selecting the Hassan town, the first step undertaken was to make a basic study of the town from secondary sources on location, population growth, occupation structure, etc. Five contacts and group discussions with important citizens and non-officials such as lawyers, businessmen, Council ex-presidents, representative of voluntary organizations, etc., and officials were made during the periodic visits to the town.

Contact drive and information collection: The views of non-officials on various infrastructure facilities available gave a picture of the prevailing conditions in the town and also the problems. Naturally the problems led to options for solutions.

These are followed up with discussions on markets, shops, parks and play fields in the town, some of which are remunerative. These meetings lead to the listing and prioritization of municipal services and remunerative projects desired and required for improvements. The services were: (a) augmentation of water supply; (b) new roads and improvement to existing roads; (c) improvement in street lighting; (d) improvement in management of solid waste collection and disposal management; (e) improvement of the existing parks; and (f) improvement of two existing slaughterhouses for hygienic functioning.

The remunerative projects were (a) daily market area, (b) weekly market area, and (c) a commercial complex.

With the views expressed on service and remunerative projects gathered from the public, the next step was discussions with the municipal officials, officials of the other departments, the Water Supply and Drainage, Housing, Slum Clearance Board, in two or three informal group meetings, to arrive at the possible proposals for meeting the problems and needs of the community. This was followed by field visits to the places identified for action.

Financial appraisal of the projects: Estimates were then prepared for the identified projects in consultation with the technical persons.

The estimated capital costs of providing the recommended service projects and remunerative enterprises are presented in Table 15.1.

In the case of remunerative projects, they were tested for their financial viability. The financial appraisal was undertaken by the use of two indicators, the IRR and NPV. The viability tests have been carried out with four sets of options (sensitivity tests) for each project—one with prevailing rates and three with pre-determined variations in project cost and revenue.

Financial Operating Plan (FOP): Along with the project cost, the operation and maintenance cost, the resulting annuity payments of loan with interest were also worked out. The already existing municipal budget with receipts, expenditure, existing debt-service ratio (ratio of loan repayment to total receipts excluding grant) was projected for the next five years and to these were added new projects, their income, expenditure and debt-service. The outcome was a consolidated picture of receipts and expenditure with new debt service ratio of existing and new projects and the net financial status.

Table 15.1: Capital Costs of Service and Remunerative Projects

Project	Amount (Rs. millions)
I. *Service Projects*	
1. Water supply	3.50
2. Roads, footpaths, storm-water drainage	7.41
3. Street lighting	1.50
4. Solid waste management	0.75
5. Improvement to slaughterhouses	0.20
6. Improvement to the existing parks	2.65
Total I	**47.50**
II. *Remunerative Projects*	
1. Daily market	3.26
2. Weekly market	4.10
3. Commercial complex	10.70
Total II	**18.06**

Alternative scenarios: Five scenarios were developed with the following workable assumptions:

(i) Revenues can be increased through traditional and innovative methods.

(ii) Expenditures can be reduced.

(iii) New projects can be undertaken to generate more funds.

(iv) Cutting down some projects or pruning down some items of one project or more, to bring down the capital cost requirements.

(v) If grants are available for service projects, to work out a loan-grant mix.

Different scenarios were tried to bring the debt service ratio below 25 per cent and at the same time aim at surplus balances. The summary of the iterations of FOP for Hassan town is provided in Table 15.2.

The Scenario C is found more appropriate and suitable for undertaking a medium-term infrastructure development plan for Hassan town.

Inputs to IIPP

(i) The inputs of IIPP have mainly come from interaction between the officials of the municipality, developmental agencies, senior citizens, voluntary organizations of the town and the consultants.

(ii) Field visits by the consultants and discussions with the local officials and citizens through participative group meetings.

Table 15.2: Summary of Iterations of the FOP for Hassan

Item	1993–94	1994–95	1995–96	1996–97	1997–98
Scenario A					
Surplus/Deficit (Rs.lakhs)	−23.88	−79.42	−142.32	−213.23	−255.93
Debt-Servicing Ratio (%)	4.16	18.44	28.69	37.32	34.61
Scenario B					
Surplus/Deficit (Rs.lakhs)	3.17	−30.65	−64.83	−100.61	−110.39
Debt-Servicing Ratio (%)	3.93	15.43	23.54	30.71	28.68
Scenario C					
Surplus/Deficit (Rs.lakhs)	−13.04	−13.80	−25.61	−42.13	−24.01
Debt-Servicing Ratio (%)	4.19	12.80	17.76	22.32	19.68
Scenario D					
Surplus/Deficit (Rs.lakhs)	−8.43	−28.12	−54.03	−73.32	−64.97
Debt-Servicing Ratio (%)	4.12	13.43	17.13	19.07	16.90
Scenario E					
Surplus/Deficit (Rs.lakhs)	−13.04	26.76	1.61	−37.66	−27.44
Debt-Servicing Ratio (%)	4.19	11.29	16.49	22.07	19.83

(iii) The meetings between IHSP and the consultants on the contents of the IIPP.

Conclusion

This is in brief the operation involved in working out a programme to assess the capacity of a municipality to raise internal resources and the extent to which it can go to raise external resources.

With an IIPP in its hand the municipality has options. If can approach different lending agencies, study their interest rates, loan period, possibility of moratorium period, grants availability and extent, and work out and arrive at a convenient and favourable arrangement.

Three remunerative projects costing Rs.181 lakhs, six service projects including water supply for uplifting the quality of life costing Rs.475 lakhs were programmed for Hassan. These were to be implemented within three years and finance is to be generated internally and externally. The external funding limits are derived to match the financial resources of Hassan municipality for enabling it to repay the loan within 15 years at 15 per cent interest rate. It also provided flexibility for continuing with its capital improvement programme within or after five years of IIPP.

BIBLIOGRAPHY

Project Management Group (PMG) and STEM (1993a), *Project Appraisal Report for Municipal Urban Development Fund, Attur Town*, Tamil Nadu Urban Development Project, Government of Tamil Nadu, Madras (unpublished report).

Project Management Group (PMG) and STEM (1993b), *Project Appraisal Report for Municipal Urban Development Fund, Thirchungode*, Tamil Nadu Urban Development Project, Government of Tamil Nadu, Madras (unpublished report).

Project Management Group (PMG) and STEM (1993c), *Project Appraisal Report for Municipal Urban Development Fund, Hosur Town*, Tamil Nadu Urban Development Project, Government of Tamil Nadu, Madras (unpublished report).

Project Management Group (PMG) and STEM (1993d), *Project Appraisal Report for Municipal Urban Development Fund, Guddiyattam Town*, Tamil Nadu Urban Development Project, Government of Tamil Nadu, Madras (unpublished report).

Project Management Group (PMG) and STEM (1993e), *Project Appraisal Report for Municipal Urban Development Fund, Arani Town*, Tamil Nadu Urban Development Project, Government of Tamil Nadu, Madras (unpublished report).

Indian Human Settlements Programme (IHSP) and Centre for Symbiosis of Technology, Environment and Management (STEM) (1993a), *Thematic Report on Methodology and Analytical Frame*, IIPP, Vol. I, IHSP-STEM, Bangalore (unpublished).

Indian Human Settlements Programme (IHSP) and Centre for Symbiosis of Technology Environment and Management (STEM) (1993b), 'Case Study - Hassan IIPP, Vol. II, IHSP-STEM, Bangalore (unpublished).

STEM (1989), *Municipal Finance - Bangalore, Hubli-Dharwad & Gulbarga, Karnataka Urban Development Project*, STEM, Bangalore (unpublished).

16

INTEGRATED PROVISION OF BASIC SERVICES IN URBAN INDIA

Harjit S. Anand

The coin of basic services has two sides — physical and social. Physical services refer to availability of potable water, drainage, low-cost sanitation, affordable shelter with proper ventilation, electricity, paving of streets, garbage disposal and a pollution-free environment. Social services refer to provision of a balanced diet to expectant mothers, proper ante-natal care, adequate post-natal care, facilities for early children education, tasty supplementary nutrition for children combined with nutritional education, persuasive and collaborative family planning service, high level of admission and retention of children in primary schools, non-formal education for school drop-outs, appropriate education for adult illiterates, training for dissemination of vocational skills and provision of an integrated package for promotion of income-generating activities.

At the present level of its development, basic services are available to the middle and upper classes in India to a considerable extent but the access of the urban poor to such services is extremely limited. Although it is accepted that the provision of basic services must be planned at the city level and so must the resources required be raised from multiple financial sources in an integrated manner, the level of deprivation suffered by slum-dwellers necessitates that a special strategy be designed to focus on such provision in low-income settlements. This paper offers an evaluation of the manner in which India has sought to provide urban basic services in low-income settlements, the lessons learnt from this experience and the development of an alternate model that can improve the access of the urban poor to such services.

Window of the Urban Poor to Basic Services

Having defined the framework of our analysis, let us examine the position of India with respect to the provision of basic services in urban areas. On the physical side, 27.1 per cent of the urban population is without access to water supply, but for low income households, this figure is as high as 38 per cent (Sivaramakrishnan and Mathur, 1991). A study of fast-growing slums of Bangalore instituted by the National Commission on Urbanization shows that the per capita water consumption in these slums was between 16 and 23 litres per day and the number or persons per tap varied between 40 and 428 (National Commission on Urbanization, 1988). With such a large number of persons drawing water from a single tap, the time for fetching one bucket of water would stretch from 30 minutes to a couple of hours.

In relation to sanitary means of excreta disposal, a study of the National Institute of Urban Affairs (1991) shows that private toilets are limited to 15 per cent of urban households, community toilets to another 21 per cent whereas more than 60 per cent of the urban households resort to open spaces for defecation.

A striking feature of urban India, especially in the large cities is the acute shortage of housing, the low affordability of the urban poor in relation to shelter and the poor quality of housing stock. A staggering 40 per cent of urban India lives in one-room tenements. This figure is a high as 70 per cent in Calcutta and 82 per cent in Bombay. The scenario is further aggravated by the fact that 75 per cent of the one-room tenements do not have proper windows and consequently suffer from poor ventilation (Himachal Pradesh Institute of Public Administration, 1991).

The quality of housing stock is the poorest in slums. The growth of India's urban population has been skewed in favour of the larger cities. Whereas there were 12 million plus cities in India in 1981, their number has increased to 23 by 1991. Further, according to the 1991 Census, 65.20 per cent of the urban population lives in Class-I cities (<100,000 inhabitants) and more than half of the population of Class-I cities lives in 23 metropolitan cities. Moreover, one-fourth of the population of the Class-I cities lives in the mega cities of Bombay, Delhi, Calcutta and Madras. The rapid growth of medium and large cities has contributed significantly to the growth of slums in India. A Task Force of the Planning Commission estimated the slum population of the country in 1981 at a "low" estimate of 32 million and a "high" estimate of 40 million and projected that these figures will increase to a "low" estimate of 45 million and "high" estimate of 56 million in 1991 (Town and Country Planning Organization, 1991, Annexure III).

In the sphere of social services, it is pointed out that 9,000 children die everyday in India which constitutes one-third of all the child deaths in the world. The infant mortality rate (IMR) in India is 74 per thousand. Field studies indicate that birth and death rates in slums are higher by 40 to 50 per cent and the IMR is higher by 1.8 times as compared to non-slum areas (UNICEF, 1995).

In relation to the epidemiological pattern of diseases leading to child mortality, it is pointed out that 28 per cent of child deaths are due to diarrhoea, 22 per cent on account of acute respiratory infections, 11 per cent on account of measles, 7 per cent due to malaria, 6 per cent due to neo-natal tetanus and 28 per cent due to other ailments. A significant aspect of child mortality in India is malnutrition. Two-thirds of the children under five in India suffer from various degrees of malnutrition. More than half the pregnant women in this country suffers from anaemia. One-third of all babies born have low birth weight (UNICEF, 1995, pp. 19 and 20). The incidence of malnutrition is especially severe between the age of 6 and 23 months when children require supplementary food besides breast milk.

In relation to educational status, it is pointed out that the urban literacy rate in India is around 60 per cent while the literacy rate among the urban poor is less than 30 per cent. About 27 per cent of urban children between five and nine years of age do not attend schools. The problems is much more severe in slums where school enrolment and retention rates are alarmingly low (UNICEF, 1991, p.62). Further, a study of several squatter settlements in Delhi showed that as many as 91 per cent of the squatters were illiterate and 80 per cent of the parents wanted their children to help in domestic work or earn additional income rather than go to school. A significant factor in the apathy of the urban poor towards education is the poor facilities and quality of instruction imparted in schools servicing the urban poor.

A very large segment of the urban population lives on pavements, illegal squatter colonies, poorly serviced *chawls* and in shanty tenements surrounded by squalor and disease. According to the National Sample Survey data (43rd round) relating to consumer household expenditure, 22.1 per cent of the urban population or approximately 42 million persons were living below the poverty line in 1987-88 (National Sample Survey Organization, 1989). These figures do not reflect the true picture of urban poverty in India since the poverty line in urban areas has been pegged at a meagre Rs. 11,850/- annual household income based on the monetary equivalent of a basket of goods providing 2100 calories per capita per day. This poverty line estimation does not take into account the substantial expenditure incurred by the urban poor from their family budget on housing, transportation and health. In case these factors are duly accounted for the number of persons living below the poverty line will be much larger. According to the Lakdawala Committee Report (Planning Commission, 1993) the number of persons below the poverty line in 1987-88 was about 83.3 million.

A study of the demographic profile of the urban poor under the aegis of the National Institute of Urban Affairs (NIUA) estimated that 68 per cent of this category consists of women and children (National Institute of Urban Affairs, 1991). India has 330 million children under 16 and 26 million children are born every year. The 1981-1991 decadal increase showed that whereas the total Indian population increased by 23.57 per cent, the urban population increased by 36.19 per cent. These demographic trends of urban India highlight the need for focussing special attention on women and children and slums.

Unemployment, both apparent and disguised, is an everyday companion of the urban poor. According to the National Sample Survey (NSS) (43rd round 1987-88), there were 4.6 million unemployed persons as per usual status in urban areas as compared to 7.1 million in rural areas despite the fact that the urban population is about 26 per cent of the total Indian population. The total number of educated unemployed with matriculation and higher qualifications was estimated by the NSS to be about 5 million. This figure according to the estimates of the Institute of Applied Manpower Research has gone up to about 6 million (Institute of Applied Manpower Research, 1992). It has been estimated by the Planning Commission that 48 per cent of the educated unemployed reside in urban areas.

An overwhelming majority of the urban poor work in the informal sector and follow vocations like rag-picking, porterage, watchkeeping, rickshaw-pulling, domestic help, serving at roadside kitchens, repair of household gadgets and automobiles, masonry, painting and polishing, and street-vending. In short, a majority of the urban poor perform either unskilled or semi-skilled jobs. The informal sector is, generally, outside the pale of social security regulations pertaining to working hours, safety precautions, maternity leave or compensation for injury.

Deviant behaviour by adolescent boys in slums is quite common. A study of the riots in the city of Baroda showed that a significant part of looting and arson was perpetrated by slum gangs (National Commission on Urbanization, 1988).

Physical and social deprivations supplement each other in developing "a vicious circle" around the urban poor. The "cumulative deprivations" which constitute this vicious circle relate to low educational attainments, limited skills, low wages, poor working conditions, unhygienic living conditions, multiple episodes of illness in the family, malnutrition, traces of juvenile delinquency and recurrent unemployment. Such are the "features" of the "face" of urban poverty in India.

Indian Policy Perspective on Provision of Basic Services

Having examined the status of the provision of basic services in low-income, urban settlements in India, it would be useful to ask the question: What is the Indian policy perspective for provision of basic services to the urban poor?

The Directive Principles of State Policy enshrined in the Indian Constitution, based on the ideas of Sydney and Beatrice Webb, Jeremy Bentham, tenets of Fabian Socialism and the social charter of the Irish Constitution, seek to promote "a social order in which justice, social, economic and political shall inform all the institutions of the national life" (Government of India, 1951, article 38 part IV). This chapter of socio-economic justice is further defined by the Directive Principles in relation to the right to an adequate means of livelihood equally for men and women, equal pay for equal work for both men and women, ensuring that the health and strength of women workers is not abused, just and humane conditions of work, provision of free and compulsory education for children up to 14 years of age, promotion of the educational and economic interests of the Scheduled Caste and Tribes (SC/ST), improving public health and raising the level of nutrition, assistance in cases of undeserved want, provision of a living wage and development of such conditions of work which ensure a decent standard of life and full enjoyment of leisure and social and cultural opportunities (Government of India, 1951, articles 39, 41, 42, 43, 45, 47).

The central government has adopted the National Programme of Action (NPA) with a view to operationalize the convention on the rights of the child and the broad Plan of Action adopted at the World Summit for Children in 1989. The aims of NPA are: improve the IMR and MMR, improve child immunization to 80 per cent, eliminate neo-natal tetanus, eliminate poliomyelitis, eliminate mortality from measles and reduce its occurrence, reduce "at risk" couples to less than 50 per cent of the current family planning status, eliminate vitamin A deficiency in children, eradicate guinea-worm disease, ensure provision of water and pour-flush latrines, universalize primary education, and empower women and adolescent girls through functional literacy, skill upgradation and income supplementation.

The 74th Constitutional Amendment Act further empowers the local governments in urban areas to boldly address issues relating to regional planning, provision of basic services, slum improvement and poverty alleviation.

Programmes Stemming from Policy

In the context of the policy enunciated, let us now examine the key programmes formulated by the Indian government which aim at provision of basic services especially in low-income settlements. A scheme of Integrated Child Development Services (ICDS) was launched in 1975 which is an important medium for achieving the NPA goals relating to women and child health, early childhood education and nutritional supplementation for children/mothers as well as nutrition education for their mothers. The ICDS programmes has about 300,000 Community Child Care Centres in more than 3,000 Community Development Blocks and is reaching out to offer early learning services to 15 million pre-school children and health-cum-nutritional facilities to 3 million pregnant or breast-feeding women. The focal point of the ICDS programme is the *Anganwari*—a child-care centre run by a female worker chosen from within the community and covering a population of about 1,000 persons. Each *Anganwari* provides facilities of a day-care centre, immunization, food supplementation and pre-school education with a view to enabling older siblings to attend school and mothers to work. There are, today, about 600,000 female, grassroots workers who are charged under the scheme to act as agents of social change for improving the health and educational status of women and children.

The scheme of Environmental Improvement of Urban Slums (EIUS) seeks to provide low-cost water supply, drains, sewerage, community baths and toilets, widening and paving of streets and street lighting in identified slums. An expenditure of Rs.300 per slum-dweller was permitted during the Seventh Five-Year Plan for provision of these physical amenities. The Ministry of Urban Affairs and Employment in consultation with the Planning Commission, has increased the per capita limit to Rs.525 and has included community facilities such as community centre, creche, dispensary, reading room, garbage disposal and an expenditure of 10 per cent on maintenance within the ambit of the Scheme.

The *Nehru Rozgar Yojana (NRY)* poverty alleviation scheme was launched by the central government in 1989 with a view to generating self-employment and wage-employment opportunities for the urban poor. The *Yojana* consists of three schemes: the Scheme of Urban micro-Enterprises (SUME), the Scheme of Urban Wage Employment (SUWE) and the Scheme of Housing and Shelter Upgradation (SHASU). SUME seeks to upgrade the technical skills of potential beneficiaries and to assist them in setting up micro-enterprises with the provision of 25 per cent subsidy up to a ceiling of Rs.5,000 for Scheduled Castes/Scheduled Tribes (SC/ST) and women beneficiaries and Rs.4,000 for other beneficiaries and 75 per cent loan from banks. SUWE seeks to provide wage employment opportunities to the urban poor through the construction of public assets in low-income neighbourhoods. SHASU seeks to provide training in construction trades to beneficiaries belonging to the weaker sections of the society and to assist them in upgrading their shelter with the provision of 25 per cent subsidy up to a ceiling of Rs.1,000 and a 75 per cent loan from the Housing and Urban Development Corporation (HUDCO) up to a ceiling of Rs.3,000. Beneficiaries requiring funds in excess of Rs. 4,000 can procure the same under the Economically Weaker Sections (EWS) Scheme of HUDCO. So far, about 6 lakh micro-enterprises of poor beneficiaries have been assisted under SUME and about 1.38 lakh beneficiaries have been provided technical training. Over 368 lakh mandays of work have been generated under SUWE. Under SHASU, 131 lakh mandays of work have been generated, about 50,000 beneficiaries have been trained in construction trades and about 4 lakh dwelling units are in the process of being upgraded.

The scheme of Urban Basic Services (UBS) was launched in 1986 with a view to providing inputs for mother and child survival and development by converging the efforts of different specialist departments and organizing neighbourhood committees of slum-dwellers. During the Seventh Plan period, expenditure on the scheme was shared on 40:40:20 basis between UNICEF, state governments and the central government. The National Commission on Urbanization (NCU) commended the scheme and as a consequence the central government launched the revised scheme of Urban Basic Services for the Poor (UBSP) in 1990. The UBSP seeks to bring about functional specialization with social services being provided by it in collaboration with other specialist departments, physical amenities being provided under the EIUS scheme and skill training as well as employment opportunities being provided under the *Nehru Rozgar Yojana*. The cardinal feature of this scheme is the creation of community structures such as neighbourhood development committees of slum-dwellers, community development societies and housing cooperatives with a view to empowering the urban poor. So far, the UBSP is being implemented in 280 cities where about 3,400 Neighbourhood Development Societies and 290 Community Development Societies have been set up. With the objective of grassroots planning, 2,779 Mini Plans and 208 Community Development Plans have been prepared.

A Critique of Programme Implementation

Having examined the essential features of India's major programmes for the provision of basic services, it would be useful to critically analyse their shortcomings. Most of the programmes in India work within the framework of rigid, departmental hierarchies. Funds are also released by each department to its own organization units at various levels. The release of funds, as also the actual utilization, is concentrated towards the latter half of the financial year. Very often, a substantial proportion of the funds is released in the last quarter of the financial year (January-March) thereby involving undue haste in expenditure.

There are considerable overlapping areas in the programmes of different departments. In this manner, funds meant for similar activities tend to get very thinly spread-out. In several programmes, field workers at the cutting edge of public contact are paid meagre honorarium or very low salaries. As a consequence, field workers of social programmes are often "rejects" from potentially better-paid jobs. Many of these workers, especially when they do not receive appropriate motivation from superiors, try to seek better opportunities in other programmes/offices leading to a high turnover rate of workers. Further, very few effective institutional linkages exist between different departments and their programmes. Whatever committees exist for inter-departmental coordination meet infrequently and their proceedings are not only of a formal nature but are often not properly followed-up.

Each department providing basic services is known to indulge in "empire-building". Take the *Anganwari* (neighbourhood) worker under the ICDS Programme, for instance. She has such a large charter of responsibilities under the programme that it is not feasible for her to perform all of them effectively. Recently, the central government has announced the launching of the *Indira Mahila Yojana* (IMY) which also seeks to perform many functions which other departments are already involved in. There is a dire need for clearly demarcating the areas of focus of different ministries/departments and for developing better inter-department linkages for integrated implementation of government programmes aimed at providing basic services in urban India.

Another significant problem faced with reference to government-sponsored programmes is the comparatively lower levels of community participation in their formulation and implementation. Notwithstanding a few success stories under the Universal Immunization Programme or Urban Basic Services for the Poor, community participation in the formulation, resource generation, implementation and evaluation of programmes relating to provision of basic services in low-income settlements is well below the required level. In a sense this situation is a legacy of the British *Raj* and the authoritarian provider-beneficiaries hiatus handed-down over centuries of imperialist rule. The secretion tradition of dialogue and the sociological method of participant- observation have yet to take strong roots in the Indian bureaucratic soil.

The EIUS programme has suffered from an overdose of engineering bias and has not been grounded in the fertile soil of community involvement. Further, facilities developed under the EIUS programme have not been provided uniformally and even partial provision has been counted towards coverage. As a consequence, a false scenario has emerged that comprehensive improvements have taken place in the "identified slums" whereas the actual position is to the contrary. Till recently, the EIUS programme had also not paid sufficient attention to repair and maintenance of public facilities once they are provided.

The *Nehru Rozgar Yojana* (NRY) has been adversely effected by the formulation of the Prime Minister's *Rozgar Yojana* (PMRY) especially after non-matriculate beneficiaries have been made eligible under the latter. The total project ceiling under the PMRY is higher than the NRY as also the maximum subsidy available. As such, potential beneficiaries are making a beeline for the PMRY thereby giving a setback to the NRY. The clientele of the two *Yojanas* needs to be clearly differentiated with the NRY concentrating on the urban poor with a matriculation or less than matriculation qualification and the PMRY focussing on beneficiar:es with higher educational attainments accompanied by technical knowledge.

A professional project organization aiming at convergence of various government-sponsored programmes has is to be properly developed. The broad framework of such an organization can be visualized in relation to Community Organizers (COs) at the grassroots level followed by Project Officers and the Humanitarian Municipal Services cell under the City Project Officer at the city level, the Chief Executive Officer and subject-matter specialists in the District Urban Development Agency (DUDA) at the district level and officers of the State Urban Development Agency (SUDA) comprising the Executive Director and representative of different specialist departments at the state level. This broad framework needs to be considerably strengthened through the joint commitment of various functional departments at the state government level.

Each department at the state level today has its own Management Information System (MIS) along with complementary supervisory hierarchy. A common Management Information System for different departments needs to be put into place so that field functionaries of different departments fill up the same Family Development Book at the grassroots level.

Organization of the community to assist in formulation, implementation and review of government programmes is still in its infancy. The system of women Resident Community Volunteers (RCVs) and male Resident Infrastructure Volunteers (RIVs) operating under the programme of Urban Basic Services for the Poor (UBSP) needs to be fully institutionalized and accepted by different functional departments. Community-based Organizations (CBOs) such as Neighbourhood Development Committees, Neighbourhood Infrastructure Committees, Community Development Societies and *Mahila Mandals* (neighbourhood committees) need to be made strong exponents of community action. There is also a dire need for encouraging the NGO movement in the country if basic services are to be provided in an integrated and time-bound manner in low-income settlements.

Community-led Integrated Development Model

Having etched out the broad contours of a critique of the existing governmental programmes, a question arises: is there is a better alternative? Indeed, there is. This alternative model can be described as the Community-led Integrated Development Model (CIDM). The strategy of this model is working with the people and for the people. The local community living in slums is the epicentre of this model.

This model emphasizes a bottom-up approach to programme formulation, implementation and evaluation through the instrumentality of the Urban Basic Services for the Poor (UBSP) programme. At the grassroots level of this model is the Resident Community Volunteer (RCV)—a slum woman representing 20 families located in a cluster or in a lane and a young male worker called Resident Infrastructure Volunteer (RIC). Ten such women volunteers constitute a Neighbourhood Development Committee (NDC), catering to 200 families. Similarly, 10 male volunteers constitute a Neighbourhood Infrastructure Committee (NIC) also covering the same 200 families. Ten NDCs and the 10 NICs together form a Community Development Society (CDS) covering 2,000 families. Each CDS is to be a body registered under the Indian Societies Registration Act so that it can be the focal point of community action at the local level as well as serve as a rallying-point for bargaining with municipal and district authorities for better provision of basic services. From the RCVs to the CDS the entire structure is community based.

Whereas CDS are the critical building blocks at the locality level serving on an average 10,000 residents, the Urban Local Body is the critical structure at the city level. This is all the more so in view of the 74th Constitutional Amendment Act of 1994 which has made poverty alleviation and provision of physical and social services an integral part of the mandate for municipal governments. The CDSs should have a vital interface with the Ward Counsellor at the ward level. Further, there should be a Humanitarian Municipal Services Unit in every urban local body under the charge of a full-time City Project Officer/Area Project Officer (APO) catering to both poverty alleviation schemes and provision of basic services in low-income settlements. In this manner, the community as represented by RCVs, NDCs and NICs and CDS should work in active partnership with the elected Counsellors of each Urban Local Body. Amongst the various government programmes dealing with provision of basic services, the programme of Urban Basic Services for the Poor (UBSP) must play the role of an "integrating catalyst". The cornerstone of the UBSP programme is the Community Organizer (CO) who should be carefully selected from within the same city and should generally be a woman with a graduation in social work, home science or psychology. It is the mandate of the CO to identify potential women leaders at the cluster level in the form of Resident Community Volunteers and to organize them further into Neighbourhood Development Committees. Similarly, it would be her task to organize enterprising young persons, generally male volunteers, into Neighbourhood Infrastructure Committees. Thereafter, every CO would be expected to take this community organizational process to its logical conclusion by forming registered CDSs with representatives of various NDCs and NICs as its members.

In case the Community Organizer is to be motivated to be a dedicated community worker, then she must be made a part of a professional Project Organization with appropriate opportunities for promotion. Such a professional Project Organization can be formed by a Project Officer overseeing the work of five COs and various POs reporting to the Humanitarian Municipal Services Unit under the immediate control of the City/Area Project Officer and the overall control of the Municipal Commissioner. With a view to bringing about a subtle interface between the community organization and the municipality, it is essential that COs and POs report to the HMS Unit and the Municipal Commissioner at the city level. The annual performance reports of the COs, POs and CPO/APO should be reported through the Municipal Commissioner to the DUDA. The COs, POs and CPO/APO should be borne on the personnel cadre of the SUDA and should be transferable from one city to another and one district to another. In this manner, efficient officers can be rewarded with promotions after reasonable intervals and a subtle system of checks and balances developed between ULBs and DUDAs.

The urban local bodies are now to be represented on the Planning Committee of the *Zila Parishad* (district-level council). The autonomous Project Organization in the form of the DUDA should be charged with providing the technical inputs to the planning process at the *Zila Parishad* level.

At the district level, the DUDA needs to be strengthened by associating Project Officers (middle-level departmental officers) from different specialist departments as an integral part of the DUDA reporting to its Chief Executive Officer. Their salaries should continue to be paid from the parent departments with a special pay/honorarium being paid by the DUDA. These Project Officers should manage the legitimate concerns of their parent departments in relation to persons living in low-income settlements by adopting the DUDA strategy and Plan of Action. In this way an efficient Project Organization can be crafted with minimum expenditure and with in-built linkages with sectoral departments like health, education, women and child development, and social welfare. Besides Project Officers, local consultants for specific tasks should also be appointed on a contractual basis to provide vital, technical inputs.

At the state level, the SUDA should have the secretaries of the other specialist departments as members of the Governing Body under the chairmanship of the Chief Secretary with Secretary Urban Development/ LSG as its Member Secretary. The SUDA should also have an Executive Council under the Chairmanship of Secretary Local Self-Government (LSG) or Urban Development with the directors of various social sector departments and managing directors of relevant Corporations as its members. A full-time, senior-scale officer should be the Executive Director of SUDA. The technical arm of SUDA should consist of secondment from sectoral Departments and consultants from the open market appointed on a contractual basis. The SUDA should constitute both a "think-tank" for the state government and the professional project organization for implementing community-based programmes in collaboration with sectoral departments.

The CIDM is fundamentally based on "functional specialization" of different ministries and departments both at the central and state government levels. The Ministry of Human Resource Development and the State Departments of Education should concentrate on primary education, school education, non-formal education for school drop-outs and adult education with special emphasis on girls and women. The Ministry of Health and Family Welfare and the State Departments of

Health should concentrate on child survival and safe motherhood, universal immunization, paediatric surveillance — especially in relation to diarrhoea, acute respiratory infections, measles and malaria — growth-monitoring of adolescent girls and persuasive methods of family planning. The Departments of Women and Child Development at the central and state levels should focus on pre-school education, supplementary nutrition for young children and expecting/breast-feeding mothers, provision of day-care services, immunization and special programmes for adolescent girls and women. The Ministry of Social Welfare and State Departments of Social Welfare should effectively address themselves to the promotion of educational and economic interests of Scheduled Castes and Tribes on the one hand, and work for the rehabilitation of street children, juvenile delinquents, alcoholics and drug addicts on the other hand. The Departments of Science and Technology at the central and state levels should aim at popularization of smokeless *chullahs* (stoves), use of solar and wind energy and conservation of energy. The Ministry of Industrial Development and the State Departments of Industries should provide high quality technical training, manage entrepreneurial development programmes and implement industrial promotion programmes. The Ministry of Urban Affairs and Employment should concentrate on facilitation of low-cost housing especially for the urban poor, convergence of basic physical and social services in low-income settlements through community action and assisting the residents of such settlements to undertake skill upgradation and income-generating activities with supportive backward and forward linkages.

Whereas such sectoral departments are to provide specialized services through their various schemes, the Project Organization deve-loped under the Urban Basic Services for the Poor (UBSP) Programme is to play a coordinating role. The UBSP Programme, with its emphasis on developing CBOs is to ensure a high quality of community involvement.

Attention is drawn to a diagram of the Community-led Integrated Development Model (Figure 16.1) where an effort has been made to link "needs" with programmes and programmes with "instrumentalities" within the framework of a community-centred approach. Part A of the model diagram also focusses attention on the critical role assigned to the Urban Basic Services for the Poor (UBSP) programme as "the Integrating Catalyst".

Part B of the model diagram elucidates the bottom-up approach starting from individual women RCVs and young, male Resident Infrastructure Volunteers (RIVs) representing a cluster of 20 households moving on to neighbourhoods represented by Neighbourhood

Figure 16.1: Community-led Integrated Development Model

Part A: Functional Specialization

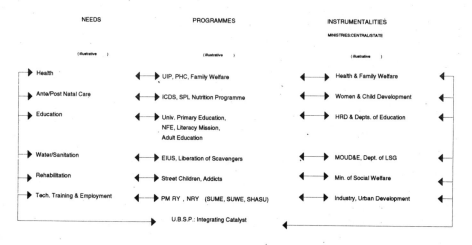

Part B: Community-centred Bottom-up Approach

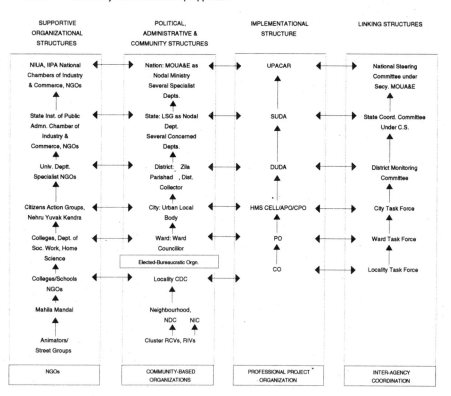

Development and Infrastructure Committees and culminating at the locality level in the form of Community Development Societies.

The model diagram focusses the spotlight on the professional Project Organization sought to be developed at the locality, ward, city, district and state levels through the instrumentality of the Community Organizer, Project Officer, City Project Officer, District Urban Development Agency and State Urban Development Agency. At the national level, the model advocates the setting up of the Urban Poverty Alleviation through Community-Action-Resources (UPCAR) Agency as an autonomous body overseeing the involvement of NGOs in the task of providing basic services in urban areas.

The model diagram highlights the synergy sought to be developed between the Project Officer of UBSP, the Ward Counsellor and local NGOs at the Ward Level as well as City Project Officer leading the Humanitarian Municipal Services (HMS) Cell, the Urban Local Body and the non-governmental organization called the Citizens' Action Group at the city level. In this manner, the model seeks to develop a harmonious interface between the Urban Local Body and the Project Organization.

The model diagram brings into bold relief the required correlation between the various levels of the Elected Bureaucratic Organization (EBO) from the Ward to the State and National levels on the one hand and highlights the interface of the EBO with the CBOs, the Professional Project Organization (PPO) and NGOs on the other hand.

Further, the model diagram emphasizes the development of "linking structures" from the locality level to the national level with a view to strengthening inter-agency coordination and for effective monitoring of the various schemes aimed at convergent provision of basic services.

In order to give a concrete shape to inter-agency coordination, it is of vital importance that Inter-agency Task Forces are set up at the locality, ward and city levels. The Task Force at the locality level should be headed by the Community Organizer, at the ward level by the Ward Councillor and at the city level by the Municipal Commissioner.

At the locality level, all members of the Locality Task Force should perform the following functions:

i) Assist the community in conducting self-surveys with regard to existing physical and social services as well as prioritization of their "felt needs".

ii) Foster general awareness in the community about the objectives of the National Programme of Action, the present status of the community with regard thereto and the salient features of the existing programmes for provision of basic services.

iii) Assist in the identification of RCVs and RICs formation of neighbourhood Development Committees and Neighbourhood Infrastructure Committees and culmination of the community organizations through the constitution of community development societies.

iv) Assist the NDCs and NICs to prepare Mini-Plans and the Community Development Societies to prepare Locality Development Plans.

At the Ward level, all members of the Ward Task Force should perform the following functions:

i) Ensure convergence of both physical and social services being provided under different schemes by different departments.

ii) Prepare and monitor a Programme Evaluation and Review Technique (PERT) chart regarding provision of physical services.

iii) Ensure that the basic services being provided cover the poorest or most disadvantaged 10 per cent of the residents of the ward.

At the city level, all members of the City Task Force should perform the following functions:

i) Forge an effective working relationship between the field functionaries of different departments thereby developing a well-knit team for the provision of basic physical and social services.

ii) Integrate the Special Plan for the provision of basic services in low-income settlements with the City Infrastructural Development Plan.

iii) Develop a common Management Information System (MIS) for the cluster, locality and city levels with a Family Development Book for each family as the initial monitoring format.

iv) Jointly review the efficacy of various programmes for the provision of basic services in terms of their structure, function and implementation.

Various ministries or departments of the central government need to issue appropriate instructions to the state governments, and the state governments, in turn, need to issue directives to both the officers of different departments as well as the administrative authorities in different districts to facilitate the constitution and working of the inter-departmental locality, ward and city Task Forces as well as the operation of the common MIS.

Both at the state and the central levels, Inter-departmental Committees need to monitor the integrated provision of basic services with the State

Department of Local Self-Government and the Ministry of Urban Development acting as nodal agencies.

Convergence of resources, both human and financial, is a critical characteristics of the CIDM. In relation to monitoring and implementation of schemes aiming at provision of basic physical and social services, the National Steering Committee at the central government level, the State Urban Development Agency, the District Urban Development Agency, the Inter-agency Task Forces at the city, ward and locality levels constitute appropriate instrumentalities.

In relation to financial convergence, it would be desirable to set up an Urban Poverty Fund (UPF) where resources of various departments earmarked for low income settlements can be pooled. This pool of resources would constitute the fundage for financing provision of basic services in low-income urban settlements. However, there should be one exception to this pooling, that is, funds meant for the Neighbourhood Development Committees, Neighbourhood Infrastructure Committees and the Community Development Societies should be sent by the DUDA directly to those committees or societies so that the urban poor feel empowered in relation to the developmental process.

Pooling of resources under the Urban Poverty Fund is only meant to develop a special corpus for the poorest of the poor and is not meant to isolate the development of low-income settlements from the city as a whole. Multi-sectoral Investment Planning (MSIP) is recommended as a medium for prioritization of competing needs as well as for designing an integrated plan for City Development. Financial integration is also important for enabling spatial and environmental integration.

Integrated planning is also recommended for enabling cross-subsidization between remunerative and non-remunerative projects. Local governments should be encouraged to look innovatively at the potential of both public and private partnerships as well as NGO and CBO partnerships. New forms of contractual arrangements, such as, Build, Operate and Own (BOO), Build Operate and Transfer (BOT) and Build, Operate, Lease and Transfer (BOLT) need to be carefully experimented with.

It is of critical importance to promote a pluralist culture in relation to the implementation of programmes aimed at provision of basic services. A pluralist culture refers to utilizing the services of academic resource institutions, National Social Service (NSS) wings of schools, National Cadet Corps (NCC) wings of schools and colleges, *Chetna Sanghs* (Association for Alertness), *Nehru Yuvak Kendras* (Nehru Youth Centres) and citizens' groups in the task of achieving the objectives of the National Programme of Action. In short, the strategy of organizational pluralism involves shifting the focus from the governmental departments to non-governmental organizations. Citizens' action groups like the Baroda Citizens' Council are a significant form of organizational pluralism. It would be desirable to set up such Action Groups at the city level consisting of resource persons from the fields of health, education, social service, community medicine, technical training, business and commerce who are interested in various facets of urban poverty alleviation. Those members of these groups who are interested in training and extension should serve as Trainers-on-Call (TOCs) for improving the awareness of the weaker sections of society in relation to NPA parameters and for assisting them to organize themselves for community action.

Appropriate and incremental technologies based on low-cost provision of basic services are ideally suited to the community-centred approach to development. Low-cost water supply systems such as Mark-II handpumps or low-height storage systems and *Sulabh Shuchalaya* (pour-flush, pay and use latrines) are examples of such low-cost technologies. Further, such public systems should be maintained by members of the community after receiving appropriate training. In this manner, the CIDM emphasizes local leadership and community management leading to sustainable development.

A comprehensive training effort needs to be mounted to orient and train officers at the state, district, city and slum levels in the philosophy of grassroots' planning, community participation, convergence of resources, inter-agency team-building and working hand-in-hand with the elected representatives of urban local bodies. Short advocacy seminars should be organized for MLAs, Municipal Councillors, Chairmen or Secretaries of noted NGOs and eminent citizens of major cities. Short orientation programmes need to be organized for senior-level officers at the state level. Training courses need to be organized for middle-level officers of different state departments, district-level officers, municipal officers and the officers of the professional Project Organization at various levels. Participative training also needs to be organized for Resident Community Volunteers, Resident Infrastructure Volunteers, members of Community Development Societies and special volunteers at the locality level called animators.

Participation of local NGOs is vital to the success of the Community-lead Integrated Development Model. The participation of NGOs should be based on their specialization in a given field, say social mobilization, health, education, skill upgradation or income-generation activities. Omnibus NGOs claiming to implement the entire programme in a given area should, generally, be handled with extreme caution. NGOs should be evaluated on the basis of a "performance audit" consisting of ascertaining the views of the beneficiaries and comparing objectives of the programme with achievements on the ground.

CBOs, the government represented by various specialist departments, the professional Project Organization, NGOs including academic resource institutions and the Urban Local Bodies together constitute the five operational instrumentalities of the community-led Integrated Development Model. These five instrumentalities are like the five fingers of the "developmental hand". It is this "developmental hand" moved by the spirit of community action which can provide basic physical and social services in any given city—for the entire city but especially for low-income settlements-- in a cost-effective, incremental and sustainable manner.

BIBLIOGRAPHY

Government of India (1957). *Constitution of India*, Government of India Press, New Delhi.

Himachal Pradesh Institute of Public Administration (1991), Urban Basic Services for the Poor, Workshop paper, Fairlawn, 15–19 July (unpublished), Shimla.

Institute of Applied Manpower Research (1992), *Employment Generation for Educated Persons—A Discussion paper*, Institute of Applied Manpower Research, New Delhi.

National Commission on Urbanization (NCU) (1988), *Final Report, Vol. II*, Government of India Press, New Delhi.

National Institute of Urban Affairs (NIUA) (1991), *Basic Services and the Urban Poor*, NIUA, New Delhi.

National Sample Survey Organization (NSSO) (1989), *National Sample Survey (43rd Round)*, New Delhi.

Planning Commission (1993), Expert Group on Estimation of Proportion and Number of Poor, Government of India, New Delhi.

Sivaramakrishnan, K.C. and Mathur, O.P. (1991), 'Urban Economy, Employment and Poverty', *Financial Express*, 18 August, New Delhi.

Town and Country Planning Organization (1991), *A Supplementary to the Annual Report, 1989–90—Environmental Improvement of Urban Slums Scheme*, Ministry of Urban Development, Government of India, New Delhi.

UNICEF (1991), *A Programme for Children and Women in India—Plan of Operations 1991-95*, Prepared by UNICEF in collaboration with MOUD, UNICEF, New Delhi.

UNICEF (1995), *UNICEF in India—The Continuing Revolution for Children*, UNICEF, New Delhi.

17

THE CUKUROVA METROPOLITAN REGION URBAN DEVELOPMENT PROJECT

Nihat Sayinalp

Introduction and Background

More than half of Turkey's population lives in cities and towns, and the number of urban dwellers is growing at around 4.5 per cent per year. Turkey's cities suffer from inadequate urban infrastructure which constrains economic growth and imposes heavy social costs. In the past, infrastructure investments have been limited and policies determining some design standards, pricing and cost recovery have not been adequate. Imbalances have resulted from responsibilities divided between central government agencies which have undertaken most of the infrastructure investments, and local authorities which have been responsible primarily for operation and maintenance. Heavy workloads and poor coordination among these agencies have only aggravated the problem of adequate infrastructure provision (Ministry of Environment, 1987).

In its policy reforms the Government of Turkey has taken a number of initiatives aimed at meeting the urban service delivery challenge. It has decentralized responsibilities for key municipal services to local governments. It is also stepping up the resource flows to municipalities while giving them greater freedom to raise their own resources. In addition, the rules and responsibilities of central government agencies are being reviewed and revised.

The Cukurova Metropolitan Region Urban Development Project is a pilot project which was designed to help the government to refine and implement its decentralization strategy through selective interventions in five cities located at Cukurova, the eastern coast of Turkey at the Mediterranean Sea.

The project would strengthen the capability of these five municipalities to plan, implement, operate and maintain urban services and improve their resource mobilization and financial management. In parallel, it would take a first step towards reorienting the *Iller* Bank by establishing its capability to appraise and supervise municipal investment programmes. *Iller* Bank is the most important institution for this project because it has been responsible for financing and executing most infrastructure investment on behalf of municipalities in Turkey. During preparation of the pilot project, a blueprint for municipal reforms has been developed; during its implementation, selected policies and programmes would be tested for a wider replication in Turkey.

Population Growth

In 1985, 27 million or 53 per cent of the Turkish population (51 million) lived in cities and towns of 10,000 or more people. This represents an almost sixfold increase from 5.2 million (19 per cent) in 1950 and a current annual rate of increase of about 4.5 per cent. The rate of urbanization shows few signs of slackening in the years ahead. In the medium term, about half of the anticipated urban population growth (currently some 1.4 million people a year) will be due to natural increase and the other half will be due to rural-urban migration. Between 1962 and 1985, the contribution of agriculture to the GNP fell from 38 per cent to 20 per cent, agricultural employment fell from 9.7 million to 9.4 million, and the rural population grew at a modest rate of about 0.6 per cent (State Institute of Statistics, 1995).

Institutional Arrangements for Urban Management

Municipalities: Local services in Turkey are provided by a variety of central and local authorities, with considerable overlap of responsibilities. The most important local government institutions in urban areas include eight metropolitan cities covering a total of 1,800 municipalities (serving 70 per cent of the national population). Under the Municipalities Law 1580 of 1930, they are responsible for a wide variety of regulatory functions (including control of consumer prices, planning and building, licenses, business permits and health inspections) as well as provision of local services (including slaughterhouses, gas works, bakeries, markets, public transport, water and sanitation, roads, drainage, solid waste collection and disposal).

The actual functions of municipalities have evolved over time in response to technological change, relative better access to resources and skilled manpower by central versus local institutions, and the government policy. Electricity supply and distribution have been transferred to the Turkish Electricity Authority (TEK).

The *Iller* Bank and the State Hydraulic Works are responsible for planning, financing and implementing the main water and sewerage infrastructure. Thus, among the major municipal engineering services involving substantial investments, the municipalities are left with road investments as their only responsibilities. The ability of municipalities to guide growth was also limited since the Ministry of Reconstruction and Settlements was charged with preparing urban master plans.

Municipal authority resides in the elected assembly which approves all budgets and major policies. Day-to-day administration is the responsibility of the elected mayor, assisted by a council with statutory membership of representatives of the assembly and specific municipal staff. Municipal departments are grouped under up to four deputy mayors. The accounting system, dating from 1930, provided no guidance on the cost of various services. In addition to normal departments, municipalities typically include one or more subsidiary organizations or departments to manage revenue-earning services (water supply, public transport, gas works, etc.).

Their budgets, accounts, organizational structures and personnel were authorized separately from those of the municipality as a whole, although their operations came under the authority of the council of mayors and the assembly. The eight metropolitan municipalities in the country, one of which is within the Cukurova project area, were established in 1986 as autonomous organizations by law with their own boards (appointed by the municipalities) to handle water and sanitation.

Central Government Organizations

Overall control of local government is exercised by the Ministry of Interior, to which the governors of the 76 provinces, sub-governors of the 842 districts, and directors of the 695 communes report. Governors are charged with coordinating all central government activities within their provinces, including security. They review municipal budgets and exercise *de facto* control over the Special Provincial Administrations (SPAs) which invest in various local services beyond municipal boundaries, and execute works for central ministries, especially education and health. Ministry of Interior tutelage over municipalities is vested in its Local Government Directorate. This Directorate monitors municipal budgets and staffing, and provides training for the staff of local government. It also supervises local government controllers who are responsible for ensuring that expenditures are made in conformity with budgets and laws.

Several other central agencies carry out urban services. The Ministry of Public Works and Settlement provides advice and training in urban planning; it also defines mass transit policies and physical planning standards to be followed by municipalities if they are to qualify for central assistance or Ministry of Public Works and Settlement funds for land development under the Reconstruction Act.

State Hydraulic Works is responsible for investment in headworks and water treatment works for centres with a population of 100,000 or more, which it then hands over to municipalities for operation and maintenance.

From the point of view of infrastructure and urban investments, the most significant central organization is the *Iller* Bank. Established by law no. 4759 of 1945, the *Iller* Bank employs more than 4,000 people. It fulfills three major roles:

1. It acts as a channel for the share of total tax revenues transferred to municipalities as a recurrent grant on the basis of population.
2. It is as a major public works agency which carries out mapping, planning, water and sewerage investments, and constructs miscellaneous buildings for local governments.
3. It functions as a bank which makes loans from its own resources for projects it executes as well as for works carried out by municipalities.

The *Iller* Bank was the executing agency for the Cukurova Urban Development Project.

The State Planning Organization approves all municipal investments over a certain amount (expenditures of $100,000 or more), as well as any new municipal project with an estimated cost of $ 1 million or more. The State Planning Organization is also responsible for approving the *Iller* Bank programme and for monitoring implementation of projects.

The preparation of the Cukurova Metropolitan Region Urban Development Project and partly its design were carried out by the State Planning Organization.

The Cukurova Municipalities and the Pilot Study

In 1984, a pilot study was started by the State Planning Organization, Undersecretariat of Prime Ministry. The Cukurova Metropolitan Region was selected for the project because it exemplifies the problems of rapid urban growth and service deficiencies, and because future growth in this important area will be jeopardized if services were not provided more efficiently. The region comprises the agriculturally-rich Cukurova region in the southern plain of Turkey within the provinces of Icel, Adana and Hatay. These provinces recorded a population of 3.8 million at the time of the 1985 census, having grown at a rate of 3.5 per cent per annum since 1945 (compared with the national growth rate of 2.5 per cent). The five cities included in the proposed project (Adana, 776,000; Mersin, 315,000; Tarsus, 160,000; Ceyhan, 73,000; and Iskenderun, 174,000) had population of 1.5 million in 1985, or about 6 per cent of the country's total urban population. Since 1945 they have grown at 5.3 per cent per annum (compared with about 4.5 per cent for all centres with 10,000 or more population). This growth accelerated, reaching 6.2 per cent from 1980 to 1985, and added about 90,000 to 100,000 persons per annum (IBRD, 1990).

Population growth in this region has responded to economic growth, and both are expected to continue above the national averages in the future. Migrants from the surrounding agricultural areas make up more than half of the urban population increase. Many new urban dwellers who were enticed from Eastern Turkey by prospects of seasonal employment in Cukurova agriculture have remained in the region and joined the industrial labour force.

Economic growth in Cukurova was initially based exclusively on agriculture (irrigated cotton and a variety of food crops) and agriculture-linked industries and services. In the last two decades, heavy industries (the largest steel plant in Turkey, fertilizer industries and a refinery), and light industries serve the region and its hinterland as well as export markets, and trans-shipment have become important economic activities. The region is accessible through the ports of Mersin and Iskenderun, with additional ports at Yumurtalik (for fertilizers), Dortyol (pipeline terminus) and Isdemir (steel mill).

A new duty-free zone had been established at Mersin, and another was planned for Yumurtalik, the terminus of the new Turkey-Iraq natural gas pipeline.

Urban service deficiencies limit welfare and growth prospects. Almost half of the population of the five largest Cukurova cities live in *gecekondus* (unauthorized settlements). Some *gecekondus* were built on squatted public land. Unoccupied public lands had largely disappeared and most buildings constructed on private land which is generally sub-divided and sold without planning approvals. The majority of these settlements were served (formally or informally) with water and electricity, some with roads, but few with sewers (95 per cent of households are connected with public water systems, of which 15 per cent are illegal, and only 20 per cent have sewer systems).

The low-lying areas with high water tables where most *gecekondus* are located, and where water is drawn from individual wells, face particularly high health risks from poor sanitation.

Drainage is also a problem in large parts of these cities, and malaria, after being eradicated in the 1960s, re-emerged in recent years as a major health threat.

Unmanaged urban garbage dumps also pose a health hazard. Lack of basic infrastructures (water, electricity and telecommunication) increasingly constrain development of light industry, although major increases in power and telecommunication are planned or are underway. With growth in the number of motor vehicles at over 15 per cent per annum in the Cukurova province, traffic would require increasing attention in the short run if costs of transporting people and goods were to be restrained. Disposal of industrial effluents has not yet become a major issue, although it is likely to emerge in response to greater density of industry, use of more chemicals, and rising consciousness of environmental matters in Turkey.

Objectives of the Cukurova Metropolitan Region Urban Development Project

The pilot study project was supported by the World Bank, and covered all municipal issues: organization, finance, accounting, capital investment, operation and maintenance of water supply, sanitation, solid waste management, roads, drainage, environmental issues, urban and transportation planning, and relations with central government agencies.

The project was formulated within the framework of the government's decentralization policy. Its main objectives were to:

1. Assist the municipalities of Adana, Mersin, Tarsus, Iskenderun and Ceyhan to overcome service deficiencies and manage urban growth through the financing of urban infrastructure;
2. Introduce in the five project municipalities policies and institutional arrangements for investment planning and implementation, cost recovery, financial management and staff development which would be suitable for replication in other Turkish cities; and
3. Build up in the *Iller* Bank a capacity for appraisal and monitoring of municipal infrastructure projects and investment programmes.

Main Features of the Cukurova Project

The project would finance part of the multi-sectoral municipal investment programmes in basic engineering services of the Cukurova Metropolitan Region Urban Development Project for the period 1987–1994. This involved, *inter alia*, analyses and projections of local revenue collection, central government revenue sharing and lending, and recurrent expenditures.

The *Iller* Bank would review the investment programmes on an annual basis, assess the credit worthiness of the municipalities, appraise sub-projects submitted for central government funding, and monitor implementation through its Project Review and Monitoring Unit (PRIMU).

The municipal investments to be financed under the project would help direct urban growth and catch up on service deficiencies through coordinated area-based programmes for construction of secondary and tertiary infrastructure and through extension of major trunk infrastructure and improvements in engineering services on a city scale. The main components were:

a) The area-based infrastructure programmes, which would deal with three different situations:

i) in urban expansion areas, large tracts of unbuilt land would be developed for subsequent sale for construction of houses (parallel to this, the government would provide the necessary social facilities);

ii) in housing areas, spontaneous private development would be guided and regularized, and the basic infrastructure and social facilities be provided; and

iii) in *gecekondu* upgrading areas land tenure would be regularized and infrastructure deficiencies be corrected. In the urban expansion areas, the cost would be recovered through the price of developed land; in the privately-owned areas, through betterment and connection charges. The area-based programmes would help to arrest the establishment of new *gecekondu* areas while at the same time upgrade the infrastructure for about 90,000 existing *gecekondu* households and provide services for some 86,000 new households or about 50 per cent of the new households in these cities during 1986 to 1994.

(b) The trunk infrastructure and city-wide engineering programmes, which would provide linkages to the area-based programmes and help overcome deficiencies in the existing main networks for water, sanitation, drainage, roads, and solid waste management. They would include works, equipment, design and supervision services.

(c) The institutional development programme, which would support a restructuring of the municipalities and strengthen their ability to plan and implement investment programmes, to operate and maintain existing facilities, and to manage their finances. This component would include equipment and selected technical assistance to the five municipalities and to the PRIMU, and the establishment of a regional training centre for municipal staff.

Implementation of the Project and Problems Encountered

Completed feasibility studies, final designs and tender documents for the project municipalities of the Cukurova Metropolitan Region Urban Development Project were handed over to the *Iller* Bank from the State Planning Organization for implementation in June 1987. The project was scheduled to be completed in 1994.

During the first phase of the implementation, the Project Review, Implementation and Management Unit (PRIMU) has been instituted in *Iller* Bank. A PRIMU Directorate in Ankara and a liaison office in the project area Adana have been established. On the other hand, the *Iller* Bank and State Planning Organization selected an international joint venture consultant to assist the PRIMU to execute the Cukurova Urban Development Project. However, the consultant's contract was effective only in late February 1988, and implementation of the project started with a delay of one year. Since then, on-the-job training of PRIMU staff has been undertaken.

First major problems were encountered in the contracts made by the municipalities in accordance with the prior agreements. The contracts required following the principles and procedures of the World Bank; but according to the State Contract Law number 2886 there were considerable problems in procedural matters.

On the other hand, one very important component of the project was to improve the old accounting systems. The implementation of the improvements executed by the finance team of PRIMU required the permission of the Ministry of Interior. The second phase of the project was also greatly influenced by the municipal elections in March 1989, which brought new mayors from the opposition party to all five municipalities. The new administrations wanted to review one by one the project and its components; and as a result of this review, one of the municipalities decided to withdraw from the project without implementing the physical and institutional improvements. The other four municipalities decided to continue with the project but with considerable changes and modifications.

Subsequently the government reviewed the project and decided on a major reduction in the scope of the project. The modified project is expected to be completed by the end of June 1995.

Discussion

Service Deficiencies

In addressing the need to assist in overcoming municipal service deficiencies, the project objective was to provide the incentive for installation of new, and upgrading of existing services and for the maintenance of services such as sewage, water, roads, drainage and solid waste. The municipalities involved in the project had services which were inadequate for their existing and increasing urban population and lacked certain essential components.

Project Objectives

a) Provision of potable water was adequate in terms of source availability and treatment, but required increase in the necessary storage and distribution networks. Existing networks were subject to high degree of leakage. With the exception of the networks provided in the urban expansion areas which are discussed later, this project concentrated on the design and the provision of increased storage capability and improved distribution efficiency by the provision of designs for additional storage reservoirs and provision of equipment, and training of municipal staff to enable the identification and analytical assessment of existing networks and the reasons for leakages.

b) Existing urban road networks were increasingly and detrimentally affected, both in terms of capacity and structural capability, which the project sought to improve by the provision of structural designs and traffic management schemes. This was supplemented by training of municipality management and the technical staff. The project also included a limited number of actual construction projects. Such works were based upon existing international specifications for design and supervision.

c) Existing sewerage systems and networks were incomplete in terms of capacity and coverage of the respective municipalities and failed to provide any centralized treatment of recognized standards. By provision of designs for sewage treatment plants, trunk sewers and secondary and tertiary networks, the project attempted to readdress these problems. Phased construction of trunk sewers and networks and treatment plants designed to attain current World Health Organization (WHO) standards also formed part of the project along with provision of facilities and training for the monitoring of achieved treatment standards.

d) Solid waste treatment generally consisted of traditional collection and landfill disposal methods, although at least one constituent municipality had a small solid waste treatment plant. The major contribution of the project regarding solid waste was the provision of recommendations and some equipment for collection and disposal.

Project Achievements

In considering the achievement of project objectives and the effects of the political changes which occurred between the conception and the implementation phases of the project some aspects need to be recognized. As a result of political changes and the overall complexity which resulted in rescheduling and in consideration reduction of the achievable objectives of the project, the success of the project has to be assessed against difficulties:

a) The increased water storage capacity, the training in network leakage assessment and the provision of equipment were among the achievements. However it is recognized that the scope of the project was severely limited in this regard, and in order to maintain these improvements it is essential that in future the funding and training of the necessary technical staff will also be provided.

b) With respect to roads the project objectives were achieved in terms of design and preparation of new schemes. However, as a result of the financial rescheduling, the intended construction works were substantially reduced, which resulted in reduced effectiveness of this project component.

c) The initial project objectives of sewage installation and sewage treatment were achieved in accordance with the planned system designs, and the construction of the sewage networks and treatment plants was partly executed. However, the achievements were considerably limited in terms of actual construction during the project period as a result of the previously mentioned financial cutback. This construction limitation prevented full integration of the sewer systems and treatment in the respective municipalities.

d) The project objectives with regard to solid waste management were achieved. However, it is recognized that considerable future planning and construction would be required to provide an effective integrated solid waste management system in the constituent municipalities.

Managing urban growth: As previously indicated it was recognized that the actions required in respect of urban management consisted of two main objectives, namely, provision of infrastructure on large tracts of unbuilt land which would subsequently be developed for planned housing and recreational purposes, and provision or upgrading of infrastructure services in unplanned or uncontrolled housing areas.

Increased capacities in planning, execution and management of services and cost recovery: It was recognized that there was a need to restructure existing management systems of the constituent municipalities in order to achieve the necessary improvements in planning, operation and maintenance of existing facilities, and the management of local budgets and financial programmes.

The central government recognized the constraints of the municipalities and hence the project objectives were restricted to the provision of equipment, technical assistance and establishment of a training centre for municipal staff. Under the project, provision was made for the supply of necessary computer equipment which enabled the municipalities to modernize their financial management control, and the system of water rate and property tax collection, and to integrate their town and area planning capabilities. Numerous accounting and financial programmes were provided to upgrade municipality financial systems. At an early stage in the project, implementation of the regional training centre for municipality staff was cancelled with the result the intended training in managerial, financial and technical matters was limited to very specific demands.

Summary

In the early stages of the formulation of the project it was recognized that creating an integrated approach which was to be long-term would require continuous efforts, even after the initial input by the central government and external funding agencies. The provision of training for all involved staff, whether political, financial or technical was considered essential.

As part of the project it had been intended that a centralized training body, designated as the Cukurova Metropolitan Training Agency, would be established at Adana, being the only metropolitan city located centrally within the project territory.

The purpose of this centre was to train all staff in the project municipalities, from the most senior to the lower managerial levels, in the setting up and control of internationally recognized financial and operational structures, which would allow the integration of all aspects of the project.

As previously described, the proposed project objectives and routes for implementation were different in many major respects to those existing nationally and required a basic change of approach in terms of political and managerial control. The existing municipal structures were politically controlled, and hence any development was directed towards political benefit. This situation tended to prevent integrated infrastructure development because such development did not have a high public profile or carry political prestige.

As a result of political changes during the initial phase of project implementation, Adana Municipality decided to opt out of the project and consequently prevented the establishment of the proposed training scheme. This had a considerable negative effect upon the institutional changes within the municipalities by preventing the political and technical staff within these bodies to be trained.

This failure to provide an overall training scheme contributed more than any other reason to the inability of the participating institutions, whether local or national, to recognize the fact that such an integrated approach could be both politically and financially beneficial. Hence, with the exception of availability of finance, which is and will be dependent on the national economy, the absence of training probably had the greatest impact in limiting the replication of the integrated approach elsewhere in Turkey.

Having recognized the limitations it must be noted that in promoting the project at a reduced financial level, certain changes were instigated in the remaining participating bodies which, while not providing the intended shift of emphasis, or long-term training, did enable the independently acting municipalities to achieve their revised project aims.

Through the project, financial accounting and reporting methods were greatly improved by the introduction of computerized systems. On-the-job-training, under the guidance of international consultants during the construction phase of the projects, made technical staff aware of the need for and benefits of complying with international standards and of integration of all stages of development.

The formulation of the Cukurova Urban Development Project as an innovative multi-sectoral investment scheme has provided many challenges and learning experiences to these institutions involved, and to those which implemented their investment schemes. This in turn allowed to maintain the political impetus and generated sufficient support to ensure that at least those projects with reduced scope were completed satisfactorily.

The achievements and experiences of the project indicate that the impact of such projects is dependent upon a number of factors which are essential for success:

   i) Political willingness of central government and associated agencies to support the objectives of integrated development.

   ii) The consensus of national and local government policy in respect of development objectives.

   iii) Financial affordability of national and local investments.

   iv) Expectation of the grass roots electorate and their willingness to insist upon the quality of governmental performance.

   v) Preparedness of municipalities and central government to change traditional practices.

   vi) Re-politicization of technical and administrative matters in order to allow unbiased assessment and action based on technical requirements.

   vii) Specialized training, as originally envisaged under this project, to be carried out at all levels of government if project objectives of transformation of local government functions are to be achieved.

   viii) The quality of staff available to implement and maintain the project aims and the permanent employment of such staff, despite local government political changes, must be a prime objective of any on-going programme.

   ix) The expectations of government staff, in particular local technical staff, and their necessary encouragement in their duties, forms an essential part to achieve the objectives of such an ambitious project.

However, replication of this pilot project is unlikely, not because the objectives are unreasonable, but because the pre-conditions mentioned above are not given in Turkey's present political and institutional scenario.

BIBLIOGRAPHY

IBRD (International Bank for Reconstruction and Development) (1990), *Cukurova Metropolitan Region Urban Development Project*, IBRD, Washington.

Ministry of Environment (1987), *National Report-Turkey*, Ankara.

State Institute of Statistics (1985), *Census of Population*, Prime Minister's Office, Ankara.

PART III

GENERAL THEMATIC PAPERS

MUNICIPAL FINANCE AND INTEGRATED URBAN INFRASTRUCTURE DEVELOPMENT[1]

Kyung-Hwan Kim

Introduction

Asia has the largest urban population in the world. By 1990 cities in the region accommodated almost 41 per cent of the world's urban population. By 2020, the share is likely to rise to 56 per cent as its urban centres are projected to hold an additional 1.5 billion people. Asia's urbanization is also marked by the growth of large cities. In 1990, 49 of the world's 116 cities with two million or more population were located in Asia. The region is expected to be the home of 71 of 157 such cities and 13 of 21 mega-cities with population of 10 million or more by the year 2000 (ESCAP 1993, pp. 2–1, 2–5, 2–7).

Rapid urbanization has increased the demand for basic services and infrastructure beyond a level which financial resources and institutional capacity of many urban local governments in the region can cope with. As a result, the quality of basic urban services and urban infrastructure has failed to improve or even declined over time, damaging urban productivity, the quality of urban environment and aggravating the problem of urban poverty by burdening the urban poor most seriously.

A major underlying problem is the large and growing gap between revenue generation and the expenditure needs at the local level. Although local governments are responsible for the provision of various urban services and development of infrastructure, they do not have commensurate financial resources and technical capacity. Their own narrowly prescribed and inelastic revenue sources, which are often poorly tapped due to ineffective administration and lack of political will, yield an income that is barely sufficient to pay for wages and salaries to their personnel and maintain existing infrastructure. As a result, they depend

---

[1] Helpful comments on an earlier draft from Emiel Wegelin are gratefully acknowledged.

heavily on higher level governments for funds, especially for new infrastructure investments.

Typical urban infrastructure investment activities planned and financed by central ministries and parastatal agencies have been carried out on a project-by-project basis and not in a coordinated manner from a broad sectoral perspective on the part of the affected cities. Experience of implementing such projects has demonstrated the inefficiency inherent in this top-down and supply-driven approach. Integrated urban infrastructure development has recently emerged· in an attempt to rectify the defects of the project approach by treating the various interlinked sub-sectors of the urban economy as an integral system.

Examples of broadly defined integrated urban infrastructure development programmes range from those focussed on investment planning and programming to those with comprehensive institution-building orientation. The Integrated Urban Infrastructure Development Programme (IUIDP) in Indonesia, the Integrated Development of Small and Medium Towns (IDSMT) and the Calcutta Urban Development Project (CUDP) in India, the Metro-Manila Capital Investment Folio (CIF) approach in the Philippines belong to the first category, whereas the Regional Cities Development Project (RCDP) in Thailand and the Municipal Management Improvement Programme (MMIP) in Sri Lanka are examples available in the region of the second category (Suselo, Taylor and Wegelin 1995).

This paper discusses interactions between integrated urban infrastructure development and municipal finance looking at both revenue mobilization and expenditure management aspects. The paper builds on the Asian experience in implementing the integrated approach and decentralization of local government administration and finance, although examples from other regions are also discussed where relevant.

Municipal Finance and Integrated Urban Infrastructure Development: An Overview

Integrated urban infrastructure development is a tool for urban management which seeks to promote efficient and equitable delivery of basic urban services of acceptable standards. The key instrument for the implementation of the integrated approach is multi-sectoral investment planning (MSIP). MSIP is an action-oriented process of setting investment priorities designed to   produce a multi-year development plan with identified sources of financing the capital investments as well as recurrent expenditure for the operation and maintenance of the planned infrastructure. Such a plan can guide private sector participation in the provision of infrastructure as well as define the framework for policy decision-making within the public sector.

In order to achieve the objectives of an integrated approach, it is necessary not only to build infrastructure in a coordinated and cost-effective manner but also to secure a sustainable system of operating, maintaining and expanding the network of infrastructure. Therefore, the availability of adequate financial resources and institutional and technical capacity to mobilize and manage resources becomes crucial to the success of integrated urban infrastructure development. For this reason, a typical MSIP includes measures designed to strengthen the revenue generation capacity of the affected local government units. The Revenue Improvement Action Plan (RIAP) of Indonesia's IUIDP is an example.

Resource mobilization at the local level is conditioned by the legal and regulatory environment as well as the institutional incentive structure and technical capacity of local governments. Therefore, efforts to enhance revenue-generating capacity of local government as an integral part of MSIP are likely to succeed only if inter-governmental institutional arrangements provide local autonomy over financial decision-making on the one hand and adequate incentives for the local decision-makers to fully exercise their power to raise revenue on the other hand. Conversely, the stronger the resource base of local governments and their capacity to tap the resource base, the easier it is to support the integrated approach to develop and maintain their urban infrastructure.

Similar reasoning applies to local resource management. Cost-effective and efficient utilization of financial resources achieved by weeding out waste and minimizing duplication through prudent and coordinated planning is the most concrete product which integrated urban infrastructure development programmes can deliver. However, a major lesson learnt in implementing integrated programmes is that bottlenecks in delivery systems could hold back budgeted investment (Suselo, Taylor and Wegelin, 1995, p.224). The point is that the impact of the integrated approach can be maximized when responsibilities are clearly defined among levels of government and an effective system of resource management exists at the local level.

The institutional incentive structure plays a critical role in municipal finance and also in implementing MSIP since it influences the level of local government endeavour to mobilize revenue from available sources and to save costs of providing services. Examples presented in the following sections on this point demonstrate that capacity-building exercises can bear fruits only when a good incentive system is in place to sustain the strengthened capacity.

It is fair to say that the MSIP procedure has raised the level of awareness in and boosted the momentum to carry forward decentralization, although in some cases the integrated approach was introduced by the central government in a highly centralized environment in terms of assignments of responsibilities and financial resources. On the other hand, MSIP becomes more meaningful in a decentralized setting because its very nature being a bottom-up approach to planning and coordination. Therefore, the larger the scope of service provision local governments are responsible for, and the greater financial autonomy they are granted, the more compelling reason will they have to be more careful in planning and coordinating infrastructure development.

Local Revenue Mobilization and Integrated Development

In this section the discussion is focussed on revenue mobilization from own sources of local government in the form of user charges, property tax and other local taxes, and borrowing. Inter-governmental transfers are discussed briefly in conjunction with access to credit for local governments.

User charges and capital contributions: User charges are a local revenue source with ample room for improvement even in developed countries with effective systems of local government administration. User charges are an equitable and efficient means of recovering costs of construction and maintenance of urban infrastructure which produces services to identifiable beneficiaries. An efficient level of investment can be achieved by setting the charge equal to the incremental cost of infrastructure.

User charges are also an effective pricing scheme to control the demand for urban services, most obviously in the case of urban roads. Suppose that a city decides that its two-lane highway is congested because the volume of traffic has exceeded the carrying capacity of the roadway. If the city expands the highway to four lanes to alleviate congestion but does not levy a toll on vehicles travelling the roadway, the expanded highway will soon be congested with a larger number of vehicles than before. The city will have to incur larger costs to further expand the highway next time. This phenomenon is known as Down's fundamental law of roadway congestion. An important implication is that so-called "infrastructure investment needs" could be substantially reduced by correct pricing of services through user charges, i.e., demand management.

Adequate cost recovery through charging is crucial in encouraging the private sector to participate in financing urban infrastructure development. Financial feasibility of an investment project financed by a commercial loan and the breakeven point of a project financed by a build-operate-transfer (BOT) scheme are greatly affected by the level of charge on the use of the service emanating from the infrastructure.

Integrated urban infrastructure development makes it easier for affected cities and municipalities to calculate the adequate amount of investment in various types of urban infrastructure together with the necessary user charge to recover costs. By providing such information about investment options and their financial implications to the potential consumers of the services, the integrated approach could facilitate the process of consensus building as to the acceptability of proposed investment programmes and associated user charges.

In order to make the most out of user charges, an accurate system of measuring and monitoring the quantity of services consumed is essential. Local governments should also overcome the temptation to use the charging system to address the needs of the urban poor. Equity concerns for low-income households can best be addressed by targeted subsidies financed out of the general budget independent of pricing and cost recovery schemes.

User charges discussed so far are levied directly on the beneficiaries of services as they use the facility. An alternative way is to require "up-front" capital contributions, in cash or in kind, to finance the capital cost when the infrastructure investment is put in place. They are known as development charges or impact fees and are most widely implemented in cities of the United States. Although such capital contributions are paid by private developers, they are at least partially passed on to home buyers, the ultimate beneficiaries, in terms of higher prices.

Property tax and other local taxes: The property tax is one of the most common taxes levied mainly at the local level, but its potential is seldom exploited to the fullest extent. A major conclusion drawn from projects to strengthen property tax administration in the Philippines and Indonesia is that improvement of collection efficiency is not sufficient to fully achieve the revenue potential of the property tax in a sustainable manner. Local governments should be allowed to adjust nominal tax rates and valuation at least within some limit. Coverage of the tax should be also broadened through a continued process of identifying new properties and reducing exemptions.

In the case of the Philippines, the Real Property Tax Administration Project contributed to raising additional revenue by improving tax map and assessment techniques. However, the extent to which additional revenue could be collected was limited by mandatory assessment ratios and rate ceilings imposed by the central government (Dillinger, 1989). The Local Government Code of 1991 exacerbated the problem even further by lowering the assessment ratios and introducing extensive exemptions for residential property. As a result, the share of property tax revenue as a percentage of GNP remained stagnant at 0.34 per cent despite improved collection performance.

Indonesia's property tax reform was implemented together with IUIDP. The structure of property taxation was overhauled in 1986 by a new law and wide-ranging measures were introduced subsequently to improve its administration. Major emphasis was placed on improving collection through the Payment Point System (SISTEP) which required that the tax be paid against pre-printed receipts at a designated bank office within the specified date. A delinquency list was produced and some property was seized for the first time in 1991. Consequently, collection efficiency improved to 79 per cent by 1991 and the share of property tax revenue in total own source revenue jumped from 15 to 26 per cent between 1985 and 1991. However, property tax revenue is less than 0.4 per cent of GDP and the current effective tax rate is 0.1 per cent of the market value, still low by international standards leaving further room for improvement (Shah *et al.*, 1994; Kelly 1992; Government of Indonesia, 1994).

An incentive system rewarding local government efforts to raise the maximum possible amount of revenue from the property tax is essential especially because the tax is one of the most visible and politically unpopular taxes. Even when the law is clear about the frequency of revaluation, local authorities hesitate to take action because of political ramifications of substantially increasing the tax burden. One way of dealing with this problem would be to make grant allocations conditional upon regular revaluation of taxable properties. In those countries in which the process of billing and collecting the tax leaves room for negotiation on the terms of payments through personal contacts between the tax officials and the tax payers, computerization helps.

Although every effort to generate more revenue from the property tax should be encouraged, the local revenue base must be broadened further. A lengthy list of local taxes may not be good enough if it includes nuisance taxes whose revenue potential is small relative to the cost of administration. For example, the vast majority of the locally levied taxes in Indonesia fall into this category. On the other hand, taxes on motor vehicles in Korea provide a highly elastic revenue source as automobile ownership increases rapidly as urban income grows and also because the cost of administrating the taxes is relatively small.

Local borrowing and inter-governmental transfers: Prudent local borrowing is an appropriate means of financing infrastructure investment projects which generate benefits over a long period of time. It also promotes inter-generational equity to the extent the debt service payments match the services emanating from the projects financed by debt. In reality, local governments in developing countries have very limited access to credit due to underdeveloped domestic financial and capital markets as well as low marketability of local government projects due to their poor finances and hence inadequate capacity to service the debt.

But one of the most fundamental constraints is the central government control on debt financing. When decentralization laws lifted all forms of state control on local government borrowing and at the same time financial deregulation took place in France, local governments attained access to all credit institutions and to financial markets at market conditions (Cacheux and Tourjansky, 1992, p.33). Some cities and municipalities in the Philippines started floating bonds at the market rates to finance projects on housing, markets and transportation when they were given the power to borrow under the Local Government Code of 1991. With the approval of the Ministry of Finance, Seoul Metropolitan Government in Korea issued Yankee bonds in the US market to raise some of the funds needed to expand its subway system.

When local governments have no access to market-based credit, municipal credit institutions (MCIs) can be a reasonable means of channelling funds to local authorities. For example, the Regional Development Account (RDA) in Indonesia was established to help local governments find capital to finance investment projects within the framework of IUIDP. However, the track record of MCIs in developing countries is poor with a few exceptions including that of Colombia. One important reason is that the financial viability of MCIs tends to be compromised by other government development interests in project selection.

In order for MCIs to be sustainable it is important to operate them on commercial terms. Lending rates should be set close to competitive rates reflecting the opportunity cost of funds. Projects eligible for funding should be selected mainly on the basis of their economic feasibility. Delinquent borrowers should be penalized through a practically enforceable mechanism in lieu of a collateral. An arrangement which allows the lender to intercept transfers to local governments from the central government is an example being implemented in the Philippines and Pakistan. The loan could be disbursed in phases conditional upon the satisfactory servicing of the debt in the previous phases. The central government could reduce the regular budget transfer to local authorities with poor repayment records.

The success of FEDU/FINDETER of Colombia is attributable to these factors. It is an autonomous agency operating under the finance ministry, relatively protected from political pressures. It does not lend directly to municipal governments but operates as a discount agency to private sector and state-owned commercial banks that make the loans, appraise the projects, and monitor the performance. They charge competitive interest rates on the loans, and retain the right to a portion of the borrower's revenue source as a guarantee. Since these financial intermediaries bear 100 per cent of the risk on debt service obligations, the system is foolproof against financially unsound projects. In fact, FINDETER has no bad debts. The system's funding does not rely on government budgetary appropriations but rather on bonds, recycling of its loans, and foreign credits from bilateral and multilateral sources (World Bank, 1994, p.103; Garzon, 1992).

On the other hand, Indonesia's RDA is a revolving fund managed by the Ministry of Finance. It is funded by central budget allocations, repayments of loans by local governments and local public enterprises, and foreign loans and grants. Loans are made based on a set of clear and uniform eligibility criteria up to 20 years including a grace period of up to five years. Although the lending rate is higher than that of inflation, it is much lower than the market rate, even considering the fact that the projects financed by RDA loans are less risky than those financed by commercial loans. Although RDA has contributed to providing access to credit for regional governments, large arrears on loan accounts, reported to be 29 per cent on principal and 24 per cent on interest (Shah *et al.*, 1994, p.151), could jeopardize the financial viability of the fund.

Whether or not MCIs should be regarded as an interim solution to the problem of the lack of source of raising capital to finance local government capital investment is somewhat controversial. There is a view that MCIs should be a transitory way station until local governments become capable of raising capital directly from financial and capital markets. In fact, Credit Locale of France has evolved from a directed credit institution to become a commercial-base lending institution mobilizing funds in both domestic and international capital markets.

The above view can be supported by the prediction that specialized financial institutions will find it increasingly difficult to survive the stream of financial integration and globalization. The changing composition of the international flow of capital from predominantly debt to equity instruments may also make MCIs less attractive to local governments in the future. However, the fact that the vast majority of local governments have a long way to go before they become bankable to private sector financial institutions suggests that MCIs may be the only realistic option for some time.

Technical expertise and financial discipline gained through integrated urban infrastructure development can be valuable to local governments in identifying economically feasible projects, prioritizing them and preparing project proposals to seek funding within the limit of their debt carrying capacity. Technical assistance from the central government or MCIs could further strengthen such capacity. The central government can make a more fundamental contribution by providing greater local financial autonomy so that the local government units can improve their ability to service the debt and hence make themselves more creditworthy.

It is also important to coordinate the credit system with the inter-governmental grant system to provide the right incentive to local governments. A relatively rapid increase in development grants from the central government during the 1988-92 period is believed to have limited the increase in regional government borrowing in Indonesia (Shah *et al.*, 1994, p.149). On the other hand, grants, rather than subsidized loans, should be used as an instrument to achieve equity objectives.

Reform in inter-governmental transfer systems is crucial for the successful implementation of integrated infrastructure development because local governments rely heavily on grants from the centre for infrastructure financing. Transfers should be made compatible with and responsive to the preferences and expenditure priorities of recipient local governments through the use of broadly defined block grants. Grants should be allocated in a predictable, reliable and timely manner to facilitate integrated capital planning and budgeting.

Inter-governmental transfers should be carefully designed to strike a balance between addressing fiscal disparity across local authorities and encouraging them to increase their own source revenue. Rewarding local government units with strong revenue mobilization record is likely to penalize those with weak economic base unless performance is carefully evaluated on the basis of efforts.

Increasing the willingness-to-pay: One last point about resource mobilization concerns the need to expand public relations efforts. Research suggests that even the urban poor are willing and able to pay for infrastructure because they are most severely hurt when adequate basic services are not provided. The challenge is to find the mechanisms to translate their willingness to actual payment. For this purpose, it is important to engage citizens from early on in the design of the projects and the selection of service standards by providing them with information on available options and financial implications of each option. Integrated infrastructure development offers an excellent opportunity for this.

By convincing the customers of the close relationships between what they pay and what they get, such efforts can contribute towards arresting the vicious circle of inadequate services lowering the willingness to pay for the services which in turn reduces local revenue, thereby leading to further deterioration of service delivery. Improved communication of financial information to the constituents will also enhance transparency and accountability of local government finance. Of course, local government units also need to increase the level of willingness-to-pay of the constituents by improving service delivery. We will turn to this in the next sub-section.

Expenditure Planning, Resource Management and Integrated Infrastructure Development

Expenditure Planning and Management: Rationalizing expenditure planning and management is equally important as enhancing resource mobilization capacity since the ultimate goal of strengthening local government finances is to provide quality services to local residents who contribute to the revenue base of local governments.

Integrated urban infrastructure development is designed as a tool aiming at achieving the above goal by enabling local governments to plan for replacement and maintenance of existing infrastructure as well as new investments, helping them minimize costs through careful sequencing of projects, horizontal integration and coordination among sectors and vertical integration among different levels of government, and by facilitating private sector participation.

In principle, the integrated approach to infrastructure development could improve capital planning and budgeting by incorporating pricing of services derived from the capital investment projects as well as taking into consideration the implications of new investments on the recurrent expenditure requirements to be met to operate and maintain the facilities. This way, capital budgeting can be made a more demand-driven process rather than an attempt to mobilize a fixed amount based upon estimates of physical investment needs unrelated to the willingness to pay on the part of potential beneficiaries. In other words, investment programmes can be selected through a process reflecting the preferences of the end-users informed of available options and required contributions instead of being determined by bureaucrats.

A capital investment programme produced by MSIP does not however, translate into a meaningful capital budget if the funds are neither apportioned nor committed. Although realistic and time-bound revenue enhancement programmes are supposed to establish the linkage, the experience of Indonesia's Revenue Improvement Action Plans (RIAPs) suggests that implementation could be hampered by uncertainties about government policy toward fiscal decentralization and inter-governmental transfers. Moreover, RIAP is inadequate in strengthening the overall financial capacity of local governments since it does not address financial management or financial controls on expenditure (Suselo, Taylor and Wegelin, 1995, p. 134 and 197). Dependency on various donors for funding and technical assistance could cause further complications.

These and other bottlenecks in programme implementation and disbursement may explain the fact that per capita real capital spending by regional governments in Indonesia has remained essentially stagnant since the implementation of IUIDP (Government of Indonesia, 1994, p.16), although it may be correctly argued that this indicator fails to capture efficiency gain in the form of reduced cost.

In rationalizing local expenditure management it is very important to establish incentives to encourage local governments to behave as entrepreneurs rather than bureaucratic units. For instance, line-item budgeting system provides perverse incentives by monitoring the input instead of the outcome of the expenditure (Osborne, 1991). It penalizes a manager who does not use up the budgeted funds within a given fiscal year as a result of identifying and applying cost-effective methods. The manager will not be able to retain the money saved for other activities, will be blamed for having asked for too much to start with, and will very likely get less in the next fiscal year. A programme performance budgeting system should be adopted to rectify this problem.

Private sector participation: In the light of the size of the gap between infrastructure needs and financing capacity of the public sector, it is logical to engage the private sector in urban infrastructure and service provision. An equally important gain could be the injection of entrepreneurship into the culture of resource management.

There is an emerging trend in Asia towards more active private sector involvement in the form of various partnerships in providing selected services. Examples include water projects in Malaysia, the BOT arrangements in the Philippines and Thailand and contracting out of garbage collection and disposal in South Korea. Efficiency gains from involving the private sector have also been demonstrated. A recent case study (Paik, 1994) on the effect of garbage collection and disposal under contracting reports almost a three-fold increase in efficiency as compared to the direct public sector provision.

On the other hand, there are various constraints which need to be overcome in order to benefit from engaging the private sector. Inadequate competition among potential bidders, the difficult task of offering a sufficiently long contract period to enable bidders to commit capital as necessary, while at the same time maintaining the leverage to rectify non-performance during the contract period, the political problem of dealing with surplus labour arising from increased participation of the private sector in municipal service delivery, and identifying and unbundling various risks associated with private sector financing are among the problems encountered generally. There may be other specific legal and regulatory issues more pertinent in particular countries (Lorentzen, 1994).

Another pre-condition for successful engagement of the private sector is that the service boundary is large enough to realize economies of scale in operation. Creation of large numbers of small municipalities and autonomous districts with inadequate resource base in the process of decentralization may be a problem in this regard. Joint service provision among adjoining local government units through special service districts could be a realistic option.

Conclusion

Integrated urban infrastructure development offers an excellent opportunity to improve municipal finance by raising cost awareness and reducing costs through better financial planning, budgeting and programming, as well as encouraging mobilization of own source by local governments. Conversely, fiscal, institutional and technical capacities of local governments affect the success potential in implementing integrated programmes.

In order to maximize the impact of the integrated approach on urban productivity and the quality of urban life in a sustainable manner, it is critical to place it in the broad context of promoting decentralization with accountability and private sector participation in urban service delivery. The development of an appropriate institutional incentive structure should be given greater attention.

Systematic efforts should be made to decentralize planning and programming responsibilities on the one hand and to strengthen vertical and horizontal coordination on the other. Improving inter-governmental fiscal transfer systems and vertical coordination among different levels of government is a critical element of viable decentralization. Horizontal coordination among local government units in metropolitan areas becomes especially relevant as decentralization will make it more difficult to deal with the not-in-my-backyard (NIMBY) attitude. Adequate regulation and ennoblement by government is essential in realizing the potential continuation of the private sector contribution towards urban infrastructure development and service delivery. While actual sectoral scope of multi-sector investment planning naturally may vary from one country to another depending on the existing arrangements of service provision and coordination in respective countries, it seems logical to include the transport sector in MSIP where relevant in the light of an overarching concern in large cities in the region over serious social costs arising from traffic congestion and environmental degradation. Incorporating land management would further enhance the synergy effect of MSIP by enabling spatial and economic concerns to be addressed simultaneously.

It would be also ideal to fully integrate the finance sources for various parts of an integrated programme within the framework of medium-term overall municipal planning. In order to facilitate this to happen, it would be necessary for local governments to be given substantial autonomy over their finances, for inter-governmental transfers to be delivered in a predictable and timely manner, and for the scope of revenue enhancement programmes to be broadened to include all major aspects of local financial management.

Formal reporting and evaluation systems using indicators will contribute to enhancing accountability as well as enabling the central government to make better-informed decisions about inter-governmental fiscal relations in general and the size of transfers in particular. Korea's municipal yearbook published by the Ministry of Home Affairs is an example which can form a basis for comparison of performance among cities.

BIBLIOGRAPHY

Cacheux, J.L. and Tourjansky, L. (1992), The French Decentralization Ten Years On: Local Government Finances, *Local Government Studies*, Vol. 18, pp. 28–38.
Dillinger, W. (1989), 'Philippines Real Property Tax Administration Project', in UNCHS Economic Development Institute/ National Institute of Urban Affairs, *Urban Management in Asia: Issues and Opportunities*, New Delhi, pp. 95–115.

ESCAP (1993), *State of Urbanization in Asia and the Pacific*, Bangkok: United Nations.

Garzon, R.H. (1992), *Municipal Credit Institutions: The Case of Colombia*, INURD Working Paper #17, The World Bank, Washington D.C.

Government of Indonesia (1994), *Monitoring Indicators of Replita V Urban Policy Action Plan Implementation Results*, Municipal Finance Project, Jakarta.

Kelly, R. (1992), 'Implementing Property Tax Reform in Developing Countries: Lessons from the Property Tax in Indonesia', *Review of Urban and Regional Development Studies*, 4: 193:208.

Lorentzen, J. (1994), *A Note on Involving the Private Sector in the Provision of Urban Services in Thailand*, UNCHS, Nairobi.

Osborne, D. (1991), 'Ways to Improve Your Performance', *Urban Perspectives*, 1, USAID Office of Housing and Urban Programs, Nairobi.

Paik, S.W. (1994), 'A Case Study on Partnership Between City Government and Private Sector for Municipal Infrastructure Service in Korea', *Proceedings of Regional Seminar on Partnerships in Municipal Infrastructure Services*, National Institute of Urban Affairs, 7–11 February, New Delhi.

Shah, A., Qureshi, Z., Bagchi A., Binder B. and Zou. H. (1994), *Intergovernmental Fiscal Relations in Indonesia: Issues and Reform Options*, World Bank Discussion Paper 239, The World Bank, Washington D.C.

Suselo, H., Taylor J.L. and Wegelin, E.A. (eds.) (1995), *Indonesia's Urban Infrastructure Development Experience: Critical Lessons of Good Practice*, UNCHS (Habitat), Nairobi/ Jakarta.

World Bank (1994), *World Development Report 1994*, Oxford University Press, Oxford.

19

INSTITUTIONAL ISSUES OF URBAN INFRASTRUCTURE FINANCING

Michael Lindfield

Institutional Development—the Basis for a Infrastructure Financing

This paper seeks to explore the linkage between successful financing of urban infrastructure projects and the institutional context of these projects. Current experience of institutional development efforts is reviewed. Examples mainly from Indonesia, the Philippines and Thailand are cited in this review; other examples are also used as found appropriate.

The analysis suggests that a new approach to institutional development will be required to implement future urban projects. In the context of a vastly more complex range of options for implementation and financing available to urban managers, and given the variety of skills now available in many countries, it is suggested that a new "enabling" approach is needed at programme and project levels. Standardized approaches to support institutional development—except at the very general level—will not be able to creatively utilize the plethora of options now available. The day of standardized projects —in the sense that these projects are focussed on preparing bulk feasibility studies to the standards of multilateral donors and carrying out institutional strengthening for implementation activities—may be over.

Institutions in Urban Infrastructure Development: A History

The importance of institutions in the development of urban infrastructure projects has been gradually increasing as experience with the implementation of these projects has grown. During the seventies urban projects did not focus on infrastructure—they focussed on building housing and the occasional water supply system. They did not consider the place of these projects in the context of the urban institutional system and of the socio-economic circumstances of the target groups. It was often the case, then, that these projects catered to middle and upper-middle income groups who probably could have been served by private suppliers and did little to relieve the pressure of shelter need or the backlog in supply of urban infrastructure.

An alternative approach, based on early experience with projects which had a significant number of sector components, such as the Indonesian *Kampung* Improvement Programme (KIP), was put forward by Lea (1979). These approaches emphasized the need to consider the wider implications of physical investments made in urban projects. In particular they argued that provision needed to be coordinated across sectors and that this provision should be matched to the characteristics of target groups. Projects which embodied this approach, which developed progressively through the eighties and into the nineties, became known as "Integrated Urban Development Projects" and included, in one way or another, elements of the approach we refer to as Multi-sectoral Investment Planning (MSIP).

This development has been characterized by two inter-related trends:

— An increasing emphasis on the need to strengthen the institutions responsible for implementing these projects — particularly at local government level; and

— An increasing emphasis on the financing structures of these projects in general and on augmenting the financial strength of the institutions responsible for implementing the project, particularly at local government level.

The objective of strengthening local government institutional and financial viability was to foster decentralization. This, in turn, was considered essential to increasing the efficiency of investment performance. This increase in efficiency would stem from investment decisions which more closely met the needs of local areas as the selection of projects would be done at local level; and from better operation of the resulting infrastructure as those responsible would be accountable at the local level.

Thus, the formulation of integrated urban development projects — for example, the project of the Integrated Urban Infrastructure Programme (IUIDP) in Indonesia; the Programme for Essential Municipal Infrastructure Utilities Maintenance; and Engineering

Development (PREMIUMED) and Regional Municipal Development Projects (RMDP) in the Philippines; and the Regional Cities Development Projects (RCDP) in Thailand—evolved away from an emphasis on the technical aspects of the project, although this was never lost entirely for reasons we will examine later. First, the emphasis shifted to the strengthening of the central institutions implementing these projects and their role in strengthening local government. Second, the emphasis moved to:

— Direct support to institutional strengthening of local government in its role as manager of investments provided through the projects through the implementation of Institutional Development Plans (IDPs); and

— Strengthening of the ability of local government to make financial contributions to the capital and operation and maintenance (O&M) costs of investments through the implementation of Revenue Improvement Plans (RIPs).

This is the stage in which most countries still find themselves (the "second generation"), with actual fiscal decentralization going better or worse according to the economic success, political confidence and size of the urban areas concerned.

Without losing sight of second generation concerns and concurrently with the implementation of second generation projects, the third step in the evolution of urban projects moved the main areas of concern for institutional strengthening again. These projects focussed on central, province levels in order to develop new institutions, or adapt existing institutions, to support the autonomy of local governments. Three key areas of institutional change related to this third wave are:

— Financial institutions catering to the capital financing needs of local governments—for example the successful Local Government Infrastructure Fund (LGIF) in the Philippines, the Tamil Nadu Municipal Urban Development Fund (MUDF) in India; and the less successful Regional Development Account (RDA) in Indonesia;

— Legislative and/or organizational changes enabling local governments to tap private local and/or international capital markets—for example, the ability of Philippine local governments to issue bonds and to engage in Build-Operate-Transfer (BOT) activity; the new Financial Institutions Reform and Expansion (FIRE) programme for the financing of urban infrastructure in India; and the capacity of Thai local authorities to contract out services (including BOT activity); and

— The development of training institutions dedicated to on-going improvement in the cadre of local government—for example, institutions such as the proposed Urban and Regional Development Institute (URDI) in Indonesia; the decentralization of the Human Settlements Management Institute (HSMI) activity in India; and the National Institute of Local Government (NILG) in the Philippines.

These activities are, as yet, rather tentative—but some of the results of this third generation activity are visible and, are an *ad hoc* response to changes in the fundamental context of urban projects. It is further argued that this response should be consolidated.

Before we return to this third stage in the evolution of integrated urban projects, more should be said in respect of the experiences with institutional strengthening of local governments on-going in second generation projects.

Second Generation Institutional Strengthening

The art (or science) of institutional analysis has reached impressive levels of sophistication in Indonesia and it is to this country that we turn for generic examples of this analysis.

As a standard feature of all current projects of the Integrated Urban Infrastructure Development Programme (IUIDP), institutional strengthening measures are set out in plans known as LIDAPs (Local Institutional Development Action Plans) and are related to the implementation of the medium-term investment plans (PJMs). These plans cover three broad categories of local urban management:

— Municipal management—overall improvement of the management and of the organizational structure of the local government agencies;
— Inter-municipal management—coordination and management of issues which affect two or more local governments or involve provincial activities; and
— Sectoral management—management of sector-specific agencies, in particular the water enterprises (PDAMs) and local government roads and sanitation departments.

In addition, some more advanced LIDAPs (Frenkel, 1995) attempt to integrate community organizations into the institutional strengthening programme having specified implementation roles for these organizations.

The organizations in each of these categories are assessed in respect of:

— The organizational structure—whether or not it is appropriate to the tasks required of it for IUIDP implementation;

— The procedures employed by these organizations—whether or not they are the most efficient and effective for undertaking implementation; and

— Staffing—in the light of the above findings, the adequacy of the existing staffing situation is assessed both in terms of its quantity and quality.

This assessment is undertaken through the LIDAP process. The LIDAP is developed by the local authorities. Consultants provide extensive support for this process. The process comprises several phases. These phases are:

— Analysis of the current situation, carried out under the categories set out above;

— Documentation of the conclusions of the analysis—weaknesses in the organizational structure, procedures and staffing are identified and documented together with representatives of the organizations concerned;

— Formulation of institutional strengthening options:

  • Options for improved organizational structures and required legislative supports are documented and organizational performance criteria designed;

  • Performance criteria for systems and options for improved systems/procedures are developed; and

  • Personnel programmes and options for adequate and responsive training programmes are set out;

— Development of strategy—organizational development, systems development, staffing and manpower development strategies are developed in consultation with the concerned organizations;

— Formulation of an action planfor each of the strategies the steps required for implementation, and the equipment required for support of implementation are identified and documented (this constitutes the LIDAP).

The major activities involved in each of these phases may be summarized under the three analysis areas discussed above.

Organization: The first step in the process of developing a LIDAP attempts to identify the local government agencies and community organizations that are involved in and/or responsible for each stage of the project development cycle. In Indonesia, this cycle has five stages:

(i) project identification; (ii) planning, programming and budgeting; (iii) project implementation/execution; (iv) project monitoring and evaluation; and (v) operation and maintenance. In addition, the legal basis (existing laws and regulations) for the operations of each of the identified agencies the specific responsibility of the agencies, and organizational problems being encountered (if any) are identified.

The results of this initial step serve as the basis for the succeeding steps in the methodology. Specifically, the key implementation organizations identified become the focus of subsequent analysis and of the LIDAP.

Applicable laws and regulations are then reviewed and compared in respect of their efficacy in furthering the objectives of the identified organizations. The focus of this review is on those laws and regulations pertaining to the scope of responsibilities and functions of, and institutional linkages among key agencies as well as of the units and sub-units within these agencies. The objective, aside from developing familiarity with the nature and purpose of these organizations, is to identify possible ambiguities, redundancies, overloading and gaps in the distribution of responsibilities and functions.

Procedures: In order to assess the systems which are utilized by these agencies, a systems survey can be conducted. The survey form identifies a number of systems that concerned agencies most likely need to accomplish their respective functions in each of the five stages of the project development cycle. The respondents, mostly the organization heads, are required to tick off whether a nominated system exists. If it does exist, then the respondents are asked to assess whether it is adequate or needs improvement. If it does not exist, they are asked to assess whether it is needed or not.

Systems and procedures that are deemed critical to the implementation of the IUIDP project, particularly those used in development planning and institutional development, can then be documented. They are subsequently analyses, and problems being encountered in their use were identified. These problems formed the basis for the recommendations pertaining to procedures.

Staffing: Analysis of staffing issues for the LIDAP is based on a manpower inventory which determines the manpower-supply profile in each of the concerned agencies. Standard data, such as name, employee identification number, birthday, education (level and field of concentration), position, rank and work experience (field of work and number of years), are gathered. In addition, inventory takers identify each employee by working designation—a title that indicates an employee's duties and responsibilities. This can be done on the basis of information furnished by supervisors.

The manpower data base that resulted from the inventory is used in identifying manpower deficiencies (both in quantity and quality). Manpower development programmes, including training and incentive systems, are formulated primarily on the basis of skills deficiencies that can be detected by examining the qualifications profile of personnel and from discussions with supervisors.

The experience with LIDAPs is now reviewed.

Institution Building by Numbers

The experience of institutional development has been limited to actual implementation of IDPs. As yet, little detailed evaluation of the efficacy of these plans in respect of their targets has been carried out. This is understandable as the second generation IDPs really came into effect only after 1990 and are still being implemented.

As Indonesia constitutes one of the most advanced examples of such second generation projects, it is again useful to review the experience of that country in the implementation of LIDAPs. Only in a few other countries has such an extensive programme of institutional strengthening been so uniformly applied to integrated urban projects. Although as yet no evaluation of the relevance and success of training and other forms of institutional development activity—based on an objective set of criteria—has been carried out, some observations can be made using the headings of analysis discussed above.

Organizations: The impact on the organizational structures at any level in the urban management hierarchy has been minimal. These structures are locked in by central government legislation and are not subject to real influence at local level.

Procedures: The impact on procedures, when painstakingly supported by consultant input, has been more significant. Small-scale seminars involving the officers actually involved in implementation of construction and revenue improvement have been successful. However, this activity requires long-term consultant contact and commitment—both of which have been lacking in some IUIDP projects.

The amount and duration of consultant input is extensive and this finding raises the issue of the ability of institutions to assimilate training and consultant on-the-job training inputs. In order to effectively assimilate knowledge, long-term exposure is needed. The effectiveness of such exposure is seen in the rate at which Indonesian consultants are replacing expatriate consultants in IUIDP projects. Over 10 years, this process has proceeded to the point where only short-term expatriate inputs are generally required. The six-month exposure of consultants to local government staff cannot be expected to provide the required transfer of skills to local government.

Staffing: The institutional strengthening programmes may be judged a success in terms of uptake and the amount of training conducted. In general, the training identified has been carried out to schedule and on the scale recommended in LIDAPs. This is the visible impact of institutional strengthening and the one used to evaluate performance. We judge institution building by the numbers of seminars delivered, numbers of people trained overseas, etc. The focus, however, should be the impact of this activity and this is, in the absence of systematic assessment, necessarily subjective. Where training was designed in real consultation with local governments, it has gone a significant way to addressing their needs. There is a general consensus that the impact of the training in respect of technical matters has made an improvement in the operational efficiency of government agencies, in particular the PDAMs.

Overview: Programmes formulated with the local governments concerned have been tailored to local needs and some are confident enough to initiate extensions of existing IUIDP projects based on their own resources—Surabaya, for example, and several central Java cities. However, with such notable exceptions as Surabaya, there is no clear evidence of improvement in the actual efficacy of institutional strengthening in respect of the general ability of the local governments to plan and implement their own projects.

The reasons for this diversity of results can be attributed to two factors:

— There is a widening range of skills, and scope for action, available to local governments—in general, large and rapidly developing urban areas have options quantum levels above smaller, slower growing areas; and

— The variety in the quality and quantity of consultant resources provided—in particular, their ability to effectively define and address institutional issues with local government.

In respect of the availability of resources for institutional development, the inter-dependence between the sustainability of the IDP (LIDAP) on the one hand and the success of the RIP (RIAP) on the other should be obvious—institutional development cannot be sustained in the absence of financial resources allotted for this purpose. We will turn to this question in more detail in the next section, but it may be noted here that current projects do not provide the opportunity to tap private and community resources (where available) for institutional development.

In addition, the variation in the quality and quantity of consultant inputs needs to be addressed. An approach which tailored inputs to the circumstances of local governments would be more efficient than a blanket approach to project preparation.

The conclusion of this analysis is that while the standard, highly subsidized, IUIDP approach is appropriate for some urban areas, others can go substantially beyond .this approach in terms of institutional strengthening and resource mobilization, and the standardized approach could be made more flexible so as to accommodate these potentials.

Revenue Mobilization on the Margin

The position in respect of local revenue mobilization in Indonesia is also illustrative. In terms of increasing the mobilization of local resources in order to ensure that local governments can fund their share of IUIDP projects, the Revenue Improvement Action Plans (RIAPs) have been successful. This share is, however, often rather small, with local government contributions sourced from their own revenue often constituting less than 10 per cent of investment cost. Targets for larger urban areas (over one million people) are set at 30 per cent and for smaller cities at 10 to 20 per cent. The picture is somewhat brighter for larger water enterprises (PDAMs) which can afford to finance almost all capital expenditure.

Another issue is that of return on assets. RIAPs are mechanisms designed to augment the revenue generation capacity relative to existing revenue performance—that is they improve relative performance. Sometimes such a plan does not squarely address the issue of objective performance. For example, if market revenue can increase by 22 per cent annually, this may achieve the revenue generation targets required to (partially) fund the local authority's share of investment—the fact that this income may constitute a 1 per cent return on asset value is not addressed by the plan. Clear cost recovery procedures are not always applied in practice, despite the existence of numerous IUIDP-related manuals detailing such procedures.

In addition, RIAPs are focussed on governmental resources—there is little scope for the integration of private sector or community resources into the plans. This reduces the flexibility and scope of the investment programme—and the institutional development programme—available to the urban area.

Thus, as RIPs make an impact on the margin of revenue generation for most local governments and as local revenue funds small proportions of required investment, the question must be asked as to the sustainability of investment activity in the absence of large international and/or central government transfers. The same question could be asked in respect of experience in most integrated urban development projects.

The questioning could be taken two steps further. Should we accept this diversity of resource mobilization opportunities and factor these into programme and project formulation? How do we strengthen institutions to deal with this diversity?

The Third Generation?

Although the success of second generation projects can hardly be said to be consolidated, experience has shone some light on important institutional aspects of third generation activity. These institutional structures, in turn, provide the context of integrated urban development projects at local level and determine the extent to which they can be effectively initiated and implemented at that level. Since the mid-eighties substantial resources have been utilized to address the institutional structures described above and it is these structures we now examine in more detail.

Direct financing of local government investment: Although some countries have a long history of institutions which finance local government capital works—the Housing and Urban Development Corporation (HUDCO) in India and the Thai Municipal Development Fund (MDF), for example—these bodies have often constituted yet another source of subsidized finance for local agencies. In the mid-eighties, the attitude to such financing, led by attitudes of World Bank staff in the field, began to change. The idea of independent financing institutions for local government was considered good, provided it fostered real decentralization by providing finance at market rates. Such independent institutions were to be given a much stronger mandate for achieving cost recovery—preferably full recovery of both capital and O&M costs. In addition, the need for institutional strengthening was explicitly recognized and many of these institutions were designed/established with the facility to provide technical assistance for strengthening the institutional capacity of borrowers.

Experience has been mixed however. The reactions to such institutions have ranged from outright rejection of additional funding and more stringent financing terms in the case of the Thai Municipal Development Fund, through the rather lukewarm reception of the Regional Development Account (RDA) in Indonesia—while the RDA disbursed all available funds (from USAID), the proponents did not succeed in persuading the relevant Indonesian government agencies to channel existing government capital finance streams through the RDA—to the more successful Local Government Infrastructure Fund (LGIF) in the Philippines.

In respect of institutional strengthening activity related to these institutions, no evaluation seems to have been undertaken. Where it has occurred, such activity has focussed directly on the need to strengthen institutions to implement the project. LGIF will finance such activity through its loans, but in practice a small proportion of resources are devoted to such purposes. In addition, experience in some countries with such institutions was that they were co-opted and utilized in less-than-transparent ways to finance less-than-viable projects.

Such experience has cooled the fervour of the advocates of local development funds and, in any case, this mechanism has been replaced as the preferred method of financing by the mechanisms discussed in the following paragraphs.

Private capital market financing: Leaping rather ahead of the state-of-play in many countries, international development institutions have now begun to focus on financing local development through (private) capital markets. In the climate of privatization and deregulation, this activity responds to right-wing criticism of development activity as not fostering productive activity. This is undoubtedly a welcome trend, but requires even higher levels of institutional competence on the part of governments and consultants than does the mechanism described above. It is thus curious that most programmes designed to implement mechanisms of private capital market financing do without significant institutional strengthening components—and have had less impact as a consequence.

There are two mechanisms of private sector financing of urban development. These are:

— Private sector financing of government entities which provide the service—this usually entails operation of these entities, or parts of these entities that supply the service, on a commercial basis; and

— Private sector financing and operation of the service—either through contracting arrangements, BOT arrangements or as a result of privatization.

It is useful to set out the advantages of private sector financing of urban infrastructure from the viewpoint of the nation. Three significant advantages are:

— Where investment must be financed by government-deficit spending, the resort to private capital reduces the deficit and consequently the cost of government borrowing;

— The internal efficiency of private sector organizations providing a service is often higher than a government organization providing the same service; and

— Private sector organizations have an incentive to recover the full costs of provision and thus produce a pricing regime which encourages the use of scarce resources more efficiently.

In addition, the use of private sector entities can remove one of the constraints to effective decentralization—refusal of central institutions to transfer substantial private sector financial resources to local governments.

USAID is the prime promoter of such private sector mechanisms and provides significant funding through its housing guarantee window for programmes supporting private sector involvement/commercialization in the urban field. The operations of the USAID Financial Institutions Reform and Expansion (FIRE) programme in India are focussed on financing private/ public commercial provision of infrastructure. It was USAID which funded the Thai Office of Urban Development (OUD) in its programme to support local governments in contracting out services. The proposed Infrastructure Credit Guarantee Corporation in Thailand is also sponsored by USAID. In Indonesia, USAID is now trying to move the RDA on to a commercial basis and has initiated the Private Participation in Urban Services (PURSE) Project in Indonesia. However, few other donors are involved in this crucial activity. Even USAID activity, constrained by budgetary cuts, has not paid sufficient attention to the full range of institutional supports required to implement such a programme.

There are several levels of specific institutional supports that are required to be substantially in place before private sector financing systems are operable. These are:

— A national policy context specific to the urban/infrastructure sector (legislation for privatization of state enterprises will not do);

— Legislation to enable local/state authorities to enter into the legal arrangements required of such funding mechanisms;

— Agencies to support local or state authorities in the formulation and approval of projects; and

— Agencies capable of filling, or arranging to fill, any financing gaps in respect of major projects where the private sector is not sufficiently confident to take on the full project risk or where the capital markets cannot take on the full financing.

The Philippines is arguably the furthest along the road towards a transparent procedure encompassing these institutional elements, followed closely by Malaysia. In virtually all countries, the above areas of institutional supports are not fully operational and, in some countries, are seriously wanting. Further support to institutional strengthening in these areas would seem to be a high priority.

In addition to these specific requirements, contextual legislation and institutions need to be in place if they are not there already. Laws relating to contract enforcement, and fair courts etc. are a must. This can vary significantly even between countries of comparable stages of economic development—by and large, India has these, China does not.

Capacity building: In support of continuing institutional development efforts, national institutions have been established to foster improvement in the planning and implementation of integrated urban projects. These institutions can be added to existing institutions—for example, the role of the Philippine National Institute of Local Government (NILG). Or they may be established for the purpose—for example, as the proposed Urban and Regional Development Institute (URDI) in Indonesia, or extended to decentralized levels as with the assistance of the Human Settlement Management Institute (HSMI) in India.

These institutions have been established in support of a programme of integrated urban infrastructure development, but do or will not focus exclusively on capacity building for implementation. Part of their role is to institutionalize the process of multi-sectoral investment planning (MSIP). In this regard their success cannot yet be evaluated in that most are effectively not fully operational. The Philippines programme has just been established. The Indonesian institution is not yet established, however the IUIDP training programme of the Ministry of Public Works continues to extend training support to provincial and local levels throughout Indonesia. The Indian training programme of the Human Settlement Management Institute (HSMI) programme (with assistance for decentralization provided by the Dutch Government) has supported such initiatives as the Integrated Development of Small and Medium

Towns (IDSMT) scheme and the Tamil Nadu Urban Development Project (TNUDP) and more integrated projects are under preparation as the integrated small and medium towns project of the Asian Development Bank in Karnataka.

The problem for such institutions is to achieve an organizational legitimacy. This legitimacy can be easily established in theory by the need for effective MSIP, but in practice legitimacy often goes to institutions capable of directing flows of investment funding. In view of the way planning organizations have been marginalized in many countries it remains to be seen if this capacity building role can be sustained once donor support is withdrawn.

On the other hand, one example of an organization which has been relatively successful at sustaining itself provides some lessons in respect of channelling too many resources through an "outsider" agency. The Office of Urban Development (OUD) in Thailand rose rapidly in importance and size during the eighties as a result of its role as a channel of substantial external assistance. The OUD undertook substantive institutional strengthening activity on behalf of Thai municipalities. The result was, however, to alienate line departments which, in turn, were able to restrict the activities of the OUD.

Conclusion: Third generation activity responded to the perceived need to: (i) supply independent lines of financing and institutional strengthening capacity in support of decentralization initiatives; and (ii) respond to a general climate of privatization initiatives and deregulatory pressures. Such activity was *ad hoc* in that it did not systematically address:

— The policy context of urban development (programme level institutions);

— The legislative basis for the scope of both government and private sector activity in urban development (programme level institutions);

— The full range of financing opportunities available (programme level institutions); and

— The formulation of urban projects in this context—specifically the lack of a linkage of integrated planning (MSIP) to investment financing, the inappropriate focus on government institutions and the variation of circumstances found in different urban areas (project level institutions).

The following section, drawing on project experience, examines how it may be possible to address such issues.

Back to Basics

The Concept: The results of project and programme activity should be evaluated against the two basic, interrelated objectives of urban development:

— To support (equitable and sustainable) economic growth; and
— To improve the quality of life in a particular urban area.

With respect to the first objective we see that the scope of activity of traditional urban projects has been limited in the extreme—limited to the provision of a limited range of physical infrastructure and financed from and through a limited range of sources. Direct support to economic activity (such as community-based loans schemes in Bangladesh and inner-city Chicago) is integral to the ability of a community to improve economic circumstances and this, in turn, enables it to improve the quality of life. Tapping of private finance through contracting out, BOT and privatization projects can improve efficiency and provide needed investment in social and physical infrastructure.

The second objective, improvement in the quality of life, has been addressed through the provision of infrastructure. Substantial improvements have been made, especially in "formal sector" areas of cities. In doing so, however, some projects have displaced substantial numbers of people without adequate compensation—impacting negatively on their quality of life.

How do we increase the scope of urban integrated projects to encompass such issues without losing focus? In order to answer this question, we revert to the weaknesses in the programmes identified earlier. In the following sections, examples of *ad hoc* approaches to countering these weaknesses will be examined. Given that these weaknesses are structured, these examples, seen as a group, may indicate a structured approach to an answer.

The policy and financing context of urban development: The policy context of urban development is dominated by the need to open up the processes of urban development—in particular investment financing and the financing of economic development/poverty alleviation activity—to participation by private sector and community actors. Institutional development activity needs to be focussed on developing the capacity of the concerned government organizations to foster investment activity in a given urban area from as wide a range of organizations as possible.

Private participation in investment financing: The Philippines, Malaysia and Sri Lanka have laid down clear guidelines and procedures for structuring of private sector participation. They were initiated by central economic planning agencies—National Economic Development Agency in the Philippines, the Economic Planning Unit in Malaysia and the Ministry of Policy Planning and Implementation in Sri Lanka. These guidelines, unlike guidelines for the sale of publicly owned producer enterprises (for example, factories), set out the processes of project formulation and tendering which must be applied for such projects. While the guidelines are not always followed to the letter of the law and, with the exception of the Philippines, do not provide for integration into a process of MSIP and do not address the small-scale investment needs of communities, they provide a context for activity in this field.

It may not be necessary to have guidelines approved by a national planning agency, provided that the agency promoting such guidelines has sufficient relevance to the planned private sector participation process—for example, a key financial institution could set down such guidelines.

These agencies also serve as nodes of information in respect of private sector participation—gathering information relevant to agencies wishing to initiate such a process and acting as initial contact point for some parts of the private sector wishing to become involved.

Financing of economic development and poverty alleviation activity: With the exception of Bangladesh, it is rare to find large-scale programmes which incorporate credit schemes for income generation activity into projects. The fashion for industrial estates (of any scale) is passed. Many countries have experimented with such credit schemes, but these tend to be scattered in their application and are not the result of a comprehensive MSIP process aimed at supporting urban economic development. The private sector in Thailand and Indonesia is now in the business of establishing large-scale industrial estates—usually without the benefit of any MSIP input.

The above does not imply that one must wait for a fully integrated MSIP process to be completed before undertaking any economic development and poverty alleviation activity, but it does imply that it is preferable for MSIP to incorporate detailed consideration of such activities.

The legislative basis for the scope of government and private sector activity: Policy is one thing but, in respect of tapping a wider pool of resources, legislation is needed to establish the ability of the relevant level or agency of government to, among others, issue bonds; take equity in companies; withdraw from direct provision of services; and make staff redundant if such legislation does not already exist. The agency promoting the above guidelines normally takes the lead in identifying the required legislative programme and fostering its implementation. Again, the Philippines lead in providing the raft of required legislation. However, it is not necessary that the whole legislative programme be in place before such programmes are attempted. It is usually the case that significant activity can occur in the absence of a full legislative framework—indeed such countries as Australia and the United Kingdom undertook major infrastructure privatizations in the absence of detailed legislation, depending instead on normal contract law.

In respect of economic development/poverty alleviation activity, the issue is more of the traditional scope of work and any legislation which prevents the relevant institutions widening their scope of work into areas of relevance for this activity. In practice, this is not usually a problem, the problem is of perception of the responsibility for these activities.

Another legislative issue is the need to ensure that planning agencies do have a legal basis for oversight of major physical investments and associated infrastructure—whether by public or private entities. This issue is highly political and solutions range in effectiveness from the Philippines (where it is solved in theory if not in practice) to Thailand (where it is simply not on the agenda).

The formulation of projects: The institutions involved in formulating and implementing projects need to be able to put the above policy into practice and take advantage of the opportunities afforded by the legislative context. Two areas are crucial in this respect—the linkage of MSIP to investment and the provision of support to agencies so as to enable them to avail of the financing opportunities for investment and economic development activities. These two areas are examined below.

Linkage of MSIP to investment financing: The Philippine Capital Investments Folio (CIF) (Einsiedel, 1995; Villá, 1995) integrates the availability of funding with the investment programme of Municipalities. Loan funding for projects is available to the Municipalities on the basis of a structured approach to project appraisal and prioritization across sectors.

The CIF process has the ability to include a variety of funding sources and to adapt to the (changing) circumstances of local governments. Some capacity for institutional "handholding" is included within the project in order to guide local governments in their investment planning activities.

Project formulation activity: The key element of project formulation activity taking place in the context of MSIP must be a process of identifying the most appropriate institutional structure for implementation of a specific project and the most appropriate funding associated with this structure. As discussed above, these two issues are interdependent. The institutional structures and the funding possibilities will vary with the type and scale of project and with the location of the project site. Thus any approach based on a standard formula for funding is inappropriate.

The Philippine CIF process enables a more flexible approach in this respect, but provides limited support to the actual formulation process in the local authority. The Sustainable Cities Programme (SCP) of the UNCHS as utilized in Tanzania, Poland and (soon) India (Madras) involves broad-based participatory processes which uses working groups focussed on specific problems. The working groups structure community input identify, prioritize and find solutions to the problems/issues, and find the finance to implement these solutions.

It is preferable that the project preparation process is resourced/monitored by an independent programme inputs acting to raise issues, introduce new concepts, suggest different forms of organizational structure and additional financing sources—a "ginger group". Such inputs raise the potentials for integration, but only in the interests of the more effective execution of specific projects - integration is dependent on the MSIP process.

It is important that the project formulation process has the flexibility to adapt to the circumstances of a particular urban area and to involve the maximum number of participants in investment and economic development activity.

Conclusion

The analysis in this article has identified significant gaps in the institutional framework of urban projects, particularly the lack of access to the wider range of financing options now available, the lack of clear evidence of the impact of implementation-oriented institutional strengthening activity and the lack of legitimacy of agencies undertaking MSIP activity. A fresh approach is required.

Given the variety of institutional circumstances encountered in the implementation of integrated urban development projects, it is important to focus support to institutional strengthening activity on providing an "enabling framework" through which agencies involved in urban development (central, regional and local) can obtain the technical assistance and funding resources required to implement the investment programmes identified by MSIP. The key elements of a new "enabling" approach are:

— Institutional strengthening of central, regional and local governments to provide for integrated MSIP systems—including planning for widening the range of investment financing sources and delivery mechanisms; and

— Institutional support to the formulation projects which, in the context of these MSIP systems, are designed to tap the available opportunities for investment financing and efficient delivery mechanisms.

Linking this activity to financing streams will add to the credibility and legitimacy of the agency(ies) undertaking MSIP and support project formulation.

The logical next step in this argument is that the focus of support to urban projects should not be on providing resources for project feasibility studies and institutional strengthening for project implementation. These should be the responsibility of the national project proponents. The traditional approach usually looks in a given formula of financing tied to a given set of funding agencies—this may not be an efficient outcome. Project proponents will have to prepare feasibility studies to the standards of the financing agencies identified as appropriate to specific projects. These feasibility studies and the institutional strengthening for implementation required by these agencies should be part of the project cost and financed. This will give an incentive for both feasibility and institutional strengthening funds to be used efficiently.

BIBLIOGRAPHY

Frenkel R. (1995), 'Pilot Base and Turning Point', in Suselo, H., Taylor, J.L. and Wegelin, E.A. (eds.), *Indonesia's Urban Development Experience: Critical Lessons of Good Practice*, Nairobi/Jakarta: UNCHS.

Lea, J.P. (1979), *Policies for Efficient and Eligible Growth of Cities in Developing Countries*, World Bank paper no. 342, The World Bank, Washington, D.C.

Villa, V.A. de (1995), 'Metro Manila Capital Investments Folio', Paper presented at International IHSP Seminar on Integrated Urban Infrastructure Development, 1–4, February, New Delhi.

Einsiedel, N. von (1995), 'The Capital Investments Folio: An Innovative Approach to Metropolitan Management in the Philippines', Paper presented at International IHSP Seminar on Integrated Urban Infrastructure Development, 1–4, February, New Delhi.

20

TRAINING FOR INTEGRATED
INFRASTRUCTURE DEVELOPMENT

Forbes Davidson, Harry Mengers and Hans·Teerlink

The Challenge

Integrated development programmes present a special challenge to the professionals involved because the effective working of these professionals requires new skills and attitudes. These include understanding and techniques of inter-disciplinary working; attitudes supportive of decentralized decision-making; and abilities to work cooperatively between organizations within government and outside government. These skills and qualities are not easy to develop, and there is very little existing capacity to provide training support.

This paper aims to provide an overview of some of the key issues in the changing environment of today, and to examine how training is developing to meet the needs. The paper starts with a brief overview of changing needs and responses. It then examines two experiences of developing and implementing training support programmes for integrated infrastructure development—one in Indonesia and the other in India. The final section draws common lessons from the experience.

Changing Environment, Changing Needs

Increasing pressures of rapid urbanization in many parts of the world, coupled with urban decay have meant that there is an ever-increasing demand for effective action to fund, supply and maintain infrastructure services (Davidson, 1991). This need is operating within changing perceptions of what makes for effective actions. Key concepts and their impact on training include:

1. *Enabling Role of Government:* This implies that government works to facilitate actions by other organizations rather than directly doing everything itself. This means new requirements including how to plan with uncertainty, working with partners, i.e., private sector and community and finance from loans rather than grants.

2. *Decentralization:* Decentralization is necessary for effective integrated development programmes. It requires learning of new skills and taking of responsibility at local government level. However, it also makes new demands from the higher level government departments which used to make decisions. Such departments have to learn to let go, and to adopt the new role of support, monitoring and evaluation.

3. *Integrated Development:* Integrated programmes are more demanding than sectoral programmes. This is not only because of the technical complexity, but perhaps even more important is the complexity of inter-departmental jealousies. New skills are needed for how to assess, when and how to integrate, and how to plan together with a wide range of interest groups.

Changing Concepts on Training Support and Key Issues to be Addressed

In the sixties the concept of training applied in developing countries was based on *transfer of (western) technologies.* During the seventies this changed *into transfer of knowledge* (knowledge necessary to create local or appropriate solutions). Currently training approaches are tending towards *exchange and gaining of local experience,* and *developing analytical and problem solving skills.* Exchange of experience and options for gaining practical experience are programmed into the training process. At the same time the training should allow for innovations and be responsive to the problems and needs as identified during the training process, especially the ones faced in on-the-job situation.

The traditional focus on improving individual and single disciplinary competencies is changing to performance improvement of teams: processes of change, although sometimes initiated/driven by an individual, need the involvement and support of a range of disciplines and stakeholders.

In this approach, training needs assessment becomes more complicated. It has to address multiple agencies and actors at different working levels. The programming and sequence of the different training events related to the integrated development programme becomes more critical for the total training effectiveness.

Changes in Training in Relation to the Policy and Operational Environment

On-the-job training and coaching offer most opportunities to tailor the training to the specific needs and problems in the operational environment. It is applied in large organizations which can afford the considerable costs for design and conduct. For organizations where the number of people to be trained is too small, or where the content of training focusses on problems felt by a number of organizations, training courses are offered "off-the-job", often by trainers from institutions, with no direct exposure to practical experience. The training approach of incorporating "hands-on experience" in the training programme, brings the training and the trainers (partly) back in the operational environment (see Figure 20.1).

Trainers with a mainly educational or theoretical background can thus learn from the professional experience (through field follow-up and on-the-job training, action research and consultancies), while trainers drawn from professional practice need to develop skills as trainers. Sometimes training also takes place in the policy environment, for example, in the framework of decentralization policies. Training becomes a mechanism to facilitate the operationalization of policies. Training has been defined as "a planned learning process to modify attitudes, skills and knowledge"[1] of its participants. However an important question is how the feedback from the training or work-floor can also contribute to a learning process for the policy makers. It is an opportunity to gain insight into additional needs such as organizational interventions, technical assistance, guidelines, manuals and elaboration of operational procedures.

Training and technical assistance working together: For new programmes, technical assistance (TA) is often mobilized to fulfil the immediate needs for professional inputs. If training is also introduced for capacity building, and is directly linked to the operational environment, the question arises how and what type of creative links can be made between the training and TA so that they can mutually reinforce each other (Figure 20.2)?

---

[1] Manpower Services Commission, UK, 1981

Figure 20.1: Relationship between Capacity Building for Urban Development Operations

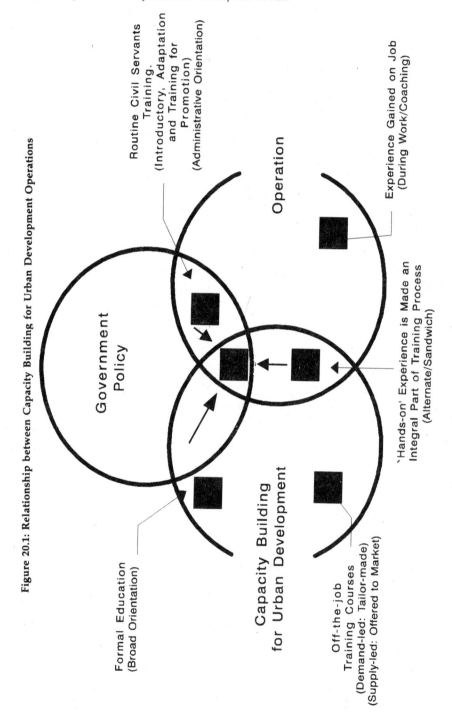

Figure 20.2: Relationship between Physical Development and Institutional Development

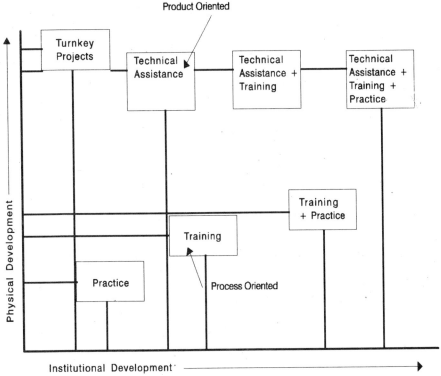

Source: Davidson, 1991.

Training for capacity building — capacity building for training: Capacity building for sustainable training support is the challenge for the future in meeting the growing and widespread needs for staff development.

Capacity building not only entails "training of the trainers" to conduct specific courses effectively. Capacities are also needed for training needs assessments, for training design, curriculum development, training material production, and for measuring training effectiveness (impact evaluations). In addition it is necessary to have capacities for training management functions, such as the formulation of (national) training strategies, marketing and mobilizing funding for training, training programming, organization, intake of participants, and the operation of monitoring, information and support systems.

The way in which all training functions are institutionalized and how the issue of sustainability of the training is addressed become very important.

In the following sections, the Indonesian and Indian experiences provide some insight in these issues. In the final section we will try to draw some lessons from these experiences.

The Indonesian Experience: Training for IUIDP[2]

This section reviews the experience of the ambitious and ongoing training support programme for the Integrated Urban Infrastructure Development Programme (IUIDP) (Hoff and Steinberg, 1992 and 1993; Suselo, Taylor and Wegelin, 1995). The long-term objective is that local government staff who are trained will design and implement more effective and efficient infrastructure programmes, and that these programmes are developed and supported locally.

The programme is remarkable for the consistent, high level and long-term promotion and support that has been there for training. Not only has training been the only means of building capacity, it has also been used creatively together with technical assistance, communication, information and hands-on experience.

The benefits of training have been both in what trainees learn, and in what the programme can learn through training. Training requires clarification of the programme itself, and provides senior officers and field staff an opportunity to interact which is not normally possible. The programme has also shown that it is necessary to be capable of continuous change in order to stay responsive to needs.

Perhaps the most difficult aspect is the institutionalization of the programme. The training programme has itself survived the end of its project support, and continues to be active. It does, however, have problems in that it is located in a government department where long-term career and promotion is not linked to performance as a trainer. The survival of institutional memory and building of a long-term capacity is still not secure.

Effectiveness of training programmes is notoriously difficult to assess, but signs are positive. One thing which is clear is that there are no easy, rapid solutions. Training has to be seen as part of a long-term, continuous process rather than a one-off project-related exercise.

---

[2]   This section is adapted from Davidson and Watson (1995); see also Sidabutar, Rukmana, Hoff and Steinberg, (1991); Rukmana and Hoff, (1992).

Training need: A new programme, such as the IUIDP, provides an apparently very clear new need. In theory you take the needs of the new programme, subtract staff's current capability and there is your training need. For a national programme, however, there is the problem of how to do this exercise for every local government, plus every provincial government plus all the central government ministries involved. Add the fact that the "goal" posts are constantly being shifted as the programme develops and the process becomes even more complicated. Even if it was possible to calculate the quantitative and qualitative dimensions (the needs differ over a large and very varied country) it would still be an academic exercise as the training capacity to provide the training is not available.

For IUIDP, the training needs assessment was rather pragmatic. It had four important elements. The first was a workshop in 1985 to develop the concept of the training programme using senior staff from central government and from the provinces. This developed a practical basis, and also ensured interest and support of key figures at provincial and central levels. The second was a high-level meeting which took place at the World Bank's Economic Development Institute (EDI) in Washington. This included very senior professionals from the main ministries involved, from EDI and the Institute for Housing and Urban Development Studies (IHS), which were providing assistance to the Indonesian Government to set up the training programme. At this meeting the experience of senior staff was pooled and the commitment and support for the programme was fostered. The third element was a rapid appraisal of the situation in local governments in Java by the training team. This gave a strong enough basis to get the programme moving. Later this was supplemented by a more detailed training needs assessment when the programme started in 1986.

The process accomplished two things which were closely interconnected. First, it established a basis of support amongst key actors in the process. Second, it was able to draw on experience and observation to develop a reasonable starting point for the programme.

Substantially, needs were identified for information about IUIDP, skills to implement new tasks and attitude changes to cope with the implications of new roles. For example, decentralization means that the staff who once handled projects directly from the centre were expected to "facilitate" the work of local government This situation may be attractive to local government, but represents, at least initially, a threat to central government staff, and thus resistance. These aspects are perhaps amongst the most difficult to deal with. Training can help, but not as the only measure. A consistent and well supported and financed government policy is required over a considerable time period.

The programme did not initially address the needs of groups outside government. This was understandable given the size of the task. However, over time additional target groups, such as private consultants and community-based organizations have been recognized and catered for.

Training approach: The approach was to try to link training as closely as possible to the needs of the IUIDP. This involved generating the support required by different levels of government — the bosses needed to be clear as to what was required, and to know, in broad terms, what their staff would be learning and why. It also meant integrating the programme timing with the needs to develop new products. Training and experience were seen as complementary. Figure 20.3 illustrates the relationship between training, experience and technical assistance in developing and supplementing capacity. Over time, both training and technical assistance will contribute to building experience. The overall capacity required, as indicated by the top line in the figure, will vary over time. For example, there is a peak when new projects are being developed and implemented. It is not necessary to have capacity sufficient for all demands available constantly in-house.

An interesting aspect of the programme has been the relationship between training and technical assistance, which is illustrated in Figure 20.4. This has worked best where technical assistance has had the main objective of capacity building and where training has come first. Where the consultants have had the prime responsibility of preparing the infrastructure proposals, the local staff have not been able to have a close involvement. This means that they have had only a limited opportunity to develop capacity through on-job experience.

Training content: A series of mutually supportive training activities were developed. Table 20.1 outlines the main programmes which have been run. It is typical of the first year of the programme. Senior decision-makers attended short seminars, middle-level managers had special one-week workshops which explained the new programme and also briefed them on what their staff would be learning in their more intensive training. The core of the training activity was the intensive technical training known as the "Programme Cycle Course". This helped participants to go through the process of developing their own integrated infrastructure plans. The programme was designed so that participants would go through the process in class in teams from local governments. They would then return to their offices and work on the development of the IUIDP plans. In this they were supported by a team of trainers and technical specialists to provide assistance and also to get feedback on the field conditions and

Figure 20.3: Relationship between Training and Other Forms of Capacity Building

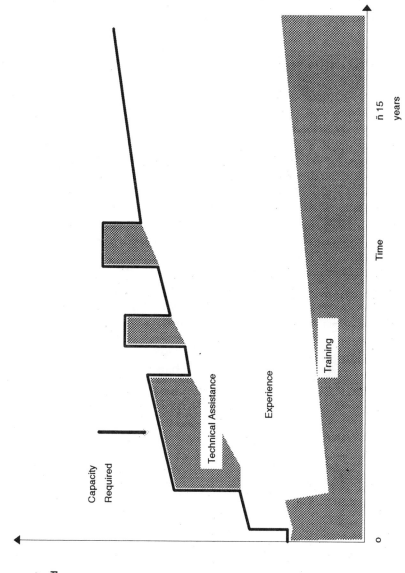

Figure 20.4: Relationship between Training and Technical Assistance

Order of Assistance Provision First → Second	Advantages	Problems	Provinces
A: Technical Assistance → Training	This model allows a Rapid Start where there is no experience. Technical quality of product is higher and quicker.	Institutional building. Gaining of experience is weaker. Training not reinforced by doing.	East Java, Central Java, Sulawesi, Metro and large cities.
B: Training → Technical Assistance	Training prepares staff to make good use of consultants. Institutional development stronger. Better chance proposals are "owned" locally.	Initial products may be weaker.	West Java.
C: Training / Technical Assistance	Can get more creative links between technical assistance and training.	Danger of conflicting objectives between institutional development (which is slow) and products such as plans (which can be fast).	Kalimantan, East Java and Bali, Eastern Islands.

Table 20.1: Target Groups and Training Programmes During the First Years

Target group: Level of Government	Core Programme	Special Programmes
Central Government ministry officials and Consultants	Policy seminars and workshops	Programme and project appraisal
		Information and communication
	Three and five months and Master's Degree courses in the Netherlands for key personnel	Special training programme for consultants
Provincial Government officials and Consultants	Provincial policy seminars	Programme and project appraisal
	Provincial management workshops	Training-of-trainers (TOT)
	Appraisal	
	Three and five months and Master's Degree courses in the Netherlands for key personnel	
Local Government staff and Consultants	Policy seminar	
	Local management workshop	
	IUIDP programme cycle Course	
	Implementation course, Appraisal course, Operation and maintenance course	
	Programme start up and Implementation course	
	Three and five months and Master's Degree courses in the Netherlands for key personnel	

the practicality of the training. This process was repeated twice so that the total time of the training was over a period of months. This allowed interaction between the field experience and the class. It also allowed sharing of experience between municipalities. This process was followed for the first years of the programme. Later, the emphasis changed to shorter courses focussed on facilitating programme implementation. This was due to changing perceived needs and to limited funding and staffing available.

The Indonesian government recognized that the bulk of training had to be carried out locally in Indonesia. At the same time there was a recognition that some staff who were regarded as agents for progressive change and innovation required more advanced training. For this, complementary programmes of three and five months in Integrated Urban Development Management were developed and run at the IHS in the Netherlands. There participants were exposed to international experience as well as that of the Netherlands. This programme was later strengthened with participation in a Master's Degree Programme in Urban Management.

Training capacity and management: Development of capacity requires building up knowledge and experience in individuals. However, it also requires building up institutions or developing institutional capacity so that there is the capability to grow and adapt to needs over time. In Indonesia, four approaches were used:

— A Central Training Management Unit was set up in the Ministry of Public Works.
— Capacity of the Provincial Training Organizations was developed.
— Involvement of universities was encouraged.
— The use of consultants was promoted.

Figure 20.5 illustrates the organization of training. So far the strongest continuity has been with the Training Management Unit situated in Central Government, and in the Provincial Training Organization in the province of West Java. In both institutions a substantial effort over a number of years went into development. Funding of training was initially through development assistance from the Netherlands and later has been funded domestically, partly through the use of the training components of loans for IUIDP.

Sustainability : The sustainability of the programme is based on five main elements:

— Institutional sustainability.
— Personnel sustainability.
— Sustainability of knowledge.
— Sustainability of innovation.
— Sustainability of funding.

Institutional sustainability: Institutional sustainability is critical, especially when a training cell is set up in a non-training institution. This was the case in Indonesia, and although the unit is doing a good job, both as a client to commission training, and in providing training directly, it has

Figure 20.5: Organization of Training

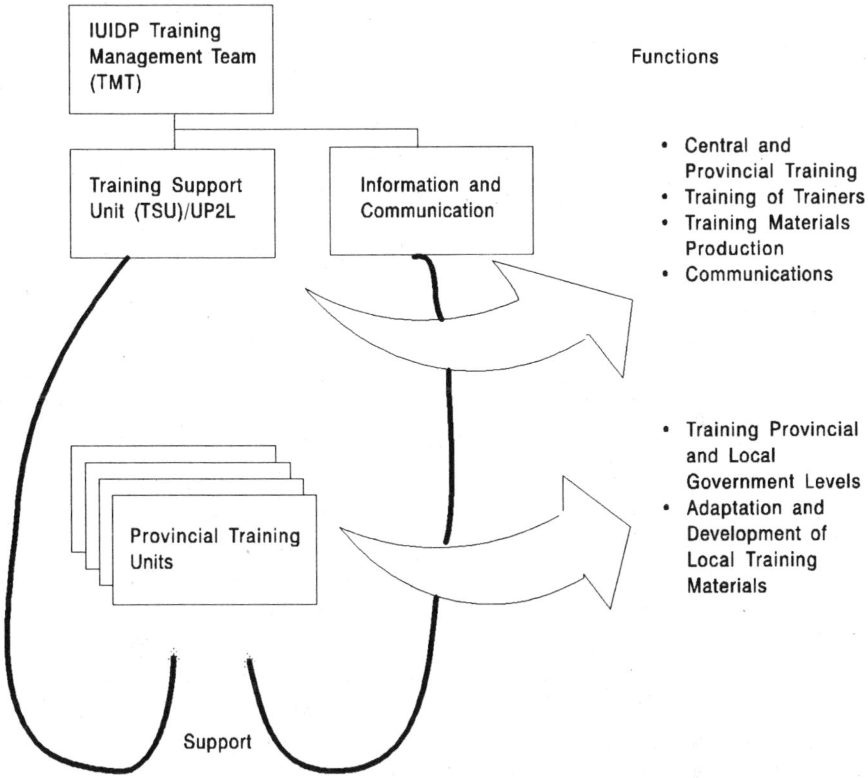

limited sustainability as a training provider. This is because training is not a core activity of the Ministry of Public Works where it is presently located. Training of local government is otherwise a responsibility of the Ministry of Home Affairs. The recent initiative to create a national, independent training and receival institution which will support training on behalf of all central initiatives which are associated with urban development is an important, new development. Which role the Urban and Regional Development Institute (URDI) can play to sustain the national urban development training is, however, yet to be seen.

Personnel sustainability: Personnel sustainability is closely linked to the institution. If promotion means moving to other departments, the knowledge and experience will be lost to training. This is already happening in Indonesia. A positive element is the use as trainers of experienced but retired staff (retirement in Indonesia takes place at a relatively young age).

Knowledge sustainability: Knowledge sustainability requires institutional sustainability plus good organization of information and a culture of networking or sharing of information rather than keeping it as a source of personal power.

Innovation sustainability: Sustainability of innovation means to continuously develop and innovate training and training materials. This is critical if training is to remain responsive. It requires both that there is a demanding client and the ability and willingness to respond.

Funding sustainability: Sustainability of funding is a very critical element where aid is used to start the process. In Indonesia so far there has been sustainability—but it is still related to project funds—through loans rather than grants. The transition to a routine form of funding, ideally by a means that allows local government to exercise choice, has not yet been made. This is a critical area and requires strong support.

Assessing effectiveness: Follow-up surveys were carried out at an early stage in the Netherlands programme. Results of these were very positive. Unfortunately, later planned evaluations were not carried out due to the Indonesian break with Netherlands aid. The World Bank carried out some assessment of Bank-funded training, but this was more indicative rather than conclusive. It highlighted some of the problems of expansion of the programme through the use of consultants—where the experienced staff necessary were often not used, and overtight budgets resulted in the skipping of important parts of the training programme. A follow-up survey of the overseas training was very positive in its findings.

Conclusions

The experience in Indonesia suggests the following:

- Strong support at high level is vital to ensure the continued backing and flow of the necessary resources.
- Incremental build up from a simple programme start is advisable. Too rapid and widespread an increase towards the scale can result in a waste of resources.
- Training integrated with operations is very effective. The process requires a lot of flexibility and effort to implement, particularly if it is organized centrally. It is best undertaken in a decentralized situation.

- Sustainability of a programme should receive considerable attention at the point of starting a programme—especially in terms of finding the appropriate institutional setting. Ideally it should be in an institution where training is the main activity, which is responsive to change and which has an open attitude to information. Funding is a key element. It must be capable of running on normal funding for local government training. This requires high level central government commitment.

The Indian Experience: Training to Support Integrated Infrastructure Programmes in Karnataka[3]

Recent developments in India aim for empowerment of the population through decentralization of administrative and financial powers. The recent *Panchayat Raj* Act and *Nagarpalika* Act aim to materialize this. While decentralization has made some headway, city governments have yet to acquire power and capacity to be able to achieve the desired objectives.

One effort for strengthening city governments is the training programme in Karnataka, which is part of the Indian Human Settlement Programme (IHSP). In this programme the Housing and Urban Development Corporation (HUDCO), New Delhi, and the Institute for Housing and Urban Development Studies (IHS), Rotterdam, collaborate in training and research.

HUDCO, together with its training wing, the Human Settlement Management Institute, approaches these challenges with a two-pronged strategy (see Figure 20.6):

1. Capacity building in the local bodies and other nodal agencies to formulate viable projects for funding; and
2. Financing viable projects in small and medium towns.

Training need: Training need was identified initially through a rapid appraisal process. A training team visited a sample of municipalities and discussed their needs. Requirements and changes in procedures were also discussed with state-level departments, funding agencies and local training organizations. Based on this, an outline strategy was developed and discussed in a widely attended forum meeting. This gave sufficient basis to enable the start of the programme. Further modification was

---

[3] This section has been partly based on Shivkumar and Mengers (1995). See also Krishnamurthy (1993), Mengers (1993), Steinberg, Mengers and Maltha (in press).

Figure 20.6: Training Approach in Karnataka

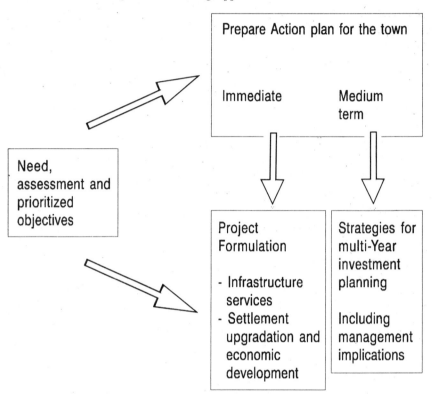

then made as the programme implementation progressed. This was based on the evaluation of courses and the responses received during follow up in the field.

Training approach and content: An important complementarity is developed between short- and medium-term planning and between actions that can be undertaken without special funding and those that require multi-year investment programming.

The following considerations were important for the chosen training approach:

- The preparation of an Integrated Action Plan (IAP) by city governments would be on a voluntary basis and, thus, an IAP would need to have a high utility value for the participants.
- The average skill and training of participants from local bodies would not allow for complicated approaches, concepts and methods.

- There would be limited support from consultants to prepare IAPs. IAPs would basically need to be prepared by the participants themselves.
- Given the overall pressures on municipal staff, assistance for preparation of IAPs would need to be organized through intensive and short workshops and on-the-job technical assistance.
- To secure continuity in a situation in which municipal staff is regularly transferred and Presidents and Chairman of Committees are regularly changed and to find a broad base for any decision on development issues, a team of elected representatives and municipal staff (two to three participants from each municipality) is invited.

Two mutually supporting areas for training support were identified: *Integrated Infrastructure Action Planning and Multi-year Investment Programming (IAP/MIP)*. The training for the support of integrated action planning and multi-year investment planning was structured as follows:

— *Pre-programme briefing*: Two to three weeks prior to the first part of the programme, nominated municipalities are invited for a day. The briefing aims to explain the possible benefits of the programme and to seek their interest and cooperation. The briefing not only explains the programme but also introduces concepts of planning, long-term development scenarios and identification of local strengths and weaknesses.

— *Part A: Integrated Action Planning (IAP)*: During a five-day programme participants are guided to formulate development objectives for a five-year period. These objectives provide a reference for later project selection. A range of problems are identified that hamper development or need to be tackled because of social or environmental implications. After having gone through a process of integrated action planning, the participants are prepared to undertake project identification and collection of necessary data, based on articulated development objectives.

— *Follow-up technical assistance*: Follow-up support is given during in-field meetings and a visit by a team to assist in the finalization of objectives, project identification and data collection.

— *Part B: Multi-year Investment Planning (MIP)*: During another five-day programme, the training is targeted towards preparing the MIP. It provides a document which becomes the basis to approach financing institutions for funding the proposed projects. The programme concludes with a presentation and first discussion with concerned state level and financing institutions.

The preparation of a MIP is thus the start for getting proposed projects formulated and for securing project finance.

Project formulation programmes: These programmes aim to provide the necessary support to elected representatives and municipal staff to make better use of existing urban development schemes. These schemes are supported by central and state government funds, often a combination of loan and grant. Aspects of project preparation, project justification and application for financial support from state-level agencies and financial institutions are addressed. In addition, modalities and requirements for successful implementation, operation and maintenance are given equal emphasis. These programmes are conducted as five-day programmes and as two-day local orientation programmes.

Training capacity: The agreement to develop and implement this training support programme in Karnataka was established by a collaboration with the state Administrative Training Institute (ATI) through a Memorandum-of-Understanding. ATI is the prime state training institute for training of higher- and middle-level administrators. Belonging very much to the state government apparatus and headed by a senior administrative officer, it is easy to connect with various departments and to ensure commitment. Moreover, the ATI has the responsibility of 18 District Training Institutes in the state from where specific training programmes can be organized.

Initially there was strong support and involvement of the management and staff of HUDCO and HSMI, which has helped to conceptualize, prepare and implement the training programmes.

Training management: Training management includes the preparation and execution of training programmes, preparation and execution of research, evaluation and project management. It also involves the establishment of institutional and financial arrangements so that the training and research programme can be continued when external financial assistance is stopped or reduced. The training management was initially done by IHS and HSMI, based in the HUDCO regional office in Bangalore. As programme activities developed, this base was gradually shifted to ATI in Mysore, involving ATI in the overall management and monitoring functions and keeping formal contacts with state and local governments in Karnataka.

Assessing effectiveness: The effectiveness of the integrated infrastructure planning and programming support and infrastructure project formulation support can be assessed as follows.

Integrated infrastructure action planning and multi-year investment programming: In all, 13 municipalities had participated in two batches till August 1994. When assessing the training impact it has to be realized that there would be no obligation by any state agency or financing institution to prepare an IAP in order to obtain project sanction or finance. Moreover there would be no separate procedure and funding line for projects prepared by IAP.

Despite these limitations, four municipalities have been invited by the Karnataka Urban Infrastructure Development and Finance Corporation for detailed discussion about project formulation and implementation of their proposed schemes. As may be expected, these four have shown good financial performance and annual surpluses. Another four municipalities have gone ahead with the implementation of some of the components by realizing funding through specific central government schemes, e.g., the Integrated Development of Small and Medium Towns (IDSMT) scheme.

Project formulation programmes: There was a great interest in project formulation programmes, and as a result the overall participation was high. The post-course evaluation indicated high appreciation, and the feedback from the field and state officials indicated that the participants were better able to be active partners in the formulation stages of projects. Whether projects in these municipalities have indeed been implemented in more responsive and in a better monitored manner is still to be assessed.

Sustainability: The sustainability of the training support programmes is now discussed and related to the policy context, the organizational set-up, and the human and financial resources.

The policy context: The implementation of the *Nagarpalika* Act in Karnataka has made good progress and the state government feels that a huge training effort is required to strengthen local bodies in their functions. In this context support has been expressed for similar and expanded training programmes in a State Training Centre for Urban Development. The overall objective for the new institution would be to become a platform for training, information and advisory support to urban development in general, and to the effective preparation and implementation of urban development programmes and projects in particular. In this changing policy context the training programme is very much at the centre of development, which will support the sustainability of the programme.

The organizational set-up: The collaboration with ATI is an important basis for organization sustainability. Their experience and expertise in training administrators, the strong links with the State Government, their network of District Training Institutes and good infrastructure are important factors. The institution is not project dependent.

Human resources: Two HUDCO-sponsored chairs were created at the ATI one year after the start of the programme. This is a moderate but sufficient basis to continue the developed decentralized training programme. The staff have gradually taken over the preparation and implementation of training programmes and research. The proposed State Training Plan will, however, call for additional qualities and for a larger capacity than is currently existing. Additional staff strength, training of trainers, management and communication skills are required.

Financial resources: With financial inputs available under the Indo-Dutch collaboration (Indian Human Settlements Programme, IHSP) from HUDCO/HSMI and from ATI/Government of Karnataka, the programme was allowed to develop and to continue in a modest fashion. However, alternative sources need to be found to compensate for these funds when they are terminated. The financial requirements for the proposed State Training Plan and the State Centre for Urban Development will be many times the above expenditures.

Lessons Learnt in Karnataka: The training programme provides a good support and incentive to the urban local governments to initiate projects and programmes that are responding to local needs, are affordable and manageable. The participation of elected representatives was difficult to materialize, but in half of the participating municipalities at least one or two officials attended. In all cases, the participants responded positively about participation as a team.

The training programme provides a good insight in the requirements of existing urban development schemes, provides a unique opportunity to exchange project-level experiences and offers practical ways and means to overcome day-to-day management problems of implementation and maintenance. In addition, the expansion of training activities to District Training Institutes facilitates a larger access to basic knowledge for local administrators and elected representatives on how they could avail of available funds and schemes. The feedback from these participants has been very encouraging and seems to satisfy a need for information.

With regard to IAP/MIP support programme, it is at present not embedded in any statutory framework or required in procedures for

369 Forbes Davidson et al.

project identification. There is a need to establish IAP/MIP and link them to statutory town planning, district planning and project formulation procedures. Financing institutions could take a lead in this process as sponsors of the programme.

Linkage with project funding would work as a justification for organizing such training programmes as well as be a major incentive for municipalities to take part in the programme. Such funding could come through:

— Existing urban development and poverty alleviation schemes in the state.
— Infrastructure funding, either directly to the urban local government or through a state-level agency.
— Through other financial institutions funding infrastructure.
— Though none of the municipalities have yet been able to secure direct funding from HUDCO or the state government, a positive observation is that some municipalities have found other avenues to get the proposals funded and have started the implementation of some of the proposals. Urban local bodies in Karnataka face a number of administrative and financial limitations as a result of an outdated Municipal Act and its bye-laws. Fortunately, the Act and bye-laws are revised under the 74th Amendment to the Constitution and the urban local bodies may expect more powers soon.

Lessons and Conclusions

The Indonesian case presented a training programme in direct support of the national Integrated Urban Infrastructure Development Programme (IUIDP) which aims to support decentralization. It was well funded and supported.

The Indian case presented training for integrated infrastructure development in a general framework of decentralization and improvement of infrastructure delivery. This was not yet embedded in a statutory framework or in procedures for project formulation and funding.

Related to this, the motivation of local authorities to participate in the training programmes was quite different in both countries, and the absence of such an embedding in India was indeed felt as a limitation for the ultimate impact of the training.

Reviewing the Indonesian and Indian cases we can draw some lessons and conclusions relevant to training programmes for integrated infrastructure development. These are now discussed.

Training needs assessment: In both cases only a broad scenario for staff competence (required knowledge, skills and attitudes) was available at the start of the training programme. Detailed guidelines and operational procedures for integrated infrastructure development were not yet available at the start of the training programmes. Because of the scale of the programmes, a pragmatic approach was chosen for training needs assessment: rapid appraisal of the situation in the provinces/states and local governments of a region (institutional and manpower), followed by a more detailed assessment in a limited number of local bodies, and during the training as a continuous process (especially during the in-field follow-up support periods). Responsiveness to identified needs and subsequent adaptation of the training programme should be part of the training approach. The advantage of this approach is that a quick start to get the training moving, while at the same time capacity building for training can take place. Close and systematic monitoring and training evaluation is necessary to get the required information and feedback.

Training approach and programme: In both cases the training and building of practical experience were seen as complementary: alternate classroom training (off-the-job) with field-follow-up support (on-the-job) were programmed. The latter is an expensive part of the training (as it includes travel, subsistence allowances, etc.), and identified as a critical aspect concerning the sustainability of the training programme.

To raise awareness of the relevance, and secure support from the policy makers and managers for the on-the-job practice, short seminars and workshops were programmed before the staff training programmes, and briefing sessions were held at the end of the training. This has proved to be very successful in both cases.

To secure continuity and in recognition of the multidisciplinary nature of integrated infrastructure planning, teams of three to four participants were invited from a local body. This approach was highly appreciated by the participants and created a critical mass in a local body to continue the process of change.

In Indonesia useful links could be made between the training and contracted technical assistance, in mutual support of each other, and for improved effectiveness of the combined support efforts. Mobilization of both support activities in time, linked to programme progress and budgeting cycles was however seen as the major difficulty.

Training capacity and management: In India the capacity for training development and conduct is developed in a state training institute (ATI), with initial support from a national training institute (HSMI, New Delhi) and HUDCO. There are plans to expand the decentralized training to other states in India, and it is envisaged that HSMI will play a more elaborate role in support for both capacity building and for training management support.

In Indonesia the central training management function is embedded in a unit in the Ministry of Public Works, while at the provincial level the training management function is with a committee of representatives from a number of agencies (Public Works, Provincial Planning Agency and Provincial Training Institute). The training development function is coordinated from the central unit, including the dissemination of training through training-of-trainers (TOT) programmes. Training conduct is organized by provincial training institutes (from the Ministry of Public Works or the Ministry of Home Affairs) who have a good access to the local government agencies, and standard procedures for invitation and selection.

In both cases trainers were drawn from both educational and professional practice. TOT courses were organized to develop trainer skills, while action research and on-the-job follow-up visits during the training programmes strengthened the knowledge of the trainers in professional practice.

Sustainability: In Indonesia the location of the central training unit in the Ministry of Public Works is considered to be vulnerable, as municipal and provincial government training is, by nature, a marginal activity for this Ministry, while in India this function is in a national training institute. In both cases the decentralized training function is successfully embedded in provincial or state training agencies.

The Indonesian training started, and still operates in the centre of development: the overlapping fields of the changing policy context (Ministry of Public Works) and the operational environment at the local level. Training has proved not only to be a manpower development tool but also a mechanism to get things moving: a feedback to policy makers for refinement of policies and operational procedures, and for making additional local needs more transparent.

In India, through the experience in Karnataka, a similar role for training is recognized, and options are considered for expansion of the programme.

The sustainability of funding is considered to be the most critical issue in both countries: funding of training, ideally from the routine budgets of local governments, is not yet in place. However, there are encouraging signs of increased commitment from central government, particularly in Indonesia, where training is starting to receive some serious funding, and where presently the creation of a central, but

Independent Urban and Regional Development Institute (URDI) for training support and resource is being initiated. If governments and professional organizations are not serious about training, as shown by sufficient budget allocation, then little progress will be made. The demand must be real, and be made effective.

Equally important is the sustainability of drive and responsiveness on the side of training organizations. This requires well-trained, well-motivated, reasonably paid individuals working in organizations where training and supporting research are central to their missions. This, coupled with quality-conscious effective demand is essential if training for urban development in general and integrated infrastructure development in particular, is to develop and have the necessary impact.

BIBLIOGRAPHY

Davidson, F. (1991), 'Gearing up for Effective Urban.Development', *Cities*, 8(2): 120–133.

Davidson, F. and Watson, D. (1995), 'Training for IUIDP: Ideas, Integration and Implementation', in Suselo, H., Taylor, J.L. and Wegelin, E.A. (eds.), *Indonesia's Urban Infrastructure Development Experience: Critical Lessons of Good Practice*, UNCHS, Nairobi/Jakarta.

Hoff, R. van der and Steinberg, F. (1992), Innovative Approaches to Urban Management: The Integrated Urban Infrastructure Development Programme in Indonesia, Avebury, Aldershot.

Hoff, R. van der and Steinberg, F. (1993), *The Integrated Urban Infrastructure Development Programme and Urban Management Innovations in Indonesia*, IHS Working Paper No. 7, IHS, Rotterdam.

Krishnamurthy, A.N. (1993), 'Training Support for Integrated Urban Development and Formulation of viable projects for institutional funding', Paper for the seminar on Effective Preparation, Implementations and Management of Urban Infrastructure in Karnataka and the Role of Training, IHSP-Karnataka, Bangalore, 5 March (unpublished).

Mengers, H.A. (1993), 'IHSP Decentralized Training Programme Karnataka, September 1992 -December 1993: State-of-the-Art', IHSP, Karnataka, Bangalore, December (unpublished paper).

Rukmana, N. and Hoff, R. van der (1992), 'Status and Progress of the IUIDP Training', in Hoff, R. van der and Steinberg, F. (eds.), *Innovative Approaches to Urban Management: The Integrated Urban Infrastructure Development Programme in Indonesia*, Aldershot, Avebury.

Shivkumar, S. and Mengers, H. (1995), 'Decentralized Training Programme in Support of Urban Development in Karnataka: A Performance Review', in Indian Human Settlements Programme (IHSP)/Human Settlement Management Institute (HSMI), *Integrated Urban Infrastructure Development*, seminar papers, HSMI, New Delhi.

Sidabutar, P., Rukmana, N., Hoff. R. van der and Steinberg, F. (1991), 'Development of Urban Management Capabilities: Training for Integrated Urban Infrastructure Development in Indonesia', *Cities*, (Oxford), 8(2), 142–150.

Steinberg, F. Mengers, H.A. and Maltha H. (in press), 'Towards a Training Strategy for Urban Management', in Singh, K. and Steinberg, F. (eds.), *Urban India in Crisis*, New Delhi.

Suselo, H, Taylor, J.L. and Wegelin, E.A. (eds.) (1995), *Indonesia's Urban Infrastructure Development Experience: Critical Lessons of Good Practice*, UNCHS, Nairobi/Jakarta.

21

ENVIRONMENTAL MAPPING FOR INTEGRATED URBAN INFRASTRUCTURE DEVELOPMENT

Dinesh B. Mehta, Usha P. Raghupathi and Rajesh Sharma

Urbanization and the Environment

The process of urbanization in developing countries leads to transformation of economic and social structures. The pace of such transformation is contingent upon macro-economic growth rates and the role that cities play in national and global economy. The linkage between rates of growth of economy and levels of urbanization are well established. It is also recognized that the distribution of economic gains is uneven. Urban centres in developing countries thus represent both prosperity of the nation as well as the poverty and abysmal living conditions.

Rapid economic growth in developing nations is a relatively recent phenomenon. This economic growth is largely led by the forces of global economic order. Most cities have an inadequate infrastructural base on which the necessary infrastructure for economic prosperity has to be built. The increases in urban population put pressures on existing infrastructure services. The increases in incomes of urban residents leads to shifts in demand for higher level and quality of services. But given the limited capacities of the local and national governments to finance and manage urban infrastructure, rapid expansion and augmentation of basic infrastructural needs has not taken place.

Environmental conditions in urban areas have been deteriorating rapidly as a result of inadequate infrastructural services. While national governments and the "green" lobbies are concerned with the global environmental issues, the need to focus on the "brown agenda" for improving the environment of urban areas is now becoming important and urgent. The recent incidence of the plague in 1994 in many parts of

India is but a preface to what is likely to follow in future if urban environmental problems and the "brown agenda" are not accorded adequate importance.

This paper focusses on urban environmental problems which result from inadequate infrastructure provision. It is based on work done at the National Institute of Urban Affairs (NIUA), New Delhi, on mapping environmental status in the four cities of Bombay, Delhi, Ahmedabad and Vadodara. The primary objective of such an exercise was to initiate a process of consultation at the local level among all the stakeholders — the local government, the business and industries, and the community. Such an exercise was felt necessary in the 74th Amendment to the Constitution on decentralization. The new mode of urban governance that is envisaged in these initiatives is beyond the realm of the conventional roles assigned to local governments. The new mode recognizes the crisis of urban management and visualizes a partnership in infrastructure provision among the local government, private sector and community groups. For such partnerships to be initiated and motivated, it is necessary to provide a synoptic view of the status of urban infrastructure and environmental conditions. The series of maps for four Indian cities (National Institute for Urban Affairs, 1994) provide a facilitative tool for initiating such local partnerships, and serve as support to plan and implement comprehensive, integrated urban infrastructure development schemes.

Local Governments and the Urban Environment

Local governments in India have always been entrusted with responsibilities related to water supply, sanitation, solid waste disposal, drainage, etc. However, protection of the environment was not a specified task either under the obligatory or discretionary functions of these bodies. Under the 74th Amendment to the Constitution Act 1992 on municipalities, the role and responsibilities of municipal bodies have been enlarged and new functions have been added to their activities under the "Twelfth Schedule" (Article 243W). Urban forestry, protection of the environment and promotion of ecological aspects have been specifically mentioned in the Twelfth Schedule as a responsibility of the municipal bodies. With this Act in place, it is expected that management of urban environment at the local level would become more effective, especially if it is undertaken in a partnership mode with the private sector and the community groups.

Sustainable Cities and Carrying Capacity

The unmanageable growth of cities in the developing world is posing serious threats to the environment. With inadequate infrastructure, inefficiency in the delivery of services and lack of financial resources to bring services to the desired levels, cities are crumbling under their own pressure. While financial solutions are sought to tackle this problem, planning solutions must also be pursued.

The role of cities in the development process is well recognized. They are productive places which make significant contribution to national economic growth. As a locus for population growth, commercial and industrial activities, cities consume energy and national resources and thus generate a variety of wastes to an extent that exceeds the assimilative capacity of urban ecosystems. The situation is further exacerbated with rapid population growth leading to increased resource consumption and increased waste generation. The resulting environmental damages threaten the productivity of cities, and health and quality of life of its citizens (World Bank, 1994).

Urban services (e.g., water supply, sanitation, public transport and roads) are already overloaded beyond their sustainable capacities. Increasing population, commercial and industrial activities further deteriorate urban environment in addition to poor urban management. As a result, the resources are diminished and polluted at a fast rate, posing a serious threat to the health of our cities. Resource development costs are rising (e.g., new water supply schemes) as accessible resources are depleting. The traditional problem of excreta disposal still remains a serious concern for the civic authorities, while increasing air and noise pollution further aggravate the problematic situation problems in cities.

The deterioration of global environment has long been a cause of concern for policy makers, planners, municipal officials, voluntary groups and citizens. The scientific community has been showing its concern for over-exploitation of natural resources since a long time. Global warming, acid rain, desertification and ozone layer depletion are all related to poorly managed resources. Cities, with concentration of population and their high per capita energy consumption, contribute significantly towards these problems (Kalbermatten and Middleton, 1992; Blowers, 1993).

Agenda 21 and the Role of Local Authorities

The 1972 United Nations Conference on Human Environment held in Stockholm, brought together the developed and developing nations to delineate the "right" of human beings to a healthy and productive environment. Twenty years later, in 1992, in the United Nations Conference on Environment and Development held at Rio de Janeiro, the countries of the world came forward with Agenda 21, an Agenda for the twenty-first century, for sustainable development. It was realized that most of the problems and solutions being addressed by Agenda 21 have their roots in local activities and hence the cooperation of local authorities in managing cities will be a determining factor in achieving sustainable development. Local authorities, as the level of governance closest to the people, play a vital role in educating, mobilizing and responding to the public to promote sustainable development (see for instance Rabinovitch and Leitmann, 1993). Local authorities construct, operate and maintain social and environmental infrastructure and oversee planning processes in cities. Chapter 28 of Agenda 21, also known as "Local Agenda 21", suggests that by 1996 most local authorities should have undertaken a consultative process with their citizens to achieve a consensus on "a local agenda" for the community. To formulate strategies for sustainable development, the local authorities would learn from local, civic, community, business and industrial organization. This process of consultation is expected to lead to an increased awareness among the citizens about local environmental issues (United Nations, 1993).

Urban Environmental Infrastructure for Sustainable Development

Cities are engines of economic growth. Nearly 60 per cent of India's gross domestic product is produced in urban areas. Being the growth centres of the economy, cities depend upon a vast hinterland for their resources and in the process of resource exploitation, generate ubiquitous pollution which damages the resources. Poverty, homelessness, crime and diseases add further to the non-sustainability of cities.

The urban environmental infrastructure plays a very important role in the development of cities — it is a medium through which resources are consumed in a city and generated wastes are disposed of. Therefore the sustainability of a city is dependent on how efficient its infrastructure is. For instance, a good water supply network in a city minimizes loss of water, discourages its theft and thus leads to maximum utilization of the resource. In promoting sustainable development of cities, the urban environmental infrastructure has to be strengthened. Inadequate or poorly managed infrastructure affects urban economic development in several ways:

— It exposes the urban population to greater health risks.
— Economic productivity gets limited when services are not reliable.
— It adds financial costs to individuals and institutions for maintaining a minimum level of infrastructure.
— It creates chaos and disorder because of congestion leading to loss of productivity.
— It leads to increased consumption of resources and hence adversely affects the sustainability of cities.

Our cities are inherently non-sustainable as they consume resources from a vast hinterland and discharge untreated wastes into the hinterland, causing ecological imbalances. City planning efforts are based on a "linear" planning model which assumes that there are unlimited resources to be exploited to cater to the increasing number of people. This model was suitable for smaller populations in the past, when one-time use of goods and resources followed by discharge was practiced. These discharges, when in small quantities, were within the assimilative capacity of the ecosystem and were not harmful to the environment. But with increasing populations demanding more and more goods and resources, single use of resources, followed by discharge, has led to not only scarcity of resources but also their contamination because the wastes have exceeded the assimilative capacity of urban ecosystems. Such a practice is no longer viable. There is a need to adopt a "circular" planning model which requires resource consumption with maximum efficiency, reuse and recycling to reduce the volume of waste to bring it within the self-purifying capacity of the environment.

Rapid Environmental Assessment

Under the Urban Management Programme, rapid environmental assessment was undertaken for many cities. Leitmann (1993) reports initial results of the environmental assessments conducted in a few cities. The major conclusions of such exercises were:

i) Urban environmental degradation has a disproportionate negative impact on the poor.
ii) Economic structure and location of economic activities shape environmental problems.
iii) The level of urban wealth is linked to certain environmental problems — basic sanitation is a problem of low-income cities, while hazardous wastes, ambient air pollution are problems of higher income cities.

iv) Environmental management is complex as a large number of actions are involved over many jurisdictions and government.

v) Institutions and policies dealing with urban environmental problems are not synchronized. The capacity of local government to address local environmental problems is crucial to resultant environmental quality.

In these exercises, it was also realized that an adequate information base on urban environmental conditions is essential for the formulation of local strategies.

Environmental Mapping

Information is a lever for change and action. Formulation of any policy or action plan on urban environment is dependent on adequate and comprehensive information base. While aggregate data at the city level can indicate the status of urban environment, desegregated data is required for a complete understanding of intra-city differences in environment. Mapping is a useful tool to indicate the environmental differentials within cities. Local environmental planning is possible with such desegregate information. While information on various aspects can be collected from different sources, it is far more important to develop tools which can put such diverse information on environment in cities together for managing local environment. Mapping also makes city-wide environmental monitoring possible.

To evolve a local agenda for sustainability, it is important to have an assessment of urban environmental infrastructure highlighting the deficiencies to pinpoint the areas requiring immediate action (Pickering *et al.*, 1993). The distribution of services within a specified geographical area, such as a city, can be a very effective management tool for city managers. This would help them to prepare development plans and programmes for each specific service. It is in this respect that environmental mapping becomes an important tool for planning and implementation of integrated urban infrastructure development.

Urban Environmental Maps

To draw the attention of planners, local government officials, service managers, non-governmental organizations (NGOs), researchers and private entrepreneurs and to educate the public at large about urban environmental problems, the National Institute of Urban Affairs (NIUA) has prepared a set of maps called the "Urban Environmental Maps" (National Institute of Urban Affairs, 1994). These sets of maps show the spatial distribution of environmental infrastructure and status of environment in different parts of the selected cities (Delhi, Bombay, Ahmedabad and Vadodara). These maps were used to acquaint community groups, institutions and local government official with the problem of their cities and help evolve an action agenda in consultation with the local government.

The information for the preparation of these maps was based on secondary sources and was obtained from the respective cities. Information was not only obtained from official sources but activist groups, NGOs and other concerned organizations were also contacted to fully comprehend the nature of environmental problems in the city.

Preparation of such maps requires a vast and updated information base as well as considerable amount of time so as to make them meaningful and easy to comprehend. Some of the major limitations encountered in the preparation of these maps was the lack of information on a city-wide basis, outdated information base and lack of uniformity in data between cities which considerably constrained comparative analysis.

The urban environmental maps cover various indicators. These are given in Table 21.1. While maps on each aspect such as population, housing, water supply, sewerage, drainage, solid waste, air and water and noise pollution are useful by themselves, these become much more meaningful when superimposed on land use, population and transport maps, and maps showing the location of industries and commercial activities. The impact of environmental pollution on health is basic to understanding the seriousness of environmental problems (Organization for Economic Cooperation and Development, 1978). However, detailed information on health problems at a desegregated level (ward-wise) is not easily available for most cities. Information on problems related to water supply, sewerage, solid wastes, pollution, etc., are also not available in the desegregated form required for mapping. These limit the utility of these maps which would otherwise be a very effective tool for environmental management at the local level.

Examples of Maps Depicting Impact of Infrastructure and Services on Urban Environment

A few maps from the full report are presented in this paper to illustrate the linkage between poor infrastructure facilities and the resultant environmental quality.

Table 21.1: Analytical Framework for Urban Environmental Mapping

Urban environmental indicators	Parameters for mapping	Inferences for evolving local agenda
Population	• Population density in different wards of the city • Population changes in different wards over past decades • Number of households and sex-ratio in each ward	Indicates areas requiring dedensification and densification. Highlights needs for improving/strengthening social infrastructure.
Housing	• Number of dwelling units in each ward • Dwelling conditions (*kutcha/pucca*)[2] - ward-wise Number of persons per room—ward-wise • Location and number of slums • Level of services in slums (per capita availability) • Average house rents and land prices in different areas/wards of the city • Housing supply by government/public/private sector in the city	Availability of affordable housing, crowding and living conditions. Mis-match in demand and supply of housing across the city.
Water supply	• Sources of water supply (surface/ground), including community-based sources (handpumps, wells) • Location and capacity of water treatment plants • Average per capita supply (at city level and in different wards) • Areas in the city facing acute shortage of water and with poor quality of drinking water • Total supply and consumption of water for different uses in all the zones/wards of the city • Water supply network showing trunk lines, distribution lines etc. • Zone-wise/ward-wise number of connections (for each type of use)	Spatial availability and quality of potable water in the city. Highlights areas having excessive consumption of water and requiring conservation measures. Estimation of total available quantity and consumption of water will suggest the population that a city can support for sustainable development.
Sewerage and drainage	• Total quantity of sewage generated in the city • Location and capacity of sewage treatment plants	Suggests areas in the city requiring sewerage facilities like public latrines, septic tanks, etc. and drainage

(contd.)

[2] *Kutcha:* Semi-permanent; *Pucca:* Permanent

(Table 21.1 contd.)

Urban environmental indicators	Parameters for mapping	Inferences for evolving local agenda
	• Mode of disposal of (un)treated sewage (land/surface water etc.) • Zone-wise/ward-wise number of individual connections, number of public latrines in each slum/community group • Sewerage network in the city • Topographical map of the city depicting prominent water-logged areas and all the open drains • BOD and DO values for all drains, stream or river passing through the city	facilities. Poor availability of sewerage facilities and untreated sewage create unhygienic conditions affecting the health of urban citizens.
Solid waste	• Total and per capita generation of solid waste • Mode of disposal of solid waste (land filling, composing, incineration, etc.) • Collection and disposal of hazardous industrial waste, hospital waste, abattoir waste, etc. • Zone-wise/ward-wise generation and collection of solid waste	Highlights areas with uncollected garbage and facilities for disposal of hazardous industrial waste and hospital waste.
Transport	• Growth of vehicles and road network in the city • Peak hour traffic volume on major roads • Accidents on major roads • Accident-prone areas and bottlenecks on different corridors • Routes of the public transport and residential areas well connected with major commercial centres, office complexes, etc., by the public transport	Identifies roads requiring widening and/or better traffic management and suggests the need of remedial measures in different parts of the city.
Green spaces	• Location and area of forests, public parks and other green spaces in the city • Temporal variation in the green cover of the city	Action for saving trees in certain pockets of the city and areas devoid of any vegetation.
Air pollution	• Ambient air quality in the city (at different monitoring stations) • Emissions from transport sector identifying polluted corridors during peak hours.	Delineation of areas exceeding 'prescribed' air quality standards. Measures to reduce air pollution menace on polluted

(contd.)

(*Table 21.1 contd.*)

Urban environmental indicators	Parameters for mapping	Inferences for evolving local agenda
	• Emissions from air-polluting industries • Prevailing wind direction affected areas by industrial air pollution.	corridors and use of appropriate technology to reduce industrial air pollution.
Noise pollution	• Ambient noise levels in commercial, industrial and residential areas and near hospitals • Peak hour noise levels at major roads intersections.	Helps to identify the causes of noise pollution in different areas and to evolve measures for reducing them.

Note: The parameters mentioned here are indicative only. Depending on the type of city and its urban environmental problems, there may be a need to emphasize one or more parameters in detail.

For example, in the city of the Delhi, there are 900 slum pockets which are estimated to house nearly 20 per cent of the city's population. These slum pockets are poorly serviced. On the whole, the water supply to the city is inadequate and there are proposals for bringing water from 500 km away. Delhi's sewerage system has the capacity to treat only three-fourths of the waste water generated. The ambient air quality is quite poor and nearly 80 per cent of the air pollution is attributable to vehicular emissions. Ambient noise level, even at night time, is far above the acceptable limits.

Similarly, other city maps depict the quality of environment in terms of air pollution, water supply, location of slums, depletion of ground-water and distribution of water across various zones (Figures 21.1 to 21.10[1]).

Process of Consultation

These maps were found to be useful to initiate local-level consultation among the various actors. In such meetings, the local government officials typically attributed the environmental conditions to lack of resources for infrastructural development. The community groups and

---

[1]   1. MPD—Master Plan Delhi
   2. DWS & SDU—Delhi Water Supply and Sewage Disposal Undertaking
   3. CPCB—Central Pollution Control Board
   4. MCGB—Municipal Corporation of Greater Bombay
   6. AMC—Ahmedabad Municipal Corporation

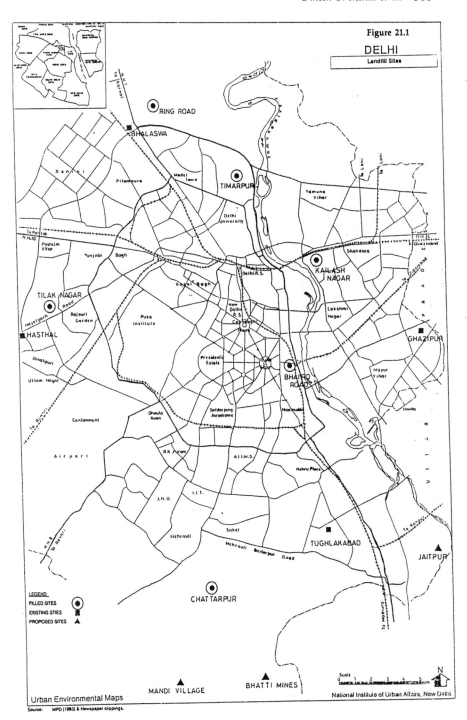

Figure 21.1
DELHI
Landfill Sites

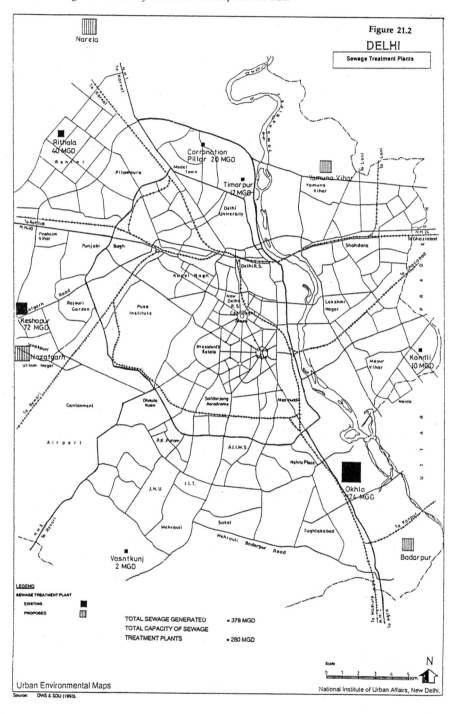

Figure 21.2

DELHI

Sewage Treatment Plants

LEGEND

SEWAGE TREATMENT PLANT

EXISTING

PROPOSED

TOTAL SEWAGE GENERATED = 378 MGD
TOTAL CAPACITY OF SEWAGE
TREATMENT PLANTS = 280 MGD

Urban Environmental Maps

Source: DWS & SDU (1993).

National Institute of Urban Affairs, New Delhi.

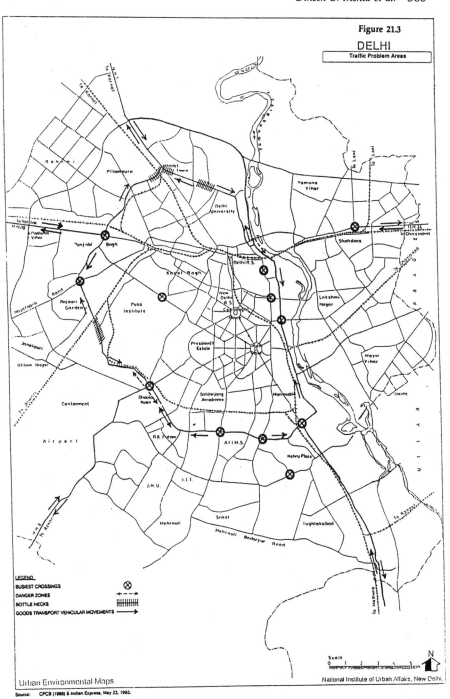

Figure 21.3

DELHI

Traffic Problem Areas

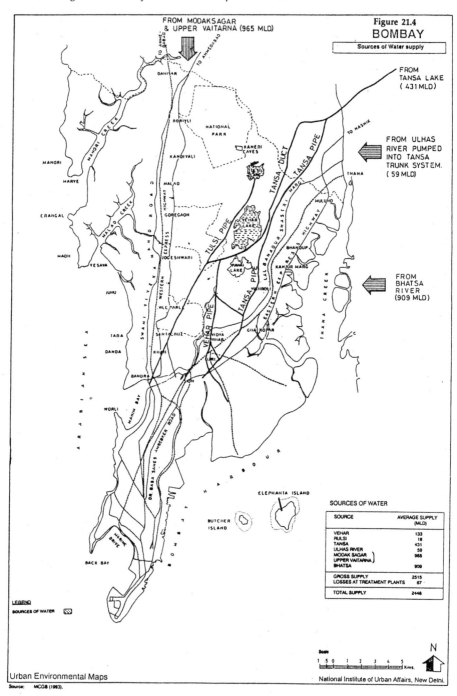

Figure 21.4
BOMBAY
Sources of Water supply

FROM MODAKSAGAR
& UPPER VAITARNA (965 MLD)

FROM
TANSA LAKE
(431 MLD)

FROM ULHAS
RIVER PUMPED
INTO TANSA
TRUNK SYSTEM.
(59 MLD)

FROM
BHATSA
RIVER
(909 MLD)

SOURCES OF WATER

SOURCE	AVERAGE SUPPLY (MLD)
VEHAR	133
RULSI	18
TANSA	431
ULHAS RIVER	59
MODAK SAGAR UPPER VAITARNA	965
BHATSA	909
GROSS SUPPLY	2515
LOSSES AT TREATMENT PLANTS	67
TOTAL SUPPLY	2448

LEGEND
SOURCES OF WATER

Urban Environmental Maps

National Institute of Urban Affairs, New Delhi.

Source: MCGB (1993).

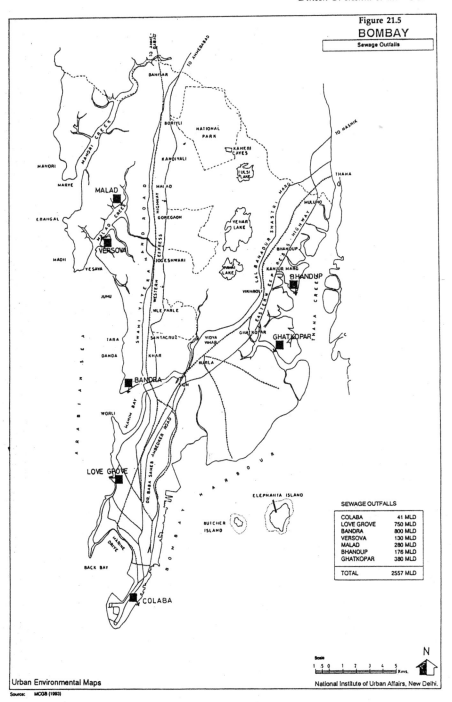

Figure 21.5
BOMBAY
Sewage Outfalls

SEWAGE OUTFALLS

COLABA	41 MLD
LOVE GROVE	750 MLD
BANDRA	800 MLD
VERSOVA	130 MLD
MALAD	280 MLD
BHANDUP	176 MLD
GHATKOPAR	380 MLD
TOTAL	2557 MLD

Urban Environmental Maps

National Institute of Urban Affairs, New Delhi.

Figure 21.6
BOMBAY
Landfill Site

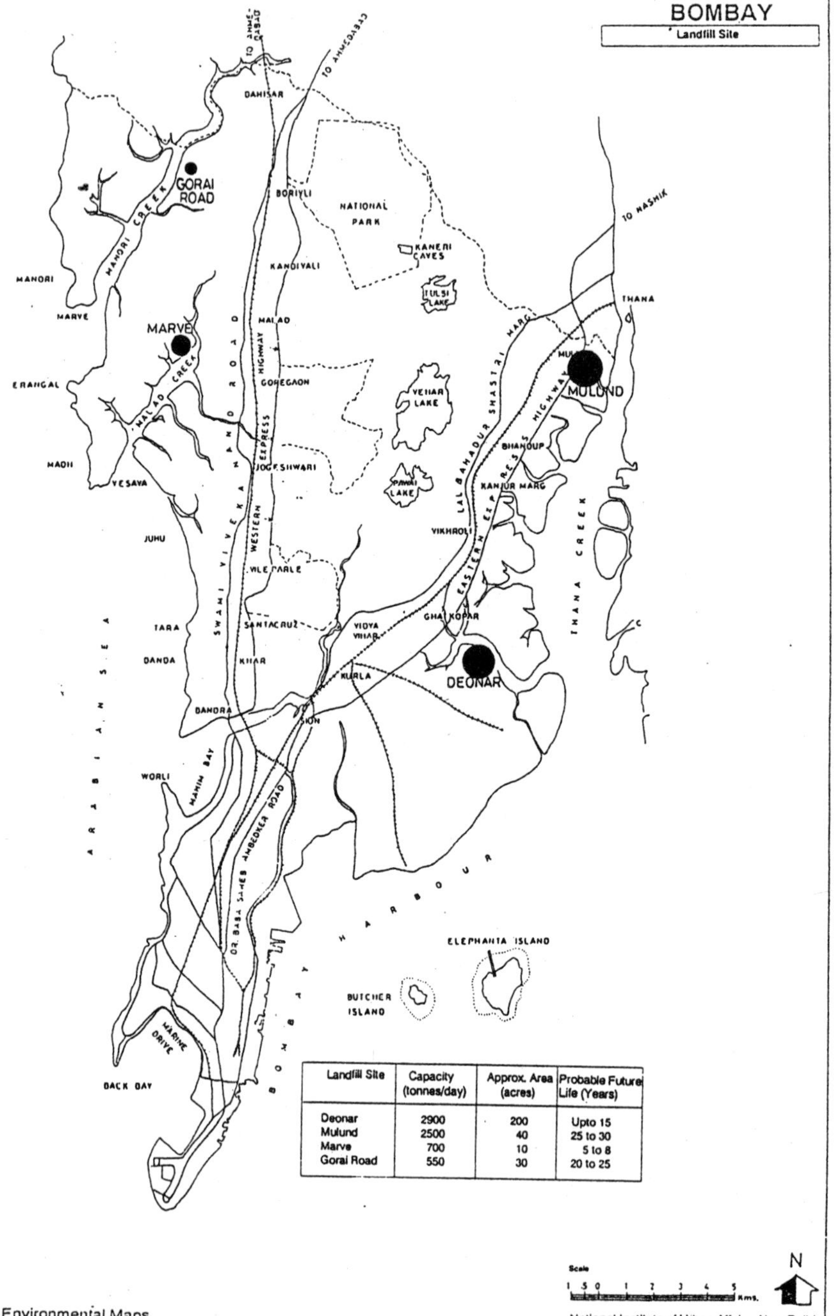

Landfill Site	Capacity (tonnes/day)	Approx. Area (acres)	Probable Future Life (Years)
Deonar	2900	200	Upto 15
Mulund	2500	40	25 to 30
Marve	700	10	5 to 8
Gorai Road	550	30	20 to 25

Urban Environmental Maps

National Institute of Urban Affairs, New Delhi.

Source: MCGB (1993).

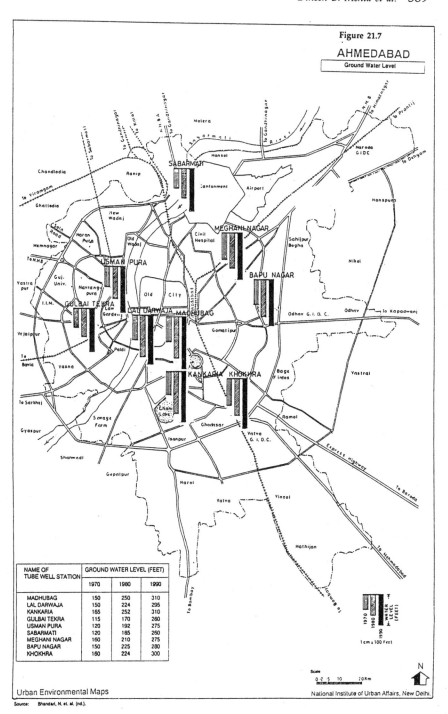

Figure 21.7

AHMEDABAD

Ground Water Level

NAME OF TUBE WELL STATION	GROUND WATER LEVEL (FEET)		
	1970	1980	1990
MADHUBAG	150	250	310
LAL DARWAJA	150	224	295
KANKARIA	165	252	310
GULBAI TEKRA	115	170	260
USMAN PURA	120	192	275
SABARMATI	120	185	260
MEGHANI NAGAR	160	210	275
BAPU NAGAR	150	225	280
KHOKHRA	160	224	300

Urban Environmental Maps

National Institute of Urban Affairs, New Delhi.

Source: Bhandari, N. et. al. (nd.).

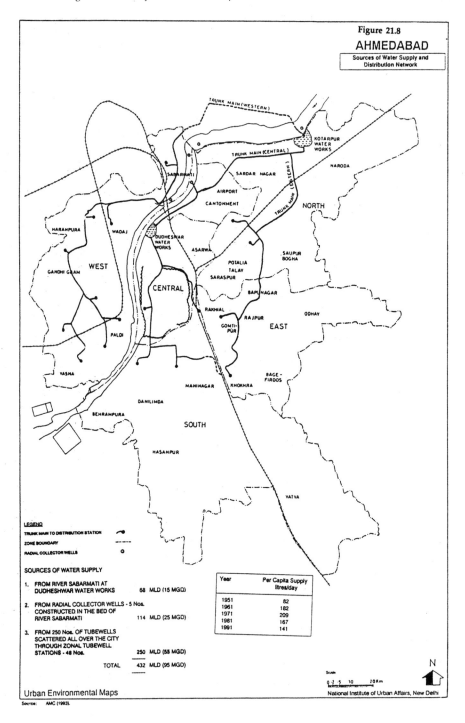

Figure 21.8

AHMEDABAD

Sources of Water Supply and Distribution Network

LEGEND

TRUNK MAIN TO DISTRIBUTION STATION

ZONE BOUNDARY

RADIAL COLLECTOR WELLS

SOURCES OF WATER SUPPLY

1. FROM RIVER SABARMATI AT
   DUDHESHWAR WATER WORKS   68 MLD (15 MGD)

2. FROM RADIAL COLLECTOR WELLS - 5 Nos.
   CONSTRUCTED IN THE BED OF
   RIVER SABARMATI   114 MLD (25 MGD)

3. FROM 250 Nos. OF TUBEWELLS
   SCATTERED ALL OVER THE CITY
   THROUGH ZONAL TUBEWELL
   STATIONS - 48 Nos.   250 MLD (55 MGD)

   TOTAL   432 MLD (95 MGD)

Year	Per Capita Supply litres/day
1951	82
1961	182
1971	209
1981	167
1991	141

Scale
0 2.5 10   20 Km

N

Urban Environmental Maps

National Institute of Urban Affairs, New Delhi

Source: AMC (1993).

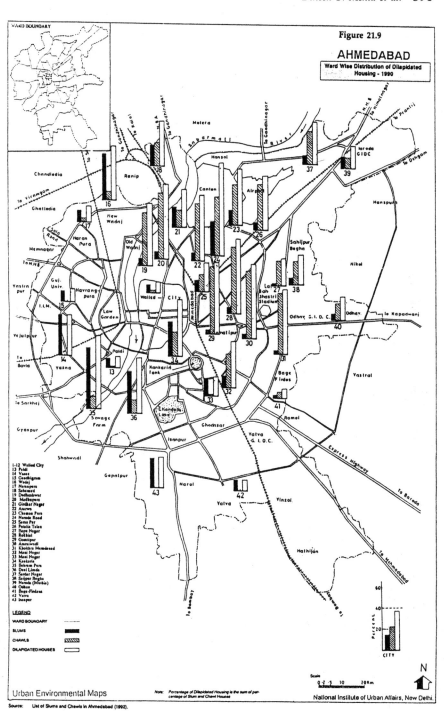

Figure 21.9

AHMEDABAD

Ward Wise Distribution of Dilapidated Housing - 1990

Urban Environmental Maps

Note: Percentage of Dilapidated Housing is the sum of percentage of Slum and Chawl Houses

National Institute of Urban Affairs, New Delhi.

Source: List of Slums and Chawls in Ahmedabad (1992).

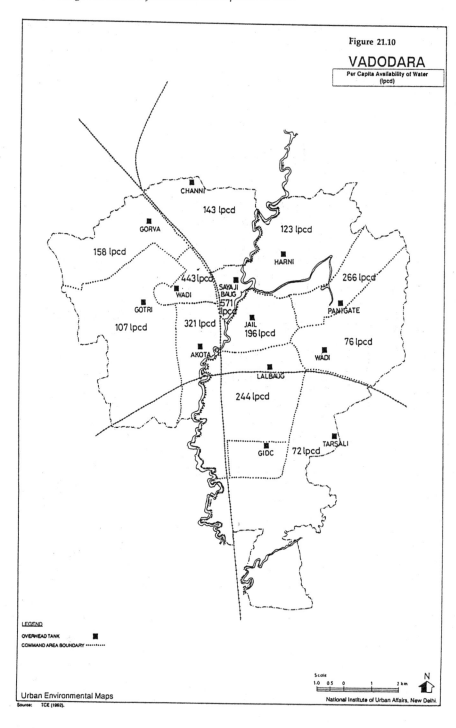

Figure 21.10

VADODARA

Per Capita Availability of Water
(lpcd)

Urban Environmental Maps

Source: TCE (1992).

other institutions, however, highlighted the need for management of scarce resources like water and improving institutional arrangements for basic services like solid waste collection and sewage treatment.

Through these consultations it became apparent that the "brown agenda" is the foremost in any discussion on environmental quality among all the stakeholders. It is imperative that institutional mechanisms, preferably outside the domain of local governments, be established to carry out such consultations and develop action strategies. Such strategies, collectively identified, would also have the prescribed roles for each stakeholder in the city. Environmental maps and status reports have been found to be an extremely useful tool for such a process and it is necessary to carry out such exercises for as many cities as possible.

BIBLIOGRAPHY

Blowers, A. (ed.) (1993), *Planning for a Sustainable Environment: A Report by the Town and Country Planning Association*, Earthscan, London.

Kalbermatten, J.M. and Middleton, R.N. (1992), 'Challenges in Environmental Protection in Cities: New Approaches and Strategies for Urban Environmental Management', Paper presented at the Conference on Enforcing Urban Environmental Management: New Strategies and Approaches, 4–6, February, Berlin.

Leitmann, J. (1993), *Rapid Environment Assessment: Lessons from Cities in the Developing World, Vol. 1, Methodology and Preliminary Findings*, Urban Management Programme, World Bank, Washington D.C.

National Institute of Urban Affairs (1994), *Urban Environmental Maps*, NIUA, New Delhi.

Organization for Economic Cooperation and Development (1978), *Urban Environmental Indicators*, Paris.

Pickering, D. *et al.* (1993), *Utility Mapping and Record Keeping for Infrastructure*, Urban Management Programme, World Bank, Washington, D.C.

Rabinovitch, J. and Leitmann, J. (1993), *Environmental Innovation and Management in Curitiba, Brazil*, Working Paper No. 1, Urban Management Programme, World Bank, Washington, D.C.

United Nations (1993), *Report of the United Nations Conference on Environment and Development, Vol. I, Resolutions Adopted by the Conference*, 3-14 June, Rio de Janeiro.

World Bank (1994), *World Development Report: Infrastructure for Development*, Oxford University Press, New York.

22

LAND MANAGEMENT FOR INTEGRATED URBAN DEVELOPMENT IN ASIAN CITIES: IMPLEMENTING THE FORMULA L + P + F + NI = SUD

Ray W. Archer

Most of the rapid growth of Asian cities is accommodated by their outward expansion through the physical conversion of rural land to urban uses. This conversion is normally by a two-stage process of land development followed by building development. The land development should be by the integrated provision of the roads, drains, water supply, sewerage and electricity supply lines necessary for the planned urban uses. This paper focusses on achieving the integrated development of these key items of network infrastructure in urban-fringe areas by the combined efforts of the government and private sectors.

It is proposed that the government sector should construct the road, drainage, water, sewerage and electricity line networks at the mainline and distributor/collector line levels, and should do this in advance of the private sector land and building development. This will create both a supply of subdivision land and a physical framework to guide the private development activity. The private land subdividers should then construct the networks of local roads, drains and utility services lines within their land subdivision projects. The main issue is: How can the government sector agencies achieve the integrated provision of the key network infrastructure at the mainline and distributor/collector line levels in the areas designated for urban development, and do so in advance of the private sector land and building development?

Introduction

In mixed-economy countries most of the urban-fringe land is privately owned and its conversion to urban land is mainly by private land subdivision and building development projects undertaken for private profit and benefit through the urban land market. But government is also very much involved in this urban expansion by its land-use planning and regulation and by its construction of network infrastructure. Governments can manage these activities so as to guide urban expansion.

Land management is the government management of its planning, network infrastructure and regulatory functions in urban expansion so as to create a physical and legal framework to facilitate and guide the private land subdivision and building projects being undertaken through the land market. It is designed to achieve planned urban expansion, adequate land supply and sustainable urban development. The land manager works to implement the formula $L + P + F + NI = SUD$, which means Land plus Plans plus Finance plus Network Infrastructure creates the physical foundation for Sustainable Urban Development, i.e., a sustainable healthy and pleasant environment.

The formula can be implemented along the following lines. As the city expands, the government selects and designates the future urban areas, plans and zones them and then constructs public road and utility service lines at the mainline and distributor/collector line levels·in these areas so as to convert the rural land into subdivision land. This network infrastructure creates both a supply of subdivision land and a physical layout (a framework) that will guide the private developers and land-owners undertaking land subdivision and building projects in response to the market demand for new urban plots and buildings. The government administers the land subdivision regulations to ensure the sound layout and construction of the local road and utility service networks within each subdivision project. (These projects include all the housing projects, shophouse projects, etc., that include the subdivision of land into building plots.) It also has to administer the land-use zoning and building regulations to limit the building development within each area to the capacity of the network infrastructure serving that area so as to prevent its overload and failure. In summary, the government sector converts the designated rural land into subdivision land, and the private sector converts this subdivision land into building land and buildings, i.e., into urban land.

The formula $L + P + F + NI = SUD$ is a simple and commonsense equation but it is not generally recognized and implemented by governments in the rapidly growing cities of Southeast and South Asia. In many cities private land subdividers implement the formula and construct the local roads and utility service lines within their projects, but the government agencies fail to construct the distributor/collector roads and utility lines in urban fringe areas until after the private land and building development is well advanced.

This paper discusses how the formula can be implemented, focussing on how local governments can construct planned networks of distributor/collector roads and utility service lines in advance of the private land and building development. The paper is divided into four parts. The first part explains and justifies the formula. The second part outlines the barriers to government agencies implementing the formula at the mainline and distributor/collector line levels. The third part discusses the implementation of the formula through self-financing land development projects. The fourth part outlines the value of the formula, and then recommends local governments to begin implementing it by using special assessment projects and land pooling/readjustment projects to construct networks of distributor/collector roads and utility lines in selected parts of their urban-fringe areas. This project approach is not proposed as the solution, but as an early step forward.

Meaning and Justification of the Formula

The meaning of the formula is shown in Box 22.1, and the justification of the formula is given in Box 22.2.

The formula $L + P + F + NI = SUD$ can be sketched as follows. The land is the rural land in urban-fringe areas that is selected and designated for urban development on the basis of its suitability for conversion to urban land. The plans are a combination of the urban land-use and circulation plans, plus the public road and utility service network plans (designs) for each development area, plus the infrastructure layout and subdivision plans (designs) for each land subdivision project. Government agencies plan the urban land-use pattern, and plan the road and utility service line networks at the mainline and the distributor/collector line levels, while the private developers plan the networks of local (access) roads and local utility service lines within their land subdivision projects. The network infrastructure to be constructed is a combination of roads, drains, water supply lines, waste-water and electricity lines, as urban households desire all-weather vehicular access for their plot and house together with storm-water flood protection, piped water, safe sanitation and electricity connection. (Some of these items, such as the water supply and waste-water treatment, might be provided on site.) There is a three-level hierarchy in the network infrastructure—the mainlines, distributor/collector lines and local (access) lines—with the government sector being responsible for providing the mainlines and distributor/collector lines while the private landowners and developers are usually responsible for

Box 22.1: Meaning of the Formula : L + P + F + NI = SUD

(Land plus Plans plus Finance plus Network Infrastructure creates the physical foundation for Sustainable Urban Development)

Land	— Rural land in urban-fringe areas that is selected and designated for urban development.
+ Plans	— Urban land-use (and density) and circulation plans, and the supporting zoning regulations, for the designated development areas.
	— Government plans (designs) for the network infrastructure works to service the planned land uses.
	— Private plans (designs) for the land subdivision projects.
+ Finance	— Funds to pay the cost of the infrastructure construction, including the cost of land acquisition.
	— Funds from current revenue/income, from reserves/savings, from loans/credit, and from grants/subsidies.
	— Private developers recover the cost of the network infrastructure within their land subdivision projects from their plot sale revenues.
+ Network Infrastructure	— Networks of public roads and drains with a hierarchy of main roads, distributor/collector roads, and local (access) roads.
	— Networks of public utility service lines for the key utilities, these being drainage, water supply, sewerage and electricity supply. There is a hierarchy of mainlines, distributor/collector lines and local lines for each utility service.
	— Government construction of the main and distributor/collector roads and lines, and private construction of the local roads and lines within the land subdivision projects.
= Sustainable Urban Development	— Creating urban areas where the activities of work and living, and the **urban** movement of people and goods can be carried out safely, efficiently and **development** with amenity, and where any pollution is within the capacity of the environmental systems to absorb it.

providing the local lines within their land subdivision projects. (The term "lines" here includes the roads.)

The funds needed to finance the construction of the network infrastructure (including the cost of land acquisition) come from a combination of sources. The government road (and drainage) agencies are usually funded by central government budget allocations and petrol tax collections, while the public utility agencies fund their capital works mainly from medium/long-term borrowings (including bond issues) and from their annual revenue surplus. Additional funds to enable these agencies to expand their programme of network construction so as to provide it in advance of private development, can be raised by taxing the

Box 22.2: Justification of the Formula : L + P + F + NI = SUD

Land	— The rural land designated and zoned for urban development is selected according to suitability criteria that recognize the environmental systems and land features, e.g., avoid flood lands.
+ Plans	— Urban land-use and circulation plans recognize these systems and features, and design for urban land use efficiency and amenity.
	— Plans specify the type and density of urban land use for each area so that the network infrastructure can then be designed with the capacity to fully service each area without overload.
	— Plans (engineering designs) of the road and utility networks guide the construction of the network infrastructure with the needed capacity for each area.
	— Plans guide the setting of the regulatory standards and the enforcement of the regulatory controls, so as to limit development to the capacity of the network infrastructure that is installed.
+ Finance	— Additional funds for the increased government construction of network infrastructure can be raised from the rising urban land values, and by user charges and taxes.
	— At the project level, the revenues from the plot sales at market value can recover the cost of the on-site network infrastructure within each land servicing and subdivision project. Larger projects will include the on site distributor/collector roads and lines.
+ Network Infrastructure	The networks of main, distributor/collector and local roads designed for the planned urban land use pattern will:
	— avoid and minimize traffic congestion, air pollution and accidents;
	— facilitate efficient public transport services and reduce private car usage;
	— assist efficient solid waste collection,;
	— assist access for emergency service vehicles for public safety; and
	— provide the layout and land for the drainage system, and for most of the water supply lines, sewerage lines, electricity lines and the telephone lines;
	— Drainage system prevents storm-water flooding.
	— Water supply system provides clean, safe water, and avoids land subsidence from on-site deep-well pumping.
	— Sewerage collection and treatment system avoids pollution and health hazard.
	— Electricity supply system reduces use of fossil fuels for heating and lighting.
= Sustainable Urban Development	— Efficient urban areas with a sustainable safe, healthy and pleasant environment.

rising urban land values, and by levying user charges and taxes, with the monies collected being paid into special funds reserved for financing specified infrastructure works.

The construction of the networks of roads and utility service lines designed to service the land use in each area provides the means of reducing energy usage, and minimizing pollution and limiting it to the capacity of the natural environmental systems to disperse/absorb it, and they enable the urban households and business firms to carry out their activities with safety, efficiency and amenity. The construction of the network infrastructure in the areas designated for urban development attracts the land and building developers and the urban land users to these areas, and away from the other urban-fringe areas that are less suitable for conversion to urban uses.

The functions and many potential benefits of a planned network and hierarchy of public roads that are shown in Box 22.2, indicate that governments should give top priority to planning the networks of main roads and distributor/collector roads in the designated development areas, and then acquiring the roadway land in advance of the private land subdivision and building development. When the planned networks of main and distributor/collector roads are fixed to the ground by the acquisition of the roadway land, this provides a strong visible framework to guide the private developers when they are buying land for their projects and then in designing their project layouts. It also guides and assists the public utility agencies locating and designing their networks of mainlines and distributor/collector lines. The acquisition of this roadway land in advance of private urban development activity also enables it to be done at the least financial cost and the least social cost. Figure 22.1 shows the chaotic pattern of local roads and utility service lines that is emerging in Bangkok suburbs due to the failure of the Bangkok Metropolitan Administration to plan and implement networks of distributor/collector roads within each of the city blocks encircled by main roads.

The implementation of the formula in the newly urbanizing areas will result in the desirable sequence of physical urban expansion. This is shown in Figure 22.2. The government agencies designate and plan the future urban areas and construct the required networks of public roads and utility service lines at the mainline and distributor/collector line levels in these areas. This converts the rural land into subdivision land, which is rural land parcels with public road and utility service line connections and zoned for urban land uses, and is therefore physically and legally suitable for subdivision into serviced building plots. The private landowners and developers then convert this subdivision land into building land by designing, servicing and subdividing it into

Figure 22.1: The Suburban Road Pattern in the Ladprao/Ramintra "Superblock", 9 km. N.E. from Bangkok G.P.O. A chaotic maze of subdivision project roads.

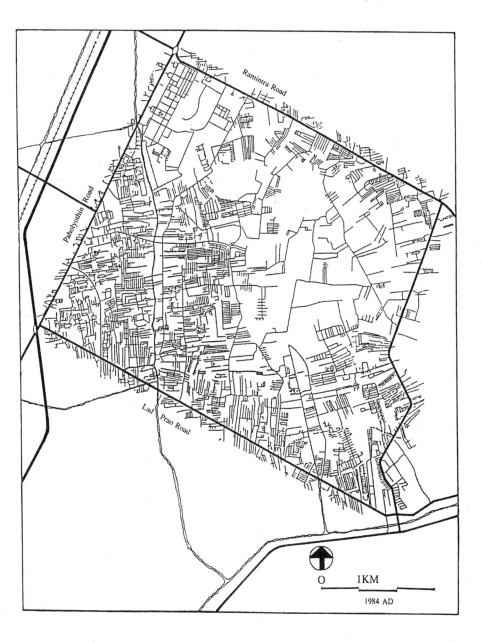

Figure 22.2: The Stages of Urban Land Development as a City Expands

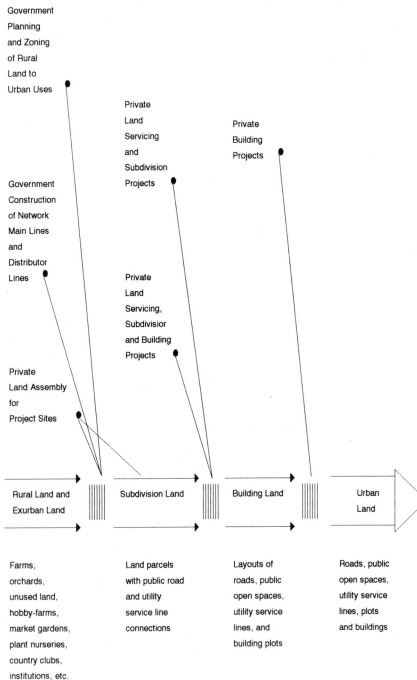

layouts of streets, open spaces and serviced building plots. The building developers and individual households, business firms, etc., then convert this building land into urban land by buying the plots and constructing buildings on them. The land subdivision and building construction stages are often combined into land and building projects, including rowhouse projects, shophouse projects and factory/ warehouse projects.

Figure 22.2 shows that the main role of the government sector in urban expansion is to combine its urban planning, regulatory and public road and public utility construction functions so as to convert the rural land into subdivision land, while the main role of the private sector is to carry out its land assembly, land servicing and subdivision, and building development functions so as to convert the subdivision land into urban land. The layout of the public road and utility service mainlines and distributor/collector lines creates a supply of subdivision land in the designated development areas and also provides a physical framework to guide the location, timing and design of the private land subdivision projects.

When the network infrastructure is constructed as planned, then the land-use zoning regulations and the building construction regulations have to be enforced on building projects so as to limit the density of building development (and hence population) in each area to the capacity of the network infrastructure installed to service the area. The public utility agencies should support the land-use regulatory agencies in enforcing the agreed limits on development density by withholding their services from buildings that exceed the regulatory limits.

The formula $L + P + F + NI = SUD$ can be applied at:

- the metropolitan or city scale;
- the metro-corridor or metro-sector scale;
- the district or neighbourhood scale; and/or at
- the land development project level.

Although it is desirable to implement the formula in all the urbanizing areas around a city, or at least for large areas such as a development corridor, doing this requires a combination of increased funding, additional personnel, re-organization, inter-agency cooperation and other measures that usually take years to arrange. However, at the present time the formula is being widely implemented at the project level and this paper focusses on the project level as local governments can begin implementing the formula in selected urban-fringe areas at the project level.

These projects are mainly the private land subdivision projects where a planned layout of local roads and local utility service lines is constructed by the developer within his project site, who then recovers the cost of these works from his plot sale revenues. (The land subdivision projects include all the land and building projects that involve the subdivision of land into building plots with separate titles.) The land subdivision projects construct the on-site infrastructure which is usually only the local roads, drains and utility service lines. It is possible to use other types of projects to construct planned layouts of distributor/collector roads and utility service lines for relatively large areas, such as for a neighbourhood or district. These are the large-scale land development projects, land pooling/readjustment projects, and special assessment projects.

Barriers to Implementing the Formula

The formula is not being implemented by governments in most of the developing countries of Southeast and South Asia and this is one of the main causes of the degradation of the urban environment in these countries (Foster, 1989, p.29). In most of their cities there is inadequate and delayed government provision of network infrastructure, particularly the distributor/collector roads and lines in their newly urbanizing areas. Many parts of this network infrastructure are being provided years after the private land and building projects have transformed the land.

There are many explanations for the non-implementation of the formula by governments. The first is that most governments do not recognize the formula and are not attempting to implement it in a conscious way. The second and more obvious explanation is the shortage of funds for public works. The cities are expanding rapidly and the network infrastructure is costly so that large amounts of money are required and there are many other demands competing for the limited development funds. The cost of the network infrastructure is also increased by the frequent failure of government to acquire the land for roads and utility service works before the private land and building development, plus land speculation, has increased land values and the cost of land acquisition. The cost of providing the network infrastructure is also increased by the wide scatter of private land and building development in urban fringe areas. Along with the financial barrier there are also planning and administrative barriers as well. There is a shortage of trained urban planners and much of the planning is directed to regulating urban land use rather than to guiding urban development. There is little cooperation and coordination between the urban planning and the network infrastructure agencies, which are usually separate organizations with their own planning, their own funding and their own priorities.

Although the government sector is short of funds for the construction of network infrastructure, the urbanization of rural land generates large increases in the market value of this land which are received by the rural landowners, speculators and developers as windfall profits, i.e., as "unearned increments" in land value. These rising urban land values are the most obvious and appropriate source of additional funds to finance the increased construction of network infrastructure, as the market land values anticipate and depend on the provision of this infrastructure. There are a number of techniques for "capturing" part of the rising urban land values so as to finance the construction of network infrastructure, either by internalizing the construction and cost recovery within each land subdivision project or by collecting a special tax or levy or charge on land which is paid into a fund reserved for financing infrastructure construction (Alterman, 1982, p.40 and 1988). The following sections describe some of the main techniques at the project level, and refer to examples from Bangkok.

Implementing the formula at the project level: The formula is widely implemented through urban land development projects. These are projects to physically convert the land by subdividing or reshaping the rural land parcels and constructing network infrastructure, and to also increase its market value by an amount significantly greater than the project costs. These projects include land subdivision projects, new town projects, land pooling/readjustment projects and special assessment projects. Each project contains the four elements of L, P, F and NI, and each project manager has to combine them for a successful project. In a typical project the land is assembled or designated, the project is designed (planned), a short- or medium-term loan is raised to finance the construction of the network infrastructure, and this construction is carried out. The land is converted and part of the increase in its market value is used to recover the project cost and repay the project loan.

Land Subdivision Projects under the Subdivision Regulations: Since World War II many countries have extended their land subdivision regulations to require land developers to construct the network infrastructure within their project site, and this regulatory requirement has coincided with the preference and the affordability of many plot buyers for fully-serviced plots. The land developer constructs the roads, drains, water supply lines, etc., within his project and sells the serviced building plots at higher prices which enable him to recover the additional cost of installing the network infrastructure. The construction of part or all of the network infrastructure within private land subdivision projects has become well established in many countries. In the case of land and house projects, the house buyers normally require all-weather road access, storm-water drainage, piped water, a sanitary system and electricity supply to their plot and house, so that these are standard elements of these projects.

The land subdivision regulations apply to projects to subdivide land into say 10 or more building plots with separate land titles. The regulations also apply to all the land and building projects that include the subdivision of land into plots with separate titles. The subdivision regulations usually:

- Set out the procedure and requirements for obtaining the subdivision permit, together with measures for consumer protection such as developer ownership of the project land, and a bar on the preselling of plots before project approval;
- Regulate the road and plot layout and specify the minimum permissible dimensions of the roads and plots for residential areas, industrial areas, commercial areas (e.g., shophouse projects) and semi-rural areas (e.g., hobby-farm projects);
- Require and specify the minimum permissible allocation of land for public open spaces and facilities;
- Require the construction of the on-site network infrastructure and set out the minimum permissible standards for this infrastructure; and
- Require the transfer of the network infrastructure when the project is completed to the appropriate government agency, at no charge.

The regulations are usually administered by the Lands Department which administers the land ownership record and transfer system. They can be a very effective land-use control because the Department can refuse to issue the title documents for the new plots unless the subdivision regulatory requirements have been met by the developer.

The land subdivision regulations provide only a partial means of implementing the formula. Their impact is usually limited to the provision of the on-site infrastructure within each project and there are often large tracts of empty rural land between the projects. Often, some of the public utility lines, such as for waste-water, are not constructed. This is frequently the case in smaller projects (Archer, 1991a).

Large-scale land development projects (private enterprise new towns):
Private developers are sometimes able to assemble large areas of rural land near the metropolises into large sites that they plan, develop and

market as new towns. They buy the land at rural land values and then plan, service and subdivide it into urban housing land, industrial land, commercial land, and recreational land, which they sell at urban land values. Their urban land sale revenues enable them to recover the project costs and make a profit. These "new town" developers usually provide all the on-site network infrastructure and also provide open space, recreational facilities and social infrastructure (and some off-site infrastructure such as a connecting main road, bridge or utility service line) that will make their projects more attractive to industrial and business firms, to households, to investors and to building developers. They often emphasize amenity, environmental quality and recreation features in the planning and marketing of these projects.

Although there are relatively few private, new town projects in progress, there can be many larger subdivision projects, and the theory of large scale urban land development explains why larger subdivision projects can produce better urban development than can many small separate projects for the same areas (Archer, 1977).

Nava Nakorn (46 km north of Bangkok) and Muang Ake (29 km north of Bangkok) on Paholyothin Highway provide two examples near the Asian Institute of Technology (AIT). Nava Nakorn is a 1,000 ha new town and industrial estate commenced in 1970 in which all the network infrastructure has been constructed or funded by the company. The layout of Nava Nakorn is shown in Figure 22.3.

Government land development and new town projects: Government agencies can undertake land subdivision projects and large-scale land development projects that include the construction of all the on-site network infrastructure. As in the case of private sector projects, the construction of network infrastructure will usually be financed by a short/medium-term loan which is repaid out of the revenues from the sale of the serviced building plots (with or without buildings on them). Most mixed-economy countries have some government agencies, such as the public housing authority and/or local governments, undertaking land subdivision projects such as sites-and-services projects, and land and house projects.

In theory, the government sector should be able to undertake urban land development projects more efficiently than private land developers because government agencies can use the compulsory purchase power to assemble land for project sites, can borrow money at lower interest rates that can private developers, and can avoid or expedite the regulatory approval of project plans. However, the theory usually does not apply in practice, mainly because government agencies are insulated

Figure 22.3: Layout of Nava Nakorn New Town

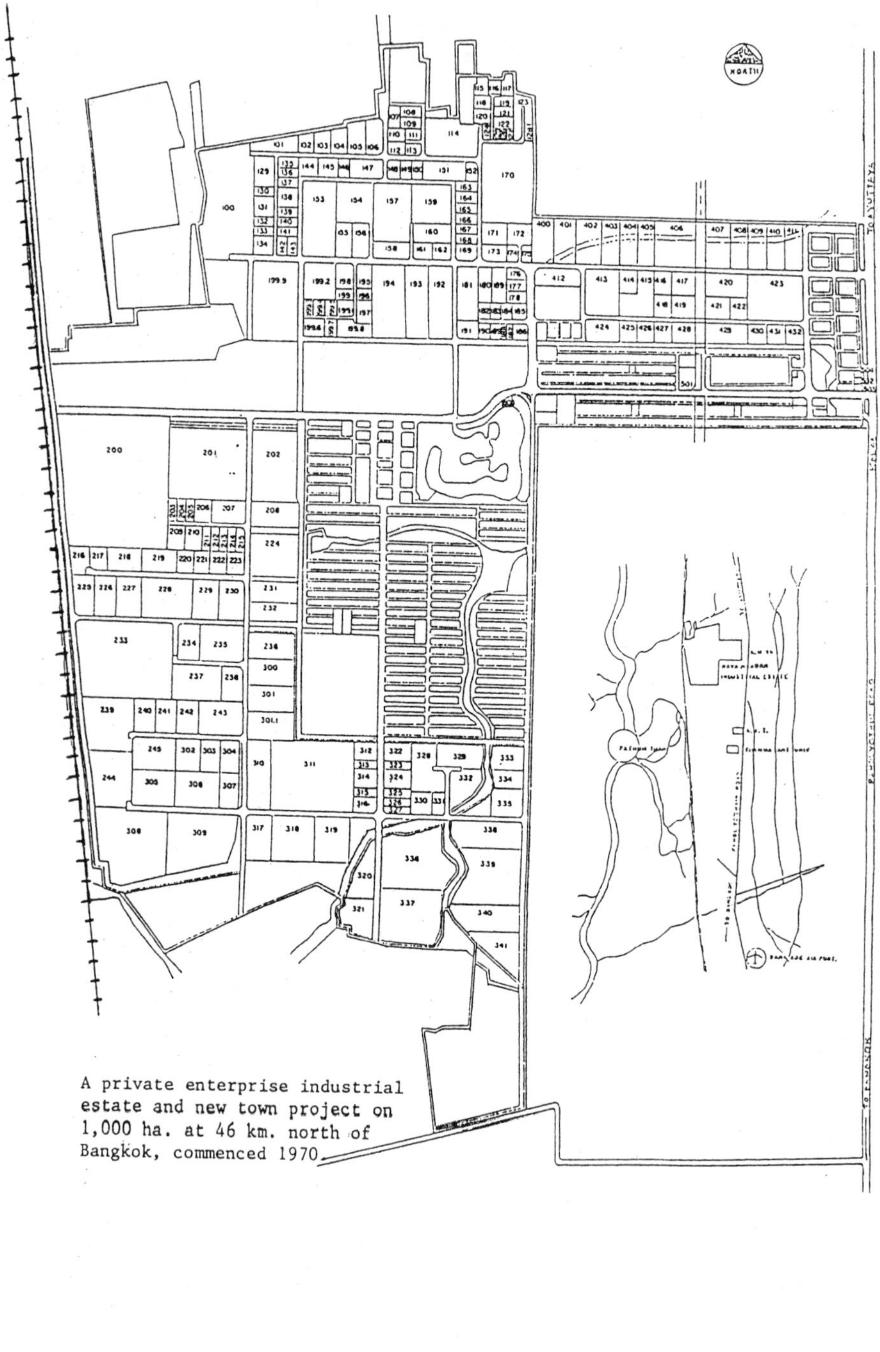

A private enterprise industrial
estate and new town project on
1,000 ha. at 46 km. north of
Bangkok, commenced 1970

from the disciplines and incentives of the marketplace and they cannot operate with the flexibility of private business firms. The compulsory purchase power over private land may not be of much benefit to those government agencies that possess it because its use is often restricted by legal and political limitations, and it can be very time consuming.

In the case of Thailand, the National Housing Authority has undertaken many land development projects, mainly as land and house projects, and they include some large-scale projects such as the Bang Pli New Town some 25 km east from Bangkok (National Housing Authority, 1993). The Industrial Estate Authority of Thailand also develops industrial estate projects with the construction of all the on-site network infrastructure in the project, including industrial waste-water treatment facilities. Since its formation in 1972, the Authority has developed six large estates and participated in the development of 14 private estates and one with the National Housing Authority (Industrial Estate Authority, 1994).

Land pooling/readjustment projects: The impact of the land subdivision regulations on the provision of network infrastructure is limited due to the small size of most land development projects, as it is often too difficult and too costly for developers to assemble many adjoining land parcels into large project sites. The difficulty can be overcome by using the land pooling/readjustment (LP/R) technique. LP/R is the temporary consolidation of separately owned land parcels for their unified design, servicing and subdivision into a planned layout of roads, open spaces and serviced building plots. Some of the plots are sold for project cost recovery and the rest of the plots are transferred to the landowners in exchange for their parcels of rural land. Alternatively, the LP/R projects can be undertaken to produce subdivision land, so that the landowners contribute rural land parcels to the project and receive back reshaped parcels of subdivision land. LP/R projects are usually undertaken by local governments but they can also be carried out by other authorized government agencies and by landowner cooperative associations (Archer, 1992).

A number of LP/R projects are in preparation in Thailand at present. The layout plan for a previously proposed LP/R project on a 329 ha site in the Minburi District of Bangkok is shown in Figure 22.4 (Foo, 1988, p. 56). The LP/R project for a 329 ha area near Minburi shown in Figure 22.4 was designed by Foo Tuan Seik to illustrate how the LP/R technique could be used to construct the distributor/collector networks in advance of private land and building development.

As special assessment is the simpler technique of the two, local governments should give first consideration to possible special

Figure 22.4: Minburi Land Pooling/Readjustment Project

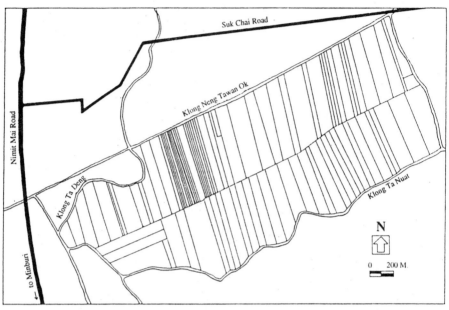

A. Site for proposed partial LP/R project near Minburi, Bangkok (329 ha in 95 land parcels)

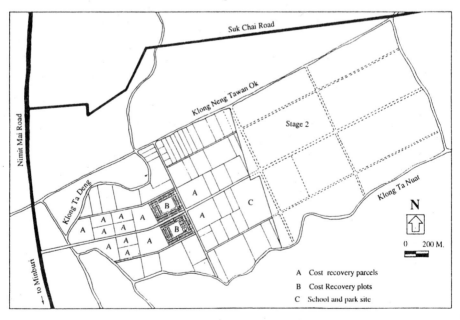

B. Layout plan for Stage 1 of proposed partial LP/R project near Minburi, Bangkok

assessment projects. One very appropriate use of the technique would be to implement some of the planned road networks shown in the general plans for provincial cities and towns as prepared by the Department of Town and Country Planning. Special assessment projects could be undertaken to acquire the roadway land and construct the roads and drains, or at least to acquire the roadway land. These projects could be undertaken with the assistance of professional consultants and could be implemented as specific plans under the Town and Country Planning Act 1975.

Special assessment projects: These are projects undertaken by local governments to construct infrastructure works that will benefit a particular locality where the cost of the project is recovered by an annual charge or tax (as a "special assessment"), on each of the land parcels that benefit from the construction of the infrastructure and increase in value. The project costs include the compensation cost of the land taken for the works, and the special assessment charge on each land parcel is calculated on the basis of the increase in value received by the land parcel. In a typical project, many of the benefiting land parcels are not physically disturbed by the project, so that special assessment projects are less intrusive and less complicated than LP/R projects which involve the subdivision or reshaping of every land parcel. Special assessment projects could be used to implement planned layouts of distributor/collector roads in selected urban-fringe areas.

The technique has not been used for the construction of urban infrastructure in Thailand but it has been used for many years for the construction of water distribution systems for existing farms in new irrigation areas. There have been proposals for urban projects and Figure 22.5 shows the layout plan for a proposed pilot special assessment project to construct a network of distributor/collector roads on a 127 ha site in the Bang Kapi District of Bangkok (Archer, 1991b, p.30).

Local governments could begin constructing these distributor/ collector level networks for selected parts of their urban fringe areas by undertaking special assessment projects and/or LP/R projects for these areas. The pilot special assessment project proposed for a 127 ha area at Bang Kapi, as shown in Figure 22.5, shows how a layout of distributor/ collector roads and drains could be constructed so as to open-up the land for development and then guide this development.

Figure 22.5: The Bang Kapi Special Assessment Project

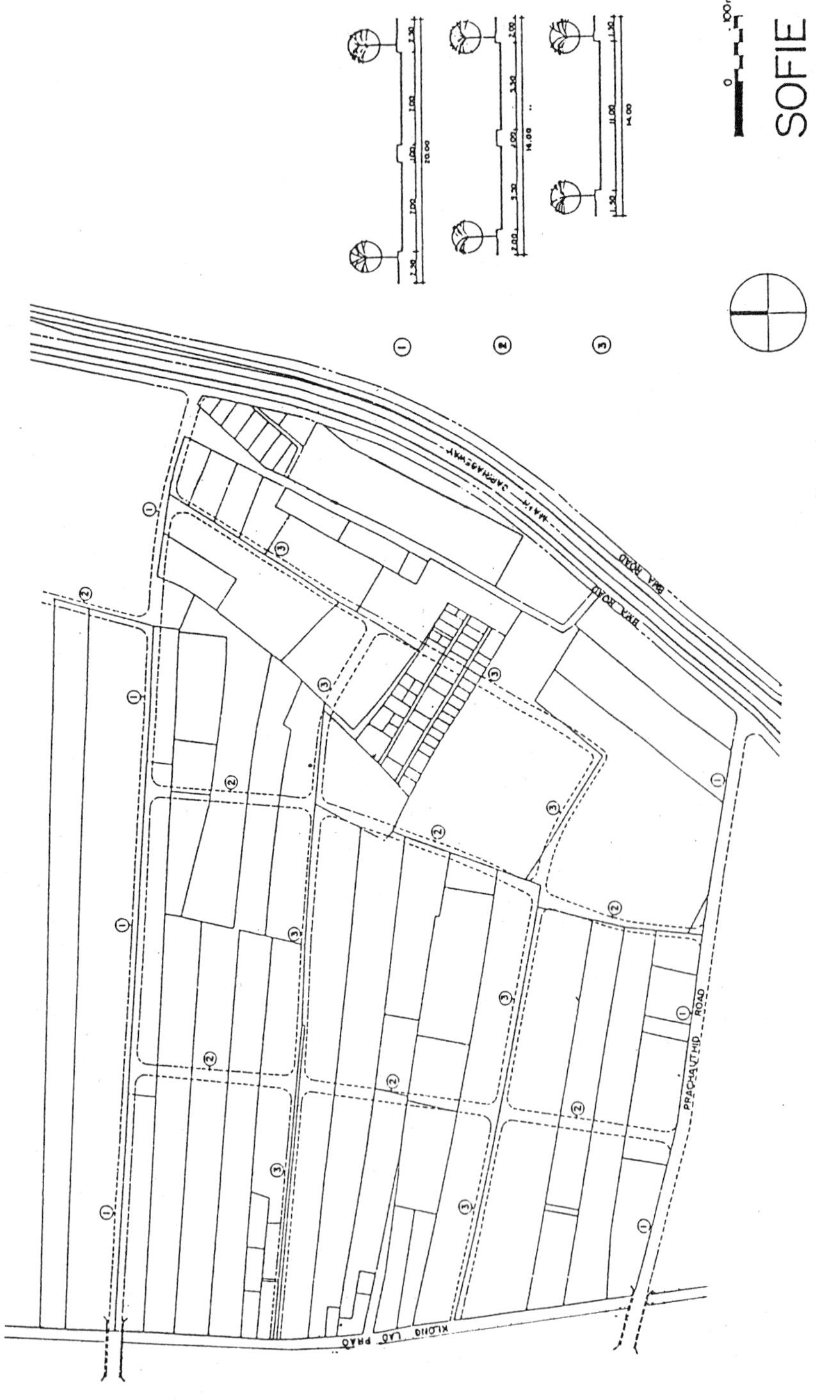

Conclusion

The formula L + P + F + NI = SUD simply says that in an expanding city the construction of planned layouts of roads, drains and water supply, waste-water and electricity lines provides the physical foundation for sustainable urban development. The formula is not a new discovery but a restatement of what is already known, although it is not being implemented in many Asian cities. The formula is a valuable restatement for seven reasons. First, it draws attention to the importance of network infrastructure in urban development. The public road, drainage and utility service networks are essential for urban efficiency and for environmental protection. Second, it clearly identifies the four elements that have to be considered together and combined so as to achieve the SUD objective. Financing the early construction of the planned networks has to be covered in the plan-making. Third, the planning of the urban land-use pattern has to be integrated with the planning of the network layouts, so as to ensure that the networks are designed with sufficient capacity to service the urban land uses in each area without overload. This integration is best achieved through cooperative planning by the urban planning, road and public utility agencies. Fourth, the formula indicates that the government sector can use its early provision of the public road and utility network mainlines and distributor/collector lines to implement the land-use plans. The advance construction of these networks will open up the designated development areas and attract private developers to them, and then guide their land subdivision and building development projects. Fifth, it indicates that the government sector can (and should) manage its construction of the public road and utility networks at the mainline and distributor/collector line levels so as to create a physical framework on the ground (alongside its regulatory framework), to guide the private sector land and building development activities. This means that the urban planners who wish to see their statutory land-use plans implemented have to become involved in the management of urban land development, particularly for the conversion of the rural land to subdivision land. Sixth, the government's advance provision of the mainline and distributor/collector line networks has to be supported with the land-use regulatory controls. The land subdivision regulations can ensure that the private developers construct the local road and utility networks within their project sites. The building construction regulations can ensure that the density of building development is within the capacity of network infrastructure to serve it without overload. Seventh, top priority should be given to planning the networks at the mainline and distributor/collector line levels, and then acquiring the roadway land in advance of private development activity. This results in land at least cost and provides the right-of-way land for most of the utility lines. It establishes the layout of the networks on the ground, and guides the private developers in assembling land parcels for their projects and then in designing their project layouts.

In summary, the formula shows that the principal task of the government sector in urban expansion is to manage its planning, network infrastructure and regulatory functions in urban expansion so as to create a physical and legal framework that will facilitate and guide the land subdivision and building development being undertaken by the private landowners and developers through the land market. This government land management should be directed to the objectives of achieving a planned pattern of urban land-use, adequate land supply and sustainable urban development. The government selects and designates the rural lands suitable for urban development, prepares land-use and circulation plans for these areas, and then designs and constructs the road and utility service mainlines and distributor/collector lines to these plans. This advance construction of the network infrastructure in the designated areas opens them up for development and creates a large supply of private subdivision land, and also provides a physical framework to guide the private land subdivision and building projects. The land subdivision regulations are administered to ensure the proper layout and construction of the local roads and utility lines within each subdivision project. (Land pooling/readjustment projects can also be undertaken by local government on a selective basis to install special infrastructure/ facilities and to close gaps in the pattern of private land subdivision.) The land-use zoning and building construction regulations are administered so as to limit the type and density of building development in each area to the capacity of the network infrastructure that has been installed to service that area. The public utility agencies should also enforce these development limits when supplying their service so as to prevent overloading their networks.

Introducing this system for a large metropolis such as Bangkok, or even for provincial cities such as Chiang Mai, would take years in order to set up the funding arrangements, to make organizational changes, to recruit and train planners, to negotiate the arrangements for cooperation and coordination between the planning and infrastructure agencies; and then prepare the plans and begin implementing them. Despite this the government should adopt the system and begin setting it up. Meanwhile, there is an urgent need for the construction of networks of distributor/ collector roads and utility service lines connected to the existing main roads and utility lines in the urban fringe areas so as to provide a physical framework to guide the private developers deciding the location and design of their land subdivision projects.

BIBLIOGRAPHY

Archer, R.W. (1977), The Theory and Practice of Large-Scale Urban Land Development, *Royal Australian Planning Institute Journal*, 15, 67–72.

Alterman, R. (1982), *Land Value Recapture: Design and Evaluation of Alternative Policies*, Centre for Human Settlements, University of British Columbia, Vancouver.

Alterman, R. (ed.) (1988), *Private Supply of Public Services: Evaluation of Real Estate Exactions, Linkage, and Alternative Land Policies*, New York University Press, New York.

Foo, T.S. (1988), *A Road-Based Land Pooling/Readjustment Scheme in Minburi District, Bangkok*, Doctoral degree special study report, Human Settlements Division, Asian Institute of Technology, Bangkok.

Foster, D. (1989), *Viewing Environmental Protection as Investment in Urban Infrastructure*, Paper PN-ABD-914, Office of Housing and Urban Programs, USAID, Washington, D.C.

Archer, R.W. (1991a), *Provision of Urban Infrastructure Through Land Subdivision Controls in Thailand*, HSD Research Paper No. 26, Asian Institute of Technology, Bangkok.

Archer, R.W. (1991b), *Report on the Bang Kapi Infrastructure Construction and Special Assessment Pilot Project*, Urban Development Coordination Division, Office of the NESDB, Bangkok.

Archer, R.W. (1992), Introducing the Urban Land Pooling/Readjustment Technique into Thailand, *Public Administration and Development*, 12, 155–174.

National Housing Authority (1993), *New Town Development Project*, New Town Project Department, National Housing Authority, Bangkok.

Industrial Estates Authority (1994), *Industrial Estates Thailand, 1994—An Industrial Edge*, Industrial Estates Authority of Thailand, Bangkok.

PART IV

LOOKING AHEAD

INTEGRATED URBAN INFRASTRUCTURE DEVELOPMENT: WHITHER NOW?

Kulwant Singh, Florian Steinberg and Nathaniël von Einsiedel

The last few years have witnessed a growing concern regarding the adequacy of infrastructure provision. In the context of economic liberalization and macro-economic development, infrastructure plays a crucial role and provides an enabling environment for the productivity of households and firms. The role of infrastructure in the social sector is equally important in a wider context of equity and affordability.

In the current phase of economic development of most Asian countries the urban sector has to play a major role. The contribution of the urban sector in the national income among most countries is significantly higher than the size of their urban population. This is particularly important in the context of these developing countries which are undergoing a rapid pace of urbanization.

There is an increasing awareness that the potential role of the urban sector in macro-economic development can be made more effective through appropriate investments in urban infrastructure. The magnitude of investment requirements to meet the backlog of urban infrastructure across many countries is so high that it is just not possible to meet this backlog through normal budgetary allocations. It will require not only stimulation of local revenue and a manifold increase in the flow of loan finance, but also innovative schemes of resource mobilization involving the private business sector. This change in the policy perception has forced the national governments in the Asian region to pay more attention towards the adequacy of urban infrastructure by way of efficiency in the delivery of municipal services. Recent insights of policy makers and development managers, however, support the view that urban centres function as generators for economic growth which can be better tapped if cities are managed more effectively. Cities can also be major centres of progress in terms of education, better health services, etc. There is a particular need for re-distributive policies in order to contain excessive urban concentration. Increased emphasis is required on development of secondary centres through access to available serviced land for development activities and communications. The present phase of urban development in Asia is characterized by the attempts to refine and develop further the management of cities. Development of infrastructure is one of the most important components in this context.

Cities are booming with internal growth and migration, putting colossal pressure on local and sub-national governments alike. This extent of urbanization also poses an unprecedented challenge to planners and city managers.

There are so many municipalities which are considered weak and which are having increasingly greater problems in meeting the infrastructure needs of its rapidly increasing populations. The crucial point is how can the financial, managerial and technical resources be mobilized and expanded to effectively cope with the situation. In the past, what has been making things even worse, generally, was that urban development has been low on the development agenda and has often been treated as a negative phenomenon. In the more recent years, the deterioration of the urban environment has placed additional strain on the management of urban areas. In the context of ecology-conscious urban development, as indicated in the United Nations' "Agenda 21", the present challenge is how to sustain urban development.

The many decentralization initiatives in Asia come at a time when the new economic policies demand improved capabilities for urban and financial management at local levels of government, supported by sub-national and central level institutions. Certain wider structural changes in the system of urban development planning, programming and management will certainly follow, such as:

— Introduction of short- and medium-term planning tools which complement the existing, comprehensive long-term development plans;

— Better correlation between urban planning, financial management and the operational management of the delivery of urban infrastructure services;

— Simplification of procedures and integration of the management of development schemes (which operate in an isolated fashion now);

— Better utilization and the expansion of the revenue base for municipal bodies; and

— Improved employment and service conditions for the professionals and staff of civic bodies and municipalities for attracting appropriate managerial/professional talent.

Civic bodies and municipalities will be required to improve and strengthen their governance, for which they are very badly lacking capacity, skills and legal basis. Their roles at the same time are becoming more complex and wide-ranging in response to new approaches in service provision, public-private partnerships, public participation in decision-making, development models for infrastructure development based on Build-Own-Operate (BOO), Build-Own-Operate-Transfer (BOOT) or Build-Operate-Transfer (BOT) strategies.

It is obvious that in this context the work of developing and managing infrastructure given the available resources, augmenting the resources to develop the urban areas further and to improve the living conditions and managing the assets are uphill tasks. Local authorities require to carry out in a responsible manner a host of tasks for which they are insufficiently equipped, and for which they do not possess adequate financial and managerial resources.

The notion here is that "integration" will contribute positively to the provision and management of urban infrastructure services. This "integration" has been attempted in some of the programmes elaborated in this publication, but we cannot yet claim that we have been successful in achieving the overall goals. If we define these as "sustainable urban development" we will require a definite acceleration and wide expansion of our infrastructure development, and the management of our infrastructure programmes will need to become geared towards "cost recovery", "replicability" and "affordability" in order to reach out to all classes of society.

There are many cases and experiences on integrated urban infrastructure which are meaningful to: (i) promote a further convergence of infrastructure programmes; (ii) establish more action-orientated urban and land development schemes; (iii) integrate the financial means of public, private sector and community sources; and (iv) strengthen the management capacities of local governments, state governments and central governments.

The methodologies for planning, programming, implementation, operation and maintenance of integrated urban infrastructure should ultimately result in acceleration of service provision, improvement of local revenues, improvement of local institutional capabilities, reduction of negative environmental impact and access of urban poor to urban services.

In this context "integrated urban development" is a promising strategy to cope with the current situation and the needs of the future. The new and innovative notion is that "integrated urban development" is necessary as a strategy to govern our cities better and create a better foundation for economic development and for extending basic amenities to our urban poor. Integrated urban development is complex and will need several and long-term avenues to materialize.

A few principles for "integrated urban infrastructure development", should be mentioned here:

Striking a balance between economic infrastructure and basic infrastructure for the urban poor: A city or town cannot do without a basic economic base that creates employment for its residents and income for the local authority. At the same time we face an increasing number of poorly housed and serviced areas. It implies that a balance needs to be found between creating an infrastructure that will attract economic activity and providing basic amenities for the urban poor so that the worst conditions are eradicated on the other. Setting development priorities and selection of projects has to keep this in mind.

Striking a balance between tackling short-term needs and providing for long-term requirements for economic development: While this principle seems similar to the first one, it requires more vision and insight into the economic opportunities and potentials of the town or city and the region at large.

Building on consensus and participation: Though it may be difficult, it is necessary to involve not only local and higher government authorities, but also key stakeholders from the private sector, communities and wards. This principle is paramount if we seriously want to promote the role of government as "enabler" and to forge meaningful partnerships.

Simplicity, transparency and incremental approach to the various forms of participation: With the general lack of understanding and appreciation for integrated infrastructure development, these principles will bear the best results to start with. Many local authorities, private enterprises and communities cannot be expected to learn and adopt complex programme approaches and decision-making procedures overnight.

Decentralization of decision-making and development: Recent legal changes in many Asian countries will allow to bank more on the development from below, entrusting local civic bodies and political entities to have a greater "say", and greater "do" in development.

Improvement of the financial position of urban local bodies: When talking about "decentralization", "local participation" and "sustainability", we must ask ourselves where are the people and the money to do all this. In the end it boils down to the financial capacity of municipal bodies to appoint staff, to invest in development, to repay development loans, etc. Better municipal financial management and resource mobilization must get equal attention.

Aim at tapping the various programmes and financial resources availed through central and state or regional governments: Although the various urban development and service provision schemes have their own objectives, targets, financial modalities, components, procedures and schedules, the main aim is directed at converging these schemes at the local level so that cross benefits can be obtained.

Aim at a comprehensive infrastructure package: The earlier principles of following social and economic needs, short- and long-term requirements and tapping various schemes and financial resource will allow the design of a comprehensive package that will serve the overall goal of development and which would otherwise not be feasible under a single scheme or from one financial source.

Strengthening of local civic bodies and municipalities: Earlier principles rely heavily on the local authorities to identify and articulate their needs, to develop a comprehensive vision of how development should take place and to initiate and manage projects. This cannot be achieved without strengthening their capacity to do so. Some efforts in that direction have been initiated under various programmes, but more are required. It will also require incentives for municipal officers and longer posting than is the practice in some countries.

Introduction of short- and medium-term strategic planning tools: The long-term physical planning tools will need to be supplemented with short- and medium-term planning tools to facilitate the thinking and decision-making process for social and economic development with a time span of five to ten years.

There are quite a number of short- and medium-planning approaches and experiences from the various Asian countries which could be moulded into more universal models without losing on local adaptation.

ANNEXURE

RECOMMENDATIONS OF THE INTERNATIONAL SEMINAR ON INTEGRATED URBAN INFRASTRUCTURE DEVELOPMENT

Introduction

The International Seminar on Integrated Urban Infrastructure Development had the objective to share various experiences of integrated urban (infrastructure) development in the Asian region (in particular, Indonesia, Nepal, Bangladesh, Thailand, the Philippines, Sri Lanka, Turkey, Malaysia, Vietnam and India). It was the intention to compare the methodologies of multi-sectoral investment planning (MSIP), and to discuss present challenges, shortcomings and impacts of integrated urban infrastructure development programmes/projects.

The objective of the recommendations made here is to try to produce a set of statements that reflect what was considered most appropriate in the papers and discussions on these various cases from Asia. The word "appropriate" is taken to mean that there is seen to be a wider applicability than the individual cases presented. It is not the idea to try to come up with a list of universal truths—but rather to identify the most important elements of the experience and to try to present this in a short but clear form.

The Seminar has focussed on the integration of "urban infrastructure" rather than "urban development" in general, as it was felt that integration in the urban infrastructure field is a tangible objective while integration of all urban development activities is far too ambitious.

The recommendations are structured into general recommendations which emerged from a large number of the papers and discussions, and specific recommendations relating to certain main sub-themes of the seminar such as Multi-sectoral Investment Planning, Services for the Poor; Municipal Finance, Capital Markets, Environment and Land, and Public-Private Partnerships.

The Seminar recognizes that an international exchange on the present experiences and practices of integrated urban infrastructure planning has started, and this in itself is a very positive development.

It is recommended that the various experiences are seen as mutually reinforcing, and the various delegations review the cases presented during the Seminar for their relevance for their own situation.

It is hoped that in more countries the concerned institutions may feel encouraged to promote a convergence and re-enforcement of the elements applicable for their own integrated urban infrastructure projects/programmmes.

However, a long time horizon — in the order of 10 to 25 years — may be required to implant and institutionalize innovative programmes which follow this approach of integration, and to incorporate these programmes/projects into the routine operations of local governments.

A. General Recommendations

A1. An integrated approach to infrastructure planning and programming is recommended as essential both for social and economic development. Integrated urban infrastructure provision implies the need for an integration of:

— technical, spatial and environmental issues;

— financial issues; and

— institutional and managerial issues.

A2. Integrated urban infrastructure development (IUID) requires a planned framework. IUID needs to be based on locally defined and supported objectives linked to a broader framework. It is important to encourage innovative working at the local level so that approaches can be tailored to local potentials and limitations. It is necessary to differentiate integrated programme/project approaches according to the local problem dimensions. Small and medium towns call for less complexity (and comprehensiveness) than large and metropolitan cities.

A3. The introduction of integrated approaches will require a lead agency at the central level, but the dissemination of the approach needs to aim at local-level institutions. Local government should normally be the lead actor at the city level for planning and implementation of integrated urban infrastructure development. Decentralization of planning and management responsibilities and resources to local government is essential, but needs genuine commitment from higher levels. Roles and responsibilities of other, higher levels of government such as provincial (state) and central-level governments need to be clear.

A4. Integration and coordination require a basis of a spirit of cooperation to succeed, and clear incentives for adopting the approach need to supplement the introduction of "integrated" schemes.

A5. Political involvement and support is essential for ensuring the allocation of resources and commitment to implementation and operation and maintenance. Integrated urban infrastructure development requires a cooperative attitude of the stakeholders. It shall not be the result of imposition or coercion.

A6. There should be a "participative" approach to planning so as to achieve ownership of projects/programmes by key stakeholders. This implies involving all actors at the earliest stage possible. This includes governmental agencies, community-based organizations (CBOs), non-governmental organizations (NGOs) and the private commercial sector, and to make use of the media.

A7. Integration should be to the extent necessary to gain clear benefits and added value above conventional, sectoral approaches (see the formula "2+2=5"), and not be for its own sake. Integration should proceed incrementally, but not try to be over-comprehensive unless this is essential.

A8. An incremental approach should be adopted so as to be able to build on and develop existing capacities. The adaptation of integrated infrastructure provision may not lead immediately to a comprehensive, all-sector-embracing form of integration. The likely development is rather a gradual build-up of integration, based on realism and pragmatism.

A9. Investments and development assistance should support positive trends in economic development rather than try to determine those trends. Integrated urban infrastructure development shall support economically positive activities which will strengthen also the position of local governments, and make them less dependent on specialized agencies and flow of subsidies.

A10. Decisions on financing of local expenditures should come under the responsibility of local government. Programmes funded from a higher level of government should allow local government enough discretion to allow integration. Block grants with local discretion are preferred provided there is effective local accountability.

A11. Integrated, i.e., multi-sectoral investment planning (MSIP) shall be linked with urban planning through the inclusion of urban development scenarios within the MSIPs. Due to the "action-orientated" nature of MSIP it is necessary to re-define conventional master planning, and to adopt more flexible urban planning tools, based on the concept of structure planning (instead of very detailed, prescriptive land use plans).

A12. Flexibility to react to financial or socio-political changes is essential and requires special management skills. It is essential to undertake reforms necessary to improve the management capabilities of local governments.

A13. External assistance needs to be carefully designed to avoid sustainability problems.

A14. Training and workshops (or "consultations") can be valuable to build up teamwork and commonsense of direction. Capacity building is necessary to support all approaches, and may be financed from and as part of integrated investment packages. Education and training should reflect the reorientation of planning approaches and support in particular the human resource development needs of local governments.

B. Multi-sectoral Investment Planning (MSIP)

B1. Multi-sectoral investment planning (MSIP) should be used as a tool for prioritization and decision-making on investment programmes at the city level, and shall encourage the convergence of public sector, private sector and community investments in urban infrastructure. Objectives should be pragmatic and related to existing capacities.

B2. Financial ·integration is important to allow technical, spatial and environmental integration. Where integration is still difficult, it is important to put together information on commitments and planned expenditures, and to structure the development process towards gradual integration.

B3. MSIP should link existing commitments, needs and effective demands with potential resources (from public and private sector as well as the capital market), and shall incorporate also social development programmes where necessary. This means it should help coordination of existing programmes and projects, and secure both their implementation as also their operation and maintenance.

B4. A participative approach to planning, involving all key stakeholders from the start is essential. Cooperation and exploration of forms of partnership between local government and community, NGOs/

CBOs and private sectors which can help urban service provision should be encouraged, while NGOs can also play useful intermediary roles.

B5. An incremental approach is most desirable and necessary, focussing on what can be achieved in the short term while building links to mid-term investment planning, operation and maintenance, urban master planning and regional planning.

B6. Links between urban and rural areas should be specifically addressed. Planning should be based on coming together of local objectives and regional/national policy.

B7. The process of planning for integration needs to be sensitive to the factor of time, utilizing rapid methods of planning and appraisal. There should be an emphasis on rapid approaches to planning and information collection.

B8. Integration levels should be related to the benefits to be achieved. A cost-benefit analysis of this should be part of appraisal procedures.

C. Services for the Poor

C1. Integrated multi-sectoral investment planning should give special attention to basic services for the poor, and bring concerns for the urban poor (especially for women and children) into the mainstream of development planning. It is advocated to emphasize less on the rather isolated, so-called typical "low-income" projects, and to concentrate on improving urban management and general services provision programmes at a city scale and give special emphasis to access to services for low-income groups.

C2. Integrated development policies directed at urban slum areas are feasible if a cross-subsidy approach is adopted. Creative urban management has to assure that revenue creation at the city level will finance those projects or project components where no cost recovery can be expected.

C3. Privatization and public-private partnerships in services provision may open new avenues also for the provision of services for the poor if appropriate service components are offered, and if adequate mechanisms of cross-subsidy are being built in.

C4. The establishment of an Urban Poverty Fund, which is well administered and targeted, may be recommended as an (additional) instrument of convergence to integrate multi-sectoral funds for slum development (integrating physical and non-physical components).

The purpose of the Urban Poverty Funds can be to reserve particular investment packages for this target group, and to make development funds accessible to the poor, and to CBOs and NGOs as their intermediaries.

C5. Innovative technologies for the cost-effective provision of infrastructure services are advocated in connection with decentralized, and incremental technologies which allow maximum participation of the users in implementation, and operation and maintenance. Standards of services should be incremental in view of the social context, actual needs and affordability of the urban poor, and not offered as standard packages for the sake of easy implementation and project budgeting and administration.

C6. The thrust of any programme should be to make people participate in the development as well as in the decision-making process of the infrastructure development process. This shall include improved access to information, involvement in the planning and prioritization process, participation in the mobilization of resources, community management of the facilities, franchises and concessions.

C7. Local government/municipal agencies as well as non-governmental agencies shall play a key role in creating a participatory environment for cooperation. This stresses again the role of local governments as facilitator of partnership arrangements, and departs from the conventional role of local government as exclusive provider of services for the poor. This may require a re-orientation and skill-development of the involved staff towards more responsive, equity-orientated and participatory approaches in settlement development.

C8. NGOs/CBOs can stipulate integration through simultaneous provision of various infrastructure services without being constrained institutionally, and thus move from small sectoral projects to multi-sectoral projects/programmes. Despite certain limitations, NGOs and CBOs are encouraged to move away from the prevailing funding practice of "sector-by-sector" projects towards more integration.

C9. Urban development programmes and so-called "priority projects" may suggest in certain cases the relocation of urban slums and other areas of the poor. Adequate policies need to be established to address relocation only as a measure of the last resort, and to protect the urban poor from indiscriminate relocation. Instead it is essential to provide positive relocation support mechanisms where relocation is inevitable.

C10. It is recommended to develop an adequate database, accessible to the public, to support policy development and evaluation of urban poverty alleviation. Such a database could be best developed and maintained by an independent research institution.

D. Municipal Finance and Strengthening of Resource Base[1]

D1. Financial resources for urban development may not be the "problem" *per se* as cities are "resourceful", and there are possibilities to strengthen the municipal resource base through higher local revenues, betterment levies and introduction of remunerative projects. Hence, it is considered necessary to address the lack of efficient municipal finance management systems and the lack of human resources. Stimulation of innovative mechanisms of improving the urban finance situation requires a set of attractive incentives to be effective.

D2. Innovative municipal finance "windows" need to be established, not only within conventional banks, but can be located within any sort of urban (infrastructure) development institution.

D3. Integration of multiple funding lines can be aimed at, and an integration is possible if these funds can be managed through the "envelope" of a municipal budget.

D4. Urban loan finance channels may be established as competitive programmes, and this competition may help to establish a healthy and innovative climate for the expanding the urban finance sector.

D5. With regard to the instrument of a Municipal Development Fund or the like, strict financial management, securing national and possible private sources and a distinct role of the executing agency in institutional management and implementation need to be ensured for long-term sustainability.

D6. The myth of the lack of creditworthiness of municipalities needs probing. Many municipalities do actually have enough financial strength and a resource base which allows to take up loans. However, their present situation only shows that they do not perform well in the field of revenue collection. Creative and business-like financial management at the city level needs promotion.

---

[1]Some of the approaches to municipal finance and capital market development may not mention explicitly the notion of "integration", but their effective potential is that urban finance is addressed as the most important component of any programme orientated towards integration.

D7. Budgetary planning processes need to be based on cost recovery and on sound principles of financial management as this will help to introduce budgets which become "developmental tools" instead of being mere "rituals" of subsidy allocation.

D8. A review of tariffs and fees for infrastructure services is essential for the establishment of cost recovery mechanisms and the financial health of municipalities, and it requires substantial improvement in municipal finance management. A good mixture of remunerative and non-remunerative projects is to be designed by municipal finance planners, and municipal expenditures need monitoring in accordance with planned investments. The particular composition of income-earning and non-remunerative projects can serve to generate funds for the cross-subsidization of non-remunerative service projects. The participation of urban stakeholders (in particular politicians) is of utmost importance for decisions on tariff setting, increase of taxes and revenue collection.

D9. Municipal finance programmes can provide incentives (for instance in the form of certain grants or low interest credit on the basis of good revenue collection performance), and thus stimulate financial decisions at the municipal level which enhance integration. Signals from central government to local governments need to be clear regarding the proportion of grant and loan funding expected.

E. Capital Markets

E1. Capital markets should be explored to fund commercially viable or remunerative (and possibly also non-remunerative) elements of infrastructure. Many of these new capital market financing forms need to be tried out and experimented with. However, this should be done in a careful manner, so as to build up trust and confidence of private investors.

E2. A combination of project and general bonds is recommended where feasible and economic viability is secured.

E3. A clear policy support and legal framework is needed from higher levels of government to support local government approaching capital markets. Nodal agencies may support local governments in the efforts to tap the capital market.

F. Environment and Land

F1. A reduction in the number of regulations should be introduced and transparency as well as simplifications in the procedures for land registrations are needed. The high costs of land control suggests to liberalize the land market altogether, and to promote "single window" procedures for planning controls and transactions.

F2. Regulations which result in constraints in land supply should be eliminated or significantly modified, and equity considerations should figure more prominently in urban land development strategies.

F3. Legal powers to acquire lands for infrastructure development need to be strengthened.

F4. A reorientation from conventional master planning (based only on very detailed, prescriptive land-use planning and zoning) towards urban management approaches in urban planning is recommended. "Blue print" master plans without the necessary elaboration of the required resource base and management responsibilities for the implementation of the proposed works and programmes/projects may not be utilized anymore. However, linkages to regional planning needs to be highlighted, particularly in the case of large and metropolitan areas as this will underscore the need for integration of various levels (spatial, technical, environmental, administrative, financial).

F5. For urban planning purposes an "action planning" approach is advocated which is based upon the principles of a more flexible version of "structure planning", encouraging regular reviews to respond to the fast urban developments, and to incorporate newly arising infrastructure needs (and demands) into the multi-sectoral investment planning process. Urban planning shall be part of the local government responsibilities, and in the context of decentralization it is essential to safeguard local participation by the private sector, the community and NGOs/CBOs.

F6. To create the necessary spatial, physical and environmental basis and linkages for multi-sectoral investment planning (MSIP) it is recommended to establish Physical and Environmental Development Plans (PEDPs). These PEDPs may have a medium-term perspective and shall be part of the urban "action plan" process.

F7. Environmental mapping—particularly for large and metropolitan cities—is recommended as a tool for quick overall urban assessment, a more rational investment prioritization, assessing risks and working out geographically integrated networks for services. It is also recommended to include information on municipal services and their management.

G. Public and Private Partnership

G1. Local government should have a clear view of the role and potentials of public-private partnerships (PPP) as they can bring important resources to play. Public-private partnerships (PPP)—through Build-Operate-Own (BOO), Build-Operate-Transfer (BOT), Build-Operate-Lease-Transfer (BOLT), service contracts and any other contractual arrangement—can be utilized as components of (MSIP) and be a substantial part of multi-year development plans.

G2. Before privatization or public-private partnerships can be established effectively, it is necessary to establish adequate regulatory mechanisms.

G3. Contracting procedures have to be developed carefully, and performance standards shall be detailed out, and risk management mechanisms be established.

G4. Relations with private sector must be transparent and there must be clear accountability. Local governments and the private sector assume the same level playing field for their partnership projects.

G5. Negotiation should aim at "win-win" situations, and not head for over-ambitious goals for either side. For sustainable relations it is important to work with strong and professional partners; this applies both to local government and to the private sector.

G6. Competition is necessary and shall be encouraged if PPP is to work. Hence, it is recommended to avoid monopoly situations where possible in order to secure the best of the possible service situations within an environment of competition for customers and quality products and services. Where unavoidable, an effective and consumer-orientated regulatory control mechanism may be required.

G7. Public-private partnership projects shall include equity concerns where possible and strive to provide services for the poorer sections of society also.